OXFORD HISTORICAL MONOGRAPHS

Gender, Modernity, and the Popular Press in Inter-War Britain

ADRIAN BINGHAM

CLARENDON PRESS · OXFORD

OXFORD
UNIVERSITY PRESS

Great Clarendon Street, Oxford OX2 6DP

Oxford University Press is a department of the University of Oxford.
It furthers the University's objective of excellence in research, scholarship,
and education by publishing worldwide in

Oxford   New York

Auckland Bangkok Buenos Aires Cape Town Chennai
Dar es Salaam Delhi Hong Kong Istanbul Karachi Kolkata
Kuala Lumpur Madrid Melbourne Mexico City Mumbai Nairobi
São Paulo Shanghai Taipei Tokyo Toronto

Oxford is a registered trade mark of Oxford University Press
in the UK and in certain other countries

Published in the United States
by Oxford University Press Inc., New York

British Library Cataloguing in Publication Data
Data available

Library of Congress Cataloging in Publication Data
Data available

ISBN 0-19-927247-6

1 3 5 7 9 10 8 6 4 2

Typeset by SNP Best-set Typesetter Ltd., Hong Kong
Printed in Great Britain
on acid-free paper by
Biddles Ltd.
King's Lynn, Norfolk

In memory of A. H. Dean

ACKNOWLEDGEMENTS

I would like to thank first and foremost my D.Phil. supervisor and Advising Editor, Janet Howarth. Her unfailing encouragement and perceptive advice have been of vital assistance throughout the period of researching and writing this book. She has read through countless draft chapters, and has always helped me to clarify my ideas and sharpen my arguments.

I would also like to thank my examiners, Pat Thane and John Davis, for their constructive comments on the thesis on which this book is based. I subsequently joined Pat at the Centre for Contemporary British History, and she has continued to offer me invaluable guidance. Philip Waller, Ross McKibbin, Jose Harris, John Stevenson, and Lesley Hall have also made useful suggestions on various parts of this book. I am very grateful to my family for always being interested in my work, and to Stephen Lucking for his generosity during my time in London. Jane and Jon Legg, Andre Katz, Rachel Mackie, Steve Dilley, Rhian Roberts, Graham Knight, Peter Smith, and Ellen Hughes have all helped far more than they probably realize, while Felicity Hay's love and support have ensured my happiness throughout the years spent on this project.

The publication of this book has been assisted by grants from the Scouloudi Foundation in association with the Institute of Historical Research, and the Isobel Thornley Bequest Fund to the University of London. I would also like to express my gratitude to the Arts and Humanities Research Board, the Leverhulme Trust, and the British Academy for funding my research.

I would like to thank the British Library, Atlantic Syndication (acting for Associated Newspapers), News International, Express Newspapers, Mirror Newspapers, and Harvey Nichols for permission to reproduce those images for which they hold the copyright. The illustrations were supplied by the British Library Newspaper Library at Colindale, and the Centre for Cartoons and Caricature, University of Kent, Canterbury.

This book is dedicated to my grandad, A. H. Dean.

A.B.

London
January 2004

CONTENTS

LIST OF FIGURES

Introduction

A new chapter of the world's history is beginning. It is for us to write it and we can write only the thoughts we have within us, draw only the figure and image of ourselves.

(*Daily Mirror*, editorial, 12 November 1918)

It is a platitude for journalists to claim that they write the first draft of history. Yet when it comes to preparing later drafts, historians have, in fact, generally been reluctant to examine the press for insights into the past. This book seeks to demonstrate the value of popular newspapers as a historical source by using them to explore the attitudes and identities of inter-war Britain, and in particular the reshaping of femininity and masculinity. The two decades after the Armistice of November 1918 were of major significance in the making of twentieth-century gender identities, as women and men came to terms with the upheavals of the Great War, the arrival of democracy, and rapid social change. These were also the years during which national daily newspapers became part of everyday life, read by a majority of the population. What follows is an analysis of how popular newspapers, in the process of reporting on this post-war world, discussed and debated male and female behaviour and contributed to the evolution of ideas of gender.

Historical and Historiographical Context

The events of the First World War posed a conspicuous challenge to conventional views about male and female roles in society. With men transferring to the front lines in their thousands after August 1914, many women were presented with unprecedented responsibilities and opportunities, and those who moved into previously 'male' spheres in factories and offices on the home front, or joined the newly formed women's military services, received considerable publicity. Their wartime efforts provided an unforgettable testimony to female abilities and powerfully reinforced the arguments of those seeking to improve the position of women. Certain concessions were made before the end of the conflict: in February 1918 most women over 30 were granted the vote, and thus the long campaign for citizenship was finally rewarded. This enfranchisement, and the opening up of some professions and public positions in 1919, further punctured the already leaky doctrine of 'separate spheres', which suggested that women should be concerned above all with home and family: now it was no longer possible to deny women's interests in politics and public life. But it was not only notions of femininity that were challenged by the war. Those ideals of honour, glory, and patriotism that were so important to pre-war conceptions of manliness were also severely tested by the bloodshed of the trenches. The sheer scale of human suffering and waste in a slow-moving war of attrition went far beyond anything described in the boys' adventure stories of the valiant British empire-builders. The manly 'stiff upper lip' was woefully inadequate amidst the unparalleled horrors and brutalities of modern warfare. Whereas women had surpassed conventional femininity, many men discovered how difficult it was to live up to the heroic masculinity described in imperial histories and fiction.

If the war offered the most obvious challenge to established notions of gender, there were also several social, cultural, and economic trends that were making a more subtle, but no less significant, impact on relations between the sexes in this period. These include, in no particular order of importance, the stagnation of the staple export industries and the emergence of mass, structural unemployment; the maturing of the 'consumer society', in the form of a major expansion in branded goods for personal or family consumption, and an associated massive increase in branded advertising; rapid suburbanization and the extension of home ownership; the growth of the leisure and entertainment 'industries', and the rise in particular of cinema, radio, and mass sport; and intellectual shifts in the understanding of personal and sexual character, especially the popularization of psychoanalysis and sexology. All of these developments influenced, in their own ways, social values and gender roles; together, they combined to produce a recognizably 'modern' society in which many of the central features of the twentieth century were present.[1] The fact that this

---

[1] Ever since Paul Fussell argued in 1975 that the events of the Great War were responsible for the diffusion of a 'modern', ironic, 'form of understanding', there has been an ongoing debate about the 'modernity' of this period: P. Fussell, *The Great War and Modern Memory* (New York: Oxford University Press, 1975); for a contrary view, see J. Winter, *Sites of Memory, Sites of Mourning: The Great War in European Cultural History* (Cambridge: Cambridge University Press, 1996). In recent years, historians of Britain have examined a broad range of 'discourses of modernity': see M. Daunton and B. Reiger (eds.), *Meanings of Modernity: Britain from the Late-Victorian Era to World War II* (Oxford: Berg, 2001), and for the later period, B. Conekin, F. Mort, and C. Waters (eds.), *Moments of Modernity: Reconstructing Britain, 1945–1964* (London: Rivers Oram Press, 1999). As Daunton and Reiger point out, scholars have used the terms 'modern' and 'modernity' in a wide variety of contexts with different meanings, and there is no generally accepted definition of either. The most

period is often regarded as one of relative retreat by the feminist movement should not be allowed to overshadow its importance in the evolution of femininity and masculinity.

The popular national daily press provides an excellent means of obtaining some insight into the way these changes affected gender identities. Daily newspapers were one of the most successful products of the inter-war period: circulation doubled in the twenty years after 1918, and by 1939 some two-thirds of the population regularly saw a daily paper.[2] They were no longer regarded as 'luxuries': when calculating a budget suitable to cover the 'necessaries of a healthy life' in 1936, Joseph Rowntree included a weekly allowance of seven pence to buy newspapers.[3] Now that the pre-eminence of the provincial press had been broken, and with radio broadcasting in its infancy for most of the period (television was still in its experimental stages), the national daily newspaper was perhaps the most important channel of information about contemporary life. Publicists certainly regarded the daily newspaper as 'a more powerful medium of advertisement than any other', while the research organization Political and Economic Planning (PEP) declared the press to be 'the principal agenda-making body for the everyday conversation of the ordinary man and woman about public affairs'.[4]

Constantly striving to maximize circulation, editors and journalists developed a template for the popular newspaper from which there has been little substantial deviation since. The popular paper of the late 1930s arguably looks closer to the paper of today than it did to that of 1914. While on one level manufacturing an ephemeral, daily publication, in a deeper sense these Fleet Street journalists were forging a long-lasting cultural product. At the same time, the leading newspaper proprietors, the so-called 'press barons', such as Lords Northcliffe, Rothermere, and Beaverbrook, had a higher profile than ever before or since, and unashamedly involved themselves in political

---

productive approach, therefore, is to investigate what contemporaries themselves understood by modernity 'through close readings within specific locales and venues' (Daunton and Reiger (eds.), *Meanings of Modernity*, Introduction, 3–4). That is the approach taken in this book.

[2] Major G. Harrison, with F. C. Mitchell and M. A. Abrams, *The Home Market* (London: G. Allen & Unwin, 1939), ch. 21; A. P. Wadsworth, 'Newspaper Circulations 1800–1954', *Transactions of the Manchester Statistical Society*, Session 1954–5 (1955); R. Williams, *The Long Revolution* (Harmondsworth: Penguin, 1965), 195–236; C. Seymour-Ure, 'The Press and the Party System between the Wars', in G. Peele and C. Cook (eds.), *The Politics of Reappraisal* (London: Macmillan, 1975), 233–9; T. Jeffery and K. McClelland, 'A World Fit to Live In: The *Daily Mail* and the Middle Classes 1918–39', in J. Curran, A. Smith, and P. Wingate (eds.), *Impacts and Influences: Essays on Media Power in the Twentieth Century* (London: Methuen, 1987), 28–39.

[3] A. Davies, *Leisure, Gender and Poverty: Working-Class Culture in Salford and Manchester* (Buckingham: Open University Press, 1992), 26.

[4] G. Russell, *Advertisement Writing* (London: Ernest Benn, 1927), 67; Political and Economic Planning (PEP), *Report on the British Press* (London, 1938), 33.

intrigue. Even if their claims of power and influence seem exaggerated in retrospect, few contemporaries thought so. In March 1931 Stanley Baldwin had to deliver one of his most famous speeches—accusing Beaverbrook and Rothermere of seeking 'power without responsibility—the prerogative of the harlot throughout the ages'—to derail the press-led Empire Free Trade campaign that threatened his leadership of the Conservative Party.[5] And while ministers worried about the political impact of popular newspapers, literary critics and social commentators debated their cultural repercussions. The national daily newspaper, with its circulation now counted in millions rather than thousands, came to symbolize the new 'mass society' and all that it brought in its wake. Understanding its significance seemed to be an urgent cultural imperative, and observers as diverse as the Leavises, Aldous Huxley, George Orwell, and Evelyn Waugh contributed to the discussions on the subject.[6] But the 'golden age' of the press would not last for much longer after 1939. Although circulations continued to rise for another decade, newsprint restrictions soon severely reduced the size of newspapers; in the longer term, radio and television combined gradually to weaken the hold of the press.

Despite the importance of the popular press, however, gender historians have made relatively little use of it in their studies of inter-war culture.[7] This is all the more surprising considering the impressive amount of work on other cultural forms in this period. Women's magazines, popular literature, films, and medical texts have all received a considerable amount of attention, as have party literature, feminist periodicals, and political rhetoric.[8] These studies are

---

[5] K. Middlemiss and J. Barnes, *Baldwin: A Biography* (London: Weidenfeld & Nicolson, 1969), 600.

[6] K. Williams, *British Writers and the Media 1930–45* (Basingstoke: Macmillan, 1996), esp. 48–61.

[7] Alison Light noted in 1991 the need for a gendered analysis of the inter-war newspaper, and this gap has yet to be filled: A. Light, *Forever England: Feminism, Literature and Conservatism between the Wars* (London: Routledge, 1991), 246 n. 19.

[8] On women's magazines, see C. White, *Women's Magazines 1693–1968* (London: Michael Joseph, 1970); R. Ballaster, M. Beetham, E. Frazer, and S. Hebron, *Women's Worlds: Ideology, Femininity and the Woman's Magazine* (London: Macmillan, 1991); M. Beetham, *A Magazine of her Own? Domesticity and Desire in the Woman's Magazine 1800–1914* (London: Routledge, 1996); J. Greenfield and C. Reid, 'Women's Magazines and the Commercial Orchestration of Femininity in the 1930s: Evidence from *Woman's Own*', *Media History*, 4/2 (1998), 161–74; on popular literature, see N. Beauman, *A Very Great Profession: The Woman's Novel 1914–39* (London: Virago, 1983); B. Melman, *Women and the Popular Imagination in the Twenties: Flappers and Nymphs* (Basingstoke: Macmillan, 1988); Light, *Forever England*. On films, see M. Rosen, *Popcorn Venus: Women, Movies and the American Dream* (New York: Coward, McCann & Geoghegan, 1973); J. Stacey, *Star Gazing: Hollywood Cinema and Female Spectatorship* (London: Routledge, 1994); J. Fink and K. Holden, 'Pictures from the Margin of Marriage: Representations of Spinsters and Single Mothers in the Mid-Victorian Novel, Inter-War Hollywood Melodrama and British Film of the 1950s and 1960s', *Gender and History*, 11/2 (July 1999), 233–55. On medical texts, see J. Weeks, *Sex, Politics and Society: The Regulation of Sex since 1800* (London: Longman, 1981), chs. 8, 10, 11; S. Jeffreys, *The Spinster and her Enemies: Feminism and Sexuality 1880–1930* (London: Pandora, 1985), chs. 8 and 9; S. Kent, *Making Peace: The Reconstruction of Gender in Inter-War Britain* (Princeton: Princeton University Press, 1993), ch. 5. On party literature, feminist

all illuminating on the state of gender discourse at this time, but still do not obviate the desirability of a separate investigation of the press. In terms of audience size (of both sexes), cultural significance, and the sheer diversity of material covered—from party politics to cosmetics and sport—the national newspaper is difficult to rival.

Perhaps one of the main reasons for the relative lack of interest in the press is the assumption made by gender historians that its content is fairly predictable. Two of the most widely known examples of press activity in these years—the *Daily Mail*'s vigorous opposition to the 'flapper vote' in 1927–8, and the rise of the same paper's Ideal Home Exhibition—both seem to suggest that the press simply championed domesticity and opposed single women trying to break out of their 'separate sphere'. This is certainly the impression that one receives from most of the work that has been published on the press. Billie Melman, who has produced the most substantial gendered analysis of the *Mail* and the *Express* so far in the first chapter of her book *Women and the Popular Imagination in the Twenties*, and whose research is often quoted by others,[9] argues that 'From the beginning of 1919 the contemporary young woman was criticised on every conceivable ground. Her appearance was derided, her manners were deplored and her newly-gained freedom was regarded with suspicion.' In this 'welter of misogyny', she continues, there was frequently an 'extraordinarily aggressive tone of utterance'.[10] Other observations on the press tend to follow a similar pattern. Dale Spender has claimed that 'the established and male-controlled press worked to censor the demands and activities of women',[11] while Deirdre Beddoe asserts that

In the inter-war years only one desirable image was held up to women by all the main-stream media agencies—that of housewife and mother. This single role model was presented to women to follow and all other alternatives were presented as wholly undesirable. Realising this central fact is the key to understanding every other aspect of women's lives in Britain in the 1920s and 1930s.[12]

periodicals, and political rhetoric, see e.g. D. Spender (ed.), *Time and Tide Wait for No Man* (London: Pandora, 1984); B. Harrison, *Prudent Revolutionaries: Portraits of British Feminists between the Wars* (Oxford: Clarendon Press, 1987); J. Alberti, *Beyond Suffrage: Feminists in War and Peace 1914–28* (Basingstoke: Macmillan, 1989); M. Pugh, *Women and the Women's Movement 1914–59* (Basingstoke: Macmillan, 1992); P. M. Graves, *Labour Women: Women in British Working-Class Politics 1918–39* (Cambridge: Cambridge University Press, 1994); D. Jarvis, 'Mrs Maggs and Betty: The Conservative Appeal to Women Voters in the 1920s', *Twentieth Century British History*, 5/2 (1994), 129–52; C. Law, *Suffrage and Power: The Women's Movement 1918–28* (London: I. B. Tauris, 1997).

[9] See e.g. Pugh, *Women and the Women's Movement*, 77–9; J. Alberti, '"A Symbol and a Key": The Suffrage Movement in Britain 1918–28', in J. Purvis and S. S. Holton (eds.), *Votes for Women* (London: Routledge, 2000), 273–4.   [10] Melman, *Women and the Popular Imagination*, 17–18.

[11] Spender, *Time and Tide*, 4.

[12] D. Beddoe, *Back to Home and Duty: Women between the Wars 1918–39* (London: Pandora, 1989), 8.

More recent work reinforces this interpretation of the press. Cheryl Law notes that 'newspapers were full of articles establishing marriage as the pinnacle of fulfilment for women and thereby alternately ridiculing or patronising the single woman', while Sue Bruley agrees that single women were 'vilified' as 'useless members of society'.[13] In general, the emphasis of the press on domesticity and motherhood is usually regarded as part of a concerted effort to reassert 'traditional' gender boundaries after the 'blurring' experienced during the First World War.[14]

Only those whose primary focus of study is the press itself, rather than gender or women, have diverged from this line. Dan LeMahieu, in his study of mass communications in the inter-war period, points out that from its foundation in 1896 the *Daily Mail* actively sought to attract female readers and that its women's pages 'did provide a forum . . . where the self-esteem of women might be enhanced'.[15] Tom Jeffery and Keith McClelland, in their article on the politics of the *Daily Mail*, use market research data to demonstrate the *Mail*'s success in attracting female readers, and observe that the paper was 'full of appeals' to middle-class women.[16] Meanwhile, Patricia Holland, writing from a media studies perspective, has drawn attention to the 'feminization' of the press in the early twentieth century, arguing that this opened up an important new democratic space for women.[17] None of these insights have been followed up by a detailed gendered investigation of the inter-war press, but they do reaffirm the need to delve further than present stereotypes of gender historians.

Yet this study is more than just an attempt to plug a historiographical gap, important though that task is. There is a further intellectual reason for choosing the popular national daily press to explore gender identities. Few, if any, cultural forms contain as diverse a range of material as the newspaper. Inside the covers of the morning newspaper one found reports on not only high politics but also housewifery, on football as well as foreign affairs, on both court cases and the latest fashions. By using newspapers as source material, it is possible to explore a wide range of images and debates, to see how a variety of dif-

---

[13] Law, *Suffrage and Power*, 205; S. Bruley, *Women in Britain since 1900* (Basingstoke: Macmillan, 1999), 62.

[14] For clear expressions of this interpretation, see M. R. Higonnet, J. Jenson, S. Michel, and M. C. Weitz (eds.), *Behind the Lines: Gender and the Two World Wars* (New Haven: Yale University Press, 1987), Introduction; Kent, *Making Peace*, Introduction, chs. 5–6.

[15] D. LeMahieu, *A Culture for Democracy: Mass Communication and the Cultivated Mind in Britain between the Wars* (Oxford: Clarendon Press, 1988), 43.

[16] Jeffrey and McClelland, 'A World Fit to Live In', 50.

[17] P. Holland, 'The Politics of the Smile', in C. Carter, G. Branston, and S. Allen (eds.), *News, Gender and Power* (London: Routledge, 1998), 21.

ferent gendered discourses interacted, interlinked, and contrasted. This is important because femininity and masculinity are complex and fragmented identities, shaped by a multitude of different influences. Too many works on gender concentrate only on one particular theme or stereotype—for example, the 'masculine woman' or the housewife—without exploring how the meaning and impact of these representations were altered when placed alongside other material and contrasting images. Billie Melman, for example, gives a rather misleading impression of the gender discourse of the *Mail* and the *Express* by not only focusing solely on the young single woman, the 'flapper' of the 1920s, but also reproducing almost exclusively hostile comments about her.[18] From her reading it appears as if the popular press was entirely dominated by a deep-seated fear and dislike of the 'surplus' woman, who threatened the basis of political and social stability. In fact, this was only one thread of a much more complex and nuanced pattern, a pattern that can only be appreciated by standing back and observing how all the strands properly weave together. Many other newspaper articles (including several in the very same issues as the hostile comments reproduced by Melman) celebrated the 'modern young woman' and encouraged her to grasp her new opportunities; at the same time, anxieties about modernity were contained by more traditional images of women, as prudent housewives or beautiful companions. Similarly, some works have exaggerated the conservatism of the inter-war period by concentrating solely on the articulation of domesticity and consumerism in the media, without exploring other contemporary perceptions about modernity that significantly influenced attitudes to women. A wide-ranging approach is, of course, just as necessary for the study of masculinity. Disturbing images of shell-shocked soldiers must not be allowed to obscure features venerating manly sportsmen and heroic explorers, or vice versa. This book is an attempt to survey the traditional as well as the modern and new, the areas of consensus as well as of conflict, the sports columns and the women's pages as well as the political articles and editorials.

The final reason that makes the daily press a compelling source lies in its position at the boundary of politics and popular culture. As Amanda Vickery has recently pointed out, historians should beware of defining the 'political' too narrowly.[19] This investigation allows gendered political rhetoric to be placed alongside, and considered in relation to, apparently non-political

---

[18] L. L. Behling's similar study of American culture *The Masculine Woman in America 1890–1935* (Urbana: University of Illinois Press, 2001) has similar limitations.

[19] A. Vickery (ed.), *Women, Privilege and Power: British Politics, 1750 to the Present* (Stanford, Calif.: Stanford University Press, 2001).

constructions: the domestic 'chancellor of the exchequer' of the political columns alongside the 'prudent housewife' of the woman's page, for example. Political imagery inevitably gains or loses potency according to the way in which it resonates with broader, 'non-political' attitudes. The press is also a useful arena in which to examine the possible disjuncture between the political efficacy of the 'feminist' movement, and the more general acceptance of 'feminist' ideas in popular culture. Too often the success of 'feminism' is judged in terms of its legislative fruits or the numbers of people mobilized as avowed supporters. It is just as important to trace its impact in the wider debates of popular discourse—to uncover, for example, general attitudes to the working woman or the female politician—and to determine the extent to which what were at one time regarded as 'feminist attitudes' gradually became more commonly accepted.

The Press and Society

One of the defining features of my research has been a desire to take popular newspapers seriously, on their own terms. Popular newspapers then, as now, did not seek to perform the same functions as the deeply political 'minority'[20] newspapers, nor were they written for the same audience; therefore they should not be measured according to the same yardstick. There is no reason to dismiss as unimportant the content of these papers merely because the emphasis was on brightness rather than on analytical depth and detail. Yet such attitudes have often marred historical investigations of the press. Franklin Reid Gannon, for example, examining the press's assessment of the German threat in the 1930s, argues that it 'would be ludicrous to devote as much space or attention to Lord Beaverbrook's or Lord Rothermere's few unsophisticated and obsessive ideas as to the development of important ideas and attitudes in the columns and offices of the quality newspapers'.[21] Why should such a study be 'ludicrous'? Millions of people read the *Mail* and the *Express*—and Neville Chamberlain, for one, was very concerned about the content of what they were reading.[22] The war that eventually broke out after the failure of 'appeasement' relied on the service

[20] This term is not an ideal label for newspapers such as *The Times* and the *Telegraph*, but I find it preferable, because it is more neutral, than the other usual labels: 'quality', 'class', or 'traditional' press. The popular papers in this study, except the *Mirror*, were broadsheets in this period, so the modern broadsheet–tabloid distinction is not appropriate.

[21] F. Gannon, *The British Press and Germany, 1936–39* (Oxford: Clarendon Press, 1971), p. vii.

[22] As can be seen by his careful 'management' of the press during these years: R. Cockett, *The Twilight of Truth: Chamberlain, Appeasement and the Manipulation of the Press* (London: Weidenfeld & Nicolson, 1989).

of British men and women from across society, and it is impossible to understand their support, especially after the horrors of the First World War, without some knowledge of how the international crisis had been presented in the media.

Nor do I accept the argument that the popular newspapers were merely the ideological tools of entrenched class interests. This interpretation has a long lineage, and has been most recently restated by Jean Chalaby. She claims that 'the press, under the influences of market forces, has essentially become a magic mirror journalists hold to society, with the effect of keeping the popular classes, in particular, in a state of ecstasy and to deny them knowledge about the world and knowledge about their position in the world'.[23] This viewpoint undoubtedly offers some important insights. Powerful interests in society, including the owners of consumer industries, certainly had (and have) a privileged access to the press. The *Daily Herald* in the 1920s, for example, often struggled to secure advertising as a result of its uncompromising left-wing views and its working-class readership; the *Daily Worker* in the 1930s was similarly disadvantaged. An ethos of consumerism permeated the press, sometimes at the expense of engagement with the realities of readers' lives. The contention that the press emphasis on personalities and 'human interest' had the effect of obscuring underlying social structures and inequalities also has some force.[24] Feminists, as I will suggest in Chapter 4, often found it difficult to overcome the reluctance of popular newspapers to discuss 'abstract' or 'theoretical' questions.

Nevertheless, the 'magic mirror' argument exaggerates the coercive power of the media and underestimates the intelligence of the readership. Proprietors, managers, and journalists on popular newspapers were all very conscious that they had to interest their audience sufficiently to persuade them to part with their money. They could not operate in isolation from the demands of their readers. Even before the arrival of market research surveys in the late 1920s, editors and proprietors sought to discover 'what the public wanted'; Northcliffe spied on readers in parks and on trains, and asked almost anyone he came across their opinions about the *Mail*. Newspapers were not necessities of life, and the

---

[23] J. Chalaby, *The Invention of Journalism* (Basingstoke: Macmillan, 1998), 5. Radicals of the 19th century made similar comments. In 1807, for example, William Cobbett declared that 'The English Press, instead of enlightening, does, as far as it has Power, keep the People in Ignorance': cited in T. O'Malley and C. Soley, *Regulating the Press* (London: Pluto Press, 2000), 26. In the 20th century a more sophisticated version of this argument was developed by Theodor Adorno and the Frankfurt school in their writings on the 'Culture Industry'.

[24] J. Curran, A. Douglas, and G. Whannel, 'The Political Economy of the Human Interest Story', in A. Smith (ed.), *Newspapers and Democracy: International Essays on a Changing Medium* (Cambridge, Mass.: MIT Press, 1980).

habit of reading them only became widely entrenched in this period because they offered good value and appealing material.[25] And if not radical in a conventional political sense, the unsettling impact that the popular press made by elevating the popular and commercial above the 'cultured' and 'refined' should not be forgotten. Placing 'human interest' stories about 'ordinary' people alongside the activities of politicians and diplomats, or material about housewifery opposite an opera review, carried a democratic challenge that had a significance well beyond serving the producers' interests in the market. It was this anxiety that Queenie Leavis expressed in 1932 when she observed that Northcliffe's main impact had been 'to mobilise the people to outvote the minority, who had hitherto set the standard of taste without serious challenge'.[26]

Some feminists have adapted this model of the media as a tool for class interests to argue that the press, cinema, and broadcasting operated unswervingly as instruments for the maintenance of 'patriarchy'. This has led to sweeping denunciations and dismissals of the content of popular culture.[27] Once again, I would accept many of the observations contained in these critiques. There can be little doubt that the products of the media routinely patronized and stereotyped women, and that they both shared and reinforced wider attitudes that denied women equal opportunities with men. On the other hand, generalizations about the 'interests of patriarchy' can obscure as much as they reveal, and there is a danger that ebbs and flows within the general context of inequality are overlooked. This study argues that there were significant shifts in thinking about gender relations in this period, even if women continued to be regarded as the 'second sex'. More fundamentally, however, I reject the idea that the tentacles of 'patriarchy' reached everywhere. There were many different 'voices' to be found in each of the newspapers under discussion and it is by no means possible to categorize them all as 'patriarchal'. Popular newspapers portrayed female achievers in a variety of spheres and sometimes carried powerful 'feminist' messages; they also created spaces where women spoke directly to other women about their lives. Women could obtain both pleasure and inspi-

---

[25] Joseph McAleer makes similar points when assessing popular fiction in this period: *Popular Reading and Publishing 1914–50* (Oxford: Clarendon Press, 1992), Conclusion.

[26] Q. D. Leavis, *Fiction and the Reading Public* (first pub. 1932; London: Chatto & Windus, 1965), 185.

[27] Various feminist works of the 1970s took up this position: there is a powerful strain of it, for example, in Germaine Greer's discussion of 'romance' in *The Female Eunuch* (London: Paladin, 1971). Laura Mulvey's influential 'Visual Pleasure and Narrative Cinema' argues that classic Hollywood cinema was completely structured around the male gaze and male fantasies: *Screen*, 16/3: 6–18; Angela McRobbie also sought to show how patriarchal ideology shaped the girls' magazine *Jackie*, '*Jackie*: An Ideology of Adolescent Femininity', in B. Waites, T. Bennet, and G. Martin (eds.), *Popular Culture: Past and Present* (London: Croom Helm, 1982), 263–83. For more recent restatements, see K. Davies, J. Dickey, and T. Stratford, *Out of Focus: Writings on Women and the Media* (London: Women's Press, 1987) and B. Fowler, *The Alienated Reader: Women and Popular Romantic Literature in the 20th Century* (Hemel Hempstead: Harvester Wheatsheaf, 1991).

ration from the popular press, just as they could from other mass media forms, as several recent commentators have demonstrated.[28] Women, no less than the working classes, could not be duped into purchasing a product that was invariably hostile or offensive. Rather than viewing newspapers through the single lens of patriarchy, then, I have treated them as the sites of an ongoing discursive contest between various and diverse images of femininity and masculinity in which a number of different interests were represented.

None of this is to suggest that newspapers offer the historian a convenient and unproblematic window into society, or that they operated as a mirror which accurately and unfailingly reflected the 'reality' of social attitudes. Newspapers had their own agendas, and each made their own selections of what to report, and what they judged to be significant, out of an almost limitless set of social happenings. The final product was the outcome of complex series of decisions which balanced what proprietors, editors, journalists, and outside contributors wanted to produce, what they assumed the target audience wanted to read, and what was (perceived to be) required for commercial and financial success (namely, securing advertising contracts and maximizing circulation). The journalist did not necessarily believe what he or she wrote, just as the reader did not necessarily believe what he or she read. The press did not wield an overwhelming persuasive power over its audience. Studies of high-profile political and electoral campaigns waged by the press have demonstrated the inability of newspapers to convert readers against their will, and in any case readers tend to select the paper that most closely fits their own preconceptions.[29] While texts usually contain a 'preferred' meaning, this meaning can always be negotiated, resisted, or ignored by the reader.[30] Neither the editors nor the audience, nor indeed the advertisers, were likely to get exactly what they wanted, but there was a set of 'feedback loops' between each of them, in the form of sales figures and market research, which ensured that each party had some input into the newspaper.[31]

---

[28] See e.g. A. Light, 'Returning to Manderley': Romance Fiction, Female Sexuality, and Class', in S. Kemp and J. Squires (eds.), *Feminisms* (Oxford: Oxford University Press, 1997), and Light, *Forever England*; J. Winship, *Inside Women's Magazines* (London: Pandora, 1987); C. Squire, 'Empowering Women? The Oprah Winfrey Show', in P. Marris and S. Thornham (eds.), *Media Studies: A Reader*, 2nd edn. (Edinburgh: Edinburgh University Press, 1999); B. Soland, *Becoming Modern: Young Women and the Reconstruction of Womanhood in the 1920s* (Princeton: Princeton University Press, 2000).

[29] Mass Observation reports were sceptical about the ability of the press to mould public opinion: e.g. Bodleian Library, Oxford, X. Films 200, Mass Observation, File Report 126, 'Report on the Press', May 1940. See also the comments of Tom Harrison, 'The Popular Press', *Horizon* (Aug. 1940), 172, where he discusses the suspicions of the public regarding editorials and political campaigns. For more recent studies, see J. Tunstall, *Newspaper Power: The New National Press in Britain* (Oxford: Clarendon Press, 1996), ch. 15.

[30] For a discussion of these different ways of reading, see Stuart Hall, 'Encoding/Decoding', in Marris and Thornham, *Media Studies*.   [31] LeMahieu, *Culture for Democracy*, 18–19.

Yet if these newspapers cannot offer an unproblematic guide to the attitudes of individuals, they remain of immense historical value for the contribution they made to the public and political discourse of the period. These newspapers helped to frame and shape many of the public debates about gender roles and the relations between the sexes—indeed, they supplied some of the very terms with which the discussions were conducted, popularizing, for example, the labels 'flapper' and 'the dole'. The gender historian can obtain valuable insights into the state of contemporary discourse by examining which types of material newspapers included and which they excluded; by investigating what values were regarded as controversial and what were beyond question; by uncovering the assumptions journalists held about what men and women wanted to read. And if the coercive power of the press should not be exaggerated, nor should its influence on social attitudes be overlooked. Whereas explicit, short-term polit- ical campaigns seem to have had relatively little effect, it is harder to discount the impact of the more subtle, longer-term process by which opinions on less overtly political subjects were shaped by repeated exposure to the values embed- ded in the press. The PEP Report observed that while the proprietor intervened to dictate policy on major political issues, this 'is not necessarily the sphere in which the newspaper's public influence is most potent . . . In the long run the direction of opinion from above in large matters may be less important than the uncensored treatment of a mass of small matters from day to day.'[32] The over- whelming support given to marriage, or the monarchy, in public discourse, to take two obvious examples, helped to explain the strength and resilience of these institutions in the first half of the century. It is difficult to believe that pop- ular ideas about femininity and masculinity were not influenced in some ways by the contents of newspapers that were read by many people day in, day out, for years on end. As Peter Catterall and his colleagues have argued, the impact of the press 'is none the less for being generally immeasurable'.[33]

The Limits of the Research

In this book I have focused my attention on the five main popular national daily morning newspapers of the period: the *Daily Mail*, the *Daily Express*, the *Daily Mirror*, the *Daily Herald*, and the *Daily News* (which in 1930 became the

---

[32] PEP, *Report*, 185–6. A similar point is made in Curran et al., 'The Political Economy of the Human Interest Story'.

[33] Introduction, in P. Catterall, C. Seymour-Ure, and A. Smith (eds.), *Northcliffe's Legacy: Aspects of the British Popular Press 1896–1996* (Basingstoke: Macmillan, 2000), 1.

News Chronicle). These papers dominated the market, both in terms of circulation and also stylistically, providing the models that were widely copied at the time and subsequently. These five papers also offer a useful spectrum of political and class approaches. The Liberal-oriented *News Chronicle* and Labour-supporting *Daily Herald* balanced the conservatism—if not always translated into Conservatism—of the *Mail*, the *Express*, and the *Mirror* (with the *Mirror* moving steadily leftwards from the mid-1930s). Similarly, the predominantly working-class readership of the *Herald* contrasted with the class mix of the *Express* and the middle-class circulation of the *Mail* and the *Mirror*. Of the popular daily market, this only excludes three papers, the *Daily Chronicle*, the *Daily Sketch*, and the *Daily Graphic* (which merged with the *Sketch* in 1926). The *News Chronicle* was established in 1930 through an amalgamation of the two remaining liberal dailies, the *News* and the *Chronicle*. I have chosen the *News* to represent the liberal press in the 1920s for two reasons. Firstly, the amalgamation in 1930 was in reality more of a takeover of the *Chronicle* by the *News*: the majority of the editorial staff of the *Chronicle* were released, and so there was a far greater continuity of policy after 1930 with the *News* than its rival paper.[34] Secondly, the *News* was politically to the left of the *Chronicle* in the 1920s, and so provides a better political balance for the purposes of the study. With regard to the *Daily Sketch* and the *Daily Graphic*, neither of these two picture papers was particularly innovative and they tended to follow the *Daily Mirror*, at least until the mid-1930s. The *Daily Worker*, set up in 1930 to support the Communist Party and to rival the *Herald* on the left, should be regarded as a special case, and is worthy of a separate study. It never came close to achieving the circulation achieved by its well-funded rivals, and its content was always more overtly political than the other papers under consideration here. In any case, a position to the left of the Labour Party is represented in this investigation by the early issues of the *Daily Herald*, before its takeover by the Trades Union Congress in 1922.

The popular London evening and national Sunday newspapers will also remain in the background. The two main evening papers, the *Evening News* and the *Evening Standard*, were for most of this period closely associated with the *Daily Mail* and the *Daily Express* respectively, and rarely offered a substantially different approach. The most successful Sunday papers, such as the *News of the World* and *The People*, did indeed record higher circulations than individual issues of the dailies, and were influential in suggesting the sort of content

---

[34] Trinity College, Cambridge, Walter Layton Papers, Box 85, fo. 27, May–June 1930, memo on merger of *Daily News* and *Daily Chronicle*.

that was required to tap the working-class market. Nevertheless, Sunday publications had their own traditions and idiosyncrasies, and are not entirely com-
parable with the popular dailies. Furthermore, because they were published
only weekly, it was not possible to trace events and unfolding debates in their
pages in the same detail as was possible in the daily press. Some of the issues
explored in this book received only minimal coverage in the restricted confines
of the Sunday papers. In any case, in the broader historical view, it was the
rise of the national daily press that was the most significant and distinctive
feature of the inter-war period. Although the circulation gains of the Sundays
were impressive after 1918, a mass market had already been established in this
field before the turn of the century; popular weeklies had been hugely out-
stripping the sales of dailies since the mid-nineteenth century. The spread of
the national daily throughout the population between the wars, on the other
hand, was a major new development, taking newspaper reading onto an
entirely different level. It is this phenomenon that is at the heart of this study.

Sources

Three types of primary source have been used in order to carry out this gendered analysis of the national daily press. They represent, in terms of Stuart
Hall's influential schema, each of the three 'moments' of any cultural form: its
production (encoding), the text itself, and its reception by the audience
(decoding).[35] Editorial and proprietorial archives that give an insight into the
process of producing the newspapers are frustratingly patchy for this period:
primary material for the *Daily Mail* after Northcliffe's death in 1922, and for the
Mirror throughout this period, is almost non-existent. Nevertheless, there
are some primary documents from each of the five newspapers under investigation, and when these are supplemented by the weekly journals of the
press industry, diaries, memoirs, and printed recollections (which do, of
course, have their own limitations and problems), a fairly clear picture of
editorial attitudes and aspirations can be constructed. In this way, the gendered
assumptions that shaped both the content and style of the daily press can be
uncovered.

The second primary source is the newspapers themselves. When examining
five newspapers over a twenty-year period, selectivity is clearly required. My
sampling has been determined by a desire to investigate not only the coverage

---

[35] Hall, 'Encoding/Decoding', 51–61.

of particular, 'significant' events and debates, but also occurrences and disputes not usually regarded in retrospect as historically important. Controversies over the respectability of 'mixed bathing' on beaches, for example, rarely feature prominently in the secondary literature, but they are very revealing of contemporary attitudes and the way the press portrayed 'modern women'. Therefore, I have both selected specific weeks to study (at times of general elections, feminist activity, major diplomatic occurrences, remembrance days, the Radclyffe Hall controversy, etc.), and chosen others at random. I have tried to respond to the subjects and debates regarded as significant by contemporaries. I examined several copies of each of my five newspapers from each of the twenty years under consideration, and ended with a sample of well over 1,000 issues.

The third type of source material comes from contemporary responses to the actual newspapers. Market research surveys of press readership were conducted from the late 1920s, and immediately before and during the Second World War Mass Observation carried out its own investigations into reading habits. Also available are some of the reactions of feminists, politicians, and the literary elite, in their discussions of the impact and significance of the daily press. Although the primary focus of this book is the newspapers themselves, on their discussions of masculinity and femininity and on the gendered outlook that shaped their overall format, this evidence does provide some useful pointers to the way the papers and their opinions were received. And because some of this material was available to the producers of the papers, it deepens our understanding of their perceptions of the market they were serving, and of the types of response they hoped to receive. Here is the 'feedback loop' that was an important factor in serving the mass market.

Approaching the Newspapers

At the heart of the study are the newspapers themselves, and I have suggested some of the thinking behind my sampling process. Yet how were the papers, once selected, to be 'read'? To move beyond the usual stereotypes that historians have about press content, a more sophisticated approach is required, one that uses some of the techniques practised in cultural studies.[36] The assumption that underlies most references to the press in the existing historiography is

---

[36] Margaret Beetham, for example, discusses how 'literary and social historians' tend to read magazines not as 'texts' but rather as 'repositories' from which they can remove '"facts" [or] expressions of ideas and ideology', and how this can be misleading: *A Magazine of her Own?*, 6.

that newspapers had clear and coherent gender 'policies': that they deliberately and consistently supported domesticity, for example, or maintained a systematic opposition to the 'flapper'. This supposition actually stems from a false generalization from the political material of popular newspapers. Each newspaper certainly developed a clearly established political identity, as determined by the proprietor in conjunction with his editors. Beaverbrook's *Express* supported pro-Empire, protectionist, conservative measures, just as the *Daily Herald* followed the moderate trade unionist Labour line, at least after 1922. Although not always entirely consistent—the *Mail* and the *Express* vacillated in their attitude towards Stanley Baldwin, for example—the position taken by each paper on most political questions was fairly predictable. The situation, unsurprisingly, was rather different with regard to gender. Contemporaries did not think in modern terms about the social construction of masculinity or femininity, and it was usually accepted that 'women's issues' could be left to the 'common sense' of journalists. Proprietors and editors rarely dictated particular policies on such matters as the marriage bar or women's position in the Civil Service, still less on how generally to portray the 'modern young woman' or the housewife. Only when specific issues hit the top of the political agenda—such as in 1927–8, when the equalization of the franchise was under consideration—was there definite instruction from above to achieve consistency.

Otherwise, one usually found a multiplicity of different voices and images. Moving between the political columns and the sports pages, from the women's section to the feature articles, one could come across a variety of divergent gender visions. Single women might be grossly stereotyped on one page, only to be praised on another; equal pay might be advocated by a contributor to one issue, only for it to be ridiculed by another in the same paper the following week. Celebrations of domesticity did not preclude advice to professional women on how to progress in their careers, nor did portrayals of war-ravaged ex-soldiers entail the exclusion of tales of heroic masculinity elsewhere. Moreover, editors often deliberately presented gender topics as 'talking points' to be debated with evidence printed on either side ('Is mixed education useful?') or offered an extreme view knowing that a story could be made out of the inevitable reaction ('Bishop denounces modern dress'). Obviously, certain papers tended to take up particular positions more frequently than others, and general patterns and trends can be highlighted. Nevertheless, we must jettison the assumption that newspapers contributed to the popular discourse on gender simply as *participants* putting forward coherent 'policies'. They were also *arenas* in which a variety of different opinions and images competed. The popular press did not unthinkingly champion housewifery and motherhood; its pages debated and explored what these roles meant for women and society, offered a range of perspectives, and explicitly and implicitly contrasted them with other possible roles. The task of the historian is to trace how these multivocal debates developed around particular themes and interacted with each other.

In examining the newspapers, then, I have attempted to embrace this diversity. Material from every section of the newspapers, from editorials and political reports to sports articles and film reviews, is used in this study, and photographs, cartoons, and adverts are also assessed. But the diversity has to be analysed and reduced to some form of order. The book is divided thematically to focus on each of the main sets of discussions—exploring, in turn, 'modernity', housewifery and motherhood, politics, fashion and sexuality, war and peace, and the evolution of masculinity. It will be noted that masculinity receives rather less space than femininity. This is by no means to suggest that it is any less important than femininity: it is merely a reflection of the fact that the newspapers themselves explicitly discussed women *as a sex* far more frequently than they did men. Femininity in these years was far more fluid and contested than masculinity.

Within each chapter, the material is organized into two main sections. After a brief introduction, each chapter begins with an examination of the various, sometimes conflicting, editorial policies and pressures that shaped the coverage of each subject. As my research progressed, it became clear that merely recording the different opinions presented before me as if they were plucked from discrete, self-sufficient articles would be inadequate and would only reveal part of the story. Their context in the columns of a popular daily newspaper was of vital significance. Not only did the way in which an article was presented, and the other material that surrounded it, alter its range of meaning, its actual content might well have been shaped by wider editorial policies. To take a simple example, a political columnist who privately believed that women were incapable of sound political judgement would usually have to mask his opinions to fall in with the overriding editorial desire to appeal to female voters and mobilize their support behind the paper's preferred party or cause; similarly, the inclination to condemn modern fashions and behaviour was frequently tempered by the need to attract younger readers for both circulation and advertising purposes. The study of gender discourse cannot be dissociated from an examination of the medium in which the discourse operates, and the constraints and opportunities that the medium opens up.

The second, more lengthy, section of each chapter provides an overview of how each gender theme was discussed in the five papers: the issues which received the greatest coverage, the main points of controversy, the divergences between the different papers, the ways in which the debates developed over time. What might be thought of as the 'balancing points' of these exchanges are identified: with opinions expressed on either side of most subjects, I try to demonstrate a sense of where the equilibrium rested. In the midst of all the conflicting images, what was the *general* impression that was likely to emerge of the character of the 'flapper', the housewife, or the 'modern man'? At certain points other tools are also employed. Content analysis is used to provide more detailed information about the composition of the women's pages (see the Appendix), and also the nature of the political commentary during general elections. Content analysis on its own is a rather blunt tool: categorization is often difficult to judge, and the deeper meanings invested in the material can be lost. In conjunction with other evidence, however, it does have a place, and it can bring into relief previously hidden trends.[37] Elsewhere, I decided that certain parts of the material can best be examined by focusing the spotlight closely on the reporting of a particular incident or controversy: the *Mirror*'s coverage of the Sudetenland crisis in 1938, for example, or the *Mail*'s treatment of mixed bathing in the early 1920s. These case studies are designed to prevent the general overviews from becoming too sketchy. Some cartoons, photographs, and advertisements are also reproduced, so that the visual impact of the newspapers is not entirely lost. By organizing the material in these ways, then, I hope that a coherent analysis will emerge.

Overview

Before these thematic discussions, the first chapter will set out the context by describing the evolution of the popular daily press from the late Victorian period. With the launch of the *Daily Mail* in 1896, Alfred Harmsworth (ennobled in 1905 as Lord Northcliffe) introduced the populist tendencies of the Sunday and evening press into morning journalism. 'News' was redefined to make 'human interest' and the events of 'everyday life' more prominent. Northcliffe courted female readers far more urgently than previous editors: not only could they boost circulations, they were increasingly important as the targets of the 'display' advertising that became a crucial source of revenue. Popular newspapers gradually recognized that they could no longer afford to ignore or alienate female readers, and a range of enticements was included for them, from

[37] On the problems of content analysis, see L. van Zoonen, *Feminist Media Studies* (London: Sage, 1994), 68–74.

'women's pages' to serial stories. During the inter-war years, the 'Northcliffe revolution' finally triumphed, and all of the major popular newspapers assimilated and then extended the pioneer's principles. By the end of the 1930s the female audience had moved from the margins to the centre of editorial calculations, a journey that was clearly reflected in the content of the papers.

These developments partly explain the fascination with the post-war 'modern young woman', the subject of Chapter 2. The press reinforced the powerful contemporary belief that the Great War had transformed the position of women, and it dramatized the debate between those who celebrated women's (perceived) new freedoms and those who were alarmed at the prospect of 'masculine women' invading male preserves. I argue that the media hostility to those young women who challenged convention or remained outside the home after 1918 has been considerably overstated. In general, new opportunities at work or on the sports field were presented in a positive fashion, and opponents of these changes were frequently portrayed as 'old-fashioned'. On the other hand, the widespread belief that women were inexorably striding towards equality perhaps weakened the appeal of feminism, which was often now depicted as 'superfluous' and 'out of date'.

Chapter 3 examines the portrayal of the housewife and mother in this 'post-war modernity'. While the press continued to celebrate these traditional roles, performed by the majority of women, there was a widespread recognition that domestic life needed to be reformed to make it more suitable for modern conditions and acceptable to the new generation of seemingly more assertive women. But attempts to raise housewifery and motherhood to the level of 'professions' through the 'scientific' advice of 'experts' could also have the effect of increasing women's burdens with higher standards and expectations. Meanwhile, the housewife's status as family consumer took on a new significance as the market for domestic products expanded. Again, this was a double-edged tendency: while women's spending power commanded the attention of both editors and advertisers, the consumerist focus of many articles meant that the shortages of money and space that continued to frustrate many housewives were often overlooked.

Chapter 4 looks at changes in political discourse in the wake of the enfranchisement of women in 1918. It demonstrates that each newspaper made substantial efforts to engage female voters by championing 'women's issues' and developing a 'feminized' political language. While women were encouraged to make use of their political power, however, they were often discursively confined to particular subjects, thought to be relevant to the housewife or mother.

Patronizing assumptions about a shared set of 'female' values and interests remained in evidence. Nevertheless, the hostility shown to women by the *Daily Mail* during the 'flapper vote' crusade of 1927–8 was far from typical, and I argue that this campaign was motivated more by the passionate anti-socialism of the proprietor, Lord Rothermere, than by anti-feminism.

Chapter 5 concentrates on the subjects of fashion and sexuality. It explains the intense post-war interest in women's dress in terms of the way in which short skirts and short hair came to symbolize modernity and the changed relationship between the sexes. It demonstrates that the popular press were not blithely opposed to modern fashions or the liberalization of morality, but often celebrated these very developments. Ideas about the 'companionate' marriage were aired, and problem pages placed a new emphasis on emotional compatibility. On the other hand, the perception of women as decoration for the male gaze was reinforced as pictures of 'bathing belles' became standard press features. A double standard of morality still existed, albeit in a more covert form, and while editors were happy to exploit 'sex appeal' with their photography, they were often reluctant to discuss issues such as birth control and venereal disease.

Chapter 6 examines how the experience of the Great War and the prospect of a future conflict influenced the treatment of gender. I show that pre-war notions of patriotism and imperial manliness were re-evaluated after the horrors of the trenches. As it became clear that the Great War had not in fact secured a lasting peace, there was growing disillusionment with older imperial attitudes and the ideals of masculinity that were informed by them. The *Daily Mail* under Rothermere was the one paper that stood apart from this current of opinion, and it promoted fascist policies that promised to 'invigorate' the nation. Meanwhile, after 1918 women were frequently shown bearing the sorrow of a grieving nation. Now armed with the vote, they were presented as a powerful force for peace. As another war approached in 1938–9, however, it was widely assumed that women would drop their objections and serve the nation against Nazi Germany.

Chapter 7 considers the evolution of masculinity in more detail. I argue that the fear of 'effeminacy' was a repeated feature of press discourse at this time; in particular the debates about mass male unemployment and the effects of the 'dole' revealed anxieties about the character of the 'modern man', which were intensified by the challenge seemingly posed by women entering the workforce in greater numbers. Nevertheless, a substantial amount of material celebrated and buttressed traditional masculine virtues, even if they were now exercised in different contexts: sportsmen and film stars gradually replaced imperial conquerors and explorers in the pantheon of male heroes. Between these two poles, the press was quietly encouraging a modest reformation of masculinity by advising men to become more involved in the domestic sphere and more aware of the emotional needs of their wives and children.

Because the basic approach of this book is to highlight the variety of gender discourses, images, and perspectives to be found in the pages of the popular press, it is not possible to produce conclusions that are neat and clear-cut. Nevertheless, certain generalizations can be made. My underlying argument is that the gender discourse of the press cannot be adequately understood through the model of the post-war 'backlash', which remains the dominant paradigm in much of the historiography. The potency of the 'cult of domesticity' that has been taken to characterize this period has been exaggerated: the fascination with modernity and the 'modern woman' prevented the material on marriage and motherhood from becoming too constricting or enveloping. The popular press generally embraced the new opportunities and freedoms for women: political coverage was reshaped to include and engage female voters, careers advice was offered to those seeking to enter the world of employment, and the relaxation of restrictive dress codes and social conventions was celebrated. At the same time, this re-evaluation of femininity was kept within strict limits. The reality of sexual difference pervaded the press; men and women had their own pages, were pictured differently in photographs, and were fitted into contrasting stereotypes in reports. More particularly, women remained subject to the male gaze: fashion accounted for the largest portion of 'women's material' and beauty was the most important criterion for selecting photos of women. Women were sexualized in popular culture as never before, and because sexual freedom and frankness seemed to run along the grain of modernity, this tendency was difficult to challenge. Opposition to it could be dismissed as old-fashioned prudery. Overall, it seems clear that convenient labels such as 'progress' or 'retreat' are inappropriate: this book presents a complex picture of fragmented change.

I

The Evolution of the Popular Daily Press

Inter-war popular journalism was conducted in the shadow of Lord North-cliffe, the founder of the first two million-selling daily papers, the *Daily Mail* and the *Daily Mirror*. To his admirers, such as his self-appointed heir Lord Beaverbrook, he was the 'greatest figure who ever strode down Fleet Street';[1] to his detractors he was the man 'whose interference with reading habits alone . . . effectively put literature out of the reach of the average man'.[2] Few doubted his cultural significance, however, or the influence of his model for the popular daily newspaper. The launch of the *Daily Mail* in May 1896 quickly became a landmark in press history to match the ending of the 'taxes on knowledge'. When the authoritative *Report on the British Press* issued by Political and Economic Planning (PEP) in 1938 stated baldly that the publication of the first issue of Northcliffe's paper 'may be taken as the beginning of modern journalism', it was merely echoing the sentiments of several other observers.[3]

The populism and the emphasis on 'human interest' stories that characterized the *Mail* were not, in fact, unfamiliar in the press world. After all, Matthew Arnold had coined the term 'new journalism' nine years before Northcliffe's paper hit the news-stands, and Sunday newspapers had been enticing hundreds of thousands of readers with their diet of 'sensational' stories for half a century.[4] Northcliffe's innovation was rather to transfer these populist techniques to the arena of the national morning newspaper, where traditional news values

[1] M. Aitken (Lord Beaverbrook), *Politicians and the War, 1914–16* (London: Thornton Butterworth, 1928), 99.

[2] Q. D. Leavis, *Fiction and the Reading Public* (first pub. 1932; London: Chatto & Windus, 1965), 224.

[3] Political and Economic Planning (PEP), *Report on the British Press* (London, 1938), 9. For similar assessments, see e.g. H. Herd, *The Making of Modern Journalism* (London: G. Allen & Unwin, 1927), 91; H. Fyfe, *Northcliffe: An Intimate Biography* (London: G. Allen & Unwin, 1930), 69; A. J. Cummings, *The Press and a Changing Civilisation* (London: John Lane, 1936), 34.

[4] Matthew Arnold, 'Up to Easter', *Nineteenth Century*, 21 (May 1887), 638–9.

remained largely unchallenged and respectability was the pre-eminent virtue. In doing so, he started a process which revolutionized the style, content, and circulation of the daily press, and at the same time completely changed the gender dynamics of popular newspapers. He moved the female reader from the margins to the centre of editorial calculations, ensuring that the definition of 'news' was radically altered, that the boundary between 'public' and 'private' was redrawn, and that the visibility of women in public discourse was transformed. This chapter will describe the remodelling of the daily press and show how the pursuit of the mass market brought issues of gender to the forefront of the newspaper operation.

The Reorientation of News Values

The late Victorian national morning press, against which the *Daily Mail* was to react, operated according to a narrow definition both of what was 'newsworthy' and of who its audience should be. Newspapers were dominated by reports of the happenings of the 'public sphere'—parliamentary debates and the machinations of party politics, diplomatic and imperial developments, financial and business transactions, the activities of 'high society'—leavened with a sprinkling of crime and sports stories. Political speeches and public meetings were reported at great length, with little attempt to summarize or analyse the material. After all, the projected reader was the educated 'man of affairs', participating in civic society according to the classical ideal: he could be expected to form his own conclusions.[5] The appearance of the paper was as austere as its contents. Very few illustrations were included, and there was no attempt to guide readers to important stories with informative and varied headlines (see Fig. 1.1). The reader was expected to have the leisure to work carefully through the paper column by column. In reality, as the PEP Report observed, this meant that the reading matter was 'suitable only for those who could retire to their clubs at four o'clock and spend two or three hours in digesting it'.[6] The Victorian morning newspaper was therefore an overwhelmingly masculine product. Editorial matter was almost exclusively concerned with a public world in which women could play little part. Women were largely invisible in the columns: they were located instead in the domestic, 'private' sphere, which was considered to be the proper subject of women's magazines rather than of a 'serious' organ of political affairs. As women were excluded from the franchise,

[5] L. Brown, *Victorian News and Newspapers* (Oxford: Clarendon Press, 1985), chs. 5, 11.
[6] PEP *Report*, 93.

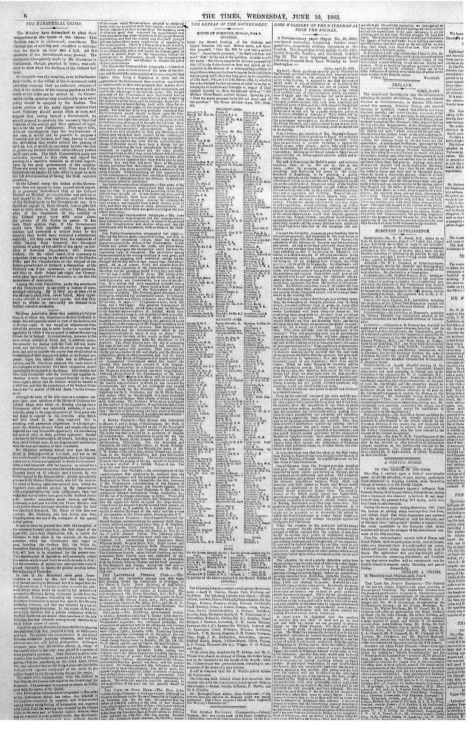

F<small>IG</small>. 1.1. The main news page of *The Times*, 10 June 1885, reporting the resignation of Gladstone's government. Little effort was made to guide the reader to the most important stories of the day; indeed, *The Times* did not include a double-column headline until December 1932

it was rarely necessary to address them in debate and discussion. Periodically, 'almost as though it were grudgingly recognised that women could read', as Northcliffe's right-hand man Kennedy Jones noted, an occasional half-column would be devoted to fashion or food prices.[7] In general, however, editors were too busy pursuing the intricacies of party politics to be concerned with broadening the readership of their papers. As Lucy Brown concludes in her wide-ranging survey of the Victorian press, the morning newspapers 'made no attempt . . . to adjust their presentation of the news to people of limited education' and 'did not try to attract readers through a simplification of thought and vocabulary'.[8] Political influence at Westminster, not a large circulation, was the most sought-after prize.

Other publications had demonstrated well before the end of the nineteenth century that higher circulations could be generated with a different set of news values and brighter, more readable articles. From the 1840s Sunday papers such as *Lloyd's Weekly News* and the *News of the World* developed a successful mixture based essentially upon human-interest stories spiced in some way with sex, crime, or both, supplemented with sport and music features. During the 1880s Newnes's *Tit-Bits* demonstrated the popularity of the magazine miscellany, while the *Pall Mall Gazette* and the *Star*, under W. T. Stead and T. P. O'Connor respectively, increased the prominence of 'personal journalism' in the metropolitan press by conducting interviews and launching high-profile campaigns.[9] In the provinces, furthermore, a new breed of halfpenny evening papers capitalized on greater prosperity and the growing popularity of sport to extend the readership of the daily press. Northcliffe learnt from all these ventures, and from America, where James Gordon Bennett at the *New York Herald* and Charles Dana at the *New York Sun* had successfully developed a new concise style with snappy headlines and a more attractive layout.[10] Using elements from each of these publications, but moderating the sensationalism of the Sunday press and rejecting the more daring typography of the American papers, he launched the *Daily Mail*. Hamilton Fyfe, a trusted contributor, recalled that 'the Chief' wanted his new paper to 'touch life at every point . . . He saw that very few people wanted politics, while a very large number wanted to be

[7] K. Jones, *Fleet Street and Downing Street* (London: Hutchinson, 1920), 84.

[8] Brown, *Victorian News*, 30, 100.

[9] On *Tit-Bits*, see K. Jackson, 'George Newnes and the "Loyal Tit-Bitites"', in L. Brake, B. Bell, and D. Finkelstein (eds.), *Nineteenth Century Media and the Construction of Identities* (Basingstoke: Palgrave, 2000). On Stead, O'Connor, and the 'new journalism', see J. H. Wiener, *Papers for the Millions: The New Journalism in Britain, 1850s–1914* (New York: Greenwood, 1988).

[10] William Randolph Hearst told how Northcliffe admitted being heavily influenced by the American press, and especially Dana's *Sun*; letter to *Editor and Publisher: The Fourth Estate* (US), 17 Aug. 1929, clipping in House of Lords Record Office, Beaverbrook Papers, H/65.

entertained, diverted, relieved a little while from the pressure or tedium of their everyday affairs.'[11] Selling at a halfpenny, half the price of its rivals, the *Mail* sought to reach the huge market as yet untapped by the daily press.

Northcliffe demoted the masculine public sphere from its position of over-whelming dominance in the news pages. 'Four leading articles, a page of Parliament and columns of speeches will NOT be found in the *Daily Mail* on 4 May', promised advertising posters before the first issue, and the pledge was kept.[12] No longer would dry parliamentary orations be recorded in full, and political events would now be reported not for the educated elites, but for the average reader. Kennedy Jones told his staff to 'Make the news clear. Avoid technical terms or explain them. State who the persons are whose names are mentioned . . . Don't forget that you are writing for the meanest intelligence.'[13] In much of the paper, the complexities of politics or diplomacy were passed over in favour of intriguing material from everyday life. Northcliffe repeatedly told his staff that 'people are so much more interesting than things' and called for stories that would feed the curiosity of readers about their fellow citizens.[14] As Robert Graves and Alan Hodge observed in 1940, Northcliffe decisively abandoned

the convention that news was only what men talked about in clubs. He knew it to be also what people talked about in the kitchen, parlour, drawing-room, and over the garden-wall; namely, other people—their failures and successes, their joys and sorrows, their money and their food, their peccadilloes. The *Daily Mail* was thus the first to cater for women readers.[15]

Northcliffe may not have been 'the discoverer of the woman reader', as he was labelled by the *Manchester Guardian* editor and press historian A. P. Wadsworth, but his pursuit of the female audience was far more consistent and committed than previous pioneers of popular journalism, and it was his success that ensured competitors followed the lead.[16] His experiences before founding the *Mail* had convinced him of the potential of the female market. As editor of *Bicycling News* in the late 1880s, Northcliffe had taken the unusual step of employing a female correspondent to write articles promoting riding for

[11] Fyfe, *Northcliffe*, 343.

[12] S. J. Taylor, *The Great Outsiders: Northcliffe, Rothermere and the Daily Mail* (London: Weidenfeld & Nicolson, 1996), 32.   [13] Jones, *Fleet Street*, 145.

[14] e.g. Bodleian Library, Oxford, MS Eng. hist. d. 303–5, Northcliffe Bulletins, 13 Nov. 1919; British Library, Northcliffe Papers, Add. MS 62234, Northcliffe to Alexander Kenealy, 'The Ten Commandments', undated.

[15] R. Graves and A. Hodge, *The Long Week-End: A Social History of Great Britain 1918–1939* (first pub. 1940; Harmondsworth: Penguin, 1971), 55.

[16] A. P. Wadsworth, 'Newspaper Circulations 1800–1954', *Transactions of the Manchester Statistical Society*, Session 1954–5 (1955), 30.

women, and following the popularity of his *Answers* publication, he launched two magazines for women, *Forget-Me-Not* and *Home Chat* in 1891 and 1895 respectively.[17] By 1896 he was determined that the *Mail* should make a direct address to the woman reader. Having decided that the content of the newspaper needed to be broadened by including a page of features—heralded in the first issue as the 'Daily Magazine, An Entirely New Idea In Morning Journalism', which would provide every week 'matter equivalent to a sixpenny monthly'—space was explicitly marked out for women's interests.[18] Northcliffe ignored the advice of his editorial partner Kennedy Jones, who was sceptical about the suitability of such material, and made a firm commitment to female readers:[19] 'Movements in a woman's world—that is to say, changes in dress, toilet matters, cookery, and home matters generally—are as much entitled to receive attention as nine out of ten of the matters which are treated of in the ordinary daily paper. Therefore, two columns are set aside exclusively for ladies.'[20] This section was not to be a haven for amateurs. The paper announced that the 'department will be under the direction of a lady who till recently occupied the editorial chair of a leading fashion weekly' (Mary Howarth) and underlined that the various subjects under consideration 'will all be treated by experts'. Across the page, a signed article by 'Lady Charlotte' gave readers a hint of the aristocratic sophistication that would be put at their disposal.[21] Every effort was made to ensure that the audience did not share Kennedy Jones's belief that these features were inappropriate or 'vulgar'.

In this way, Northcliffe brought sexual difference to the forefront of popular journalism. Previously, daily newspapers had been gendered only implicitly, by the absence of material specifically directed at women. In the *Mail* editorial matter became explicitly gendered. 'The man who has not time for this class of reading', the editor remarked of the women's columns, 'can leave it severely alone and lose nothing; he gets his Money Market and all the latest news on the other pages'.[22] This gendering of the material was double-edged. On the one hand, there was a danger that women would be discursively confined to the 'woman's realm', as this feature material was labelled. As the initial announcement made clear, female interests were defined fairly conservatively, following the tradition of the nineteenth-century women's magazine.[23] Mrs

---

[17] R. Pound and G. Harmsworth, *Northcliffe* (London: Cassell, 1959), 61.

[18] *Daily Mail*, 4 May 1896, 7.

[19] For Kennedy Jones's doubts, see Pound and Harmsworth, *Northcliffe*, 200–2.

[20] *Daily Mail*, 4 May 1896, 7.   [21] Ibid.   [22] Ibid.

[23] On 19th-century women's magazines, see M. Beetham, *A Magazine of her Own? Domesticity and Desire in the Woman's Magazine 1800–1914* (London: Routledge, 1996).

Peel, who became editor of (what had by then become) the women's page during the First World War, recalled with frustration how *Mail* journalists 'expected women to be interested solely in knitting jumpers, in caring for their
complexions, looking after babies, in cooking, in a "good murder" and in silly
stories about weddings'.[24] It could be argued that women were being admitted
into the pages of the national press only for their distance from the 'public
sphere' to be reinscribed.

On the other hand, the *Mail* was challenging established conceptions
of what constituted 'news' and what was 'important' enough to be reported
in a morning newspaper. If this women's material was as worthy of inclusion
as 'nine out ten matters' that were usually covered, then the conventional
privileging of the 'public sphere' as the location of the 'serious' business of
life was brought into question. In practical terms, moreover, it gave women
an important foothold in the male-dominated national press, ensuring both
a greater visibility and opportunities to voice their concerns; once the space
had been established, more challenging material could, and would, be included. In any case, the value of this fashion and domestic advice should not be dismissed: it proved to be popular with large numbers of female readers, for it
engaged with actual interests and concerns in a pragmatic way. Rebecca
West, herself briefly the editor of the *Daily Herald*'s women's section, stoutly
defended the domestic advice found in newspaper women's pages and women's
magazines:

Because *Home Twitters* [an imaginary publication West used to represent women's
pages and magazines] talks of nothing but recipes and babies, we are not to think that
it supports an ideal in which women would concern themselves with recipes and
babies; it is simply dealing with the needs of those who happen to be serving the State
by using recipes and rearing babies. The *Financial News* is deficient in references to the
beauties of art or religion, but men are not shamefaced regarding the readers and writers of such a paper . . .[25]

Northcliffe himself displayed a genuine determination that the women's
section should be treated as seriously as any other department. He ordered that
recipes be checked by his own chef, and insisted that articles and stories were
accurate and consistent: those he suspected of being casual were, as Norman
Angell recalled, 'flayed alive'.[26] As time went on, Northcliffe carried out his
own forms of market research to ensure that the women's page remained rele-

    [24] C. S. Peel, *Life's Enchanted Cup: An Autobiography* (London: John Lane, 1933), 227.
    [25] R. West, 'On a Form of Nagging', *Time and Tide*, 31 Oct. 1924, repr. in D. Spender (ed.), *Time and Tide
Wait for No Man* (London: Pandora, 1984).
    [26] N. Angell, *After All: The Autobiography of Norman Angell* (London: Hamish Hamilton, 1951), 120–1.

vant and readable: he sent one of his famous bulletins to the office warning that he had 'fifty women of all classes' giving their opinion of the features.[27] 'Don't be bluffed by journalists with only a men's outlook,' he counselled staff. 'Read the woman's page every day.'[28]

The articles of the 'woman's realm' were not the only means by which the *Daily Mail* sought to attract the female audience. The first issue also contained the opening instalment of a fiction serial, directed above all at women. Northcliffe hoped it would soon encourage wives to remind husbands to bring their paper back home.[29] He continued to place great store by this device: when the serial had to be dropped owing to newsprint restrictions during the First World War, he reminded the editor that it was 'one of the means by which we gained the great influence we have among women . . . [it] must be revived at the earliest possible moment'.[30] More generally, the reorientation of news values allowed women and 'women's interests' to enter the main body of the paper. Northcliffe sent bulletins to his news editors reminding them to 'look out for feminine topics for the news columns'.[31] One of these editors, Tom Clarke, recalled his proprietor's exhortations: 'Don't forget the women, Tom. Always have one "woman's story" at the top of all the main news pages.' Northcliffe made clear his determination not to return to the time when newspapers were 'written only for men [and] women and their interests were despised'.[32] He urged journalists to consider the news from perspectives other than that of the metropolitan man: 'I think the *Daily Mail* might have had some reference to the great sale week,' he told the editor in July 1918, despite the limited space and the mass of war news to fit into the columns. 'The whole feminine population of the village where I am is *en route* for London this morning for the great day.'[33] He praised the paper when it had a 'good wedding exclusive', for these were 'always very valuable to a newspaper so largely read by women'.[34] Northcliffe wanted his newspapers to set people talking, and this meant engaging female readers as well as male readers.

The Advertising Incentive

These attempts to attract female readers formed part of a conscious strategy from the very first issue of the *Mail*, and were regarded by Northcliffe as

[27] Northcliffe bulletins, 11 May 1920.
[28] T. Clarke, *My Northcliffe Diary* (London: Hutchinson, 1931), 279.   [29] Ibid. 136.
[30] Northcliffe bulletins, 21 Feb. 1917.   [31] Ibid., 10 Apr. 1916.   [32] Clarke, *Diary*, 197.
[33] Northcliffe bulletins, 1 July 1918.   [34] Ibid., 27 Apr. 1921.

indispensable tools for achieving the mass circulation that was his primary target. Yet the value of the female market was soon significantly increased in a way quite unforeseen in 1896: as a result of pressures from the advertising department. Advertising in the late Victorian press was dominated by small, private advertisements, supplemented by various public announcements, company prospectuses, and a handful of notices from high-street shops. Brand advertising was very limited, largely owing to the dislike of illustrated or 'display' advertisements, which were regarded by most national newspapers as vulgar. For most advertisers, reaching a high circulation was unimportant as long as their messages were seen by a sufficient number of the wealthy, educated classes. So while advertising finance was vital for the Victorian press (usually contributing around half of a paper's annual income), it did not create any momentum to broaden the paper's audience.[35] Originally, Northcliffe believed that many readers were irritated by the amount of space taken up by advertising in their papers, and predicted that his publication would be able to reduce this burden. The first issue boasted that

The main difference between the *Daily Mail* and its competitors is the absence of the advertisement supplements of two or four pages added to most of them some years ago. The *Daily Mail* gives exactly the same news, but fewer advertisement sheets . . . the 'note' of the *Daily Mail* is not so much economy of price as conciseness and compactness. It is essentially the busy man's paper. The mere halfpenny saved each day is of no consequence to most of us. The economy of the reader's time effected by this absence of the usual puzzling maze of advertisements is, however, of the first importance.[36]

This was effective flattery: the large number of readers for whom the saving of a halfpenny was indeed of significance could feel that the purchase of the paper was justified by its status as the 'busy man's paper'. But when the *Mail* quickly achieved record circulations, it was clear that this policy was letting major revenue-raising opportunities slip by. With retailing and consumer industries developing rapidly, and branding increasingly significant, advertising space was becoming ever more valuable, especially where large audiences could be delivered. Guided by the entrepreneurial instincts of Wareham Smith, the *Mail's* advertising department began to expand the space allocated to display advertising, especially for the products of major drapers and department stores. This illustrated advertising gradually came to occupy a central place in newspaper finances; indeed one advertising historian argues that these pioneering operations in the *Mail* 'effectively ushered in the industrialization of

---

[35] Brown, *Victorian News*, 15–23.   [36] *Daily Mail*, 4 May 1896, 4.

the press'.[37] Here was a powerful extra incentive to chase the mass circulation: the greater the number of readers that could be promised to advertisers, the more expensive was each inch of space.

These were the calculations that provoked the bitter battle for readers in the inter-war years. But every reader was not of equal significance to the advertiser. Just as those with a greater spending power were more attractive than the less prosperous, so too female readers were more keenly sought than male readers. Women were the major spenders of the domestic budget, and the prime targets for retailers. Inevitably, they became crucial targets for the popular press as well. Kennedy Jones, who had initially doubted the wisdom of including a women's section, came to recognize the commercial imperative behind the appeal to women: 'We realized that women are by nature more loyal and conservative than men, and that if we had them with us and got a firm footing in their homes, the value of our papers from the advertisers' point of view would be greatly enhanced.'[38] Likewise, Mrs Peel understood that the whole newspaper enterprise 'depended upon the goodwill of women—for it is women who spend the greater part of men's earnings and so make advertisements pay, and without advertisements no paper can live'.[39] Northcliffe found that advertisements had a circulation value as well. Attempting to lift rather flat early week sales, he offered concessions to department store advertisers—and was rewarded by circulation increases.[40] When space became limited during the First World War, he made clear where the advertising priorities should lie: 'Wareham Smith should be careful to ration advertisements, giving preference to those which appeal to women. Drapery advertisements are news to them and are so regarded by the American newspapers. Now that we have abolished the women's column, it is more than ever necessary not to neglect this important department.'[41]

When, after the war, Wareham Smith received reports that other newspapers were more effective than the *Mail* in enticing women into London shops, investigations and concerned correspondence followed.[42] The female audience had become of structural importance to the *Mail* and it could not be allowed to dissipate. So long as it was advertising convention to target women—and one inter-war manual was entirely typical in advising that 'the business man has

[37] G. Dyer, *Advertising as Communication* (London: Methuen, 1982), 42. See also R. Williams, *The Long Revolution* (Harmondsworth: Penguin, 1965), 225.

[38] Jones, *Fleet Street*, 331.   [39] Peel, *Autobiography*, 229–30.

[40] Major Harrison, London Press Exchange, to Royal Commission on the Press, *Minutes of Evidence* (London: HMSO, 1948), Day 8, Cmd. 7336 6.   [41] Northcliffe Bulletins, 9 Mar. 1918.

[42] Northcliffe Papers, Add. MS 62213, Wareham Smith Report on Advertising, 15 Mar. 1921; Northcliffe to Smith, 21 Mar. 1921.

come to the conclusion that he has to consider the woman's point of view almost exclusively in advertising and selling'—this would remain the case.[43] Newspapers literally could not afford to alienate too many of their female readers.

The introduction of display advertising also had a substantial visual impact on the daily newspaper. Victorian newspapers had generally consisted simply of columns of closely printed type: line illustrations of any kind were few and far between. Display advertising ensured that a significant amount of space was devoted to pictures—and pictures, more often than not, of women. Drapers and department stores tried to tempt female readers with drawings of their latest fashions, and cheery housewives appeared extolling the virtues of various household products. Such was the importance of the corset and underwear market, moreover, it was not long before pictures of scantily clad female figures were included. The first publication of an advertisement portraying a woman in 'combinations' in 1898 provoked an uproar. Wareham Smith recalled how letters of protest 'poured in from villages, vicarages, provinces, Brixton, Tooting . . . and every other hill and vale in the country, "We cannot have our sons' morals contaminated in this way"'. When Northcliffe ordered an end to the 'vulgar' advertisements, Smith resisted, pointing out that

combinations were an essential part of a modest woman's attire, that drapers wanted to advertise them, in addition to other articles, and that we could not afford to offend them, and that they could not, in any case, illustrate combinations properly without putting a woman's body inside them. I also urged that we were on the edge of the greatest revenue producer we had yet found, and that millions sterling were involved in the principle.[44]

Smith eventually overcame Northcliffe's caution: letting the controversy subside, he gradually slipped in further advertisements of this kind.

By the early years of the century, the front page of the *Daily Mail* regularly consisted of a collection of illustrations of women in the latest fashions, and the 'feminization' of the press was unmistakably affirmed in visual terms (see Fig. 1.2). The traditional organ of (male) public affairs had become a retailer for women's clothing. Several newspapers, lamented the playwright and critic St John Ervine in 1933, 'are now, in effect, drapers' circulars and are kept, so to speak, for the purpose of informing ladies in the provinces of cheap lines of goods in departmental stores'.[45] In practice, the overt dialogue between the advertiser and the female consumer could be disrupted by the male gaze (hence

[43] A. J. Greenly, *Psychology as a Sales Factor*, 2nd edn. (London: Pitman, 1929), 201.
[44] W. Smith, *Spilt Ink* (London: Ernest Benn, 1932), 42.
[45] St John Ervine, *The Future of the Press* (London: World's Press News, 1933), 13.

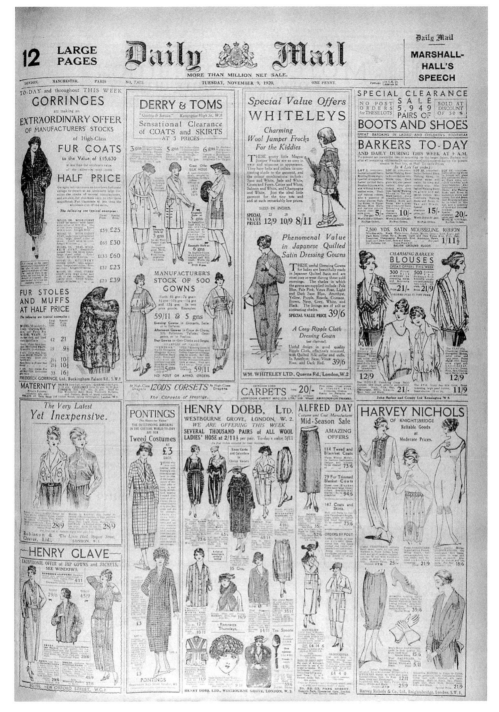

FIG. 1.2. The front page of the *Mail* was a lucrative advertising space, frequently taken by drapers and department stores marketing women's clothing. The *Express*, the *Mirror*, the *News*, and the *Herald* all put news on the front page, but they competed fiercely to secure similar advertising for the inside pages

the uproar about underwear): these advertisements served up the female body to male scrutiny, starting a practice that would become increasingly common as photographs entered the columns. At the same time, women became even more visible in the papers, and the fact that a large female readership was being targeted became inescapable. Perhaps more clearly than any feature, these advertisements showed that women had come in from the margins of the newspaper enterprise to a place of centrality.

The *Daily Mirror*: A Paper for Women?

In 1903 Northcliffe's confidence in his ability to attract the female reader emboldened him to go a step further: to establish a daily newspaper specifically for women. Encouraged by the success of a similar paper in France, *La Fronde*, and hopeful of securing lucrative advertising revenue, he launched the *Daily Mirror* with an all-female staff under the original editor of the *Mail's* women's columns, Mary Howarth.[46] The paper was a spectacular failure, eventually losing him £100,000. Complacent after a string of successes, Northcliffe neglected to carry out essential preparatory work and market research. Misreading the demands of his audience, the mixture of crime and human-interest stories, fashion advice, and domestic articles did not hit the right note for a 'high class' journal for 'ladies'. As circulation plummeted, the *Mirror* was rescued only by removing the female staff and turning it into an illustrated paper—as which it became the first daily to rival the readership levels of the *Mail*.

This ill-fated experiment revealed once again the different aspects of Northcliffe's attitudes to women. His faith in the potential of the women's market led him to take extraordinary risks. At a time when women had barely gained a foothold in the world of journalism, he demonstrated his willingness to place a great deal of responsibility onto an inexperienced female editorial team, while simply by launching a 'women's newspaper' he continued to challenge assumptions about gender and popular publishing. Nor did the failure of the *Mirror* seem to alter his perceptions about the female audience. 'While we learnt there was no room in London for a women's daily paper,' recalled Kennedy Jones, 'we also discovered there was room in a daily paper for more letter press that directly appealed to women.'[47] The *Mail* therefore increased its efforts in this area, even advertising itself as 'the woman's daily'. Similarly, Tom

---

[46] Jones, *Fleet Street*, 227.   [47] Ibid. 232.

Clarke noted that the setback to the *Mirror* did not undermine Northcliffe's 'faith that the future for popular newspapers and magazines depended on a big woman readership'.[48] In 1920, indeed, he declared to his staff that 'as many women read the *Daily Mail* as men' (a claim that later research suggests was unfounded—a mid-1930s survey recorded about nine female readers for every eleven male).[49]

On the other hand, Northcliffe clearly shared many conventional gender prejudices and stereotypes. He continued to view women as being largely defined by their roles as wives and mothers, and the 'women's material' for his papers was produced on these terms. When he told staff to find 'feminine matter', he assumed that his meaning was self-evident: he wanted domestic articles, fashion tips, or society 'gossip'. He was sceptical about the need for female suffrage, a scepticism that was reproduced in the columns of the *Mail* and which only evaporated during the First World War. His social conservatism and his imperialistic, jingoistic instincts—emerging in the *Mail's* coverage of the Boer War, and its consistent hostility to Germany—further ensured that the editorial line of his papers did little to challenge traditional gender prescriptions. Just as his populism was held in check by a profound concern for respectability, so too his forward-thinking with regard to the female market was tempered by what the new *Mirror* editor Hamilton Fyfe described as 'an old-fashioned doubt' as to whether women were 'really the equals of men'.[50]

Although the *Mirror* no longer advertised itself as paper for 'ladies' after its relaunch in January 1904 as an illustrated paper, it maintained a distinctly 'feminine' identity, and circulation evidence suggests that it continued to attract a much higher percentage of female readers than any other paper until well into the 1930s.[51] Demoting politics and the public sphere even more firmly than the *Mail*, it took the much derided 'snippet journalism'[52] to new levels and gave even more space to human-interest and feature articles. Its main appeal rested on its pioneering photography, however, which at certain dramatic moments—such as when it famously secured pictures of the recently deceased Edward VII—enabled it to reach circulations exceeding the *Mail*. But its

[48] T. Clarke, *Northcliffe in History: An Intimate Study of Press Power* (London: Hutchinson, 1950), 23.

[49] Northcliffe Bulletins, 29 June 1920; PEP, *Report*, 28.   [50] Fyfe, *Northcliffe*, 94.

[51] Hugh Cudlipp revealed that research showed that 70 per cent of *Mirror* readers were women in 1935, falling to 49 per cent in 1943: H. Cudlipp, *Publish and be Damned! The Astonishing Story of the Daily Mirror* (London: Andrew Dakers, 1953), 122. The female predominance is confirmed by the PEP *Report*, 28, and by the findings of Mass Observation, which suggest that it lasted longer than 1943: Bodleian Library, Oxford, X. Films 200, File Report 1420, 'Report on the Daily Herald Readership', Sept. 1942, 9.

[52] This was the insult levelled by the *Saturday Review*. Taylor, *The Great Outsiders*, 35.

unusual tabloid format and its partiality to pictures of glamorous society women allowed it to be stereotyped by traditionalist critics as more of a fashion magazine than a newspaper. The *Mirror* was regarded as a 'feminine' and 'low-brow' paper—the two were often conflated—and thus not to be taken seriously. This was a complaint of which Northcliffe was all too aware. Writing to Alexander Kenealy, the editor, in 1911, he lamented that the paper 'frequently contains news which is below the intelligence of the average fourth housemaid. You can imagine what educated readers think of it.'[53] The *Mirror* found these prejudices difficult to shake off, and it inadvertently encouraged the assumption that pictorial journalism itself was inherently 'feminine', appropriate for the practical female mind, which found abstract ideas difficult to grasp. Greenly's advertising handbook noted in 1929 that 'Woman has demanded fewer references in the news to the obviously remote idea and the laboriously exact particular: she prefers the concrete and the personal aspects, and . . . to suit her taste the picture newspaper with its intimacy and gossip has been developed.'[54] The lesson for the advertiser was clear, argued Greenly: the average woman 'is able to understand a clear situation shown by illustration better than she would if she had to read a longish paragraph to grasp its essentials'.[55] Writing on 'The Dictatorship of the Lay-Out Man' in 1938, meanwhile, the cultural critic Holbrook Jackson lamented the increasing use of photography in the popular press, a tendency which he pinned on the influence of women readers. 'When men think pictorially,' he claimed, 'they unsex themselves.'[56]

Despite its high female readership, then, advertisers did not believe that the *Mirror* received the level of attention devoted to other newspapers and penalized it accordingly.[57] Market research surveys throughout these years continued to group the 'picture papers'—the *Mirror* and its competitors, the *Daily Sketch* and the *Daily Graphic*—in a separate category from the rest of the popular press, suggesting that they were somehow not quite 'proper' newspapers.[58] Only with its substantial editorial reinvention in the 1930s was the *Mirror* able to shed this 'feminine' tag. While Northcliffe demonstrated the benefits of winning over a substantial female readership, the

[53] Northcliffe Papers, Add. MS 62234, Northcliffe to Alexander Kenealy, 11 Mar. 1911.

[54] Greenly, *Sales Factor*, 201.   [55] Ibid. 202.

[56] Holbrook Jackson, cited in D. LeMahieu, *A Culture for Democracy: Mass Communication and the Cultivated Mind in Britain between the Wars* (Oxford: Clarendon Preess, 1988), 265.

[57] J. Curran, A. Douglas, and G. Whannel, 'The Political Economy of the Human-Interest Story', in A. Smith (ed.), *Newspapers and Democracy: International Essays on a Changing Medium* (Cambridge, Mass.: MIT Press, 1980), 292.

[58] e.g. the Mass Observation surveys: File Report 1339, 'Report on Daily Express Readership', June 1942; File Report 1420.

experiences of the *Mirror* also indicated the problems that could hinder a paper regarded as too 'feminine'.

The Revolution Triumphant

The introduction of the *Daily Mail* and the *Daily Mirror* transformed daily journalism. Imitations were soon launched to try to capitalize on the reading potential uncovered by Northcliffe. The *Daily Express* was established in 1900 by Arthur Pearson, Northcliffe's rival in the magazine sector, while in 1908 the *Daily Sketch* was published by Edward Hulton as a 'picture paper' to compete with the *Mirror*. The editors of these new papers were keenly aware of both the circulation and the advertising significance of the female market. 'Never forget the cabman's wife,' Pearson famously warned his staff.[59] R. D. Blumenfeld, editor of the *Express* from 1904 to 1929, had served both on the *New York Herald* and under Northcliffe, and was well acquainted with the value of reaching a broad audience. He believed, like his mentor, that 'women number at least half, if not more, of the readers of a national daily newspaper'.[60] Established papers were also forced to react to the challenge to conventional news values. The *Daily Telegraph* and the *Daily News*, among others, began regular women's columns and increased their display advertising. The introduction of 'feminine material' became a standard technique for reviving flagging circulations: a women's page was one of the first changes made when Beaverbrook took over the ailing *Globe* in 1911.[61] It was not until after 1918, however, that the press revolution was fully realized. Before 1914 competition remained relatively restricted. No popular daily paper was able to acquire much more than half of the circulation achieved by the *Mail* and the *Mirror*—and these two were, of course, both owned by the same man.[62] The amount of consumer advertising had not reached the level it would attain in the inter-war years, and newspaper production prices remained favourable. The war increased the demand for national papers, but newsprint restrictions ensured that pagination levels had to be kept down, leaving little room for editorial innovations. Northcliffe was largely content to consolidate the pattern that he had developed, and the rest of the press world was content merely to try to catch up with him.

---

[59] S. Dark, *The Life of Sir Arthur Pearson* (London: Hodder & Stoughton, 1922), 90.
[60] R. D. Blumenfeld, *The Press in my Time* (London: Rich & Cowan, 1933), 94.
[61] A. Chisholm and M. Davie, *Beaverbrook: A Life* (London: Hutchinson, 1992), 107.
[62] Northcliffe transferred his interest in the *Mirror* to his brother Lord Rothermere in 1914.

It was in the two decades after 1918 that the logic of Northcliffe's populism was fully worked out. Competition intensified dramatically, with the *Express* and the *Herald* eventually overtaking the *Mail* and the *Mirror*, while other papers folded or merged. The importance of advertising revenue to the newspaper operation increased as production costs rose. When the manager of Associated Newspapers, Pomeroy Burton, wrote to Northcliffe in 1921 that the 'advertisement department [is] now, more than ever before, the mainstay of the newspaper business', 'the Chief' entirely agreed: 'we no longer profit by sales, we are dependent entirely on advertisements'.[63] As circulation auditing and market research figures became more accurate—the Audit Bureau of Circulations was established in 1931—newspapers could no longer hide, or indeed inflate, the true extent of their readership; and unless the circulation of rivals could be matched, there was a real prospect of a dramatic decline in advertising revenue. In these circumstances, there were intensive efforts to make the editorial content more enticing. Political and foreign affairs coverage continued to be reduced and more space was allocated to features, sport, and celebrity news. 'Personal journalism'—gossip columns, interviews, and signed articles— replaced anonymous reports. Newspaper layout was made more visually attractive, with headlines of different font styles and sizes, and more and more photographs were included. One of the main criteria for these changes was that they improved the appeal of the paper to women. It was during these years that Northcliffe's insights about the female market were fully accepted throughout Fleet Street and elevated to the status of conventional wisdom.

For Robert Ensor, a leader-writer with the *Daily Chronicle* until 1930, and a member of the 1947–9 Royal Commission on the Press, this 'feminization' was the most striking development in popular journalism between the wars. With editors reminded more firmly than ever before 'that for advertising purposes women readers were incomparably more valuable than men'[64]—and by the 1930s they were receiving market research data from advertisers informing them of the percentage of housewives that read their paper[65]—they were forced

to pursue two aims—more women readers and more readers. Editor and news editor and advertisement manager watched in detail day by day the play of cause and effects

[63] Northcliffe Papers, Add. MS 62195, Pomeroy Burton to Northcliffe, 6 May 1921; Northcliffe to Burton, 7 May 1921.

[64] R. C. K. Ensor, 'The Press', in Sir Ernest Barker (ed.), *The Character of England* (Oxford: Clarendon Press, 1947), 417 (proof copy in Bodleian Library, Oxford, Ensor Papers, Box 72).

[65] For example, the editorial director of the *News Chronicle*, Walter Layton, received such evidence in October 1933 from a Cadbury survey: Trinity College, Cambridge, Walter Layton Papers, Box 85, H. T. Weeks to L. J. Cadbury, 25 Oct. 1933.

. . . Such observation sustained over sufficient periods enabled them to discover with certainty what features and subjects do and do not attract readers, and particularly women readers.[66]

For Ensor, who believed passionately in traditional notions of the press as a political 'fourth estate', these developments were disconcerting, and he left the *Daily Chronicle* of his own accord when it merged with the *Daily News* in 1930.[67] Others learnt to adjust to the altered conception of news value. In 1926 Sydney Moseley, an experienced reporter and later the editor of the *Daily Herald*, produced a book of advice for aspiring freelance journalists. He made clear how important it was to be conscious of the female audience: 'No study of the daily and weekly press, however casual, can fail to impress one with the efforts that are being made to "play up" to the woman reader. In point of fact, many editors devote a preponderating share of space to articles and "stories" having a special appeal to women.'[68]

If unable to come up with an idea for a feature article, there were few more reliable angles than one based on sexual difference, Moseley suggested: 'A comparison between the sexes on practically every subject under the sun can be exploited . . . There is always something new happening to the sexes.'[69] As an encouragement, he gave the example of a young woman on his staff: 'In three months she "placed" no fewer than twenty-four articles, all on topics of interest to women.'[70] Class was never mentioned in his work as a fruitful journalistic perspective: this was too politically fraught and controversial. Sexual difference, on the other hand, provided perfect subject matter for dining table conversation; features of this type were regarded as 'light' and entertaining rather than 'serious' and divisive.

The success of Moseley's female staff reporter hinted at the greater opportunities that were being extended to women journalists after the war as a result of this interest in 'feminine' reading matter. Contributing to the periodical *The Writer* in 1925, Gertrude Allen was optimistic about the prospects for women: 'The professional woman writer has explored practically every corner of the journalistic field and found many tenable spots which were, at one time, considered the exclusive territory of the male journalist.'[71] Seven years later, in a handbook for aspiring female freelances, Myfanwy Crawshay claimed that women journalists were now 'indispensable to editors' owing to the

[66] Ensor, 'The Press', 417–18.

[67] D. Griffiths (ed.), *The Encyclopedia of the British Press 1422–1992* (London: Macmillan, 1992), 222.

[68] S. Moseley, *Short Story Writing and Freelance Journalism* (London: Pitman, 1926), 96.

[69] Ibid. 33.   [70] Ibid. 101.

[71] G. Allen, 'The Women's Page Specialist', *The Writer* (Aug. 1925).

importance attached to the female reader: 'anyone who works in the offices of a big daily paper knows to what extent she influences policy'.[72] And surveying the scene in 1936, Emilie Peacocke, a long-serving feature-writer with the *Express*, the *Mail*, and the *Morning Post*, argued that 'the story of modern journalism, so far as it relates to the woman writer, is the Rise of the Women's Story'. She was confident that women had managed to secure a significant and lasting place in the profession: 'It is because of the insistent demand for the woman's point of view that the sphere of the woman journalist has widened and, not withstanding temporary setbacks from time to time, must continue to grow.'[73]

In retrospect, it can be seen that this optimism was not entirely justified. The presence of some high-profile female reporters, such as Margaret Lane and Hilda Marchant, alongside a substantial number of female feature-writers and freelances, could not disguise the failure of women to reach positions of power or disperse the masculine atmosphere of Fleet Street offices and drinking holes. After all, an International Labour Organization study in 1927 estimated that there were only around 400 female journalists in Britain, out of a total of 7,000.[74] It was not until 1997 that a woman repeated the achievement of Mary Howarth and became the editor of a national daily.[75] What these upbeat inter-war assessments did reflect, however, was the increasing number of openings for those women who did make the grade, and the far greater demand for their work compared with only a couple of decades previously. Such was the need to cater for the female audience that 'women's material' took up far more space than the actual proportion of women journalists in newsrooms would have suggested.[76]

Nor was the 'rise of the woman's story' confined to the popular national dailies. The provincial press, increasingly under pressure from the metropolitan papers, also tried to broaden its appeal during these years. Arthur Christiansen, who became the editor of the *Daily Express* in 1933, recalled working at the *Liverpool Evening Express* in the early 1920s: 'News angled to attract women was new . . . [and] I was assigned the task of producing a woman's story a day for months on end.'[77] Similarly, the traditionally austere, 'minority'

---

[72] M. Crawshay, *Journalism for Women* (London: Fleet Publications, 1932), 7–8.

[73] E. Peacocke, *Writing for Women* (London: A. & C. Black, 1936), 1, 3.

[74] F. Hunter, 'Women in British Journalism', in Griffiths (ed.), *Encyclopedia*, 689.

[75] Rosie Boycott, editor of the *Independent* 1997–8, and then editor of the *Daily Express* 1998–2001.

[76] Arthur Christiansen made this point in his memoirs: A. Christiansen, *Headlines All my Life* (London: Heinemann, 1961), 249.

[77] Ibid. 25. *Newspaper World*, 25 Dec. 1920, 16, also noted that the *Berkshire Chronicle* had started a woman's page.

dailies made some concessions to the new populism. In 1922 C. P. Scott established a women's page under Madeline Linford at the *Manchester Guardian*, while in 1926 the *Morning Post* introduced 'A Woman's Pageant', a feature detailing 'happenings of particular interest to women'.[78] The editor of the *Post*, Howell Gwynne, later reminded his staff: 'Women, Women! Remember them always. They will tell you what they like, and it is not silly fashions only and cooking recipes. They are also intelligent.'[79] Even *The Times*, which felt obliged to hold out against all journalistic innovations for as long as possible—it did not include a double column headline until December 1932[80]—eventually launched a woman's page in 1937.[81]

As Gwynne's memorandum suggested, the definition of 'women's material' broadened significantly in these years, both as the amount of space allocated to it increased, and as women entered Parliament and the professions. Of course, many male journalists instinctively retained Northcliffe's notion of domestic advice and fashion hints when thinking of women's articles; Beverley Baxter, briefly editor of the *Express*, urged Beaverbrook that the paper should 'strengthen the women's appeal remembering that their interests never change and are, therefore, always available for exploitation'.[82] Yet many were conscious that such stereotypes were no longer acceptable. Sydney Moseley cautioned prospective contributors that

it is a vast mistake to think that women's interest nowadays is purely domestic. Except that there are certain subjects which appeal to women—just as there are topics which particularly interest men—the interests of the woman reader today are no more circumscribed than those of her husband or brother . . . Because women are now competing with men in business, in the professions and the arts, and in politics, it is evident that there is a limitless opportunity for the freelance writer to produce articles on almost any subject, and still present them in such a way as to hold the interest of women readers.[83]

Crawshay agreed that 'the scope of the woman's page has widened as editors have realised that women want to hear about other things besides routine domesticity'.[84]

At the *Express* editors other than Baxter were indeed aware that 'women's material' should not be too narrowly delineated. Blumenfeld recognized that 'modern women have a multitude of interests', including 'physical exercise',

---

[78] For the *Manchester Guardian*, M. Stott (ed.), *Women Talking: An Anthology from the Guardian Women's Page* (London: Pandora, 1987), p. xvii. For the *Morning Post*, *Newspaper World*, 4 Dec. 1926, 16.

[79] Bodleian Library, Oxford, Howell Gwynne Papers, Dep. 31, memo, Oct. (?) 1936.

[80] LeMahieu, *Culture for Democracy*, 259.   [81] *The Times*, 15 Nov. 1937, 19.

[82] Beaverbrook Papers, H Series, Box 91, Beverley Baxter to Beaverbrook, 5 Jan. 1932.

[83] Moseley, *Freelance Journalism*, 98–9, 102.   [84] Crawshay, *Journalism for Women*, 9.

'careers', and 'sex', as well as 'beauty culture' and 'cooking'.[85] Christiansen reminded staff that they should 'never underestimate the interest of women in news which is supposed to be outside their purview'.[86] While fashion and housewifery remained the staple subjects of the women's pages, during the 1920s careers advice and features on sport were often included. Elsewhere in the paper, political and foreign affairs articles after 1918 were often presented from a 'female viewpoint', and the various activities of 'modern young women' became a favourite 'talking point'. Certainly the assumption that it was legitimate to write about the 'female viewpoint' and 'women's issues' remained very deeply rooted; the importance of sexual difference had by now become a central organizing feature of the whole newspaper and advertising operation. Nevertheless, the discursive space in which women—or men writing about the 'female perspective'—could operate had been considerably extended, and contributors did sometimes use this space directly to challenge assumptions about women and femininity.

The *Daily Herald*: Resistance Fails

The only popular paper that was to some extent isolated from these developments, at least in the period up to 1930, was the *Daily Herald*. Edited by the Christian socialist George Lansbury between 1919 and 1922, when it was taken over by the Trades Union Congress (TUC), the *Herald* was dedicated to expounding the 'workers' perspective' against the 'dope' peddled by the 'capitalist press'. Perpetually struggling for money, it lacked the resources to match its rivals for size or brightness. But with a commitment to political and industrial news, it resolutely refused to compete with other papers on their own terms. Human-interest stories and racy crime and divorce reports were regarded as unwelcome distractions that merely obscured from the worker the need for collective political action. In 1919 Ernest Bevin outlined what the movement leaders expected from a newspaper: 'Labour's press must be a real educational factor, provoking thought and stimulating ideas. In addition it must not be full of the caprices of princes, the lubricities of courts and the sensationalism produced by display of the sordid. All these are but passing phases and are the products of a system which is rotten at the base.'[87] The *Herald* essentially maintained the news values of the late Victorian morning press in a transformed

---

[85] Blumenfeld, *Press in my Time*, 94.   [86] Christiansen, *Headlines*, 164.

[87] Bevin, cited in H. Richards, 'Conscription, Conformity and Control: The Taming of the *Daily Herald* 1921–30', D.Phil. thesis (Open University, 1992), 30.

popular market. Although it did include a women's section, it lagged far behind its rivals in its commitment to the female audience. Still only receiving 20 per cent of its revenue from advertising by the end of 1926 (its rivals were obtaining more than 50 per cent), it was not under the same pressure to attract women readers.[88] TUC directors complained that 'we feel that the cost of producing the women's page is high in proportion to the amount of space devoted exclusively to women's topics'.[89] The women's section was sacrificed when there was a lot of movement news, and other non-political features remained underdeveloped. Even the book column was more likely to review weighty tomes such as J. C. Wright's *Administration of Vocational Education* than the latest bestsellers.[90] And while it maintained a firm editorial belief in women's political and civil equality, in practice the paper was dominated by the very masculine world of trade unionism. Content analysis shows that other papers with far less 'progressive' views on sexual equality produced more material on politics and careers from the 'female perspective' than the *Herald*, as well as outperforming it in the more traditional areas of fashion and housewifery.

The *Herald* limped through the 1920s with a circulation of around 400,000 while its rivals sold up to four times as many copies. Pleas from some insiders to give more prominence to 'human emotion stories' and to counter the public impression that the paper 'is not out to give them news, but to do them good' were largely rejected.[91] By 1929 the TUC could not support the underperforming paper any longer, and half of its stake was sold to J. S. Elias's Odhams Press, the publishers of *John Bull* and the *People*. The terms of the sale ensured that the *Herald* remained committed to the TUC line in its political and industrial news, but Elias was given a free hand to develop the rest of the paper. The transformation when it was relaunched in 1930 was spectacular: news values were reoriented, human interest entered the columns, and the amount of space given over to photographs, features, and advertising increased dramatically. Although the percentage of female readers remained lower than for any other popular paper, far more attention was now paid to the women's market, and the overall sales position improved rapidly. Breaking through the 1 million circulation barrier within weeks, the *Herald* actually became the first paper to sell 2 million copies in 1933, before dropping slightly behind the

[88] Bodleian Library, Oxford, Daily Herald Papers, X. Films 77/7, LP/DH/521, Report on Advertising, Dec. 1926.

[89] Ibid., Reel 6, LP/DH/466, Sub-committee on editorial policy to Editor, 13 Nov. 1925.

[90] *Daily Herald*, 5 May 1927, 2.

[91] Daily Herald Papers, Reel 6, LP/DH/248, Report of the Printing Trades Federation to the *Daily Herald* Inquiry Committee, 9 Oct. 1923; LP/DH/465, Clifford Allen memo, Sept. 1924.

Express for the rest of the decade. The relaunch precipitated one of the most bitter periods of competition the newspaper industry has ever seen, with millions of pounds spent on canvassing and free gifts. The *Herald's* success prompted the merger of the *Daily Chronicle* and the *Daily News* to form the *News Chronicle* in 1930; and by the mid-1930s the *Daily Mirror* was forced to reinvent itself in order to survive. In the broader context, the remodelling of the *Herald* signalled the final triumph of Northcliffe's conception of news values, eight years after the pioneer had died. There would be no turning back now.

Eve of the Second World War: Transformation Complete

By the end of the 1930s the two papers which embodied the 'Northcliffe revolution' most completely, which had indeed perhaps taken it further than 'the Chief' had ever envisaged, were the *Express* and the *Mirror*. The memoirs of Arthur Christiansen and Hugh Cudlipp, two of the main driving forces behind these papers, reveal how complete had been the transformation since 1896. Christiansen, the editor of the *Express* in its heyday between 1933 and 1957, acknowledged that the 'guiding principle' of his years in journalism was whether the paper would be comprehensible to people in 'the back streets of Derby' or on the 'Rhyl promenade': 'News was not only written about but written for those Great Unknowns of this country.'[92] Whereas Victorian editors had regarded Parliament as the primary focus of their activities, Christiansen admitted that he 'was too busy producing the newspaper to pay much attention to politics', and that he always felt uncomfortable in interviews with politicians.[93] He envisaged the paper less as a tireless 'fourth estate' crusader than as a domestic, parent figure, where the 'human link' was 'an editorial attitude of mind, to which readers respond. We want readers to turn to us automatically with their confidences, their grievances, their triumphs, or the wrongs that are done to them which they want to get put right.'[94]

Hugh Cudlipp, the features editor of the *Mirror* between 1935 and 1937, and an important figure in the transformation of the paper, had similar opinions. Accepting the dictum of his mentor at the features desk, Basil Nicholson—'What was the use of worrying readers about obscure revolutions in Bolivia if they could not sleep at night through indigestion?'—he propelled the *Mirror* further in the direction of personal, domestic journalism.[95] 'The down-to-

---

[92] Christiansen, *Headlines*, 2–3.   [93] Ibid. 154, 178.   [94] Ibid. 162.
[95] Cudlipp, *Publish and be Damned*, 81.

earth feature pages became more and more like a letter home to the family,' he recalled, 'and that was their secret':

The paper was homely too: it wanted to hear readers' stories of their children's pranks on holiday . . . Prizes were offered for letters in which husbands, wives and others got off their chests the things they would like to say about their nearest and dearest . . . The relationship between reader and newspaper became more intimate, and tantalising problems of the heart were much in favour.[96]

Northcliffe had imported some of the features of women's magazines to add breadth to his daily paper; by the end of the 1930s this magazine ethos was permeating much of the content of the popular press. Unsurprisingly, many critics were disgusted at these developments. Queenie Leavis longed for a time when 'the daily papers catered for the governing and professional classes, intelligently interested in politics, the money market, the law, and current affairs'.[97] Instead, the main characteristics of the 'mass press' were 'their glorification of food, drink, clothes, and material comforts, their determined inculcation of a higher standard of living . . . their facetious denigration of serious values'.[98] This was clearly an attack on what editors regarded as an essential 'feminization' of their papers: 'food, drink, clothes, and material comforts' were some of the main topics with which they had hoped to engage women readers. Other critics were more blunt. 'How womanised the popular Press has become,' complained St John Ervine in 1933. 'Articles by, and about, women prevail in these papers, and editors, without any appearance of embarrassment, will print "powerful" articles by young ladies not long enlarged [i.e. released] from school.'[99] Three years earlier, meanwhile, Stanley Morison had been given the task of redesigning the typography of *The Times*. The typeface should reflect the character of the paper and its readership, he argued; therefore it should be 'masculine, English, direct'.[100] At a time when it was the only national daily paper without a regular woman's page, *The Times* remained committed to maintaining its distance from the 'feminized', 'lowbrow' popular press.

It is this transformation of the popular press that makes the newspaper archives of such value to the gender historian. A vast amount of material, from a wide array of contributors, explored the relations between men and women. As Sydney Moseley noted, comparisons between the sexes were carried out on almost every topic imaginable. Already, some of the gendered assumptions of

[96] Ibid. 82, 83, 84.   [97] Leavis, *Fiction and the Reading Public*, 178.   [98] Ibid. 177.
[99] Ervine, *Future of the Press*, 15.
[100] Morison, quoted in LeMahieu, *Culture for Democracy*, 259.

editorial staff should be clear: the instinctive equation of the 'feminine' with the domestic, the apolitical, and the decorative was being increasingly challenged by the recognition of a broader set of 'women's interests' and the necessity of integrating the female voter into political discourse of the press. The following chapters will examine these attitudes more closely, as well as investigating in detail the main themes of the gendered debates that took place in popular newspapers.

2

The Discourse of Modernity

We've heard an inordinate amount about the Modern Woman. So much so that a thousand years hence scientists will doubtless imagine the twentieth century responsible for a new form of animal life and they will wonder why nothing remains of it.

(Rosita Forbes, *Daily Mail*, 2 March 1931)

The behaviour of young men and women is scrutinized and criticized in the journalism and literature of all modern societies. The belief that the coming generation will challenge or undermine the standards of the present is a recurring human theme. Those women who defied the conventions of femininity in Victorian and Edwardian England were certainly no exception. Eliza Lynn Linton's famous attack on 'the Girl of the Period' in the *Saturday Review* in 1868 sparked off a heated controversy in the press; the so-called 'New Woman' of the 1890s, and the pre-war suffragettes, similarly provoked extensive debates in newspapers and magazines.[1] Yet the amount of attention devoted to 'modern youth', and in particular the 'modern young woman', or 'flapper', after 1918 was exceptional. Rarely, if ever, can there have been such a widespread feeling that society was entering into a new era as after the First World War. As Samuel Hynes has noted in his cultural history of this period, the change wrought by the conflict 'was so vast and so abrupt as to make the years after the war seem discontinuous from the years before, and that discontinuity became a part of English imaginations. Men and women after the war looked back at their own past as

[1] *Saturday Review*, 25 (1868), 339–40, cited in M. Beetham, *A Magazine of her Own? Domesticity and Desire in the Women's Magazine 1800–1914* (London: Routledge, 1996), 105–6. On the 'New Woman', see M. E. Tusan, 'Inventing the New Woman: Print Culture and Identity Politics during the Fin-de-Siècle', *Victorian Periodicals Review*, 312 (Summer 1998), 169–82. On the press treatment of the suffragettes, see M. Pugh, *The March of the Women: A Revisionist Analysis of the Campaign for Women's Suffrage 1866–1914* (Oxford: Oxford University Press, 2000), 225–31.

one might look across a great chasm to a remote, peaceable place on the other side.'[2]

The activities of women were an obvious and striking means by which this discontinuity could be measured and symbolized. During the war, women had entered factories and carried out 'men's jobs'; they had finally been enfranchised; they had even altered their appearance, wearing shorter skirts and more practical clothing. Women, contemporaries believed, had been 'emancipated'. And even if some of their gains were surrendered shortly after the war ended, others, such as entry into the professions, seemed to be only just beginning. Few doubted that a lasting shift in gender relations had occurred. To her supporters, the 'flapper' personified the new opportunities in a world finally free of stifling 'Victorian' conventions; to her enemies, she epitomized the erosion of manners and the slide into immorality and indecency.

The 'modern young woman' was, then, one of the most prominent and characteristic figures of post-war culture. 'Flapper' has been described as 'one of the defining words' of the Twenties;[3] equally pervasive was the visual image of modern femininity, slim, short-skirted, and with cropped hair.[4] The 'modern young woman' was 'the decade's most familiar female type' in literature[5] and she was almost ubiquitous at the cinema and in advertising.[6] She was also unmissable in the pages of the popular daily press. *Newspaper World*, the weekly publication for journalists, noted this development in April 1927 when discussing what types of material newspapers included to entice readers. 'In the old days,' it claimed, 'a two-page account of a murder . . . was the great attraction; now it seems to be what some-well known man or woman thinks of the modern girl.'[7] Women's 'firsts' were frequently reported on the news pages; her latest fashions were recorded in photographs; her behaviour was a favourite talking point in the correspondence columns. 'If a future chronicler were to study the files of our newspapers,' speculated the novelist Rose Macaulay in 1925 with words that foreshadowed those of Rosita Forbes six years later, 'he would get the impression that there had appeared at this time a

---

[2] S. Hynes, *A War Imagined: The First World War and English Culture* (London: Bodley Head, 1990), p. ix.

[3] J. Ayto, *Twentieth Century Words* (Oxford: Oxford University Press, 1999), 139.

[4] On this visual image, see M. Thesander, *The Feminine Ideal* (London: Reaktion Books, 1997), ch. 6.

[5] Hynes, *War Imagined*, 377; see also B. Melman, *Women and the Popular Imagination in the Twenties: Flappers and Nymphs* (Basingstoke: Macmillan, 1988).

[6] On the cinema 'flapper', see M. Rosen, *Popcorn Venus: Women, Movies and the American Dream* (New York: Coward, McCann and Geoghegan, 1973), ch. 2; on the 'modern woman' in advertising, M. Pumphrey, 'The Flapper, the Housewife and the Making of Modernity', *Cultural Studies*, 12 (May 1987), 179–94.

[7] *Newspaper World*, 16 Apr. 1927, 3.

strange new creature called woman who was receiving great attention from the public.'[8]

Historians in the 1980s and 1990s demonstrated that the First World War did not in fact bring 'emancipation' for the majority of women.[9] Even if many legal and political disabilities were removed, most women still faced a mountain of economic, cultural, and social obstacles. Almost all contemporary observers exaggerated the pace of change and the actual impact made by the war, and with the benefit of hindsight it is obvious that the rhetoric of women 'invading' male spheres and 'ousting' men was grossly overstated. Nevertheless, this discourse of modernity is far more than a historical curiosity. It is impossible to appreciate inter-war debates about femininity and masculinity without understanding these beliefs about the changes ushered in by the war. Even if equality was still far off, moreover, opportunities were indeed increasing for women, especially for those in the middle classes, and it was of real importance how these openings were portrayed and debated by the press. Gender identities were being redefined, and new images presented to the public. And, as Birgitte Soland's recent work on Denmark suggests, women often sought to emulate these media images, assimilating definitions of 'modern' behaviour into their own lives.[10]

The basic practices of the press encouraged journalists to record change rather than to remind readers of underlying continuities, and they powerfully reinforced the existing preoccupation with modernity after 1918. Newspapers contrasted 'old' and 'new' versions of femininity and emphasized the challenge that 'modern young women' posed to convention. As this chapter will show, much of this reporting was positive: the popular press was, in general, far more open-minded about the post-war freedoms and opportunities for women than has usually been allowed. At the same time, however, the persistent suggestion that sexual equality had been, or was soon to be, achieved may have weakened the appeal of feminism, which was frequently represented as 'out of date' and no longer necessary.

---

[8] *Manchester Guardian*, 13 Nov. 1925, cited in *The Guardian Century: The Twenties* (London: *The Guardian*, 1999), 5.

[9] e.g. G. Braybon, *Women Workers in the First World War* (London: Croom Helm, 1981); G. Braybon and Penny Summerfield, *Out of the Cage: Women's Experiences in Two World Wars* (London: Pandora, 1987); M. R. Higonnet, J. Jenson, S. Michel, and M. C. Weitz (eds.), *Behind the Lines: Gender and the Two World Wars* (New Haven: Yale University Press, 1987); D. Beddoe, *Back to Home and Duty: Women between the Wars 1918–39* (London: Pandora, 1989); S. Kent, *Making Peace: The Reconstruction of Gender in Inter-War Britain* (Princeton: Princeton University Press, 1993); D. Thom, *Nice Girls and Rude Girls: Women Workers in the First World War* (London: I. B. Tauris, 1998).

[10] B. Soland, *Becoming Modern: Young Women and the Reconstruction of Womanhood in the 1920s* (Princeton: Princeton University Press, 2000).

Editorial Policies and Pressures

News Values

Newspapers are essentially records of modernity, and they inevitably focus attention disproportionately on the new and the unusual. The recurrent and the typical rarely meet the news values of the press, except in specially designated feature pages targeted at particular types of reader (for example, the 'women's page'). Women performing the roles of housewife and mother were not usually worthy of comment in their own right, but, as Myfanwy Crawshay noted in 1932, women 'conquering fresh fields, setting up new records, exploiting new crazes and running new enterprises, is important news'.[11] During the war, the press had churned out endless articles on female munitions workers, bus conductors, and train drivers.[12] With stringent restrictions on what correspondents could disclose from the front, reports of patriotic British women 'doing their bit' provided colourful and cheering copy with which to fill the papers and underline that the nation was united in the war effort. But while most of the home-front workers soon found themselves demobilized, striking new opportunities for women did not dry up with the cessation of hostilities. The Sex Disqualification (Removal) Act of 1919 opened up some professions and public positions to women, and ensured that newspapers were provided with further eye-catching copy about women entering 'male' spheres. Considerable amounts of space were devoted to the first women JPs, jurors, and barristers, and the press tendency to dramatize its news ensured that grand proclamations were made about the significance of each of these first steps. 'The empanelment of women jurors . . . is another long stride towards civic equality with men,' declared the *Daily Mail* in January 1921:

the last traces of women's long dependence are quickly wearing off with increasing practice in public life now that the plunge has been taken. In fact, women are noticeably becoming more self-reliant and stoical. The Old Bailey's pioneer forewoman of yesterday is the true type of our new citizens, who are steadily steeling themselves to do all that the country expects.[13]

The *Daily Herald*, with these jurywomen on its front page, was no less effusive: 'How many of those public-spirited ladies who pioneered and carried on

---

[11] M. Crawshay, *Journalism for Women* (London: Fleet Publications, 1932), 8.

[12] For some examples of these, see J. Marlow (ed.), *The Virago Book of Women and the Great War* (London: Virago, 1998).   [13] *Daily Mail*, 12 Jan. 1921, 6. See also *Weekly Dispatch*, 16 Jan. 1921, 8.

for two generations the righteous cause of the Rights of Woman ever dreamt to what triumphs the movement would have reached by the year 1921?'[14] And when, the following year, Ivy Williams was called to the Inner Temple as the first female barrister, the *Mail* observed that 'the changed status of women in regard to public affairs grows more marked every day . . . women are finding more and more useful public work they can perform in their changed status'.[15] But it was not only female pioneers in public and professional positions who attracted attention; women pursuing any kind of new opportunity were considered newsworthy. The *Mail* reported in September 1919, for example, that a young woman had become what the paper rather awkwardly called a 'stable lad', and thus entered 'one of the few jobs left essentially for men'.[16] 'From company directors to piano tuners there is an extraordinary variety in the things women do nowadays,' noted Joan Kennedy in the *Express* in 1924.[17] With the *Daily Mirror* printing pictures of women boxing, and female aviators starting to obtain publicity, it would have been easy to believe that there was hardly anything done by men that women were not now doing themselves.[18] Sydney Moseley advised freelance journalists to 'make the most of any new movement among women, or of any fresh development or extension of feminine activities'; it seems that such advice was heeded enthusiastically.[19]

Women's 'firsts' were news and were treated as such, yet thereafter women's experiences rarely hit the headlines. Popular newspapers tended, then as now, to concentrate on concrete happenings and the particular achievements of individuals: this ensured the presence of the all-important quality of 'human interest'. More general, structural issues of progress and prejudice were much less easy to fit into the popular format. After the frequent reports of these female accomplishments, it would have been reasonable to assume that many other women were following in the footsteps of the pioneers and that their advance was relatively smooth. But the exceptional difficulties that faced women entering these new spheres, or the travails of those who failed to break into their chosen field, were not usually pursued. By focusing such attention on female achievers, newspapers tended to present a rather distorted picture of reality. Ellen Wilkinson, the Labour MP, noted in 1931 that

women doing startling new things fill the papers until one begins to wonder if men are doing anything at all. They beat flying records, carry off the architectural prize of the

---

[14] *Daily Herald*, 12 Jan. 1921, 1.   [15] *Daily Mail*, 9 May 1922, 8.
[16] *Daily Mail*, 17 Sept. 1919, 5.   [17] *Daily Express*, 21 Oct. 1924, 4.
[18] Female boxers were shown in the *Daily Mirror*, 7 May 1919, 8.
[19] S. Moseley, *Short Story Writing and Freelance Journalism* (London: Pitman, 1926), 103.

year, apparently beating men at their own games all along the line . . . the impression gets about that all England's women are barristers, or aeronauts or crack channel swimmers. Of course it is not a bit like that really.[20]

As a result, the number of women who overcame the obstacles in front of them was repeatedly overestimated. Under the headline 'The Business Woman Wins', for example, a contributor to the *Express* in 1924 complacently claimed that 'all the world over women are running big businesses and little businesses, feminine business . . . and most unfeminine businesses'.[21] At other times, the practice of 'splashing' the story of a female advance led to its real significance being exaggerated. In April 1928 the *Express* topped its front page with a banner headline proclaiming 'Woman as Conservative Party Chief— Historic Move in Politics—First Woman to be a Party Leader—Miss M. Maxse—Deputy Principal Agent of the Conservatives'.[22] In fact, this appointment was little more than a symbolic concession to the party's women's section, and did not merit the urgent headline or the celebratory report announcing that 'It is the first time that such a position has been filled in any party organisation by a woman.' But newspapers required instant judgements for their readers, and it was convenient, and it seemed convincing, to place such achievements in the wider context of women's inexorable progress to equality. In retrospect, however, it is clear that the press radar was calibrated so sensitively to spot the arrival of 'modernity' that it often failed to provide an accurate representation of reality.

The Desire for Controversy

The basic news-gathering principles of the popular press inevitably encouraged the exaggeration of women's progress. But if one primary aim of newspapers was to relay the news, another was to generate controversy and 'talking points'. Beverley Baxter's claim that 'newspapers which never carry stories that outrage their readers die a lingering death' was a restatement of Northcliffe's wisdom that would have been accepted right across Fleet Street.[23] Denunciations of 'modern women' from establishment figures provided perfect newspaper copy in this respect. As the previous controversies over the 'Girl of the Period' and the 'New Woman' had demonstrated, few subjects produced more correspondence than those concerning the behaviour of younger generations. It was an

---

[20] *Daily Mail*, 19 May 1931, 10.   [21] *Daily Express*, 14 Oct. 1924, 8.
[22] *Daily Express*, 4 Apr. 1928, 1.
[23] House of Lords Record Office, Beaverbrook Papers, H/91, Beverley Baxter to Beaverbrook, 1 Sept. 1932.

issue that had a suitably broad interest for the mass market, and required no special expertise or knowledge: anyone could have an opinion on it. At the same time, it was conveniently apolitical (in conventional terms at least), and thus attractive to editors wary of burdening readers with too much 'heavy' and politically contested material. Always sensitive to opportunities to set his readers talking, Northcliffe launched several debates relating to post-war 'modern women' before his death in 1922: subjects included the morality of 'mixed bathing' and the merits of the short skirt. In the former instance, indeed, the *Mail* generated extra controversy by paying a local councillor who was a vehement opponent of mixed bathing to tour England's beaches and write articles criticizing the practice. The effect of such material was inevitably to reinforce the impression that a whole generation of women, rather than a few daring pioneers, shared the attitudes and characteristics under discussion. The seriousness of the condemnations suggested that the whole basis of sexual relations was under threat.

Historians have often misunderstood the tactics used by the press in such instances. Flicking through a few issues of 1920s newspapers, it is possible to read the inclusion of these attacks as evidence of a widespread editorial hostility to 'modern women'. Such a conclusion is usually misleading. In fact, Northcliffe favoured both mixed bathing and short skirts, as the *Mail*'s readers doubtless realized. But he was adamant that his paper should 'give all opinions' to spark off debate. This was also the motivation behind the prominence given to clerical attacks on 'flappers', as Robert Graves and Alan Hodge recognized:

The Press used Church comment as a convenient measuring stick for popular tendencies. It was news if a bishop denounced the modern girl . . . but the scales were always slightly weighted in favour of 'modernism'. 'Modernism'. . . had become synonymous with lively progress.[24]

Some historians have given only one side of these controversies. The following article has been quoted to show the *Mail* blaming post-war women for the decay of established social values:[25]

The freedom of the modern independent girl from the supervision of her parents, the tendency to rebel against discipline . . . the cry of pleasure for pleasure's sake—all these tended to encourage a lower standard of morality . . . the social butterfly type had

---

[24] R. Graves and A. Hodge, *The Long Week-End: A Social History of Britain 1918–1939* (first pub. 1940; Harmondsworth: Penguin, 1971), 109–10.

[25] Melman, *Women and the Popular Imagination*, 18–19; M. Pugh, *Women and the Women's Movement in Britain 1914–59* (Basingstoke: Macmillan, 1992), 74.

probably never been so prevalent as at present. It comprised the frivolous, scantily clad, 'jazzing flapper', irresponsible and undisciplined.[26]

Actually, these words were not editorial comment, but taken from a report of a lecture given by Dr Murray Leslie at the Institute of Social Hygiene (his speech was also covered by *The Times* and other papers[27]). An editorial did accompany the report. Ignoring the contentious claims about female morality (and certainly not endorsing them), it criticized Leslie's proposed solutions to the 'surplus women' problem that had formed the substance of his address. By not putting forward any alternatives, the paper was clearly inviting suggestions.[28] Sure enough, the issue became a feature of both the news pages and the correspondence columns over the next few days. The follow-up article canvassed the opinions of women and allowed them to respond to Dr Leslie and the stereotypes he had invoked. One interviewee was the prominent feminist Ray Strachey. She attacked the assumptions that all women were seeking husbands, and that marriage and motherhood should necessarily mean giving up paid employment. 'There are plenty of married workers with children,' she claimed, 'who are quite frank in saying that they hope to add to their family.' She believed that the solution to the problems caused by the disparity between the sexes was employment: 'There ought to be a job for every woman who wants one.'[29]

Over the next few days, a variety of women were able to voice their opinions. A self-declared 'one of the million' 'surplus' women argued that the restricted opportunities to marry should not be a matter for regret: 'We have a glorious freedom of our own'.[30] Meanwhile a female doctor criticized the terms in which the question was discussed: 'I also greatly regret that the word "surplus" should be applied to them, however many there may be. No woman is "surplus" just because there is not a husband for her, marriage is not the only thing in life open to a woman.'[31]

Dr Leslie's comments cannot be taken to reflect the attitude of the *Mail*. They were merely the opening salvo of a debate in which the paper remained relatively neutral: if anything, it distanced itself from the controversial views of the lecture. The *Mail*—and other papers generated similar discussions—was not condemning the 'flapper', but exploiting the widespread interest in her.

---

[26] *Daily Mail*, 5 Feb. 1920, 7.

[27] Claire Langhamer notes that the *Manchester Evening News* picked up on the lecture: *Women's Leisure in England, 1920–1960* (Manchester: Manchester University Press, 2000), 53.   [28] Ibid. 6.

[29] *Daily Mail*, 6 Feb. 1920, 5.   [30] Ibid. 6.   [31] *Daily Mail*, 7 Feb. 1920, 7.

Financial Incentives

An attitude of consistent hostility to modernity and the modern generation would, after all, have been financially imprudent for newspapers. Circulation departments emphasized to journalists the importance of attracting younger readers. As Robert Ensor pointed out, 'experience showed that once people have grown up and settled down to take in a particular paper, it is hard to shift them to another. So the special attention of the circulation-getter must be directed to young people.'[32] Or, as Hugh Cudlipp of the *Mirror* put it more colourfully, every newspaper cherishes its 'younger readers for the simple reason that older folk already have one foot in the grave: the dead don't pay newsagents' bills'.[33] For Ensor, these considerations explained what he regarded as an 'extraordinary wave of youth-worship and flattery which swept over Britain between 1920 and 1930'.[34] Newspapers certainly sought to keep up with modern interests, expanding their coverage of cinema and sport and photographing the latest fashions. Northcliffe repeatedly warned his staff against slipping into a 'middle-aged somnolescence', and his news editor, Tom Clarke, recalled how young journalists became 'the Chief's obsession'.[35] Beaverbrook reminded John Gordon, the editor of the *Sunday Express*, that the paper 'is out to believe in the future; to believe in the new generation; to trust in Youth'.[36] In July 1933 the *Express* firmly tied its image to that of the modern generation in an article on the 'young men' who produced the paper: 'If the *Express* has faults, they are the faults of youth. They spring from enthusiasm, cocksureness and a restless urge for experiments.'[37] This was an image that the *Daily Mirror* sought to steal for itself in the second half of the 1930s with its new irreverent approach. Even the serious-minded editorial director of the *News Chronicle*, Walter Layton, told his colleagues that they needed to 'import a little youthful diablerie and effervescence into the paper'.[38]

Many advertisers, too, sought to reach that important group of younger readers who had a small but significant disposable income before undertaking

[32] R. C. K. Ensor, 'The Press', in Sir Ernest Barker (ed.), *The Character of England* (Oxford: Clarendon Press, 1947), 418.

[33] H. Cudlipp, *Publish and be Damned! The Astonishing Story of the Daily Mirror* (London: Andrew Dakers, 1953), 87.

[34] Ensor, 'The Press', 418.

[35] Bodleian Library, Oxford, MS Eng. hist. d. 303–5, Northcliffe Bulletins, 22 Sept. 1919; T. Clarke, *My Northcliffe Diary* (London: Victor Gollance, 1931), 120.

[36] Beaverbrook Papers, H/73, Beaverbrook to Gordon, 14 Sept. 1930.

[37] A. Christiansen, *Headlines All my Life* (London: Heinemann, 1961), 93–4.

[38] Trinity College, Cambridge, Walter Layton Papers, Box 89, fo. 7, memo to Directors of Daily News Ltd, 9 Nov. 1937.

the responsibilities of marriage and family life.[39] Cosmetics, cigarettes, and films were all directed heavily to this market. And newspapers could hardly wage war against modern fashions when they were so dependent upon revenue from the very clothing retailers who were trying to encourage readers to keep up with the latest styles. The various fashions of this period, including the short skirts and one-piece bathing suits that so concerned traditionalists, were heavily promoted in the women's pages as well as in the advertising columns.

For these reasons, editors knew that newspapers could not afford to cut themselves off permanently from the post-war generation by consistently following the standpoint of those critics whom they included in the news columns to provoke their readers. This is not to suggest that criticisms of the 'flapper' were confined to the rants of a few conspicuously old-fashioned contributors. Editorials and feature articles, as will be seen, did express suspicions about the independence and assertiveness of 'modern women'. Nevertheless, only in one instance in this period was there a sustained, deliberate, and coherent editorial attack on the 'flapper'—and that was for political reasons and largely restricted to the political columns. This was the campaign undertaken by Lord Rothermere's papers, the *Mail* and the *Mirror*, in 1927–8 against the concession of the vote to women under 30—the infamous 'flapper vote' crusade. It was actually motivated, as Chapter 4 will demonstrate, far more by Rothermere's vehement anti-socialism than by any anti-feminist instincts. The campaign was not, it is worth reiterating, typical of the output of the popular press. In general, the editorial attitude underlying the contrived controversies over 'modern women' was usually one of quiet acceptance of changing gender relations.

Inter-War Debates

The Transformative Impact of War

Popular newspapers, as a result of their basic editorial practices, focused attention disproportionately upon modernity and 'modern women'. Their scale of news values gave prominence to path-breaking female achievements rather than to the difficulties and prejudices still facing the majority; their penchant for controversy encouraged them to inflame the debates about the

---

[39] On the younger end of this market, see D. Fowler, *The First Teenagers: The Life-Style of Young Wage-Earners in Inter-War Britain* (London: Woburn, 1995). Ensor also noted the interest in reaching 'young unmarried women earning money'; 'The Press', 418.

behaviour of the younger generation; and their desire to remain relevant to younger people ensured that they did not neglect modern interests. When these tendencies were powerfully reinforced by the overwhelming contemporary sense that the war had caused a massive dislocation in British history, involving a fundamental shift in gender relations, it was inevitable that the press would be dominated by the theme of social transformation. If commentators disagreed on the nature and merit of the changes in the position of women, almost all accepted that something profound had happened. As the war drew to a close, there were numerous assessments of how society had been altered. Hardly anyone believed that there was any hope of a return to the *status quo ante bellum*. 'Intelligent women recognise that things can never be again as they once were,' declared a contributor to the *Daily Express*.[40] Florie Annie Steel, the novelist, wrote in the *Mail* that 'the world is fresh and new for womanhood . . . it is not possible for us to go back to what we were before the flame of war tried us as in a fire. And why should we?'[41] In the *Mirror*, Edith Nepean assured readers that 'women have grown a lot mentally during the last four years'. Returning home, the 'bachelor girls' would demand to be treated differently because they had 'tasted the sweets of liberty . . . [and] known the joy of liberty of action'.[42] Left-wing commentators did not demur from this analysis. Mary Macarthur, the trade union organizer, writing in the *Daily News*, observed that 'It is undeniable that the sphere of woman has been tremendously widened during the war. The national conscience has been mightily pleased by the spectacle of some five millions of women doing their share and the share of the absent men in the work of the country.'[43]

Northcliffe himself seems to have been swept along by this current of opinion. Mrs Peel, the editor of the *Mail*'s women's page at the time, recalled that it dawned on 'the Chief' 'that the women who had come out of their homes during the war to work as nurses, WAACs, Wrens, munitions girls . . . would not remain unchanged by such experiences. It was for this reason that on several occasions, he asked why more use was not made of my services.'[44] Internal memorandums confirm the latter claim. Northcliffe criticized editors for not including more of Mrs Peel's feature articles: 'Her points of view on sex matters may not be that of the hermits of Carmelite House [the *Daily Mail* offices] but it is shared by most of the folk one meets in the larger world.'[45] Northcliffe

40 *Daily Express*, 9 Nov. 1918, 2. 41 *Daily Mail*, 12 Nov. 1918, 2.
42 *Daily Mirror*, 6 Dec. 1918, 5. 43 *Daily News*, 14 Nov. 1918, 5.
44 C. S. Peel, *Life's Enchanted Cup: An Autobiography* (London: John Lane, 1933), 227.
45 Northcliffe Bulletins, 6 June 1919.

wanted to ensure that the *Mail* was quick to cater for the 'new mood' among women.

The belief in the transformative impact of the war on the position of women survived throughout the 1920s and 1930s, despite the unceremonious removal of most women from their wartime work. This was partly a reflection of the tendency of press commentators to generalize from the metropolitan middle-class society that most of them knew best, where opportunities for women had increased most appreciably. In August 1921, for example, well after the heady atmosphere of the Armistice and the post-war boom had dispersed, the *Mail* asked the novelists Stephen McKenna and Elizabeth Marc to assess the 'modern woman'. The extent of their sympathy with the 'flapper' was very different, but they were equally convinced that the events of the war had completely reshaped femininity. McKenna described how

Seven years ago, as at the striking of the clock, the modern girl threw off the control of her elders and claimed equality with men in contributing to the war, in making a career for herself, in constructing her own code of morals and in determining her own standard of conduct.[46]

Elizabeth Marc agreed that 'the girl of today is simply in tune with her generation. She is as much a war product as a high income tax and poison gas.'[47] When, two years later, Rose Macaulay had the temerity to call into question the existence of a 'post-war generation', her opinions were summarily dismissed in an editorial in the *Daily News*:

We think Miss Macaulay will find it difficult to persuade observant persons that the poignant experiences of the war have produced no plainly discernible difference in the manner of the young. The 'New Young' is not merely the invention of a novelist pursuing a conventional stunt . . . to deny that any marked change has taken place seems to us to be blind to a very notable fact of general observation.[48]

In 1927, indeed, the *Daily Mail* could declare that 'the greatest social problem of today is the impact of modern youth, impelled by the enthusiasm and force of new ideas, upon a disillusioned older generation which has passed through the grim forcing house of a world war'. Those brought up before 1914 were, the paper claimed, separated by a 'mysterious gulf' from the new society.[49] The *Mail* gave a platform to this post-war generation by commissioning a major series in which young people outlined their 'new' values and beliefs. In the first article, a 'modern society girl' used imagery that was already becoming clichéd, of the war as a flood breaking down the

46 *Daily Mail*, 9 Aug. 1921, 4.   47 *Daily Mail*, 11 Aug. 1921, 4.
48 *Daily News*, 3 Mar. 1923, 4.   49 *Daily Mail*, 6 May 1927, 9.

restrictions and certainties of Edwardian society: 'many of the old barriers have been swept away and we have now a wider horizon than ever before . . . We are inclined to doubt everything and ask "Why?" We cannot take anything on trust.'[50]

This idea of employing spokesmen or women for a generation became a popular press practice—one that merely reinforced the impression of a clean break with the past.[51] The passage of time seemed to do little to dull this sense of a nation stratified by age. In August 1931, for example, despite a fresh political and economic crisis emerging to command attention, Ursula Bloom continued to view society as being defined by the war experience and in particular by the wrenching apart of generations:

My generation, brought up according to pre-war standards, is, in a sense, exiled from the new flitting generation of bright young people; we are at heart purely imitative of their thoughts and behaviour . . . In those years of 1914 to 1918 we lived an entire century of change . . . [But] we could not keep up with the women who marched steadily forward towards their freedom.[52]

Work for Women: The Post-War Demobilization

Commentators across the spectrum of the press agreed that the war had been the cause of a remarkable transformation in the behaviour of a whole generation of women. They were far from unanimous, however, about the desirability of this change or in the images they used to describe 'modern women'. Some admired the independence and competence of the 'daughters of freedom'; others derided 'masculine women' for 'invading' male realms. Some praised the new athleticism and vigour of the 'flapper'; others lamented a loss of femininity and elegance. All of the popular papers gave space to a variety of different opinions, although, as already suggested, the balance was usually tipped in favour of modernity. Examining the pattern of the debates in two of the main areas of contention, namely employment and sport, it is clear that the popular press generally came to terms with, and sometimes even enthused about, the developments of modernity, while seeking to blunt the appeal of the more radical and threatening aspects of changes in gender relations, and underplaying the need for further feminist effort.

The historiographical consensus on press attitudes to paid employment for women is that, after celebrating the contribution of women on the home front during the war (which they were largely obliged to do for patriotic reasons),

---

50 Ibid. 10.

51 See e.g. the *Herald*'s series in May 1930 'Youth Has its Say', e.g. *Daily Herald*, 23 May 1930, 8.

52 *Daily Mail*, 25 Aug. 1931, 8.

newspapers turned viciously against women, demanding that they vacate their jobs for the returning 'war heroes' and return to a life of domesticity. Once the war had ended, writes Gail Braybon, 'the change in tone of press reports was extraordinary . . . superficial praise changed to spiteful criticism in many newspapers'.[53] The lineage of this interpretation is lengthy. As early as February 1919 Mary Macarthur told a meeting of the National Federation of Women Workers that 'with the coming of the Armistice these women, who had worked 12-hour shifts, days and nights, Saturdays and Sundays, had, according to the newspapers, suddenly become shirkers and slackers'.[54] The charge was repeated by Ray Strachey in *The Cause*, her influential history of the women's movement, and hence was elevated to historical orthodoxy: 'the tone of the press swung, all in a moment, from extravagant praise to the opposite extreme, and the very same people who had been heroines and the saviours of the country a few months before were now parasites, blacklegs and limpets'.[55] For many historians this 'backlash' signalled the start of two decades of a press-sponsored 'cult of domesticity'.

This idea of a press backlash has been considerably overstated. There *were* aggressive voices demanding the speedy removal of women workers—after all, that was what had been negotiated during the war by the unions and later became government policy as the Restoration of Pre-War Practices Act in 1919—and some of them were reported in the popular papers. The *Mail*, the *Mirror*, and the *Express* certainly wanted to stand up for the 'war heroes': the *Mail*, for example, advertised itself as the 'Soldiers' Paper'. In general, however, the popular dailies were far more restrained than has been claimed. An article by a regular *Mail* columnist, G. Ivy Sanders, written two weeks after the Armistice, gives a sense of the characteristic tone. 'In the interests of the country in general, and of the women workers in particular,' she argued, 'every encouragement should be given to the women to return to their pre-war employment until such time as normal peace conditions are resumed.' Nevertheless, she continued, 'War has created entirely new and improved conditions of service in every sphere of labour. The women are now in a position to demand fair wages and treatment from their pre-war employers. They should be assisted to grasp this rare opportunity.'[56]

---

[53] Braybon, *Women Workers*, 186. This charge is repeated by many others, including (as has already been seen) Melman, *Women and the Popular Imagination*, 17, and also Pugh, *Women and the Women's Movement*, 77, who notes that 'Where recently they [the press] had heaped praise on women they now began to identify them in a threatening light as a section of the population lacking true public spirit.'

[54] *Daily Herald*, 22 Feb. 1919, 12.

[55] R. Strachey, *The Cause: A Short History of the Women's Movement in Great Britain* (London: G. Bell, 1928), 371.   [56] *Daily Mail*, 29 Nov. 1918, 4.

The editor of the *Express* believed that the paper would be able to gain favourable publicity by helping women search for alternative work. Warning that 'a large number of war workers will soon find themselves out of employment', the paper offered for a month its advertising columns free of charge to women war workers seeking alternative employment.[57] The day after this initial offer was made (and it had been significant enough to be accorded a banner headline across the front page), the paper printed a message of thanks from a number of women parliamentary candidates; the following day another congratulatory telegram was printed from none other than Ray Strachey.[58] Both of those later critics of the press, indeed, were given space in which to put forward the women's case. Writing in the *Express*, Strachey accepted that the 'discharged soldiers have undoubtedly the first claim to consideration' but also voiced her hope that society would 'not let the women who have done us such good service be barred from the work they can do and do well'.[59] Mary Macarthur, meanwhile, was invited by the *Daily News* to inform readers 'what will happen to the women'. 'No time should be lost', she advised, 'in making the employment of women on work formerly or customarily done by men conditional upon the payment of the same rate of wages.'[60]

By the middle of 1919 discontent at the pace of demobilization was rising, and editorials became somewhat less sympathetic. Discussing women workers in the civil service, the *Mail* argued that

Women have unquestionably done great service in these departments. They can be divided into two classes, those to whom work is necessary for a livelihood and those of independent means who took up work when men were scarce and now find it a pleasant distraction. It is time the latter should be heartily thanked for their services and allowed to retire in favour of men who are obliged to earn a living.[61]

With the phrase 'pleasant distraction', the leader-writer betrayed his ignorance of the wide range of motivations that led women to take up employment, and the social, financial, and psychological frustrations that beset women who wanted to work outside the home but were unable. The spectre of the 'pin money girl' was here invoked, as it would be occasionally throughout the decade. 'If there is to be unemployment it is obviously better for the community that the women should stay at home and mind the housekeeping than that they should keep men out of work,' argued the *Mail*'s correspondent Alexander Thompson. But, he added, 'if industry were rationally organised

---

[57] *Daily Express*, 7 Dec. 1918, 1. [58] *Daily Express*, 9 Dec. 1918, 5; 10 Dec. 1918, 1.
[59] *Daily Express*, 10 Dec. 1918, 3. [60] *Daily News*, 14 Nov. 1918, 4.
[61] *Daily Mail*, 6 June 1919, 4.

neither men nor women need be idle. There is enough to be done, for all who are fit and willing.'[62]

On the left, the *Herald* was caught between its policy of sexual equality—it publicized Mary Macarthur's efforts on behalf of women war workers, including her demand for women's 'Right to Work'[63]—and its position as the defender of male union interests at a time when many unions were vigorously demanding the removal of women. Reporting a strike by Halifax engineers against women 'dilutees', the paper recorded the union's claim that 'the war necessity having disappeared the women ought to go. They object to anyone doing skilled engineering work who has not gone through an apprenticeship and especially at a time when thousands of trained engineers in the country are out of employment.'[64] Similarly, the following year there were complaints that 'women are satisfied with too little and so keep down the men's salaries'.[65] Although it felt obliged to give space to these concerns, elsewhere the *Herald* continued to defend the women's cause.

But if the escalating tensions certainly revealed a widespread assumption that female workers should be the first to be sacrificed in a crisis, this was very different to a fully fledged campaign of hostility as described by Macarthur and Strachey. For both right and left wings of the press, the main target of attack was Lloyd George's government, not women. Strachey claimed that women were described as 'parasites' and 'limpets'. Such language was indeed used in the popular press—but mainly to describe men on high salaries retaining their posts in government bureaucracies, rather than female workers. Indeed, the *Mail* claimed that the removal of women was being used to distract attention away from continued government 'extravagance'. 'We hear much on every side of the dismissal of "flappers" and pig-tailed messengers,' observed the *Mail* in September 1919, 'but little or nothing of reductions in the big salaries.'[66] The headline on the following page made clear its message: 'Cutting Down in Nibbles—"Flappers Go First"—Big Limpets Stick—Seeking New Retreats'. The paper charged that 'the Ministry of Munitions is providing an ark of refuge, to which temporary and highly paid barnacles are attaching themselves with an adaptability and tenacity only to be found in the Civil Service'.[67] Furthermore, the *Mail* continued to give space to women unhappy about the direction of the demobilization process. Mrs Peel was allowed the opportunity to put the 'woman's side', and she defended the right of women 'to decide

---

[62] *Daily Mail*, 25 Sept. 1919, 5.
[63] *Daily Herald*, 8 Feb. 1919, 12–13; 22 Feb. 1919, 12; 1 Mar. 1919, 11.
[64] *Daily Herald*, 9 Apr. 1919, 6.   [65] *Daily Herald*, 11 Nov. 1920, 7.
[66] *Daily Mail*, 1 Sept. 1919, 4.   [67] Ibid. 5.

for themselves what kind of work they shall do, whether they be married or single'.[68] Another headline asked directly: 'Are Men Afraid of Women? 100,000 Workless Girls—"Freezing Out Theory"': the report detailed allegations from women's organizations that 'men are challenging us to a bitter war of the sexes'.[69]

Away from the immediate difficulties of the post-war industrial reorganization, the popular papers continued to offer positive visions of women's role in society. In its issue celebrating the signing of the Versailles peace treaty at the end of June 1919, for example, the *Mail* invited assessments of the contribution of women to the war effort and their future prospects in peacetime. The conclusions were optimistic. The novelist George Birmingham (Canon James Hannay) argued that women had 'proved themselves' and that there was no going back:

> We know now, as we never knew before, what women can do. Women themselves are conscious, as they never were before, of their own powers . . . We have everything to hope and very little to fear from the new activities, the new powers of those who in time of trial have shown themselves noble-hearted, devoted and capable.[70]

If the tone was somewhat patronizing, the sentiments were clear. On the previous page, Lady Rhondda, an explicitly feminist voice, proclaimed that 'Women Can Direct Businesses' while Millicent Fawcett, the veteran suffrage campaigner, added that 'a vista of endless opportunities' had opened up for women.[71] Meanwhile, women's pages across the spectrum of the press included careers advice. The electricity industry offered a number of openings for women, noted the *Daily News*; photography was a 'fascinating career', observed the *Mail*.[72] Government clerks no longer in work were advised to visit the Women's Service Bureau, choose a career, and 'resolve to train and become as efficient as possible'.[73] In December 1919, indeed, the *Mail* women's page began a weekly series entitled 'Womanly Politics', whose first topic was demobilization and the 'dole'. The author of the series was Ray Strachey.[74]

This notion of a full-blooded press 'backlash' against women workers after the war needs revision. The popular national dailies have been tarred with a brush that should perhaps have been restricted to the more rumbustious weekly papers, such as *John Bull*, or they have been blamed for some of the third-party opinions that they reported.[75] As has been suggested, papers were

---

[68] *Daily Mail*, 7 June 1919, 4.   [69] *Daily Mail*, 19 Sept. 1919, 3.
[70] *Daily Mail*, 30 June 1919, 8.   [71] Ibid. 7.
[72] *Daily News*, 3 May 1919, 8; *Daily Mail*, 6 May 1919, 11.   [73] *Daily Mail*, 1 Jan. 1920, 9.
[74] *Daily Mail*, 1 Dec. 1919, 15.
[75] For the views of *John Bull* on demobilization, see 25 Jan. 1919, 3; 3 May 1919, 2; 10 May 1919, 2.

unafraid of stirring up controversy, as they did with letters such as that in the *Mail* from Major Brunel Cohen entitled 'Will the Women Go Back?'[76] When writing her criticisms of the press in *The Cause* in 1928, Ray Strachey might well also have been influenced by the *Mail*'s recent attack on the 'flapper vote'. The average unprejudiced reader at the time, however, would have been likely to receive the impression not that the press was opposed to women's perceived new opportunities, but rather that it was heavily critical of the government's handling of the demobilization process.

The point can be reinforced with another example that has passed into the historiography, relating not so much to the demobilization crisis as to those women who were entering previously male spheres in these immediate post-war years. Attention has been drawn to a *Daily News* article from March 1921, entitled 'Dislike of Women', to give substance to this idea of a groundswell of opinion against women.[77] 'The flood of praise poured out on women during the war has had its inevitable backwash,' noted the author, W. Keith: 'Women preachers, barristers, engineers, professors are regarded as evidence of women's advance towards equality. Legally it may be so. In public estimation they merely add fuel to the flame of indignation and annoyance.'[78] There had been, Keith also noted, an 'outcry against women jurors'. Yet this contributor was clearly responding only to one stream of public opinion, and not one that was dominant in the daily press. The celebratory welcome offered to jurors from across the spectrum of the press has already been noted, and the praise of the first female barristers was similarly effusive; in 1923, moreover, a *Daily News* editorial made clear the paper's support for female preachers such as Maude Royden.[79] Such one-sided pieces are significant, and clearly represented genuine fears, but they do need to be set in their full context.

Work for Women: Expanding Opportunities?

There was a widespread assumption throughout the period that a continuing expansion of women's role in public life and the workplace was an inevitable aspect of post-war modernity. Images of the convergence of the two sexes were frequent, and the popularity of the androgynous figure with a slim silhouette and short hair appeared to symbolize a much wider appropriation of masculine traits by women. Discussing the introduction of female jurors, the *Mail* wrote of the 'inexorable logic of the law which has equalised the sexes' civic rights';[80]

---

[76] *Daily Mail*, 30 May 1919, 6.
[77] Cited in Braybon, *Women Workers*, 193; Kent, *Making Peace*, 101.
[78] *Daily News*, 11 Mar. 1921, 4.   [79] *Daily News*, 4 May 1923, 4.
[80] *Daily Mail*, 4 Jan. 1921, 4.

and when the paper asked Professor A. M. Low to predict 'Our Lives in 1950', he forecast that 'The next twenty years will undoubtedly see a great advance in the position of women. With the gradual erosion of physical disabilities I do not believe that women will trouble to stay at home . . . Women will cease to expect to the suggestion of protection.'[81] 'There is little doubt that fifty years will see women almost completely supreme in most things', claimed a contributor to the *Herald*'s women's page in 1933. 'One only has to keep one's eyes and ears open to see evidence of this wherever one goes.'[82]

It seemed inevitable that remaining strongholds would soon be toppled. 'The clergywoman is surely coming,' declared a contributor to the *Express* in 1928—almost ten years after another article in the same paper had confidently outlined how social life would change 'When We Have "Curettes"' (female curates).[83] The intervening period had not been enough to dampen expectations. Male prejudice definitely seemed to be waning, argued Gladys Watts in the *News Chronicle* in 1931. 'Whereas ten or twenty years ago it was necessary perhaps for a woman to devote every ounce of energy she possessed to push her way in the world, and to force an entrance into a profession, that condition no longer holds good.'[84] The women's pages gave details of what seemed to be a spectacular array of opportunities for middle-class women. In 1920 the *Daily Express* introduced a new series of career advice for the parents of young women with the observation that 'today, when practically every profession and most industries are open to women, fathers and mothers are confronted with a bewildering field of choice'.[85] These words were echoed a decade later when the *Evening News* advertised a similar feature: 'The careers open to women nowadays are truly bewildering in their variety . . . now it is possible for a girl to be a "flying secretary", a museum keeper, a canine nurse, a policewoman, a beauty culturist . . .'[86]

In the context of the numerous reports of women's firsts and the heightened perceptions of modernity, the 'defeats' that women experienced in these years, such as the various impositions of a marriage bar to prevent married women from working, and the refusal of London hospitals to continue to admit female students, often received relatively little attention. They frequently appeared to be of little real significance in comparison with the gains that had been made. When fifty-eight married women teachers finally lost their case against Rhondda Urban Council's marriage bar in May 1923, for example, the *Herald* was paying far more attention to the Labour Party Women's Conference and the prospect of newly enfranchised women providing a fresh approach to old

---

[81] *Daily Mail*, 1 Mar. 1927, 10.   [82] *Daily Herald*, 21 Oct. 1933, 5.
[83] *Daily Express*, 30 Mar. 1928, 10; 10 Dec. 1918, 3.   [84] *News Chronicle*, 21 Oct. 1931, 8.
[85] *Daily Express*, 27 Oct. 1920, 3.   [86] *Daily Mail*, 3 July 1931, 12.

political questions.[87] Similarly, on the day in October 1924 that the *Daily News* reported the decision by St Mary's Hospital in London not to train any more women, its banner headline on the front page announced that a record forty-two female candidates had been accepted for the forthcoming election campaign.[88] Women still appeared to be marching onwards. When these 'defeats' were taken up, papers usually pursued a relatively neutral editorial line: they often framed the matter in terms of a 'sex war', and evidence was presented on either side to generate a controversy. When Westminster and St George's Hospitals followed the example of St Mary's in 1928, for example, the *Express* invited 'A Physician' to deliver 'The Truth About the Women Students': 'It is easier to run a school for men only than one for men and women,' he claimed.[89] Five days later, however, there was another article, 'A Spirited Reply' by a female doctor, who declared that 'the overcrowded state of the profession is the fault of the medical schools and their selfish and short-sighted methods'.[90] The *Mail* took a similar approach.[91] But such controversies seemed to do little to undermine the widespread beliefs about modernity. Indeed, when a new wing of the Elizabeth Garrett Anderson Hospital was opened the following year, the *Mail* could view the hospital as 'perhaps the premier manifestation of the part played by women in the modern world'.[92]

Because the evidence that women were still experiencing considerable difficulties and restrictions at the workplace was not usually given sufficient prominence to shake the conviction that women's opportunities were continuing to expand, complaints about discrimination were often received unsympathetically, and indeed rather incredulously, by the conservative papers. When the feminist and musician Dame Ethel Smyth claimed in March 1928 that women were still not competing on equal terms with men, James Douglas of the *Express* accused her of suffering from 'conspiracy mania': men would, he argued, 'in the new era of equal opportunity for both sexes hold their own against women only by being better at their job'.[93] Similarly, three years later a *Mail* editorial was sceptical about the protests of a Mrs Godfrey of the Guild of Insurance that women were being unfairly excluded from higher administrative positions:

She voices a feeling that is very natural among ambitious people, confident in their own ability, and for that very reason dissatisfied with the rate of their progress. And yet the

---

[87] *Daily Herald*, 4 May 1923, 2, 4.　　[88] *Daily News*, 18 Oct. 1924, 1, 7.
[89] *Daily Express*, 26 Mar. 1928, 9.　　[90] *Daily Express*, 31 Mar. 1928, 9.
[91] For example, *Daily Mail*, 2–9 Mar. 1922; 19, 22 Mar. 1928.　　[92] *Daily Mail*, 9 May 1929, 11.
[93] *Daily Express*, 17 Mar. 1928, 8.

outside observer, taking a broader and more detached view, sees women in every branch of commerce pushing forward with what seem to him prodigious speed, to lucrative and responsible offices that they scarcely dreamt of filling even twenty years ago.[94]

Even the liberal *Daily News* argued that the notion of a 'conspiracy' against women in the professions was a 'mischievous illusion': 'the fact is that women have been so long denied their natural right of development that when it is at last granted and no one is really denying it any longer they cannot believe it'.[95]

But this impatience with complaints from professional women did not usually translate into calls for restrictions on their employment. Popular news-papers were by no means, as has been suggested, unquestioning supporters of the marriage bar. Certainly, the implicit assumption of much of the women's page material was that most women would eventually leave the world of work to marry and raise a family. The elevation of housewifery and motherhood to the status of a profession perhaps suggested that domestic duties were worthy of a woman's full attention. The occasional attacks on 'Those Pin Money Wives' displayed hostility to women who worked merely to supplement their income. 'Can't anything be done to make them realise that their ambition leads them into the labour market, to the detriment of women who must work—to say nothing of the men?' asked a contributor to the *Express* women's page in 1930.[96] Nevertheless, many other voices were raised opposing the prejudice against married woman. On the left, the *Daily News–News Chronicle* was a fairly regular critic of the marriage bar. 'It is so stupid and short-sighted, and generally absurd, to try to deny the possibility of an alliance between matri-mony and competence,' argued Hilda Nield in 1919.[97] 'The decision should be left to the individual,' agreed Helen Hope four years later. 'No less than men, women must have the Right to Work and express themselves without let or hindrance.'[98] The *Daily Herald* also attacked the restriction on married women's employment, although it was rarely a priority. But there were also opposing voices in the conservative papers. 'Business Women Make Good Wives', argued Jane Taverner in the *Mail* in 1924: 'Women who enjoy home life and professional life have struck an almost perfect balance. And there are very many such women . . . women who work outside their homes find house-keeping a hobby, their children an unending source of happiness and delight.'[99] E. M. Delafield, the novelist, cautioned against marriage being women's only goal: 'It is extraordinarily satisfactory to be loved, admired and happy—but to achieve these ends should not really be an adult preoccupation

---

[94] *Daily Mail*, 18 May 1931, 10.   [95] *Daily News*, 24 May 1929, 8.
[96] *Daily Express*, 6 Nov. 1930, 5.   [97] *Daily News*, 1 May 1919, 8.
[98] *Daily News*, 3 Mar. 1923, 6.   [99] *Daily Mail*, 23 Oct. 1924, 8.

to the exclusion of everything else.'[100] Contributing to a series on women's employment in the *Mail*, Lady Rhondda told readers that 'Girls' careers should not be chosen with an eye to their possible temporary nature . . . choose a career with a future.' She revealed that she had received many letters from married women anxious to return to work.[101] By end of the 1930s—after the London County Council marriage bar had been overturned—it did not seem particularly controversial for women's page contributors to be advising working wives. When Sister Cooper of the *Mirror* women's page discussed the issue of working women having children in September 1938, for example, she counselled that there was no need to leave work on marriage, or even when first pregnant. Instead, depending on the nature of the business, women could realistically work for five or six months into their pregnancy: 'Such a number of wives work today, even when they are expecting a baby, and I think this is a better solution, when the exchequer is low, than to put off the coming of the first baby indefinitely.'[102]

Work for Women: The 'Servant Crisis'

Where the conservative press did take a firm stand against 'modern' tendencies, however, was on the issue of domestic service. Openings seemed to be multiplying not only for middle-class women, but for working-class women as well, and this appeared to be at the root of what a range of commentators described as a 'servant crisis' in the early 1920s. (Records confirm that there was indeed a significant decline in the number of servants in these years, with a slight recovery by the 1930s.[103]) It was widely believed that the recruitment of servants was being undermined by a growing distaste for submitting to class hierarchies inside the home, and a preference for shop or factory work that allowed more time for leisure and socializing. 'No one will be a servant,' lamented the *Mirror* in May 1919. 'The wail arises "We want freedom, we want to be out, we want to see life. We hate domestic work."'[104] A *Daily Mail* editorial in May 1923 agreed that 'the restless desire for independence, which is a legacy of the war' was one of the main reasons for the reluctance to enter service.[105] 'The shortage of domestic servants', the paper continued, 'is a serious menace to the well-being of the whole community.'[106] It was for these women, or more particularly for those who claimed the 'dole' rather than take up service positions, that the

---

[100] *Daily Mail*, 7 July 1931, 10.   [101] *Daily Mail*, 7 Nov. 1927, 19.

[102] *Daily Mirror*, 23 Sept. 1938, 31.

[103] B. R. Mitchell and P. Deane, *Abstract of British Historical Statistics* (Cambridge: Cambridge University Press, 1962), 60–1.   [104] *Daily Mirror*, 13 May 1919, 7.

[105] *Daily Mail*, 2 May 1923, 8.   [106] Ibid.

conservative press reserved its harshest rhetoric. The *Mail* columnist John Blunt lamented that 'young women would rather idle away their time or join the already swollen ranks of the unemployed' than take up this 'honourable calling'.[107] The *Express* similarly declared that it 'was monstrous that healthy young women are living on the dole and refusing jobs as domestic workers'.[108] The government was censured for allowing such women to claim assistance at all. 'The dole has gone far to dry up domestic service at the source. It is eating into this nation like a disease and undermining the independent spirit of the people.'[109] John Blunt blamed a coalition of 'busybodies, "highbrows", and people who delight in making other people discontented' for gradually 'spreading abroad the idea that there is something derogatory about domestic service'.[110] (Perhaps Blunt had in mind the *Daily Herald*, a paper that consistently called for the improvement of service conditions and encouraged unionization, as one member of this unholy alliance. Virginia Woolf, after all, had recently used a servant reading the *Herald* as a symbol of women's new assertiveness.[111]) Underlying some of this rhetoric was the belief that service was, as Blunt put it, 'the best training for her future life that the average girl could have'.[112] Most of it, however, was motivated far more by anti-working class, rather than anti-feminist, feeling and the perception that the government was being grossly extravagant in its allocation of unemployment benefits. These arguments should be seen as part of a far wider attack on the 'dole' and dependants on the state (see Chapter 7 for attacks on male 'scroungers'). The *Mail* and the *Mirror* repeatedly called for the 'dole' to be abolished altogether. But if the servant 'crisis' was only part of a broader issue, these images nevertheless provided a powerful reinforcement of the notion that 'modern women' were more independent and less subservient than ever before.

Sport and the Active 'Modern Woman'

If during working hours 'modern women' seemed to be rapidly entering previously 'male' spheres of employment, in their leisure time they appeared to be threatening male dominance in the sporting arena. After the war, the sportswoman was almost as prominent as the female professional as a symbol

---

[107] *Daily Mail*, 19 Nov. 1924, 7.   [108] *Daily Express*, 8 July 1925, 8.
[109] *Daily Mail*, 19 Sept. 1923, 5.   [110] *Daily Mail*, 19 Nov. 1924, 7.
[111] V. Woolf, *Mr Bennett and Mrs Brown*, first pub. Hogarth Press, Oct. 1924; repr. in V. Woolf, *A Woman's Essays*, i, ed. R. Bowlby (London: Penguin, 1992), 69–87; reference to the *Herald*, 70.
[112] *Daily Mail*, 19 Nov. 1924, 7.

of modernity. Working women had always performed heavy labour, of course, but their high-profile contribution to the war effort made it more difficult than ever to maintain the belief in female physical frailty that had been so embedded in Victorian medical thought.[113] In the shorter skirts and less restrictive corsets that had come into fashion, moreover, women had a greater freedom of movement. At the end of the war, press commentators observed that conventional ideas about female capabilities would have to be reassessed. Harold Saunders, writing in the *Express*, announced that 'The war . . . has taught us that, in the matter of strength and endurance, there is little to choose between the sexes.' He predicted that on the golf 'links, as well as in the rough and tumble affairs of life, it will probably be found that women can now hold their own'.[114] In the *Mail* an 'Amateur International' agreed that women were no longer 'to be despised as an opponent nor ignored as a partner' on tennis courts and golf courses.[115] The *Mail* photo pages displayed 'the splendidly healthy bodies they [women] have cultivated on active service' and the 'athletic propensities of the girls of today'.[116] Papers pictured women engaged in not just tennis, golf, and hockey, but also football, cricket, rowing, and fencing.

It became commonplace to contrast the more active and robust post-war women with Victorian women who, in the words of the *Mail*, were 'too dainty to eat, too delicate to walk and too inert to think', and who 'divided their time between crocheting antimacassars and fainting elegantly'.[117] This suggested to some, in an eugenically minded culture, that 'modern women' were not just a different generation, but perhaps even an evolutionary step forward from their predecessors. A contributor to the *Mail* in 1921 voiced these thoughts explicitly: 'The woman of the new type is taller than the average man, athletic and full of energy. In all the lighter forms of sport she can already compete on equal terms with men, and the day is not far off when she will prove herself in more violent and exacting games.'[118] In 1927 the *Mail* coined the term 'boyette' to describe young women who imitated both the dress and the behaviour of their male contemporaries, noting that 'a point of interest to eugenicists is that the boyette has a finer physique than the average boy of her age'.[119] The following year the *Mirror* agreed that there had been a 'wonderful advance in feminine physique' and observed that 'Girls nowadays, emancipated from trailing skirts, run and jump and throw the discus and put the shot much in the same

---

[113] On Victorian medical thought, see M. Poovey, *Uneven Developments: The Ideological Work of Gender in Mid-Victorian England* (London: Virago, 1989), ch. 2.   [114] *Daily Express*, 9 Dec. 1918, 3.
[115] *Daily Mail*, 2 May 1919, 4.   [116] *Daily Mail*, 13 May 1919, 6, 12; 12 July 1920, 12.
[117] *Daily Mail*, 10 Jan. 1922, 6; 6 Sept. 1923, 8.   [118] *Daily Mail*, 8 Aug. 1921, 4.
[119] *Daily Mail*, 19 Apr. 1927, 7.

way as their athletic brothers.'[120] The evidence seemed to suggest that the physical disparities between men and women would continue to decrease. Asked to produce a paper dated 1 January 2000 for the Ideal Home Exhibition in 1928, the *Mail* staff suggested that by the end of the century men's physical superiority would have been eroded altogether. The sports pages reported how a woman had knocked out the male champion boxer, and described the tremendous shock when a British man overcame the top female French tennis player.[121] Two years later the *Manchester Evening News* quipped that 'Before long we shall probably see a girl bowler dealing with Bradman.'[122]

Inevitably, such material generated a reaction. Victorian medical attitudes may have been weakened, but they had by no means been completely eroded. A doctor warned in the *Mail* in 1922 that 'one must not lose sight of the fact that the supreme function of women is motherhood. It is possible, in some cases at least, to indulge in games that may have a prejudicial effect on normal childbearing.'[123] The following year another claimed that the impressive physique of modern women could not disguise the internal damage they were causing: 'From being a sheltered, delicate piece of human mechanism whose whole destiny in life was to avoid strenuous exercise and arduous pastimes, she has developed into a vigorous Amazon, with the carriage of an athlete, but all too often with an "athlete's heart" and frayed nerves.'[124]

Other commentators were more concerned with the less tangible, but for them equally worrying, threats of inhibiting the proper expression of masculinity and of compromising the essence of femininity. Describing the 'Strange Outcry' at 'Eve's New Place in Sport' in 1927, the *Daily Herald* outlined the dilemma of men who 'don't like to beat or lose to women' at games of tennis or golf.[125] Only a week later the *Daily Mirror* took up the issue as well, asking 'Are women playing too many games? At almost all the athletic meetings today there are events for them . . . they are invading realms hitherto closed to them.'[126] Some contributors considered the possible consequences of women becoming too masculine. Writing in the *News Chronicle*, James Lansdale argued that while both men and women were growing 'taller, stronger, fitter', there was a danger that the spark of sexual attraction between them might soon be lost: 'When I observe maidens in bare feet and Grecian

---

120 *Daily Mirror*, 19 June 1928, 29.   121 *Daily Mail*, 2 Apr. 1928, 10.

122 *Manchester Evening News*, 21 July 1930, 4, cited in Langhamer, *Women's Leisure*, 55.

123 *Daily Mail*, 1 June 1922, 8.

124 *Daily Mail*, 7 Sept. 1923, 8. Similar attitudes to sportswomen are recorded in J. Hargreaves, *Sporting Females* (London: Routledge, 1994), 123.   125 *Daily Herald*, 11 Apr. 1927, 5.

126 *Daily Mirror*, 18 Apr. 1927, 12.

gowns who are so given up to the cult of sunshine and open air that their limbs rival Britannia's and grow beyond comparison with Juno, I wonder who will woo them.'[127]

Despite occasionally stoking controversy, however, the popular papers were clearly on the side of modernity on this subject. Gone were the days when women's pages would state, as did that of the *Daily News* in 1913, that 'bowls is a far more suitable game for women than hockey or golf or lawn tennis, and far less exhausting';[128] now successful sportswomen were presented as role models and heroines. In the immediate post-war years, substantial press coverage of the women's tennis competition at Wimbledon enabled the French player Suzanne Lenglen to establish, as Ross McKibbin has noted, the 'precedent of a powerful and successful female sporting personality'.[129] The *Mail*'s correspondent claimed on watching Lenglen in 1919 that 'I have never seen on a tennis-court either man or woman move with such mechanical and artistic perfection and poise,' and an editorial observed of her eventual victory in the final that 'never before has a sporting event engaged in by women aroused such whole-hearted enthusiasm'.[130] After Lenglen, the exploits of female tennis and golf players regularly reached the front pages. Newspapers even organized and sponsored sporting competitions for women. In 1924 the *Daily Mirror* and the *News of the World* combined with the journal *Sporting Life* to set up an international 'Women's Olympics', and gave the event generous coverage (see Fig. 2.1).[131] From 1925 the *Daily Mirror* sponsored a special trophy to be presented to the victorious team at the annual women's national athletic meeting.[132] During the 1930s newspapers also reflected and encouraged the growing interest in fitness and exercise, and organizations such as the Women's League of Health and Beauty received considerable publicity.[133] The *Daily Mirror*, again at the forefront, sent eight 'Physical Culture' women on a 4,000 mile tour around Britain demonstrating fitness techniques to eager crowds.[134] By September 1938 the *Mirror* was well within the bounds of convention when it argued that 'Games are good for business girls': 'physical drill before the rush for the office makes her a keen, alert, business girl . . . The staff apply sports ideals to office life. They play for

---

[127] *News Chronicle*, 12 Nov. 1935, 10.   [128] *Daily News*, 30 July 1913, 10.
[129] R. McKibbin, *Classes and Cultures: England 1918–51* (Oxford: Oxford University Press, 1998), 369.
[130] *Daily Mail*, 4 July 1919, 4; 7 July 1919, 4.   [131] Hargreaves, *Sporting Females*, 131–2.
[132] *Daily Mirror*, 19 June 1928, 29.
[133] Mollie Bagot Stack, 'How I Train my Daughter', *Daily Express*, 15 Nov.–4 Dec. 1928; 'Exercises for Health and Slimness', *Daily Mail*, 27 May–Sept. 1930; Women's League of Health and Beauty, see *Daily Mirror*, 4 June 1934, 4; *News Chronicle*, 4 June 1934, 18; see also J. J. Matthews, 'They Had Such a Lot of Fun: The Women's League of Health and Beauty between the Wars', *History Workshop Journal*, 30 (Autumn 1990), 22–54.   [134] *Daily Mirror*, 19 Sept. 1938, 5.

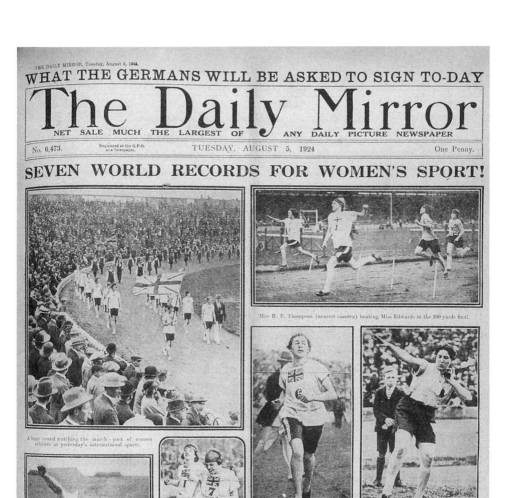

FIG. 2.1. Newspapers supported women's sports by sponsoring events and prizes, and by providing generous publicity. This international women's athletic meeting was backed by the *Mirror*, the *News of the World*, and *Sporting Life*, and produced seven world records

the side. It means team spirit instead of petty rivalry, perfect combination instead of cattiness.'[135]

Nevertheless, newspapers did work to ensure that women's sporting endeavours remained compatible with a certain degree of 'femininity'. Sport continued to have a different (and lesser) role in the construction of femininity than it did of masculinity. Reports on sportswomen tended to emphasize qualities such as elegance and grace, rather than bravery and toughness. Press fitness programmes for women concentrated on health, suppleness, and slenderness, rather than on building up a muscular appearance that would have raised Lansdale's spectre of unattractive 'masculine' women. While supporting the idea of women's participation in sports such as tennis, golf, and rowing, an *Express* editorial in 1923 affirmed the need to draw the line at aggressive and dangerous activities: 'No one would like to see a boxing contest between women, and it is doubtful if it would be permitted in this country. It certainly would not be successful.'[136] The WRAF experiments in female boxing, pictured in the *Mirror*, do not seem to have been followed up. Women were also reminded that even when playing sports they were on display and should remain both decorous and decorative. Women's pages frequently advised on the latest fashions in sportswear, reminding readers that they 'should avoid being over-masculine' in their clothing, while the annual press controversy over the attire of the female tennis players at Wimbledon underlined the continuing tension between respectability and practicality.[137] In debates such as these, press commentators sought to negotiate an acceptable compromise between the 'old' and 'new' versions of femininity.

Female Heroism: Pilots and Swimmers

There were some sporting achievements, however, that commanded unqualified admiration. In aviation, land-speed racing, and long-distance swimming, women produced landmark achievements in these years that conspicuously challenged the male monopoly on feats of heroism and endurance. Although such feats could be attributed to that select breed of 'exceptional women' found throughout history, for many they provided further evidence that post-war women were striding towards equality. In the mid-1920s press attention was focused upon female Channel swimmers, with the first successful crossing by

---

[135] *Daily Mirror*, 28 Sept. 1938, 27.   [136] *Daily Express*, 14 May 1923, 8.

[137] *Daily Express*, 10 Nov. 1920, 3. For examples of the debate about suitable attire at Wimbledon, see *Daily Express*, 27 May 1929, 10; *Daily Mail*, 29 May 1929, 10; *Daily Mirror*, 27 May 1929, 7; *Daily News*, 28 May 1929, 6.

Gertrude Ederle in August 1926 described by the *Herald* as an 'astonishing' achievement.[138] 'She accomplished with comparative ease a task that has reduced strong men to exhaustion,' observed the *Mail* admiringly.[139] The *News of the World* offered a prize of £1,000 for the first British women to beat Ederle's time.[140]

Female pilots hit the headlines towards the end of the decade, with Amelia Earhart's successful crossing of the Atlantic Ocean receiving considerable publicity.[141] Looking back over the events of 1928, the *Manchester Guardian* concluded that 'in feats of daring, especially in the air, women have more than held their own'.[142] But it was Amy Johnson's solo flight to Australia in May 1930 that truly found press commentators reaching for their superlatives. As her journey reached its conclusion, she received huge coverage, with the *Daily Mail* paying her a substantial sum for a series of exclusive articles. The completion of her voyage merited the main headline in all of the popular papers and was acclaimed as an accomplishment to rival Lindbergh's Atlantic crossing.[143] For 'the most marvellous feat of endurance recorded in the whole history of womankind' the *Mail* presented her with a further £10,000 and hired her to travel the country to promote the paper.[144] Her endeavours appeared to demonstrate the potential talents of the whole post-war generation of women: she announced herself that 'the greatest achievement of the flight was the vindication of womanhood'.[145] She was, noted Tom Clarke of the *News*, the 'embodiment of modern youth'.[146] Across the spectrum of the press, commentators called for a revision of the honours system for women, because there was no award particularly suitable for her. 'When the various honours were established to reward heroic acts of this kind, it was not imagined that a girl would accomplish such a feat,' observed the *Herald*.[147] Johnson had, however, opened up 'new vistas for the young women of our time'.[148] A new award 'must be invented', declared the *News*, 'not merely in the interest of Miss Johnson, but in the interests of the many girls who in the years to come will in one field or another desire to emulate her'.[149] The only note of caution was sounded by the *Herald*, for whom the very absence of a suitable honour served 'to remind us that women have a lot of leeway to make up before they arrive at anything like complete political equality with men'. Even so, now that women's 'power and

[138] *Daily Herald*, 7 Aug. 1926, 1.   [139] *Daily Mail*, 9 Aug. 1926, 7.
[140] *News of the World*, 26 Aug. 1928, 4.   [141] e.g. *Daily Mirror*, 19 June 1928, 1, 3, 9, 30, 32.
[142] *Manchester Guardian*, 28 Dec. 1928, copy in Fawcett Library news clippings, reel 58, 396. 1.
[143] *Daily Express*, 24 May 1930, 2.   [144] *Daily Mail*, 24 May 1930, 10; 27 May 1930, 10–11.
[145] *Daily Herald*, 26 May 1930, 1.   [146] *Daily News*, 23 May 1930, 8.
[147] *Daily Herald*, 26 May 1930, 1.   [148] *Daily Mail*, 24 May 1930, 10.
[149] *Daily News*, 27 May 1930, 6.

Fig. 2.2. Amy Johnson's solo flight from England to Australia in 1930 received huge
publicity in the press. Newspapers regarded her feat as a powerful demonstration
of the abilities of 'modern women'

influence and range of achievement are extending' there was no reason, the
paper concluded, that women would not be able to remove the obstacles that
lay before them.[150] With the sort of capabilities displayed by Johnson, there
appeared to be little that could stop 'modern women' (see Fig. 2.2).

Amy Johnson's 1930 flight was perhaps the pinnacle of female inter-war
'heroic' achievements, and Johnson herself became a household name. She
was, for example, included in a list of a dozen 'Heroes of the King's Great Reign'
in the *Mail*'s Jubilee supplement in 1935.[151] But many other less memorable
accomplishments were interpreted in the same light as triumphs of the
'modern generation'. When a woman swam the length of the Bosporus in
1931, the *Mail* noted the contemporary female desire 'to make fresh records and
like Alexander conquer new worlds':

The modern woman, having rid herself of ancestral conventions, is resolved to show
what she can do; and is making the running very hot for men. The Juliet of today would
not languish and wait for Romeo to climb up to her window. She would have a dozen
plans for reaching him; she would fly or drive or swim to him, but she would arrive. For
women are nowadays not only the restless but also the resolute sex.[152]

150 *Daily Herald*, 27 May 1930, 8.   151 *Daily Mail*, 4 May 1935, suppl., p. iii.
152 *Daily Mail*, 20 Aug. 1931, 8.

The *Manchester Guardian*, reviewing the triumphs of female 'flyers and swimmers', recorded 'a certain impatience on the part of many people when stress is laid on the achievements of women who have been the first to win distinction in a field on which hitherto women have never entered'; but society 'had not reached a stage at which these things have ceased to interest the general public, and the word woman is dotted about the headlines of the press'.[153] Some were even convinced that such material was part of a concerted policy to diminish the standing of men. Mr A. D. Seares of the Manchester University Union and Athenaeum Debating Societies contended that 'there was an attempt . . . to falsify fact in the newspapers for the purpose of exalting women'. Women were being given far greater credit than they deserved for their aviation and racing accomplishments, and 'helped on by newspapers arose this strange cult of feminism'.[154] St John Ervine held a similar opinion. 'The fuss that was made about Miss Amy Johnson's flight to Australia was astonishing,' he claimed in 1933, 'when one remembers that the more successful flight over the same route by Mr Bert Hinkler received a tenth of the attention that was given to hers.' This was proof, he claimed, that the 'tone' of newspapers was now set by women: 'whatever is interesting to them is "displayed": whatever is interesting to men is suppressed or put into an obscure corner'.[155] The fascination for female heroics was certainly ripe for satire. It is no coincidence that when Boot returns from Ishmalia in Evelyn Waugh's *Scoop* he notices that the front cover of the *Daily Beast* 'was mainly occupied with the preparations of the Ladies' Antarctic Expedition'.[156] But the impact of this material should in no way be dismissed. Winifred Holtby recognized that 'When an Amy Johnson breaks flying records, a woman driver wins races at Brooklands, or a woman carries off the King's Cup for marksmanship at Bisley, the legend of woman's delicacy and instability loses force.'[157] Similarly, the noted columnist James Agate declared that

Opening my *Daily Express* the other day I saw that some young woman flying by herself had safely crossed the shark-infested Sea of Timor. From which I am forced to conclude that she is no wee, sleekit, cow'rin, timorous beastie. She cannot be, like the girls of my youth, a mouse circumspectly dressed in brown velvet.[158]

---

153 *Manchester Guardian*, 2 Jan. 1928, 2.   154 *Manchester Guardian*, 12 Jan. 1928, 13.

155 St John Ervine, *The Future of the Press* (London: World's Press News, 1933), 15.

156 E. Waugh, *Scoop* (first pub. 1938; Harmondsworth: Penguin, 1967), 185.

157 W. Holtby, 'A Generation of Women's Progress', *Yorkshire Post*, 6 May 1935, cited in P. Berry and A. Bishop, *Testament of a Generation: The Journalism of Vera Brittain and Winifred Holtby* (London: Virago, 1985), 95.   158 *Daily Express*, 3 May 1935, 10.

The importance of tales, fictional or otherwise, of male heroism and conquest in the construction of masculinity is routinely acknowledged; given their extended coverage in the press, the significance of these inter-war female role models should not be forgotten either. Simone de Beauvoir called on young girls to 'swim, climb mountain peaks, pilot an aeroplane, battle against the elements, take risks, go out for adventure'.[159] Newspapers portrayed women doing exactly that.

The Thirties: A Decade of Reaction?

It has frequently been observed that the 1930s was a far less propitious time for the 'women's cause', broadly understood, than the previous decade. Eleanor Rathbone, among others, felt an alteration in the atmosphere as the economic situation worsened, noting in 1936 that 'when there was work for all, it was relatively easy for men to be magnanimous'.[160] Many later historians shared her judgement.[161] The idea of there being a reaction to the 'excesses' of the 1920s was actually fairly common in the press at the time. Anthony Gibbs, the son of the renowned war correspondent Sir Philip Gibbs, claimed in the *Herald* as early as May 1930 that after a post-war 'period of libertinism', 'the pendulum has swung back'; in a reaction to 'devastating modernism', he announced, 'youth is quietly putting marriage back on its pedestal'.[162] The following year Mrs Ronald Balfour told the *Mail* that 'modern brides are more domesticated . . . that mad rush from one party to another which characterised the immediately post-war young woman is lessening considerably'.[163] And two months later Ellen Wilkinson, writing in the same paper, warned that the 'cave women' of England, who 'regard it as the natural order of things that they remain in the home', were staging a counter-offensive: 'the come-back of the long skirt, the ousting of the ideal athletic dress of the twenties, is no mere whim of changing fashion. It is the outward sign of the real power of the cave woman.'[164] This widely remarked shift in fashions towards a more 'feminine' appearance in the 1930s certainly reinforced perceptions of changing attitudes.[165]

---

[159] S. de Beauvoir, *The Second Sex* (first pub. 1949; London: Picador, 1988), 357.

[160] E. Rathbone, 'Changes in Public Life', in R. Strachey (ed.), *Our Freedom and its Results* (London: Hogarth, 1936), 55.

[161] Many—and diverse—examples could be cited here. For instance, Kate Millet dated the backlash against women from 1930: *Sexual Politics* (New York: Doubleday, 1970); Martin Pugh has labelled the 1930s as a decade in which the 'cult of domesticity' really took root and feminism declined: *Women and the Women's Movement*, chs. 7–8.   [162] *Daily Herald*, 23 May 1930, 8.

[163] *Daily Mail*, 12 Mar. 1931, 19.   [164] *Daily Mail*, 19 May 1931, 10.

[165] On changing fashions, see Thesander, *Feminine Ideal*, ch. 7.

These opinions could, of course, be balanced by others, and it is almost impossible to gauge the reality, extent, or timing of any 'backlash'. Nevertheless, in terms of press content, it does seem fair to conclude that the 'modern woman' was a less prominent figure during the 1930s. Content analysis of the women's pages (see the Appendix) suggests that careers advice and articles considering women's overall position in society were less frequent in the 1930s than in the previous decade, and the political columns also took less of an interest in the female electorate after 1929. This was not, perhaps, so much the result of a 'reaction' as the inevitable dying-down of long-running controversies, combined with a lesser supply of material with which to stoke new debates. Women had entered the professions, obtained the vote, challenged dress conventions, and produced famous sporting accomplishments by 1930; throughout the 1930s, despite the efforts of the feminist movement to place such causes as equal pay and family allowances on the political agenda, there were fewer obvious issues around which the press could generate discussion. 'It is not so easy now as it was a few years ago when women were breaking down sex barriers . . . to find new subjects,' noted Myfanwy Crawshay in 1932.[166] The grave problems of economic depression and international crisis inevitably diverted attention (including that of feminists themselves) elsewhere. There is also an extent to which there had been an accommodation with 'modernity'. The admittance of women to previously male spheres had not, at least in the eyes of most observers, provoked the crisis that opponents had predicted.[167] In most cases, it was difficult to envisage the clock being turned back. As the *Evening Standard* commented on the tenth anniversary of the women's vote, enfranchisement was 'not an experiment concerning which there can be any thought of revocation'.[168] Nor did it seem likely that there could be a return to older conventions of femininity. When Mary Burdett in 1934 made an impassioned plea in the *Mirror* for the return of the crinoline to 'renew memories of a fragrant yesterday', her point was completely undermined the following day by a cartoon demonstrating how ridiculous crinolines would look on the beach alongside modern beachwear (see Fig. 2.3).[169] Indeed, this device of contrasting old and new was a favourite of cartoonists and repeatedly emphasized visually quite how distant was the pre-war world.

On the other hand, any fading of the interest in the 'modern woman' should not be exaggerated. It was only in December 1932, after all, that the famous

---

[166] Crawshay, *Journalism for Women*, 30.
[167] This is also the conclusion reached by Soland in her study of Denmark: *Becoming Modern*, Conclusion.
[168] *Evening Standard*, 4 Feb. 1928, copy in Fawcett Library news clippings, reel 58, 396. 11.
[169] *Daily Mirror*, 1 June 1934, 12; 2 June 1934, 11.

FIG. 2.3. This cartoon gently mocks Mary Burdett's article in the previous day's issue calling for the return of the crinoline. Such cumbersome pre-war styles seemed incongrous on 'modern women'

cartoon featuring the 'Bright Young Thing', Jane, appeared for the first time in the *Mirror*. She represented a type of femininity that would not have been light-heartedly portrayed in the press before 1914.[170] Both in the openings that she pursued—she was shown standing for Parliament and entering the City— and in the flaunting of her sexuality, Jane was unmistakably a manifestation of modernity.[171] More broadly, the perception that women were striding purposefully towards equality remained intact despite the difficult circumstances of the 1930s. The celebration of King George V's Silver Jubilee in 1935 generated a flood of articles reflecting on the social changes experienced since 1910, and many highlighted the progress of women. In the *Herald*, Sylvia Pankhurst declared that 'the steady increase of political and social interest among women during the last twenty-five years is remarkable' and expressed her pleasure in particular that the 'professional status of women has been revolutionized'.[172] The *Mail*'s Jubilee edition claimed that 'in the whole realm of the professions

[170] Cudlipp, *Publish and be Damned!*, 72–6.   [171] *Daily Mirror*, 5–16 Nov. 1935.
[172] *Daily Herald*, 3 May 1935, 10.

and business, scarcely a trace of sex distinction now remains', and added that 'the phrase "the stronger sex" has almost lost its meaning'.[173] Winifred Holtby, writing in the *Yorkshire Post*, argued that there had been a 'revolution in values' over the previous twenty-five years and declared the reign 'the most notable in the whole history of British women'. 'We take it for granted that women should become surgeons, engineers and ministers,' she observed, and although aware that prejudice against women remained, she believed that it was decreasing yearly.[174] Three years later, in September 1938, the *Mirror* collected together unconnected reports of female triumphs in air races, mountain climbs, and job interviews to conclude that 'women everywhere are invading what were once regarded as the preserves of men'.[175] Here, relatively minor achievements were magnified because of underlying assumptions about modernity and the progress of women—assumptions that mirrored those of 1918 and which the intervening two decades had been unable to disrupt.

Feminism and the Discourse of Modernity

The widespread conviction that there had been a profound dislocation with the past and a transformation in the position of women was the most striking feature of press gender commentary in this period. The massive social and cultural obstacles that remained in the path of women all too often lay obscured. Reviewing advances up to the beginning of 1927, for example, the *Daily Mail*'s women's page could declare that 'a casual person asked about women's achievements in the past year might think the position analogous to Alexander—"no new fields left to conquer"'. It noted that men 'are beginning to talk of the necessity for real sex equality, or, at least, a Men's Rights Defence League'.[176] Similarly, a contributor to the *Mirror* claimed in 1929 that 'Women are already equal with men. They have the right to work, the right to own property, and the right of political action. We can be fairly sure that what they want, they will get.'[177]

Such attitudes made it difficult for the feminist movement to continue to justify its existence and draw attention to issues of inequality. Vera Brittain commented that some elements of press opinion could be 'gently patronising,

---

[173] *Daily Mail*, 6 May 1935, Jubilee suppl., p. ii.
[174] *Yorkshire Post*, 6 May 1935, quoted in Berry and Bishop, *Testament of a Generation*, 93–6. Holtby, who produced a similar article for *Time and Tide*, was criticized by Philippa Polson for ignoring the struggles of working-class women: 'Feminists and the Woman Question', *Left Review*, 112 (Sept. 1935), 500–2, cited in P. Deane (ed.), *History in our Hands: A Critical Anthology of Writings on Literature, Culture, and Politics from the 1930s* (London: Leicester University Press, 1998), 259–63.   [175] *Daily Mirror*, 5 Sept. 1938, 5.
[176] *Daily Mail*, 1 Jan. 1927, 15.   [177] *Daily Mirror*, 23 May 1929, 11.

lightly chaffing those women who share in feminist activities, and jocosely suggesting that their enthusiasm is just a bit behind the times'. Some journalists believed, she thought, that 'feminism is merely hysterical, since it is now quite unnecessary'.[178] Feminist organizations and single-sex campaigning seemed all the more old-fashioned when one of the central features of modernity was a greater degree of mixing between the sexes and the cultivation of the sort of 'sex appeal' displayed by film stars. In this sense, the Jane cartoon was perhaps a sign of the times. These currents of opinion, so powerful in the press and elsewhere, help to explain the contrast between feminist optimism at the increasing opportunities available to women, and their pessimism at the reluctance of young women to join the movement; this was the context of Ray Strachey's oft-quoted remark that 'Modern young women know amazingly little of what life was like before the war, and show a strong hostility to the word "feminism" and all which they imagine it to connote.'[179]

On the other hand, the press portrayal of modernity did open up important discursive space for the redefinition of femininity. The mythology of women's heroic sacrifice in the war, and the belief in the convergence of the sexes, enabled conventionally masculine qualities and attributes to be claimed for femininity. 'Modern women' were shown embodying independence, assertiveness, and athleticism, and not just traditional 'feminine' virtues such as purity, patience, and kindliness. Female pioneers, from barristers to aviators, were placed before the public and celebrated. And the wrenching apart of feminism and modernity—these 'modern women' were generally perceived to be the product of war, and appeared to reject rather than espouse a 'feminist' consciousness—had advantages as well as disadvantages. The activities of 'modern women', while still controversial, were portrayed in *generational* rather than *sectional* terms. Opponents could thus be depicted as being 'old-fashioned', as running against the grain of 'modern' society. Feminists could be, and were, easily stereotyped as unrepresentative or embittered; the young, on the other hand, appeared to be harbingers of the future. When the *Express* celebrated the newly enfranchised female voters in 1929, for example, they were presented not as symbols of the success of a feminist campaign, or of the achievement of

---

[178] V. Brittain, *Why Feminism Lives* (London, 1927), cited in Berry and Bishop, *Testament of a Generation*, 97.

[179] R. Strachey, Introduction, in Strachey (ed.), *Our Freedom and its Results*, 10. The feminist optimism about the position of women generally is clear in all of the contributions to this collection. Rapp and Ross make similar observations on the problems facing American feminism after the First World War: R. Rapp and E. Ross, 'The 1920s: Feminism, Consumerism, and Political Backlash in the United States', in J. Friedlander, B. W. Cook, A. Kessler-Harris, and C. Smith-Rosenberg (eds.), *Women in Culture and Politics: A Century of Change* (Bloomington: Indiana University Press, 1986).

sexual equality, but as representatives of an admirable young generation living up to the example of their heroic wartime predecessors: 'they showed there was nothing in the way of sacrifice, hardship, endurance that the young women of Great Britain would not gladly meet for their country's sake. The type has not altered since then.'[180] Although this meant that the feminist case was marginalized, such a celebration would have been unlikely in any form in a conservative paper had this discursive space not been available. And it was as an accommodation with what seemed to be the inevitable progress of modernity that papers came to terms with many of the new opportunities available to women. While by no means accepting the more extreme manifestations of modernity, most editors and journalists equally wanted to avoid being pigeonholed as 'Victorian'.

The 'modern young woman' was only one of the versions of femininity to be found in the popular press. Other stereotypes, especially of the dutiful housewife and mother, and of the glamorous companion, remained powerful. Yet this assertive modern figure posed a challenge, sometimes explicit, sometimes implicit, to these other images. The unresolved question at the heart of inter-war gender discourse was whether the 'flapper', as she matured, would slip quietly into these other roles, or whether she would seek to subvert them. As the next chapter shows, it certainly seemed likely to many that housewifery and motherhood would have to become more 'modern' if they were to be accepted by the younger generation.

[180] *Daily Express*, 23 May 1929, 10.

3

Traditional Duties: Housewife, Mother, Consumer

If the 'modern young woman' met the editorial need for bright, unusual, and controversial articles after 1918, the housewife and mother was at the other end of the news spectrum: she represented the average, the everyday, the basic norm against which other manifestations of femininity were defined. While the activities of the 'flapper' were frequently the subject of the main news and feature pages, those of the housewife were more often to be found in the sedate surroundings of the 'women's section'. This section was somewhat isolated from the rhythms of the rest of the paper. Rarely conspicuously affected by the political crises or social upheavals that resounded around the other columns, the women's pages appeared to represent a haven from the travails of the public sphere. Dominated by fashion advice—which will be examined in Chapter 5—and articles on domestic life, these pages explored, according to the *Express* editor Ralph Blumenfeld's rather patronizing dictum, 'the changeable moods of unchangeable femininity'.[1]

On closer examination, however, it is clear that the dichotomies between the 'flapper' and the 'housewife', or the 'modern' and the 'traditional', were by no means absolute. Contributors to the women's pages could not, and did not, ignore the challenge posed by the much-discussed post-war generation to conventional domesticity. If young women were eventually to be attracted to the home, it appeared to many commentators that the domestic sphere would have to be reorganized and made more 'modern': otherwise, the appeal of a career and independence might prove stronger than marriage and motherhood. More immediately, the reluctance of young female workers to enter domestic service was exacerbating the 'servant problem' and increasing the pressures on middle-

---

[1] R. D. Blumenfeld, *The Press in my Time* (London: Rich & Cowan, 1933), 94.

class women. It was modern technology, in the form of labour-saving devices, that seemed to offer a possible solution to these problems, and raised the prospect of a more 'scientific' and comfortable home. Pursuing the task of 'updating' housewifery, advertisers competed to sell the products that would remove drudgery and transform domestic existence, while newspaper 'experts' outlined the management techniques and theories of child character formation that would enable the modern housewife and mother to be truly 'professional'. So even if the domestic sphere was confined physically to its own section of the paper, it was not restricted discursively in the same way: there was a dialogue with many of the other images of the paper, and the housewifery of the woman's page was very much part of the same modernity that the other columns were describing.

This updating of housewifery was by no means the exclusive concern of the national daily press. It was also being promoted, as several historians have noted, by the burgeoning women's magazine sector.[2] New publications from the middle-class monthly *Good Housekeeping* (1922) to the mass market weekly *Woman's Own* (1932) similarly flattered their female readership by describing domestic work in terms of a skilled profession, while delivering to advertisers a market for consumer goods.[3] There was a considerable cross-fertilization of ideas between these magazines and the women's pages of the daily press, and many female journalists contributed to both. The newspaper features displayed the same sort of limitations that have been recognized in the content of the periodicals. Despite genuine attempts to raise the status of housewifery and motherhood, the sexual division of labour in the home was rarely substantially challenged, and the possibilities heralded by the labour-saving technologies were often negated by the burden of higher standards placed upon women. The discourse of 'modern housekeeping' tended to obscure both how few women could actually share in the technological advances and also how much still depended on the labour of domestic servants.

This chapter will explore the portrayal of this modern domestic life, describing first the editorial and advertising pressures that shaped the make-up of the women's pages, and then looking in detail at the debates that developed over the period about the responsibilities of the modern housewife and mother.

[2] On the impact of women's magazines see e.g. C. White, *Women's Magazines 1693–1968* (London: Michael Joseph, 1970); M. Pugh, *Women and the Women's Movement in Britain 1914–59* (Basingstoke: Macmillan, 1992), 209–18; J. Greenfield and C. Reid, 'Women's Magazines and the Commercial Orchestration of Femininity in the 1930s: Evidence from *Woman's Own*', *Media History*, 4/2 (1998), 161–74.

[3] On *Good Housekeeping*, see B. Braithwaite and N. Walsh, *Home Sweet Home: The Best of Good Housekeeping 1922–39* (London: Leopard, 1995).

Editorial Policies and Pressures

The Drive for Circulation

Ever since Northcliffe included the 'woman's realm' section in the first issue of the *Daily Mail*, material directed at the housewife had been regarded as an important newspaper circulation tool. The logic of the mass market dictated that features should appeal to as wide an audience as possible, and for female readers that meant engaging with marriage, housewifery, and motherhood, the common experiences of millions of women. Successive generations of magazines, from Beeton's *Englishwoman's Domestic Magazine* to Northcliffe and Pearson's own publications of the 1890s, *Home Chat* and *Home Notes*, had demonstrated the viability of such a formula, and as it was another characteristic of mass market publishing to stick with tried and tested formulae, there seemed to be little need to experiment.[4] 'The enormous sales of the practical papers issued at Fleetway House', Northcliffe informed the *Mail*'s editor in 1921, 'should indicate to Miss Cohen [the women's page editor] that what women want is practical advice.'[5] Suggestions that the women's page was too conservative in its make-up were usually regarded with suspicion. Mrs Peel's advice at the *Mail* was frequently ignored because she was viewed as an 'exceptional woman', unreflective of the tastes of 'normal women'.[6] Similarly, when candidates to replace Mrs Peel as editor of the women's page in 1920 complained that the page was 'too stereotyped in its choice of articles and too "narrow-minded"', a memo was drawn up and action promised; yet genuine changes were slow in coming.[7] After all, one of Northcliffe's maxims that had been elevated to conventional wisdom in Fleet Street was that while it was bad not to give the public what they wanted, it was far worse to give them what they did not want.[8] In any case, survey evidence, increasingly scientific from the mid-1930s, indicated that traditional women's page features were indeed popular. Mass Observation recorded in 1948, for example, that almost 80 per cent of the women it questioned were interested in the cookery material on the women's page, a success rate that was far higher than most other newspaper

---

[4] On the formulae of 19th-century women's magazines, M. Beetham, *A Magazine of her Own? Domesticity and Desire in the Woman's Magazine 1800–1914* (London: Routledge, 1996).

[5] Bodleian Library, Oxford, MS Eng. hist. d. 303–5, Northcliffe Bulletins, 6 May 1921.

[6] C. S. Peel, *Life's Enchanted Cup: An Autobiography* (London: John Lane, 1933), 229–230.

[7] British Library, Northcliffe Papers, Add. MS 62204, Crawford to Price, 19 Jan. 1920.

[8] R. C. K. Ensor, 'The Press', in Sir Ernest Barker (ed.), *The Character of England* (Oxford: Clarendon Press, 1947), 419.

sections.[9] Few editors wanted to run the risk of tinkering with an apparently winning mixture.

Yet if the subjects covered by the women's page were defined cautiously, it was still a space which operated differently to the rest of the paper. Here, by and large, women spoke to women. Sydney Moseley, warning prospective freelance contributors in 1926 not to 'write down' to women, recalled that 'in the early days of "feminine interest articles"—when most of the work was done by men—there was a great deal of silly nonsense, sentimental bathos and, what would be called in American slang, "sob stuff" written for women'.[10] Such poor quality writing, he observed, was 'no longer tolerated by any publication of repute'. By the inter-war period, as greater numbers of women entered journalism, women's pages were largely written by women, and the worst kind of patronizing material penned by men was mostly eradicated. And with the emphasis in popular journalism placed on connecting and engaging with the audience, this ensured that on these pages an explicitly female voice emerged which contrasted with the bulk of the paper. When a husband complained to the *Daily Mirror* women's page writer Ann Bovill that he never had a change from bacon and eggs for his evening meal, for example, she told her readers that 'I wrote and told this husband he was jolly lucky to get anything at all, for I don't want to encourage husbands to grumble!'[11] Bovill acted as a loyal friend, showing solidarity with her community of readers. The women's pages deliberately sought to construct a female network that the reader could turn to as a supplement to her actual friendship group. Each paper formed their own leagues and clubs for the mutual support of housewives and mothers. Sometimes it was a maternal hand that was extended. After detailing the stresses and strains facing the average housewife, for example, the *Daily Herald* nursery expert sympathetically invited letters and questions: 'Small wonder if she sometimes feels it would be comforting to write for practical help now and again, to someone on whom she can rely for knowledge and understanding.'[12] At other times, the tone was more of sisterly conspiracy. The *Daily Sketch* produced, 'for women only', a 'page of stories of the ways of men': 'When a woman has learned the ways of men she has the secret of running the world in her hands. She pulls the strings and the man does the work. So today Page Five tells you about men, their ambitions, hobbies,

---

[9] Bodleian Library, Oxford, Mass Observation, File Report 3005, 'Reading the *Daily Herald*, June 1948, 22. The popularity of the women's page is also suggested by later surveys—see J. Curran, A. Douglas, and G. Whannel, 'The Political Economy of the Human-Interest Story', in A. Smith (ed.), *Newspapers and Democracy: International Essays on a Changing Medium* (Cambridge, Mass.: MIT Press, 1980), 301, 304.

[10] S. Moseley, *Short Story Writing and Freelance Journalism* (London: Pitman, 1926), 102–3.

[11] *Daily Mirror*, 3 Dec. 1936, 27.   [12] *Daily Herald*, 14 Nov. 1935, 5.

tragedies.'[13] These were hardly revolutionary developments, given the restrictions of space and subject matter on the women's page. Few readers seemed to want revolutionary change. Nevertheless, housewives were being taken seriously on their own terms in the national daily press, and this alone was an important contrast from the Victorian period.

Advertising Incentives

If the desire to maximize circulation was one editorial motive for appealing to the housewife, equally important was the need to secure the advertising revenue on which all daily newspapers relied. Most advertisers regarded the housewife as the chief spender of the family income and the essential target for advertising campaigns; newspapers had to be able to convince clients that their adverts would reach enough female readers if they were to win contracts. When moving 'downmarket' in the late 1930s, for example, the *Daily Mirror* reassured advertisers of its continuing hold on the women's market, boasting in the trade publication the *World's Press News* of its 'huge buying army' of housewives and claiming an average of 1.9 million female readers per issue.[14] Even by the narrowest of definitions, the importance of domestic advertising was clear. Food alone accounted for almost 9 per cent of all press advertising expenditure in 1935, at a cost of £3.7 million, with household equipment and stores responsible for another 6 per cent. More broadly, though, the vast majority of press advertising expenditure, aside from the 26 per cent spent on financial, real estate, and trade advertising, was directed at the domestic consumer and primarily at the housewife.[15]

These pressures led to newspapers generally, and the women's pages in particular, being pervaded with an ethos of consumerism. Northcliffe had to warn the editor of the *Mail* against the 'juxtaposition of reading matter and advertising matter made to look like reading matter' on the women's page, conscious of the potential legal penalties.[16] Nevertheless, he was also prepared to collude in these ploys to an extent, explaining away a weak women's page in December 1920 as 'a hotch-potch in order to attract gardening advertisements'.[17] Little changed over the period. Seventeen years later Walter Layton, the editor of the *News Chronicle*, was concerned that the women's page 'illustrations are not readily distinguishable from the advertise-

---

[13] *Daily Sketch*, 3 July 1937, 5.   [14] *World's Press News*, 29 July 1937, 15.

[15] N. Kaldor and R. Silverman, *A Statistical Analysis of Advertising Expenditure and of the Revenue of the Press* (Cambridge: Cambridge University Press, 1948), 123–7.

[16] Northcliffe Bulletins, 20 July 1920.   [17] Northcliffe Bulletins, 11 Dec. 1920.

ments'.[18] Newspapers consistently minimized the differences between editorial features and advertising by arguing that adverts merely represented news of a slightly different kind, and portrayed themselves as performing a public service by bringing the latest products to the nation's attention:

Every inch of advertising space in the *Daily Express* represents news for readers—news of an essentially practical kind. The advertisement columns are the world's shop window.[19]

Do You Watch the Advertisement Columns of the *Daily Mirror*? They are both informative and educative. From them you can gather many a useful hint, many an interesting suggestion.[20]

In 1934 an article in the *Mirror* went even further, suggesting that the adverts were actually more important than many of the reports that newspapers traditionally included:

People who do not read advertisements suffer from a sad lack of proportion. A riot in Afghanistan is extremely unlikely to influence the life of Mrs Brown at The Laurels. But the fact that Messrs Blank are offering the coat she wants at a guinea less than someone else means something real to her. It means exactly a guinea more to her summer holidays . . . A world without advertisements would be a world immensely poorer in every respect.[21]

Here was the newspaper turned upside-down, its traditional priorities reversed. The first responsibility of the housewife–reader, it seemed, was to the family budget rather than to any sense of curiosity she may have about the world.

At times, newspapers were even more blunt in their advice. 'Buy Now!' screamed the front-page headline of the *Daily Express* in November 1930 as the recession started to bite: 'Prices at Their Lowest for Years—But They Are Going Up! £1 Spent Now Means 10/- Wages for Someone—Buy British and Speed the Wheels of Prosperity'. The article reported a plea from the director of 'one of the Chief London stores' that 'People—and particularly women— should use their imagination when they are buying.'[22] Sure enough, the headline the following day recorded the success of the *Express*'s campaign: 'Women Rush to "Buy Now"—Sales Up With a Bound—Tonic Effect of *Daily Express* Appeal . . . Naturally the most enthusiastic response to the *Daily Express* advice "Buy Now" came from the women, with their natural desire to secure the

---

[18] Trinity College, Cambridge, Walter Layton Papers, Box 89, Walter Layton memo to Directors of Daily News Ltd, 9 Nov. 1937.

[19] *Daily Express*, 15 Oct. 1924, 1.   [20] *Daily Mirror*, 20 May 1929, 11.

[21] *Daily Mirror*, 8 June 1934, 12.   [22] *Daily Express*, 7 Nov. 1930, 1.

bargains which have come with low prices.'[23] The crusade continued for several days, with the gendered division of spending always close to the surface. Women, 'having the family and household cares on their shoulders', were aware of the 'exceptional opportunities . . . offered with every British manufactured article and every commodity'.[24] Indeed, not to take advantage of these low prices was little less than an abnegation of the housewifely responsibility to her family: 'who with any instinct of common sense and economy could refrain just now from replenishing themselves and their households with whatever they may be needing?'[25] When the campaign could no longer be pushed in the news pages without tiring the readers, the *Express* switched its attention to advertisers. Producing a poster for publicity agents, the paper proclaimed its power to persuade readers: 'The urge of the *Daily Express* to Buy Now had an immediate effect . . . The *Daily Express* will continue its fight against 'depressionism'. Its readers have a vast spending reserve. Tap that reserve by appealing to them through the advertisement columns of the newspaper which they read and trust.'[26]

If the *Express* was the most flagrant in its mobilization of the housewife as consumer, other papers were not far behind. The *Mail* adopted a similar strategy in 1934, for example, claiming that 'Never in recent years were prices lower than they are at present, and it is an additional reason for purchasing that the business prophets regard them as certain to rise in the immediate future.'[27] More generally, the women's pages were infused with an aspirational atmosphere. Northcliffe was adamant that 'Nine women out of ten would rather read about an evening dress costing a great deal of money—the sort of dress they will never in their lives have a chance of wearing—than about a simple frock such as they could afford.'[28] Labour-saving devices were featured in the women's pages well before the vast majority of readers would have had any realistic prospect of buying them. Myfanwy Crawshay advised the freelance journalist that she would be 'wasting her time if she does not keep pace with developments . . . To write an article on labour-saving devices that will sell you must be able to show that you have something really new to tell readers.'[29] As a result, articles declared 'It's Time You Were "Refrigerator-Conscious"!' at a time when only around 1 per cent of homes actually had refrigerators.[30] Articles detailing

[23] *Daily Express*, 8 Nov. 1930, 1.   [24] *Daily Express*, 10 Nov. 1930, 1.   [25] Ibid. 10.

[26] House of Lords Record Office, Beaverbrook Papers, H/81, Poster from 1931.

[27] *Daily Mail*, 1 Jan. 1934, 12.

[28] H. Fyfe, *Northcliffe: An Intimate Biography* (London: G. Allen & Unwin, 1930), 93.

[29] M. Crawshay, *Journalism for Women* (London: Fleet Publications, 1932), 27–8.

[30] *Daily Mirror*, 1 July 1934, 27. On the ownership of fridges, S. Bowden and A. Offer, 'The Technological Revolution that Never Was: Gender, Class and the Diffusion of Household Appliances in Interwar

extravagant room decorations based on Sheraton furniture were equally out of the price range of most.[31] It is revealing that a 1934 survey of the press carried out for the *News Chronicle* found that the popularity of the women's page tended to decrease with the income of the reader.[32] With seductive images of an 'ideal home' to be achieved by educated consumption frequently triumphing over features with a more realistic appraisal of average domestic circumstances, it is unsurprising that the less prosperous may have felt themselves excluded.

Resistance to the consumerist tide was difficult. The *Daily Herald* in the 1920s was prepared to include scathing critiques of capitalism, and suffered greatly in terms of advertising revenue as a consequence. There was some internal pressure to moderate the paper's stance. 'I should be glad if you would discourage editorial attacks on known advertisers,' requested Poyser, the *Herald*'s advertising manager, in 1926 after the paper had censured Boots the Chemists:

they only make our task harder and the securing of advertisements for the *Daily Herald*, even in the best of times, is far from easy . . . It would be a very serious thing for us if Boots placed pressure on these advertisers, whose goods they sell, and urged them to cease advertising in the *Daily Herald*. Is there not ample scope for editorial vigour in concentrating on capitalism and its attendant evils, without the necessity of referring to individual advertisers?[33]

The *Herald* was directed squarely at the trade unionist and unfailingly supported the struggles of the working class. But this identity, Poyser complained, hindered his search for advertising contracts: 'We give the impression also that we cater mainly for the worker drawing about £2 per week, and the unemployed. It would be difficult for advertisers reading our paper to realise that there is a big middle class element supporting us.'[34] The lack of advertising revenue was one of the main reasons why the Trades Union Congress had to sell half of its stake in the *Herald* to Odhams Press in 1929 to keep the paper afloat. When it was relaunched in March 1930, it was clear that henceforth the *Herald* would broadly share the consumerist ethos of the rest of the daily press. An

England', in V. de Grazia and E. Furlough (eds.), *The Sex of Things: Gender and Consumption in Historical Perspective* (Berkeley: University of California Press, 1996), 248. Bowden and Offer state that 2.4 per cent of wired homes in 1938 had a fridge; as only 65 per cent of homes were wired for electricity, then it follows that only around 1 per cent of all homes owned one.

31 *Daily Mail*, 28 Feb. 1923, 11.

32 Political and Economic Planning (PEP), *Report on the British Press* (London, 1938), 252.

33 Bodleian Library, Oxford, X. Films 77/6, Daily Herald Archives, LP/DH/490, Advertisement Manager to General Manager, 20 Jan. 1926, 6.

34 Cited in H. Richards, 'Conscription, Conformity and Control: The Taming of the *Daily Herald* 1921–30', D.Phil. thesis (Open University, 1992), 209.

editorial reminded readers that 'good advertisements in the *Daily Herald* mean good goods'.[35] A huge increase in advertising enabled the number of pages to be doubled to twenty, and when the 1 million circulation mark was reached in April 1930, the paper proclaimed its success as an advertising medium:

Advertisers have been quick to realise that the new and enlarged *Daily Herald* has enabled them to display their products before an army of readers who have been largely neglected in the past. Readers in their turn have not been slow to appreciate that the firms which advertise most freely are the firms whose products are the best.[36]

Inevitably, the emphasis on the women's pages shifted somewhat from careful economy to a more consumerist outlook. 'It Pays to Keep a Well-Filled Store Cupboard,' announced an article in August 1931, at the depths of the depression.[37] Features championed the virtues of kitchen gadgets from Moulinette mincing machines to icing syringes.[38] Poyser's hopes were finally being fulfilled.

Advertisers themselves, for all their rhetoric about 'modern' housewifery and 'scientific' domesticity, relied heavily on traditional notions of gender, even if these were now often couched in the language of psychology. Despite admitting that there was little actual evidence to justify treating the sexes differently, A. J. Greenly, the advertising authority, observed that 'much of our advertising and salesmanship is planned on the assumption that the buying psychology of men is rather different from that of women . . . Men are more active, more independent, more adventurous, more acquisitive and more constructive; women are more sensitive, more loyal and self-sacrificing, more sympathetic generally.'[39] Explaining how it was possible to capitalize on the market for children's products, for example, he noted that while for men parenting was a duty, 'in women the almost primitive functioning of the "mothering" instinct is patent'.[40] Gilbert Russell, another advertising expert, agreed that this was a profitable angle. If selling cameras, for instance, 'in papers read by women particularly, the copy might deal with the unending delight of a photograph album showing children through infancy, childhood, schooldays'.[41] It was a basic maxim that 'advertisements should offend nobody', so these images rarely challenged established stereotypes.[42]

It is important not to exaggerate the coercive effects of advertising. The housewife could not be browbeaten into buying, even if adverts did subtly

[35] *Daily Herald*, 17 Mar. 1930, 7.   [36] *Daily Herald*, 8 Apr. 1930, 1.
[37] *Daily Herald*, 5 Aug. 1931, 5.   [38] *Daily Herald*, 13 Nov. 1935, 5.
[39] A. J. Greenly, *Psychology as a Sales Factor*, 2nd edn. (London: Pitman, 1929), 199.
[40] Ibid. 194–5.   [41] G. Russell, *Advertisement Writing* (London: Ernest Benn, 1927), 203.
[42] Ibid. 124.

increase the burden of expectations by portraying the possibilities of the 'ideal home'. Women could use them to their own advantage, to compare prices and examine the range of goods on offer. Whereas the majority of men interviewed by Mass Observation regarded adverts as benefiting the producer, most women found them useful from the consumer's point of view, helping to simplify the problem of shopping.[43] Adverts were also a key site of fantasy and desire, as Sally Alexander has pointed out; they 'enabled women to imagine an end to domestic drudgery and chronic want. Images of streamlined kitchens, effective cleaning equipment, cheap and pretty clothes and make-up, added a new dimension to romance.'[44] On the other hand, the need to secure advertising revenue ensured that readers and the realities of their lives were not always the first priorities when composing the women's pages. The Political and Economic Planning *Report on the British Press* found that consumer interests were often betrayed and that 'there is undoubtedly a tendency to tone down or suppress minor items that seem likely to annoy advertisers or potential advertisers, and an even more serious tendency to soft-pedal problems that ought to be widely discussed, but which are inconvenient to advertising interests.'[45] A prime example of the latter was the press silence about the inflated claims of patent medicine advertisers; the various attempts of the British Medical Association to have these adverts removed in the 1930s failed owing to the covert resistance of newspaper proprietors.[46] More generally, these commercial pressures encouraged women's pages to suggest that the solution to all the problems and frustrations of housewifery lay in consumption and better household management. With so much space devoted to explaining the benefits of labour-saving devices and electrical appliances, more fundamental issues such as the sexual division of labour, and the lack of money and poor conditions of many housewives, rarely received the attention they deserved.

Inter-War Debates

'Reconstruction' and Domestic Life

As the Great War came to a conclusion, the press turned to the subject of 'reconstruction'. One major theme was the reorganization of the domestic sphere, which appeared to be necessary not only to reduce squalor and

---

[43] Mass Observation, File Report 2019, 'Public Attitudes to Advertisements', Feb. 1944.

[44] S. Alexander, 'Becoming a Woman in London in the 1920s and 1930s', in ead., *Becoming a Woman and Other Essays* (New York: New York University Press, 1995), 205.   [45] PEP, *Report*, 21.

[46] Ibid. 192.

drudgery, but also to give 'modern women' the opportunity to engage more fully in public life. A typical contributor to the *Daily Express* observed that 'The home we are rebuilding in our imagination must be different from the old home—most especially it must not use up our time and strength during so many hours of the day. Women will refuse to let housework occupy their whole attention when greater issues are to be met outside.'[47]

Several journalists suggested that some form of communal domestic arrangements would inevitably emerge in the near future. Reforms of the kind previously advocated by writers such as Jane Hume Clapperton and Clementina Black were now supported by women who were not explicitly feminist or socialist in inclination, but who were responding to the experiences of the war.[48] The *Express* contributor continued her piece by predicting that 'Either the work must be greatly simplified or cooperative housekeeping will become the fashion . . . a separate home for each family is likely to be abandoned. The practical economical system of flats built around a common kitchen will certainly be demanded.'[49] Over at the *Mail*, Hilda Nield foresaw a 'necessary reconstruction of home life', with the returning war workers giving a 'strong lead to cooperative housekeeping, peace-time day nurseries, and communal kitchens'.[50] Three weeks later 'D.C.P.' argued that 'trained and certified home workers, labour-saving houses, a central heating and hot-water system, communal schemes of life, all of these must come';[51] later in the month another writer called for communal nurseries.[52] These predictions were not, of course, to be proved accurate—they flew in the face of both government policy and the expressed wishes of most working-class families, who wanted a suburban home of their own[53]—but they demonstrated an impressive consensus that the conditions of domestic life needed to be improved.

The underlying fear of many commentators was that (middle-class) 'modern young women', seemingly 'emancipated' by the war, would reject domestic life altogether in favour of 'freedom', 'independence', and a career unless it was made considerably more attractive.[54] These anxieties were compounded by newspaper images of women returning from war industries and expressing, in the words of the *Mirror*, an 'almost unanimous refusal to return to domestic

[47] *Daily Express*, 9 Nov. 1918, 2.

[48] On 'collective housekeeping', see C. Dyhouse, *Feminism and the Family in England 1880–1939* (Oxford: Basil Blackwell, 1989), 111–32.   [49] *Daily Express*, 9 Nov. 1918, 2.

[50] *Daily Mail*, 13 Nov. 1918, 2.   [51] *Daily Mail*, 5 Dec. 1918, 7.

[52] *Daily Mail*, 28 Dec. 1918, 7.

[53] J. Giles, *Women, Identity and Private Life in Britain 1900–50* (Basingstoke: Macmillan, 1995), 68.

[54] This anxiety was also evident in girls' magazines: P. Tinkler, *Constructing Girlhood: Popular Magazines for Girls Growing Up in England 1920–50* (London: Taylor & Francis, 1995), 6.

service'.[55] This reluctance was attributed to the higher expectations of young working-class women, and led many commentators to conclude that the status and working conditions of servants would have to be improved as part of the wider reform of the domestic sphere. Both the *Express* and the *News* launched an investigation to find out what conditions servants themselves wanted.[56] 'Training, qualification and satisfaction' would be the three key requirements in the future, claimed Mrs Arthur Stallard in the *Mail*.[57] 'Domestic service should be no less of a career than civil service' argued another contributor: '[it] must be elevated to the rank of an organised skilled trade'.[58] For Constance Ingram in the *Mirror*, 'Simplification of life [is] the only possible solution,' while the *News* declared 'Mistresses Now Much More Considerate—Better Conditions'.[59] Yet still the servant shortages continued, amidst much middle-class frustration. 'Until the servant problem is solved there can be no emancipation for women,' lamented Alice Nield Musgrave in the *Mirror*.[60]

It is in this context that the elaboration of the 'modern', 'scientific' housewifery that has been shown to characterize the inter-war period should be placed. The evidence from the press suggests that the function of this material was not so much to reinscribe traditional gender roles after the 'blurring' experienced during the war, but rather to reconcile 'modern womanhood' and domesticity, especially now that middle-class women might be forced to carry out many household tasks themselves owing to the lack of servants. Describing the 'wise housekeeper' in May 1919, for example, a contributor to the *Express* argued that old practices were no longer acceptable:

New and better ways of preparing familiar things and progress in every household department are the results of some of the most valuable war work done by women, and few will find it possible to relapse into the old methods. The standard must be raised, and then upheld.[61]

Three pages later, in the same issue, the *Express* advertised its first Model Homes Exhibition with similarly grand claims about the transformation of domestic life:

Women are now at the parting of the ways in housekeeping methods. All the signs point to a new type of small house which can be worked, if necessary, without resident servants, and where every detail of construction has been evolved in the interest of economy in domestic labour and the comfort of the family as a whole.[62]

---

[55] *Daily Mirror*, 10 Dec. 1918, 10. [56] *Daily Express*, 31 Dec. 1918, 5; *Daily News*, 12 May 1919, 4.
[57] *Daily Mail*, 3 Dec. 1918, 4. [58] *Daily Mail*, 31 Dec. 1918, 7.
[59] *Daily Mirror*, 26 Nov. 1918, 5; *Daily News*, 28 Nov. 1918, 3. [60] *Daily Mirror*, 12 Dec. 1918, 7.
[61] *Daily Express*, 3 May 1919, 3. [62] Ibid. 6.

Clearly, some of this rhetoric was rather detached from reality. Public and private building programmes were indeed rapidly extending suburbia and creating new housing standards in these years, but the process was far more gradual than the *Express* suggested. Nor was the presentation of housewifery in a language of science and professionalism by any means unknown: Mrs Beeton's contributions to the *Englishwoman's Domestic Magazine* and her *Book of Household Management* had developed this elevated idiom in the nineteenth century.[63] Yet the newspaper women's pages—together with the press-sponsored home exhibitions, and magazines such as *Good Housekeeping*—gave this material a fresh spin and took it to a wider audience, emphasizing the capabilities of modern labour-saving devices and the opportunities available to the educated consumer as new products entered the marketplace. And this was, at least in part, a response to the huge coverage of the 'modern woman' in the post-war decade. Just as the first issue of *Good Housekeeping* in 1922 referred to the 'great awakening' of womanhood and pledged to reflect it, so too the press women's pages gradually elaborated a housewifery that would be more appropriate to the 'modern woman'.[64] Scientific and less time-consuming, it would (in theory) enable women to pursue other interests.

For it is important to recognize the extent to which 'traditional' domesticity was on the defensive throughout the 1920s as press attention focused on the 'modern young woman'. 'The girl who stays at home is treated as a servant . . . From morning till night she slaves away, attending to monotonous housework,' noted Dora Patterson in the *Mirror* in 1920. 'Who can wonder that she longs for outside employment, which affords her the daily companionship of other girls [and] a good salary with its consequent feelings of independence and self-respect?'[65] In the *Express* a concerned Joan Kennedy asked in 1924, 'Is Housework Really a Bogey?': 'you would imagine that housework was the only monotonous job that fell to a woman, to judge by some remarks made in print and out . . . Women are pictured as dreary and draggled by domesticity.'[66] And fellow women's page columnist Betty Ashmore, attacking 'wives who cheat' in 1929, was similarly pessimistic: 'the modern young woman appears to think that housekeeping is in some curious way beneath her dignity and insulting to her intelligence'.[67] In the context of the greatly increased post-war numerical

[63] Beetham, *A Magazine of her Own?*, ch. 5.

[64] *Good Housekeeping*, 1922, cited in Giles, *Women, Identity and Private Life*, 5.

[65] *Daily Mirror*, 16 Nov. 1920, 9.　　　[66] *Daily Express*, 21 Oct. 1924, 4.

[67] *Daily Express*, 17 May 1929, 5.

disparity between the sexes, and the continuing decline in the birth rate, the institutions of marriage and motherhood appeared to be under threat as never before.

The Ideal Home Exhibition and the Elaboration of 'Modern Housewifery'

The most notable elaboration of the 'modern housewifery' that promised to improve domestic life for post-war women was associated with the *Daily Mail*'s Ideal Home Exhibition. The exhibition had first been held in 1908, not, as some later commentators have claimed, as 'a celebration of the domestic values to which the paper still adheres',[68] but simply as a publicity stunt and a new means of securing advertising.[69] Northcliffe himself initially disliked intensely what he regarded as a 'sideshow': 'My heart sank', he wrote to his advertising manager Wareham Smith in 1911, 'when I read the other day that you were about to start another Ideal Home Exhibition.'[70] He refused to visit the first two exhibitions, relenting only when his wife persuaded him to attend what was the final pre-war display in 1912.[71] After the war, however, Northcliffe developed a greater enthusiasm, which he transmitted to the rest of the staff. The organizer of the exhibition, Bussey, told Wareham Smith in January 1920 of his breakthrough in promoting the project: 'It has needed the Chief's personal intervention, after 12 years effort, to persuade the Editorial side that the *Daily Mail* Ideal Home Exhibition is anything other than a very poor relation.'[72] Henceforth, the *Mail* publicized the exhibition extensively in its pages, and championed the idea of remodelling domestic life to make it suitable for the modern age. The paper announced that the 1920 show 'dates a new era in housing. From now on there is no excuse for ugly, inconvenient, time-wasting and labour-wasting houses . . . The Ideal Home has arrived . . . The virtues of a new house are economy, beauty and usefulness . . . We want ideal homes not for a few but for all.'[73] A competition was launched for readers to send in their best labour-saving ideas, and the paper called for 'intelligent planning and the

[68] P. Holland, 'The Politics of the Smile: "Soft News" and the Sexualisation of the Popular Press', in C. Carter, G. Branston, and S. Allan (eds.), *News, Gender and Power* (London: Routledge, 1998), 21.

[69] W. Smith, *Spilt Ink* (London: Ernest Benn, 1932), 66–7; D. S. Ryan, *The Ideal Home through the Twentieth Century* (London: Hazar, 1997), 9.

[70] Northcliffe to Wareham Smith, 5 June 1911, cited in R. Pound and G. Harmsworth, *Northcliffe* (London: Cassell, 1959), 419.   [71] Ryan, *Ideal Home*, 16.

[72] Northcliffe Papers, Add. MS 62214, Bussey to Wareham Smith, 19 Jan. 1920.

[73] *Daily Mail*, 5 Feb. 1920, 6.

provision of labour-saving appliances and fitments to lighten women's toil in the home'.[74] Few opportunities were lost to emphasize the transformative potential of science and technology.

The Ideal Home Exhibition came to be seen as an occasion at which several editorial demands could be satisfied: the paper could appeal to and flatter the housewife–reader, demonstrating its commitment to updating the domestic sphere for the post-war world; at the same time a consumerist atmosphere was created, with advertisers parading their latest appliances to improve the home (see Fig. 3.1). The historian of the exhibition confirms that in these years the publicity material increasingly portrayed housewives as professionals, using gadgets and rational techniques.[75] The idea of modernity was ever-present. In 1925 an 'all-Electric' house was displayed, while the stated theme of the 1928 exhibition was actually 'the future'. A 'house of the future' was displayed and a copy of the *Daily Mail* for the year 2000 was produced. That this paper predicted that the millennial prime minister would be a woman was perhaps the clearest indication that the 'modern housewifery' was not simply an attempt to resurrect traditional gender roles and confine women to the home, but that it was responding to and following post-war currents of change and the apparent improvement in the position of women.[76]

The expressed intention, after all, was to reduce the workload of the housewife. The Ideal Home material recognized that domestic duties were tiring and difficult—'drudgery' was the word that cropped up repeatedly—and sought to alleviate some of the burdens. The 1922 exhibition was described in the *Mail* as the 'Housewives' Paradise—Birthplace of Ideas that Make Work Easy'; it was carrying out a 'War on Women's Drudgery'.[77] The same phrases were used two years later: 'Paradise for Women—Housework Made Easy—Olympia Shows How It Is Done'.[78] (These claims certainly angered someone at the *Daily News*: 'Nothing is done at Olympia to make things easier for men . . . But everything is done to give women a better time. There are model homes that look as if they would take care of themselves.'[79]) The removal of drudgery was certainly the marketing approach that advertisers themselves favoured: domestic appliances and household products were presented as the means by which the 'modern woman' could find 'hours of freedom for pleasure'.[80]

---

[74] Ryan, *Ideal Home*, 34; *Daily Mail*, 17 Feb. 1920, 6.   [75] Ryan, *Ideal Home*, 38.

[76] *Daily Mail*, 1 Mar. 1928, 9–10; 2 Apr. 1928, 10.   [77] *Daily Mail*, 1 Feb. 1922, 10; 7 Mar. 1922, 7.

[78] *Daily Mail*, 3 Mar. 1924, 9.   [79] *Daily News*, 1 Mar. 1923, 5.

[80] This claim was made by Whirlwind about its 'cleaner-sweeper': *Daily Express*, 1 May 1931, 11. 'Rinso' likewise promised to remove the drudgery from washing and to allow the housewife 'hours more leisure': *Daily Mirror*, 19 May 1931, 20. For further examples of this sort of advertising, C. Langhamer, *Women's Leisure in England, 1920–60* (Manchester: Manchester University Press, 2000), 34–5.

FIG. 3.1. The *Daily Mail*'s annual Ideal Home Exhibition attracted a considerable amount of advertising to the paper, especially from retailers wishing to publicise their latest labour-saving products

In 1931 Mary Edginton celebrated the Ideal Home Exhibition with an article that had overtones of the so-called 'new feminism'. While successful women in business, the professions, and the sporting world had made impressive gains, she noted, 'these women are in such a small minority that they hardly scratch the surface of the old household-slave system. They serve to detract the diehards' attention from the field on which the real battle is being won.' And where was the 'real battle' being won? In the domestic sphere, of course: 'women's freedom begins where she will live—in the home. Her freedom is evolving quietly by means of such innovations as have been presented to her every year for 23 years at Olympia.'[81]

In some respects, Edginton had a valid point: it was important to engage with the realities of women's lives. Yet she failed to address the question of how many women could actually benefit from these labour-saving appliances. This discourse of 'modern housewifery', although directed in theory simply to 'women', was often relevant in practice only to a small section of the readership, the prosperous middle classes. As Sue Bowden and Avner Offer have demonstrated, while radio sets spread rapidly in these years, the take-up of 'labour-saving' electrical appliances was slow. By 1938, after all, only a quarter of homes possessed a vacuum cleaner. This was 'the technological revolution that never was'.[82] Driven by consumerism and heightened perceptions of modernity, however, articles on the 'new housewifery' consistently exaggerated the opportunities available to women to create this 'ideal home'. Even when not focusing on labour-saving devices, women's page features often seemed to expect considerable resources. For example, many housewives can have only dreamed of following the *Mail*'s advice when it described a well-planned programme of spring-cleaning: 'Much can be done by systematic preparation to lessen the labour of spring cleaning. Take a notebook and pencil and go over the house noting necessary repairs and decorations required . . . Engage the services of workmen, such as painters, plumbers, joiners, chimney-sweep, charwoman in good time.'[83] This is not to say that more economical advice was never published: money-saving tips were included, and a number of the 'management techniques' relied more on good organization than any real expenditure. Nevertheless, the basic pattern was clear: housewifery could be 'updated' and drudgery reduced, but only with a significant amount of expenditure and often with a continued dependence on domestic help.

[81] *Daily Mail*, 11 Apr. 1931, 10.
[82] Offer and Bowden, 'Technological Revolution', vacuum cleaner figure, 248.
[83] *Daily Mail*, 21 Feb. 1923, 15.

A Public–Private Divide? The Daily Herald

The other popular papers tended to follow the lead of the *Mail* with their women's page material. The *Express*, as we have seen, introduced its own Model Homes Exhibition, and it also started a regular feature entitled 'Modern Housecraft' in which the latest appliances and techniques were reviewed.[84] The *Daily News* launched competitions inviting readers to produce labour-saving plans 'for a house for a servant-less family with one or more children'.[85] The *Herald*, meanwhile, tried to adapt the labour-saving advice for its working-class audience. Trying to disprove the maxim that 'the housewife's work is never finished', it counselled its readers that

A little management will easily decrease the number of hours at least, and make the amount of energy thrown away considerably less . . . Arrange your rooms to give you as little cleaning as possible. Get a long-handled mop and don't stoop more than you need . . . Have saucepans and kettles close to the stove . . . if you have everything in its place and work well planned, you need not labour for more than the regulation eight hours a day.[86]

'Home Rulings', the *Herald*'s women's page, did occasionally distinguish itself from its competitors, before the Odhams relaunch in 1930 at least, by including socialist analyses of the housewife's position. John Lister informed housewives in 1919, for example, that their contribution to the family earnings was just as important as that of the husband, despite the 'breadwinner' model employed by capitalism: 'Under the capitalist system the family income is usually paid to the husband, because the capitalist pays for labour and not for maintenance . . . When an employer engages an employee he, in fact, engages two employees, the man and the woman, but he pays the wages to the man only.'[87] Content analysis (see the Appendix) makes clear, however, that such contributions were rare. The *Herald*'s women's pages usually conformed to traditional notions of gender. The interests of the housewife tended to be defined fairly narrowly. There was a patent concern with achieving respectability, and this generally entailed aping middle-class norms. One contributor discussed the dilemma of having to answer the door when in the middle of her domestic duties, and betrayed a revealing separation of public and private radicalism:

to have to 'clean-up'—turn down my sleeves, take off my blue apron, tidy my hair, answer to the social convention in that way, and yet not annoy the knocker by keeping

---

[84] e.g. *Daily Express*, 9 May 1923, 4.   [85] *Daily News*, 4 May 1923, 2.
[86] *Daily Herald*, 1 Mar. 1923, 7.   [87] *Daily Herald*, 2 May 1919, 9.

him waiting, is well-nigh impossible. Writers may say that we should always be presentable if we wore chintz overalls and caps: true, but most of us are conservatives in domestic habits, even if we may be Communists in political theory![88]

The only solution, she concluded, was to install a sliding door panel; thus could the transaction with the caller be carried out, 'without my having appeared at all or revealed the sacking apron in which I scrub!'[89]

The *Herald* no more challenged the basic sexual division of labour in the home than the other popular papers. The housewife could not escape her domestic responsibilities. And, given that so few of its readers had the resources to purchase modern labour-saving appliances, little immediate prospect of change could be offered to the toiling women. The paper was forced instead to fall back on Christian homilies about the spiritual rewards of supporting a household. One writer contributed a parable about the 'Soul Impregnable', describing the tireless work of a housewife, with little money to go round a large family and whose health every year 'came near breaking point when the family was about to be added to'. Yet still she 'was happy and radiated peace': 'She was impregnable because she knew that inner peace, which passeth understanding . . . a knowledge that though every blow might be dealt to her and her dear ones materially, yet they knew the life spiritual, and no misfortune could really touch them.'[90] Nor was much coverage given on the *Herald*'s women's pages to possible political or feminist avenues for improving the lot of the housewife; campaigns for family allowances or birth control, when reported, were usually placed in the political columns. The underlying expectation of 'Home Rulings' seemed to be that housewives would uncomplainingly make the best out of their difficult situations.

Educated Motherhood

If newspaper women's pages in this period sought to elevate housewifery to a scientific and professional discipline, the same process was being applied to motherhood—although, as content analysis shows, articles on mothering were significantly less numerous than those on housewifery.[91] Here the emphasis was not on technological improvements but upon intellectual advances which it was the duty of the 'modern mother' to master. As smaller families became

[88] *Daily Herald*, 20 Jan. 1921, 7.　　　[89] Ibid.

[90] *Daily Herald*, 11 Dec. 1923, 7.

[91] This tendency has also been recognized by many historians, e.g. D. Gittins, *Fair Sex: Family Size and Structure, 1900–39* (London: Hutchinson, 1982), 52–3; J. Lewis, *Women in England 1870–1950* (Brighton: Wheatsheaf, 1984), 101–2.

the norm, women had greater opportunities to monitor the upbringing of individual children. Newspapers were quick to popularize the findings of the growing band of psychologists and educationalists, and they informed women about the possibilities of moulding the character of their children. As early as December 1918 a *Mail* women's page article discussed the question of whether traditional forms of child-raising 'killed initiative'; mentioning the pioneering work of Maria Montessori, the piece concluded that 'The teacher of the future will let a child find out for himself what he has to learn, and not cramp his mind by trying to put in what the brain cannot absorb.'[92] The following year the *Daily News* referred to Freud as another theorist of whose findings women should be aware. Its 'child-study' dialogue between a mother and an educationalist gave a clear indication of how motherhood was becoming intellectualised:

Mother: You don't think, then, that the Freudian doctrines about antipathy between parents and children are true?
Educationist: Yes I do. But they are exaggerations. The dislikes are not innate and inevitable. They are products, generally, of mis-education. Dr Montessori comes nearer the truth by showing that, for children as well as adults, the charm of life consists in self-realisation.[93]

The work of Jung was similarly put in the spotlight in July 1920, as January Mortimer outlined in the *Mail* how the 'new method of analysis' had demonstrated that 'many persons remain on the infantile level in mental and emotional development'. This was the fault of poor parenting producing 'over-emotionally stimulated children' and could only be rectified by learning the fundamentals of psychology and 'mind-healing': 'It is the duty of conscientious and fond parents to understand the emotional growth of children.'[94]

Such was the faith invested in these new methods, indeed, that a *Daily Mirror* editorial in 1927 criticized a judge as 'old-fashioned' when he advocated the use of corporal punishment to knock sense into recalcitrant children. The *Mirror*, still at this stage under the proprietorship of Lord Rothermere, was hardly a bastion of forward-thinking. Nevertheless, it argued that 'we have psycho-analysis. We have Montessori. We have Borstal and other systems of reform without brutality. Therefore we conclude that "force is no remedy" for naughty infants. The rod is the parent's confession of failure.'[95] Nursery experts and psychologists became increasingly common contributors to the women's

92 *Daily Mail,* 13 Dec. 1918, 7. 93 *Daily News,* 6 May 1919, 8.
94 *Daily Mail,* 23 July 1920, 6. 95 *Daily Mirror,* 26 Mar. 1927, 7.

pages. Although mothers were believed to have a well-developed 'parental instinct', this 'instinct' had to be trained and guided. But if 'modern house-wifery' was supposed to save labour and remove drudgery, there was little dis-guising that 'modern motherhood' required greater involvement and more activity from the parent. 'Children Should Be Seen and Heard', insisted the *Daily Herald* 'nursery expert' in 1932, declaring the end of the 'Victorian' family regime when 'parents were beings apart, when children used to call their father "Sir", when they only put in an appearance when they were sent for': 'The movement towards making pals of the growing family has been established for some time now, and an excellent thing it is, for parents as well as children . . . The run-away-and-play-and-don't-bother-me type of parent can't expect a great deal of love.'[96]

The increasing pressure to create a close-knit, emotionally stable family unit ensured that men were urged to take their domestic responsibilities more seri-ously. Nevertheless, the bulk of the burden clearly fell on the shoulders of the mother. The fact that childcare advice was almost exclusively restricted to the women's pages underlined the point, as did the content of some of the articles. 'Father should not supervise the family's diet, even if he has just read an inter-esting article on Vitamins,' warned the *Herald* knowingly, recommending that parents should mark out 'their own spheres of influence'.[97] The so-called 'divi-sion of labour' that most experts outlined actually seemed to entail the father looking after the discipline and physical stimulation of the male children, with the mother organizing everything else.[98] Advertisers were certainly clear where to focus their attention, and reinforced the impression that it was the mother who would be accountable for any parenting failures: 'The future of the Empire is in the hands of every nursing mother,' proclaimed Glaxo: 'The physical fitness of a household rests largely in her hands,' agreed the makers of Shredded Wheat.[99] As with the material on housewifery, however, the press emphasis on 'modern parenting' as a combination of psychological knowledge and enlightened consumerism took little account of the practical and financial difficulties facing many mothers.

Newspapers themselves tried to capitalize on the desire to provide healthy stimulation for children by including increasingly extensive children's supple-ments. Northcliffe had introduced into the *Mail* at an early stage features 'designed to familiarise children with the paper from infancy upwards', and was intensely irritated when it was suggested to him that the *Mirror*'s 'Pip, Squeak

---

[96] *Daily Herald*, 8 Feb. 1932, 5.   [97] *Daily Herald*, 4 May 1939, 15.

[98] See e.g. ibid., and 'Mother's Job', *Daily Herald*, 14 Nov. 1935, 5.

[99] *Daily Mail*, 24 Apr. 1919, 1; 10 Sept. 1931, 3.

and Wilfred' was more interesting than the *Mail*'s own 'Teddy Tail'.[100] 'Bobby
Bear' was one of the *Herald*'s few publishing successes in the 1920s, with a spin-
off annual selling tens of thousands of copies and bringing in hundreds of
pounds of revenue to the cash-strapped operation.[101] By the 1930s four-page
Saturday supplements were included in some papers. The Manchester office of
the *Express* explained to the London headquarters in 1933 the advantages of a
weekly children's section for its local edition: 'Poverty in this district is acute.
Parents want to give their children little treats, and our supplement would supply them with one. Although the supplement would only appear on Saturdays
it would be a lever for all the week round sales.'[102] Popular newspapers were
increasingly defining themselves as 'family newspapers' and indeed sought to
be regarded as 'part of the family', here offering judicious 'treats'. And with a
substantial amount of 'improving' and 'constructive' material—from educational puzzles to sports training advice and scouting sections—included alongside the cartoons and fiction, these children's supplements were subtly raising
the standards and expectations of parenting just as much as the more explicit
advice directed at mothers. Even in 1929, before the full flowering of children's
features, A. J. Greenly could refer to newspaper children's sections as evidence
for his claim that 'much more is being done today for children than was
done forty years ago. This is the children's age.' His conclusion that 'the public
has been taught how to look after its children as much by advertisement
and newspaper publicity as by formal education' certainly should not be
dismissed.[103]

The Limitations on Domesticity

The general tendency of the popular press during the inter-war period, therefore, was to 'update' domesticity, in an attempt to make it more acceptable to
the 'modern woman' and appropriate for a more 'scientific' and technological
era. Ray Strachey, writing in 1936, noted a greater respect for 'domestic science'
since the war: 'women's work, in fact, has been turning into real work, greatly
to the benefit of the workers'.[104] Nevertheless, while usually assuming that

[100] Northcliffe Bulletins, 21 Feb. 1917; 9 Mar. 1922.

[101] Daily Herald Archives, LP/DH/273, Daily Herald Inquiry, Sub-committee minutes, 24 Oct. 1923;
LP/DH/366, General Manager's report, 23 Sept. 1924; G. Lansbury, *The Miracle of Fleet Street* (London:
Labour Publishing, 1925), 166.

[102] Beaverbrook Papers, H/101, L. Plummer to Robertson, 17 Mar. 1933.

[103] Greenly, *Sales Factor*, 196–7.

[104] R. Strachey, 'Changes in Employment', in ead. (ed.), *Our Freedom and its Results* (London: Hogarth,
1936), 150.

housewifery and motherhood would take a primary place in the lives of the majority of women, the popular newspapers did not, as has sometimes been suggested, seek to contain women completely in this domestic sphere. Chapter 2 has explored the press fascination with the defiantly non-domestic 'modern young woman'. On the woman's page itself, content analysis shows that in twenty of the thirty samples more space was devoted to fashion and beauty than to housewifery and motherhood combined; in five of the fifteen samples from the first half of the period, indeed, there was more space devoted to careers advice than to motherhood. Furthermore, a number of the articles on house-wifery were explicitly directed at employed women.

The frustrations and limitations of the domestic sphere were also directly addressed in some of the women's page features. Several articles insisted upon the importance of married women maintaining a rich and cultured 'inner life'—something that was an important part of contemporary middle-class notions of femininity, as Judy Giles has shown[105]—and ensuring that they were not 'drowned in domesticity'. 'Domesticity is an excellent thing, but it is not well to let it seize hold of you and engulf all your faculties,' warned a feature in the *Mail* in February 1920. Inexperienced housewives, often now unable to rely on the same amount of help as they could before the war, 'let the house-running engross all their time and thoughts and gradually other interests slip from them. This is not well . . . A woman can run the house better if she keeps a hold on her former interests.'[106] The *Daily News* offered similar advice: 'The home woman's life is naturally more narrow than a man's or than the business woman's. Her duties are such that unless she keeps herself well in hand, the whole day is devoted entirely to her home and to those dear ones in her imme-diate circle.'[107] Women at home, the writer urged, should make every effort to ensure that they were not left 'in the dark with regard to the outside world and its events' by reading as widely as possible.

In May 1927, indeed, this issue of the 'inner life' became a major talking point on the *Daily Mail* women's page after space was given to a feature fiercely denouncing 'the convention that all married women are bound to be domestic and express themselves in the same way':

Because you are a woman you need not be a domestic creature. A wedding-ring does not ensure a talent for jam-making . . . the domestic instinct is a gift. And it has always been one which has swamped all other talents. Once get absorbed in household affairs and farewell to all the arts and crafts. Become a conscientious duster . . . and you lose all interest in literature and the arts.[108]

---

[105] Giles, *Women, Identity and Private Life*, 83–8, ch. 3.   [106] *Daily Mail*, 9 Feb. 1920, 11.
[107] *Daily News*, 11 Mar. 1921, 2.   [108] *Daily Mail*, 4 May 1927, 19.

The piece prompted a flurry of correspondence. Some readers denied that the domestic life was unfulfilling—'there is as much beauty in a well-kept home', argued one, 'and even polished brasses as in polished verse or a good illustration'—but others welcomed the opportunity to discuss the mundanity of housework. 'Let every man who is blessed with a clever but undomesticated wife', declared one reader, 'reflect that though he may return to a house less efficiently or luxuriously run than those of the men he knows, his home will nevertheless radiate that brightness of intellect which is the salt of the earth and the secret envy of many husbands.'[109]

A similar controversy erupted in the *Mail* two years later. When a female doctor asked whether she should sacrifice her career to accept a marriage proposal, letters of advice poured in.[110] One businesswoman who had given up work herself warned that she had made the wrong decision and that 'housework does not satisfy the intelligence': 'I maintain, therefore, that marriage has moored me in a backwater and has robbed me of an interesting and independent existence. I admit that motherhood is a compensating fact, but will it make up for the years the locusts have eaten?'[111] While some correspondents put the contrary case, the editor of the women's page announced that 'those who advise the woman doctor not to marry are in a small majority'.[112] Readers of the *Mail*, it seems, had not been blinded by the 'cult of domesticity'.

Other columnists began to use the new language of psychology to discuss aspects of what was eventually labelled in 1938 as 'suburban neurosis'.[113] In October 1931, for example, Lynne Joyce wrote in the *Express* about the 'thousands of potentially happy homes' that had been 'wrecked by this tendency to ingrowingness of the female mind': 'The wife of today, no longer conducting her housekeeping in the grand manner, no longer producing and rearing large families, with every labour-saving device at her disposal on the hire-purchase system, has too little to do and too much time to do it in.'[114] 'Modern housewifery', she claimed, had not emancipated women but encouraged a 'stunted mentality' that was manifested in women 'nagging' and arguing with their husbands. Joyce's account was not particularly sympathetic to these women, accusing them of wasting opportunities to enrich their personality. Others were more compassionate: 'When housewives work so hard, sometimes in a depressing house with a monotonous outlook, it is no wonder that they become "rundown" and nervy,' observed a 'family doctor' in the *News Chronicle*,

---

[109] *Daily Mail*, 10 May 1927, 19.   [110] *Daily Mail*, 2 May 1929, 19.
[111] *Daily Mail*, 7 May 1929, 23.   [112] *Daily Mail*, 8 May 1929, 23.
[113] Dr S. Taylor, 'The Suburban Neurosis', *The Lancet*, 26 Mar. 1938, as cited in Giles, *Women, Identity and Private Life*, 78–88.   [114] *Daily Express*, 20 Oct. 1931, 10.

recommending trips out and holidays as the solution.[115] The *Sunday Pictorial*, meanwhile, gave a woman from Surrey the opportunity to explain 'the restlessness that is driving so many wives to boredom'.[116] Even if some remained sceptical about the reality of this mental problem, or offered fairly facile advice to counter 'neurosis'—'are there no unusual meals you mightn't like to plan?' asked the *Sketch* in 1938[117]—this psychological perspective enabled the easy platitudes of happy domesticity to be at least temporarily punctured and opened up a space where the frustrations could be considered.

Such criticisms of domesticity led some contributors to argue that single women, far from being 'redundant' and unfulfilled as in the Victorian tradition, were actually happier than their married contemporaries. 'There is no getting away from the fact', argued Lady Ankaret Jackson in the *Mail*, 'that the married woman of today is much lonelier than her unmarried sister, with her busy office life and her round of parties.'[118] In a piece for the *News Chronicle* headlined 'The Modern Spinster Grows in Power', meanwhile, Gladys Watts claimed that the single woman possessed 'a freedom of mind and body which leaves the soul in peace. No one can turn their day into night or their heaven into hell. They can develop a judgement independent of persons, and a way of life not hemmed in by other persons' prejudices and principles.'[119] The only real difficulty, she maintained, was the single woman's lack of earning potential. However, if given 'an annuity of £500 a year', sufficient, as Virginia Woolf had pointed out, to secure 'a room of one's own and the leisure to develop one's own mental resources', Watts believed that the advantages of marriage would look very unclear.

Some contributors argued that marital life should be reformed to take account of the growing independence and expectations of young women. Elizabeth York Miller, the popular novelist, declared in the *Mail* that marriage and motherhood could be combined with a career: 'Marriage is no hindrance to a business girl whose home is her hobby . . . I would rather see marriage regarded in the light of a hobby than as a mere duty. The pursuit of duty sometimes leaves the soul with a sense of empty uplift.'[120] In the *Evening News* (the sister paper of the *Mail*) Vera Brittain outlined the potential benefits of the 'semi-detached marriage', a model that she was pioneering with her husband, George Caitlin. Although there were periods of separation, she believed that the loss of intimacy was not the greatest challenge to most partnerships: 'the complete

[115] *News Chronicle*, 6 May 1935, 5.   [116] *Sunday Pictorial*, 12 June 1938, 14–15.
[117] *Daily Sketch*, 1 July 1938, 15; see also, for example, 'A Boring World?', *Daily Mirror*, 8 Sept. 1938, 11.
[118] *Daily Mail*, 19 Apr. 1929, 10.   [119] *News Chronicle*, 21 Oct. 1931, 8.
[120] *Daily Mail*, 22 Mar. 1928, 19.

waste of a woman's training and the frustration of her ambitions is a far greater threat to the success of many marriages'.[121] Brittain's great friend Winifred Holtby also used the press to call for more flexible domestic arrangements: 'Let each man and woman lead the kind of life which is most suitable to their own requirements, and let us stop this stupid attempt to acquire merit by martyrizing ourselves to an ideal of "Family Life".'[122]

These criticisms of domesticity had the effect of raising explicitly some of the questions that were often suggested implicitly by the images to be found elsewhere in the paper. To what extent would the 'modern woman' allow herself to be confined to the domestic sphere in the future? How long could the institutions of marriage and motherhood remain in their present form? Set against the hundreds of other features discussing housewifery and motherhood, however, these articles could only operate as an occasional 'safety valve' rather than posing any fundamental threat to assumptions about the sexual division of labour. Although explicitly feminist voices such as Brittain and Holtby were sometimes included in the women's pages of the popular press, there was never any chance of a coherent feminist perspective consistently shaping the content of the section, as it did in the *Manchester Guardian* under the stewardship of Madeline Linford between 1922 and 1935. Mary Stott later recalled that it was the inter-war *Guardian* women's page that educated her 'as a feminist, and indeed, a pacifist'.[123] In the mass circulation papers, on the other hand, the tone was avowedly 'apolitical': which usually meant, in effect, that it was conservative. The women's page editor was not allowed to launch campaigns of the kind that were regularly found in the main editorial columns. By giving relatively little space to the critical scrutiny posed by the feminist viewpoint, difficult questions about the division of labour could be largely avoided, and domestic advice could continue to portray technological improvements and smaller families as the eventual answer to present frustrations and discontents. Happy households were to be created by good organization and educated consumption.

Contributors to the women's page did not ignore the challenge posed by the 'modern woman', but met it head on by reshaping domesticity for a new era. When viewed in the context of the whole paper, this domestic material had the

[121] *Evening News*, 4 May 1928, cited in P. Berry and A. Bishop (eds.), *Testament of a Generation: The Journalism of Vera Brittain and Winifred Holtby* (London: Virago, 1985), 130–2.

[122] *Evening Standard*, 2 Nov. 1929, cited in Berry and Bishop, *Testament of a Generation*, 282–5.

[123] M. Stott (ed.), *Women Talking: An Anthology from the Guardian Women's Page* (London: Pandora, 1987), p. xvi.

effect of reassuring traditionalists that, despite the images of high-achieving women 'invading' the public sphere, the relations between the sexes had not been completely transformed. In the same way, features about dutiful house-wives and loving mothers helped to contain and defuse the impact of the sexualized female images on the photo pages and in the fashion columns. The popular press had moved sexual difference to the forefront, and these domestic articles had an essential role in providing the discursive balance to secure gen-der definitions at least partly to the conventional and respectable. They enabled editors to claim that their publications were 'family newspapers', a definition which enabled them to sidestep criticisms that they were brash and sensa-tional. As the next chapter shows, women's page stereotypes about 'family chancellors' and 'caring mothers' were also transferred to the political columns to help make sense of women's impact on party politics.

4

Reshaping the Political Sphere: The Female Voter

Before 1914, when the suffragettes were frequently headline news, popular newspapers were divided over the issue of votes for women. The *Daily Herald* unwaveringly defended the militant campaign of the Pankhursts; looking back in 1925, the paper's former editor George Lansbury was proud to recall that his staff had 'found time to support in every possible way the women's fight for freedom', to the extent of harbouring activists on the run from the police.[1] The *Daily News* disapproved of the Women's Social and Political Union (WSPU)'s use of violence, but advocated female enfranchisement in principle, as did the *Express*, albeit less consistently.[2] On the other hand, the *Daily Mail* and the *Daily Mirror* generally opposed any concessions to women. Northcliffe viewed the 'antics' of the militants with distaste, and encouraged his papers to deny them publicity. 'Sorry to see the outburst of Suffragette pictures again,' he complained to Alexander Kenealy, the editor of the *Mirror*, in 1912. 'I thought you had finished with them. Except in an extreme case, print no more of them.'[3] The events of the First World War rapidly eroded these differences. The conspicuous contribution of women to the war effort both made it far more difficult to deny them a political voice and offered a convenient excuse for those now seeking to recant former opinions without 'giving in' to the WSPU. By 1916 Northcliffe had been converted entirely to the suffragist cause, and even spoke to Lloyd George on behalf of the leader of the National Union of Women's Suffrage Societies (NUWSS) Millicent Fawcett: Fawcett recorded

[1] G. Lansbury, *The Miracle of Fleet Street: The Story of the Daily Herald* (London: Labour Publishing, 1925), 75–7.

[2] e.g. *Daily News*, 6 May 1911, 4; 28 July 1913, 6. See also M. Pugh, *The March of the Women: A Revisionist Analysis of the Campaign for Women's Suffrage 1866–1914* (Oxford: Oxford University Press, 2000), 225–31.

[3] British Library, Northcliffe Papers, Add. MS 62234, Northcliffe to Kenealy, 20 Nov. 1912 (?); see also Northcliffe to Kenealy, 11 Mar. 1911.

that the press baron's assistance 'was of great value' in energizing the prime minister. As a result of this dramatic change of heart, the long-standing opposition to female enfranchisement of both the *Mail* and *The Times* (which Northcliffe had bought in 1908) was reversed.[4] J. L. Garvin at the *Observer* was one of several others who performed a similar about-turn. When the vote was finally conceded to most women over 30 in February 1918, the whole spectrum of the national press was able to celebrate the measure. No one was prepared to deny that women 'deserved' the vote. If there were disagreements in subsequent years over whether the franchise should be extended below the age of 30, the principle of women's involvement in the political sphere had been settled beyond question. The inter-war popular press included women in their political discourse, encouraged women to exercise their vote, and reported with interest the activities of the new female politicians. The pictures of women entering the polling booths, and from 1919 the House of Commons chamber itself, offered striking reminders of the post-war modernity in which women seemed to be striding towards equality with men. Women had won a significant right, and newspapers competed to guide them on how to use it.

The admission of women to the political sphere was not simply a matter of increasing the number of electors and potential parliamentary candidates, however. There was an almost universal assumption among journalists that women would bring a new perspective to politics: their outlook would be crucially influenced by their sex and they would have different priorities to men. Numerous articles sought to uncover how 'women' would cast their vote and what 'women' wanted from their legislators. And if women viewed politics differently from men, most commentators also believed that they should not be addressed in the same way. Attempts were made to develop new forms of political discourse that would engage the female voter, which usually involved translating issues into the language of housewifery or motherhood.

The potential power of the new female electorate ensured that a considerable amount of political material would be directed at women throughout the period. Yet the assumption that women were, in general, rather less interested than men in politics, and especially in the abstractions and intricacies of parliamentary debate, persisted in editorial circles. Moreover, as newspapers sought to entice ever greater numbers of readers, and especially female readers, the proportion of political material in each issue inexorably declined. By the late 1930s the *Daily Mirror* had developed a format in which 'public affairs'

---

[4] R. Pound and G. Harmsworth, *Northcliffe* (London: Cassell, 1959), 517–18.

had been relegated well behind human-interest stories, sports reports, and entertainment features. Female readers of the popular press were being admitted to the political arena just at the time when coverage of it was steadily decreasing.

These tendencies did not help a feminist movement seeking to capitalize on enfranchisement to put pressure on politicians to improve the position of women. The popular press was by no means consistently hostile to feminism, especially as espoused by relatively moderate figures such as Eleanor Rathbone. But as the available space for 'heavy' news declined, it was difficult for any sectional interest groups to obtain much attention. The women's movement struggled against being stereotyped as 'old news' and found it more difficult to capture headlines now that it was attempting to remedy broad and complex problems of social and economic inequality rather than the eye-catching issue of exclusion from the franchise. It simply did not fulfil press conceptions of 'news value' on a regular basis.

Women were often patronized and stereotyped in the political columns of the press. Nevertheless, the hostility of the *Daily Mail*'s campaign in 1927–8 against the extension of the franchise to women over 21 was far from typical. The *Mail*'s fear of the 'flapper vote' was largely a product of the visceral anti-socialism of the proprietor, Lord Rothermere, rather than a reflection of the paper's inherent anti-feminism. Because historians have made generalizations on the basis of this campaign the actual nature of press political output has often been misunderstood. Newspapers usually sought to channel the political energies of women by converting them to their own causes. Rothermere's notorious attempt to exclude younger women by claiming that they were not competent to vote was highly unusual.

This chapter will examine the various editorial assumptions that informed the portrayal of the new female voters, before discussing the different ways in which competing papers tried to mobilize women, and assessing claims that the popular press did not do enough to defend women's political interests.

Editorial Policies and Pressures

Political Aspirations

The mass circulations built up by the Sunday newspapers of the nineteenth century and the daily press after 1896 were achieved by reducing political content and increasing the amount of space devoted to human-interest news and features. This pattern continued in the inter-war years, with the Royal

Commission lamenting in 1949 that such a gap had opened up between the 'quality' press and the popular newspapers that broad 'intermediate' swathes of the population were not being supplied with adequate political information.[5] Yet if politics did not loom as large in the columns of the popular press as it did in *The Times* and its competitors, this by no means reflected a lack of interest on the part of proprietors. Indeed, the huge circulations that were being obtained tempted the press barons to believe that they could sway a range of opinion far wider than ever before and perhaps even challenge the established party machines. The subtle influence columnists had long enjoyed in the corridors of power and among the 'people who mattered' was exchanged for a (perceived) ability to mobilize significant sections of the country at large.[6] In fact, the inter-war period, and particularly the years up to 1931, marks the high point of the political aspirations of the press. Lord Rothermere, the proprietor of the *Mail* from 1922, was perhaps the individual most certain of his political power. 'If Bonar [Law] places himself in my hands,' he informed Beaverbrook in April 1923, 'I will hand him down to posterity at the end of three years as one of the most successful Prime Ministers in history, and if there is a general election I will get him returned again.'[7] Nor was Rothermere deterred by the failure of his high-profile Flapper Vote campaign. After the defeat of the Conservatives in the 1929 election he assured Beaverbrook that 'You and I have the situation entirely in our hands. Without our active support, there is not the remotest chance of the ex-Premier [Baldwin] and his group of intimates returning to office.'[8] The following year Rothermere was even bold enough to demand concessions from Baldwin, writing that he would not support him 'unless I am acquainted with the names of at least eight, or ten, of his most prominent colleagues in the next Ministry'.[9] Beaverbrook was slightly more subtle than Rothermere in his machinations, but he was equally confident of his ability to influence the political scene. He admitted to the Royal Commission in 1948 that he ran the *Express* 'purely for the purpose of making propaganda', and in 1926 declared that the power of the press was so great that 'when skilfully employed at the psychological moment no politician of any party can resist it'.[10] His Empire Free Trade campaign, run in conjunction with the *Mail*

---

[5] Royal Commission on the Press 1947–49, *Report* (London: HMSO, 1949), Cmd. 7700, 152–4.

[6] D. G. Boyce, 'Crusaders without Chains: Power and the Press Barons, 1896–1951', in J. Curran, A. Smith, and P. Wingate (eds.), *Impacts and Influences: Essays on Media Power in the Twentieth Century* (London: Methuen, 1987).

[7] House of Lords Record Office, Beaverbrook Papers, C/283a, Rothermere to Beaverbrook, 26 Apr. 1923.

[8] Beaverbrook Papers, C/284a, Rothermere to Beaverbrook, 5 July 1929.

[9] A. Chisholm and M. Davie, *Beaverbrook: A Life* (London: Hutchinson, 1992), 298.

[10] Royal Commission on the Press, *Minutes of Evidence* (London: HMSO, 1948), Day 26, Cmd. 7416, 4; Beaverbrook Papers, C/283b, Liverpool speech, 12 Apr. 1926.

between 1929 and 1931, was a direct challenge to the party system in which alternative candidates were put up at by-elections. Although Baldwin eventually withstood the onslaught by channelling the resentment against over-mighty press proprietors exercising 'power without responsibility', the danger to his leadership should not be underestimated; he was, it seems, pushed to the verge of resignation.[11]

This belief in the power of the press was not confined to the proprietors of conservative newspapers. The importance that Labour Party and trade union leaders attached to the fortunes of the *Daily Herald* was a reflection of their desire for a counter-weight to the 'millionaires' press'. 'The present economic anarchy is skilfully supported by a lavishly-subsidised Press organisation,' wrote the directors of the *Herald* in 1922. 'The Press is the principal manufactory of that unscientific bias called "Public Opinion" which is the despair of progressive minds.'[12] Coordinating the campaign to relaunch the paper in 1930, two organizers reminded canvassers that 'The most powerful weapon our opponents have is the Press of the country.'[13] It appeared essential to those on the left that their own paper worked to win over as many readers as possible to prevent the spread of the 'capitalist dope' peddled by the *Mail* and the *Express*.

These aspirations to power had important effects on the political discourse of the press. Newspapers were explicitly trying to galvanize readers into action. During election campaigns they advised which party should be supported, and between elections they encouraged subscribers to back the crusades they were running to ensure that the politicians defended the 'national interest'. Given that the claims of the popular press to power rested on their mass circulation, the papers aimed to secure as wide a constituency of support as possible—and now that (some) women possessed the vote, this inevitably entailed addressing them. If their political pretensions were to be maintained, popular newspapers simply could not afford either to ignore or to alienate female electors. Editors sought to engage women readers in each of the major press crusades of these years, from Anti-Waste to Empire Free Trade. The coverage of general elections was sprinkled with features with such titles as 'Talks with Women', in which papers discussed issues of particular interest to the female audience, while female politicians and commentators were also invited to put the 'women's

---

[11] K. Middlemiss and J. Barnes, *Baldwin: A Biography* (London: Weidenfeld & Nicolson, 1969), ch. 22.

[12] Bodleian Library, Oxford, X. Films 77/6, Daily Herald Papers, LP/DH/19, memo from Directors of Daily Herald Limited, 23 Nov. 1921.

[13] Daily Herald Papers, LP/DH/776, F. J. Hopkins and G. Franns, Eastern Counties Area to Comrades, 9 Jan. 1930.

point of view'; both types of article were essentially party propaganda translated into a 'feminized' language. If the need to reach out to as many women as possible inevitably involved the use of rather crude stereotypes, the desire to involve women in the political process was genuine.

For proprietors and journalists were convinced both that women's political outlook would be influenced by their sex and that this shared perspective gave them real power. Assessing the political situation in November 1924, Rothermere wrote to Beaverbrook that 'We have definitely entered upon a cycle of rising food prices. Baldwin in his speeches has raised expectations that these prices can somehow or other be modified or reduced. Well they can't and when the women know this we shall have a series of the most sensational by-elections.'[14] Beaverbrook concurred with these predictions. 'I agree with what you say about food—like you I also expect disastrous results at by-elections.'[15] Only weeks earlier one of the *Manchester Guardian* staff had explained recent election results in terms of the contribution of women in a letter to his editor, C. P. Scott: 'I suppose the women's vote has had much to do with it—in 1923 by the Dear Food cry and now in 1924 by the Anti-Socialist clamour—see for example the figures in the sea-side landladies' constituency, the Isle of Thanet.'[16] It was the challenge of editors and journalists to capture this 'women's vote' for the paper's own preferred parties and policies.

News Value

If female voters were the targets of newspaper propaganda, they were also the subjects of numerous articles about the political situation. For these entrants to the political sphere offered an irresistible new angle for journalists always seeking to brighten their political reports. Editors of popular papers were always wary of concentrating too much on abstract issues and policies, and endeavoured to enliven political material with the all-important quality of 'human interest'. In 1918 a string of articles played on the drama of the unpredictable female electorate, with 'How Will She Vote?' headlines peppering the columns. The pattern was set for future elections. 'It used to be said that no woman could keep a secret,' observed the *Mail* in 1923. 'A puzzling factor in this election campaign . . . is that they can keep it only too well.'[17] It became standard practice

---

[14] Beaverbrook Papers, C/283b, Rothermere to Beaverbrook, 26 Nov. 1924.
[15] Ibid., Beaverbrook to Rothermere, 28 Nov. 1924.
[16] Bodleian Library, Oxford, X. Films 1643, C. P. Scott Papers, Reel 22, 336/131, F. Williams to C. P. Scott, 2 Nov. 1924.   [17] *Daily Mail*, 28 Nov. 1923, 8.

to send out correspondents to gauge the 'mood' of women voters, with reports coming to a variety of striking conclusions from claims that women were actually far more interested in politics than men, to warnings that they were a dangerously apathetic section of the electorate.[18] Female candidates themselves provided another focus for reports, as journalists described the trials of pioneering women seeking to win over their constituents. Those who succeeded, especially colourful figures such as Lady Astor, obtained more coverage than average backbench male MPs. 'Women's incursion into the field of politics has already yielded a rich harvest to article writers,' noted Sydney Moseley in 1926 in his book of advice to aspiring journalists: 'The published contributions of freelance journalists in connection with this single phase of feminine activity have ranged in subject and treatment from elaborate examination of the possibilities of the new era for women, down to the trivial comment on the question of hats or no hats for women MPs.'[19]

The enfranchisement of another $5^1/_4$ million women in the 1929 general election gave further encouragement to press speculation about the impact of the 'women's vote'. 'Does the Flapper Voter Really Care?' asked the *Express*; 'How Will Women Vote This Week?' pondered the *Mirror*.[20] A revealing exchange between the Royal Commission and the management of the *Daily Mail* in 1948 demonstrated how well established was the use of the 'women's perspective'. Addressing the issue of prejudiced reporting, they asked why a report about Labour-controlled Jarrow had concentrated on the fact that women were carrying empty shopping baskets; aside from the political implications, a Commission member, Robert Ensor, wondered: 'Could it not have been due to the sub-editor being influenced by the very prevalent motive in Fleet Street that he should show the matter through the eyes of women? If it was a long report and he was just going to pick out something like this, a sentence which began with the word "women" would appeal to him?'[21] The editor of the *Mail*, Frank Owen, agreed that this was indeed likely, and thereby gave confirmation of how far news values had travelled. Gender had become a key category in political reporting. Yet it was almost always women who were defined by their sex: men were still usually defined by their class position or occupation. While these articles ensured that the importance of the female electorate was underlined, then, they also reinforced the impression that women's voting priorities

---

[18] e.g. *Daily Mail*, 14 Nov. 1935, 9; *Daily Express*, 13 Nov. 1922, 9.

[19] S. Moseley, *Short Story Writing and Freelance Journalism* (London: Pitman, 1926), 102.

[20] *Daily Express*, 13 May 1929, 12; *Daily Mirror*, 27 May 1929, 7. Similar questions were asked by *The Times*. P. Thane, 'What Difference did the Vote Make?', in A. Vickery (ed.), *Women, Privilege and Politics* (Stanford, Calif.: Stanford University Press, 2001), 261.

[21] Royal Commission, *Minutes*, Day 32, Cmd. 7840, 8.

were determined by their shared sex. It almost appeared that women had entered the political system as a powerful pressure group, rather than being integrated into it fully.

Balancing Politics and Entertainment

Whatever the incentives for securing the support of female voters, or the rewards for structuring reports around the 'women's angle', the enfranchisement of women could not dispel entirely the belief that women simply were not particularly interested in the details of party political conflict. Discussing the make-up of the *Express* in a letter to Beaverbrook in 1932, Beverley Baxter, the editor, accepted that 'the most important thing about the *Daily Express* is its political policy and especially its Empire policy'. Nevertheless, he continued 'it is essential that we maintain our hold upon the general public, and we would be foolish if we failed to realise that not one woman in a hundred reads political, financial or industrial news'.[22] For that reason, he argued, every effort had to be made to ensure that 'heavy' material was not too prominent, and that women's other interests were adequately catered for. Looking at the inter-war popular press as a whole, Robert Ensor believed that similar calculations had been made elsewhere. Editors analysing circulation results, he claimed, concluded that 'women (in the mass that is) have no day-by-day interest in politics. They will not patronise a paper that obtrudes much serious politics upon them. They have very little interest in doctrines, arguments or serious speculations of any kind ... Women's concern is not with ideas or principles, but with persons and things.'[23]

Readership surveys from the 1930s onwards repeatedly confirmed such impressions. Research carried out by the London Press Exchange for the *News Chronicle* in 1934 found that while parliamentary and domestic news reports had a strong appeal for a significant proportion of male readers, they were less popular with women.[24] Political and Economic Planning's *Report* in 1938 presented evidence that women newspaper readers displayed a 'lack of interest in public affairs', while Mass Observation noted more than once the different levels of interest in political reports displayed by men and

[22] Beaverbrook Papers, H/91, Beverley Baxter to Beaverbrook, 5 Jan. 1932.

[23] R. C. K. Ensor, 'The Press', in Sir Ernest Barker (ed.), *The Character of England* (Oxford: Clarendon Press, 1947), 418–19.

[24] J. Curran, A. Douglas, and G. Whannel, 'The Political Economy of the Human-Interest Story', in A. Smith (ed.), *Newspapers and Democracy: International Essays on a Changing Medium* (Cambridge, Mass.: MIT Press, 1980), 294, 318–19.

women.[25] One survey concluded baldly that the proportion of male to female readers 'can be taken as dependent largely on the degree of political education of the average reader of the paper': as the analysis became less sophisticated, the percentage of female readers increased.[26] Editors were clearly aware of such results. Hugh Cudlipp, to take one example, recalled that research on the *Daily Mirror* revealed that 'women readers particularly do not know the paper's political outlook'.[27] Rather than consider why women were not engaged by public affairs reports, it was easier simply to reduce the amount of space devoted to them and expand more 'entertaining' features. Cartoons, which had a wide general appeal but were found to be especially popular with women, were one of the main types of material to benefit from these calculations. By 1936, Cudlipp noted, the *Mirror* included so many cartoons that they 'were given more space than serious news, and the reader still asked for encores'.[28]

The desire to attract female readers was by no means the only reason behind the steady diminution of political content. Human-interest features, crime reports, and gossip columns were more popular than political material among both sexes and all classes, and as competition intensified all of the mass market papers tended to focus on the most widely read items. Nevertheless, this persistent scepticism about the extent of women's interest in politics ensured that while the political and editorial columns continued to address female voters, those sections of the paper directed specifically at women very rarely incorporated political articles. In the early 1920s it had seemed possible that political material might become a regular feature of the women's pages. As noted in Chapter 2, the *Mail* in December 1919 invited Ray Strachey to write a regular column on 'Womanly Politics'. The feature would discuss 'week by week, those aspects of House of Commons business which touch women and their children most nearly'.[29] Although the series covered a wide variety of subjects in a very readable style, it was dropped after little more than a month, despite complaints at the time from candidates for the *Mail's* vacant women's page job that there was insufficient political material on the page.[30] Similar experiments at other papers suffered the same fate. Party politics subsequently tended to reach

[25] Political and Economic Planning, *Report on the Press* (London, 1938), 250; Bodleian Library, Oxford, X. Films 200, Mass Observation, File Report A11, 'Motives and Methods of Newspaper Reading', Dec. 1938, 15; File Report 126, 'Report on the Press', May 1940, 4; File Report 1339, 'Report on *Daily Express* Readership', June 1942, 18.

[26] Mass Observation, File Report 1420, 'Report on *Daily Herald* Readership', Sept. 1942, 11.

[27] H. Cudlipp, *Publish and be Damned! The Astonishing Story of the Daily Mirror* (London: Andrew Dakers, 1953), 123.   [28] Ibid. 73.   [29] *Daily Mail*, 1 Dec. 1919, 15.

[30] Northcliffe Papers, Add. MS 62204, Crawford to Price, 19 Jan. 1920.

the women's page only at the time of general elections, when there were regular articles about female candidates, discussions of 'women's issues', and advice about public speaking and canvassing.[31] By the late 1920s even this material was discontinued, and elections passed by without comment from the women's page. From the mid-1930s, indeed, the most 'feminist' women's page of all, that in the *Manchester Guardian* under Madeline Linford, reduced its political coverage.[32] Any prospect that the women's pages of the popular press might develop a regular forum for political debates was gradually snuffed out, and editors increasingly supplemented the fashion and housewifery features with horoscopes and 'problem' columns. Such decisions were justified on the basis of audience reactions, but underlying assumptions about women's interests ensured that political features were given few real opportunities to prove their worth.

Inter-War Debates

Redefining Citizenship: The 1918 Election

Popular newspapers differed as to how they portrayed the entry of women into the political arena in 1918, but they all agreed on two basic points: firstly, that the nation would benefit in peacetime from the contribution of women, just as it had during the war; and secondly, that it was the responsibility of every qualified woman to exercise her new right. 'Women demonstrated their right to the privileges of citizenship by the enthusiasm for service that they have shown since the beginning of the war,' declared the *Daily Express* on the passage of the Representation of the People Bill through the House of Commons. 'The woman politician will humanise politics, and her help will be invaluable in the rebuilding that must follow the war.'[33] Ten months later, with the war concluded and an election campaign under way, the words of the *Mail* were similar, and represented a complete reversal of the paper's pre-war policy on 'votes for women':

The need for the association of women in the deliberations and governance of national affairs was never greater than now . . . Now that we have admitted and realized the rights of women it seems almost incredible that we should have attempted to touch even the fringe of such problems [of social reform] while more than half of the population were excluded from any share in the management of the nation's affairs.[34]

---

[31] e.g. *Daily Express*, 8–15 Nov. 1922; *Daily Mail*, 15–29 Oct. 1924.

[32] M. Stott (ed.), *Women Talking: An Anthology from the Guardian Women's Page* (London: Pandora, 1987), p. xv. [33] *Daily Express*, 11 Jan. 1918, 2. [34] *Daily Mail*, 26 Nov. 1918, 2.

The *Daily News*, meanwhile, announced its 'profound satisfaction' that women had been enfranchised in time to play a full political role in 'the new era which lies before this country and the world'. In the tasks lying before Parliament, 'the interest of women is equally involved with that of men'.[35] Circumstances had changed so much since 1914 that no national press commentator was prepared to deny women a political role. The *Mirror*, by no means a progressive voice before 1914, chided readers who saw the acceptance of female MPs as catastrophic: 'we cannot foresee the end of everything in the admission of women to debates they will already be influencing by their voting capacity . . . at present, women speakers seem to be remarkable for their lucidity and swiftness'.[36]

During the election campaign of December 1918, papers emphasized time and again the importance of women involving themselves in the political process, understanding the issues under discussion, and casting a vote. The 'public sphere', for so long rhetorically constructed as a male preserve, now had to be recast as a legitimate arena for female activity, and, as the content analysis demonstrates, a considerable amount of space was devoted to this task. In the conservative papers, between one-quarter and one-third of total election coverage in the final week was dedicated to 'women's issues' and female candidates, while in the *Daily News* the proportion was about one-seventh. 'Mind You Vote', warned an *Express* editorial a week before polling day: 'the *Daily Express* appeals especially to women to vote in force. They now have the privilege; it is for them to show that they realise the responsibility.'[37] On the day itself, there was a front-page message to women from Millicent Fawcett: 'Remember you are voting for your work, your wages, the education of your children, the guardianship laws that concern them, for your homes, for your citizenship. And then do not hesitate, but Go To The Poll!'[38] 'Vote! Vote!! Vote!!!' implored the women's page of the *Mail*: 'Women Must Do Their Duty Today as Parliamentary Voters'.[39] The *News* explained that it was the responsibility of women 'to promote the welfare of the community as they see it after due consideration and reflection', while the *Mirror* commissioned an article explaining the 'dangers involved in apathy on the part of the feminine electorate'.[40] There could be no excuses for not fulfilling this duty. After all, as the papers repeatedly made clear, the new voters possessed a considerable influence on the final result. Emilie Peacocke, an *Express* columnist, pointed out that women 'might even be a decisive factor in the general election as a

[35] *Daily News*, 10 Dec. 1918, 4. [36] *Daily Mirror*, 23 Oct. 1918, 6.
[37] *Daily Express*, 7 Dec. 1918, 4. [38] *Daily Express*, 14 Dec. 1918, 1.
[39] *Daily Mail*, 14 Dec. 1918, 7. [40] *Daily News*, 29 Nov. 1918, 6; *Daily Mirror*, 11 Dec. 1918, 7.

whole!'[41] In the *News*, Mrs Bradlaugh Bonner predicted that 'the election will turn largely upon the women's votes' and headlines claimed that women enjoyed a 'Predominant Vote in Practically All London Constituencies'.[42] At times, indeed, male anxieties about the amount of power that women would wield could not be disguised. The *Mirror* published a cartoon in which the Houses of Parliament were reduced to a cradle and screaming politician–children were admonished by a giant mother figure (see Fig. 4.1).[43] This cartoon offers a salutary reminder of the genuine contemporary belief that the newly enfranchised women would have a profound impact on political life.

Newspapers even began to compete on the quality of their election coverage for women. The *Daily News* capitalized on its long history of support for the suffrage movement by including a daily advert that proclaimed it was 'The Paper that said women must have the vote, and the Paper that the woman voter must have.'[44] The *Mirror* could hardly challenge on this ground, but its editor knew that it had the largest female readership of any national daily and so gave a high profile to election appeals to women, advertising his 'special article' on 'Why Women Should Support Mr Lloyd George' in the *Daily Express*.[45] He promised that the paper would not patronize its audience in the manner of many pre-war women's magazines:

Woman, it was thought, would be merely bored if you talked to her about serious matters such, for example, as politics or real business. So you prattled of things suited to her charming, but what you thought was her somewhat limited, intelligence . . . we do not take that view in these pages—we never have . . . We write for men and women, knowing that the great human, personal and national interests, the things that matter, the deeper issues of life, touch the two sexes equally, and concern them both.[46]

Despite these fine declarations, however, most editors, as we have seen, assumed that most women were not particularly interested in the abstractions of political theories and would only be engaged if the practical issues at stake were highlighted. 'Talk of education, and the average woman remains cold,' noted M. P. Willocks in the *News*; 'but tell her that a class of sixty to a teacher is a shame and she agrees.'[47] Popular newspapers encouraged contributors to portray politics in such as way as to make it seem relevant to the everyday lives of 'ordinary women'. The *Mail* women's page published a

[41] *Daily Express*, 12 Dec. 1918, 3.
[42] *Daily News*, 29 Nov. 1918, 6; 30 Nov. 1918, 4.
[43] *Daily Mirror*, 30 Nov. 1918, 5.
[44] *Daily News*, 30 Nov. 1918, 4.
[45] *Daily Express*, 9 Dec. 1918, 2.
[46] *Daily Mirror*, 10 Dec. 1918, 7.
[47] *Daily News*, 25 Nov. 1918, 4.

FIG. 4.1. The caption below this cartoon read: 'Will they, in firm maternal manner, soothe the mere male legislator and teach him how to behave? There appears to be some fear amongst male politicians that their feminine rivals will completely control them.' In the run-up to the 1918 election there was intense speculation about the effect women voters and MPs would have on the political situation

message from the NUWSS that sought to address women's uncertainties over their new role:

You feel, perhaps, that politics are something remote, something not women's concern at all. And yet there is no one more concerned than the British woman with the politics of today. For this is what the politics of today mean—the terms on which women shall be allowed to work, the trades in which they shall work, the wages they shall earn, the education that shall be given to their children . . .[48]

The authors of the daily Labour Party column in the *Mail* (this space was donated by Northcliffe during the 1918 election campaign to compensate the

---

[48] *Daily Mail*, 7 Dec. 1918, 7.

left for the *Herald*'s inability at this time to publish more than once a week) were equally careful to tailor their message when appealing to female voters: 'Some women imagine that the things done in Parliament do not concern them, and so they are not going to bother about the election. Is a house, its healthfulness, proper construction and comfort no concern of yours? Is the food in your cupboard and its price no concern of yours?'[49]

Any fears that the new female voters would fail to fulfil their political responsibilities were comprehensively dispelled by the press when polling was finally completed. The overall turnout was disappointing—only 58.9 per cent of the electorate voted—but women were conspicuously excluded from any blame. 'Not even the most ardent women suffragists . . . anticipated such a remarkable demonstration of women's interest in their new prerogative,' declared the *Express*. 'While the men were apathetic, the women turned out everywhere.'[50] The *Mirror* agreed: 'This election has been marked by a great number of abstentions: not amongst the women. The women voted.'[51] 'Two facts stand out from the polling,' observed the *Mail*. 'First the public apathy; second the great strength of the women's vote . . . nearly as many women voted as men.'[52] And for the *News* 'the only redeeming feature of a depressing day was the way in which the women exercised their privilege'.[53] The inclusion of women into the political system appeared to have been a resounding success—and as a *Mail* editorial shortly before the election noted, the gloomy predictions of the anti-suffragists had proved to be wide of the mark: 'Those good if slightly out-of-date politicians who used to paint lurid pictures of a world which included women voters may be relieved to know that the worst results they anticipated seem quite unlikely to be realised.'[54] The key phrase here was 'out-of-date': in this post-war modernity the denial of citizenship to women seemed anachronistic.

Elections after 1918

The coverage of the 1918 election campaign set the basic template for future political reporting, although inevitably coverage of 'women's issues' and the female electorate decreased somewhat once they became more accustomed features of the political landscape. To obtain a clearer picture of the patterns in political reporting, I analysed the final week of every election campaign in the

---

49 *Daily Mail*, 13 Dec. 1918, 2. 50 *Daily Express*, 16 Dec. 1918, 7.
51 *Daily Mirror*, 31 Dec. 1918, 5. 52 *Daily Mail*, 16 Dec. 1918, 5.
53 *Daily News*, 16 Dec. 1918, 1. 54 *Daily Mail*, 4 Dec. 1918, 4.

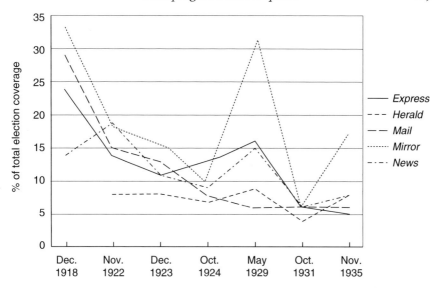

Fig. 4.2. Coverage of women's issues in the week before general elections, 1918–1935

period in each of my papers, and calculated the percentage of the total election coverage (including photographs) that explicitly focused upon 'women's issues', women voters, or female candidates. The results are presented in Figure 4.2. (The *Herald* was still only publishing weekly in December 1918, and so does not appear in the first sample.) The trends were fairly similar for each paper: a gradual decline in the coverage of the 'woman's angle' in the 1920s, followed by an increase in 1929 due to the enfranchisement of women under 30, and then a sharp fall during the crisis election of 1931. Despite opposing the 'flapper vote', the *Mirror* in 1929 invited leading female political figures to appeal to the new electorate, which explains its high figure in that sample. By contrast, the paper with the most avowedly egalitarian stance, the *Herald*, usually devoted the smallest percentage (of its admittedly more extensive) election coverage to 'women's issues': its approach was generally to highlight class rather than sex.

At each election, the value of women's political contribution and the importance of their vote was emphasised—indeed, from 1929 women formed a majority of the electorate and so they were often presented as having a 'decisive' influence[55]—while the task of breaking down the imaginary walls dividing the

---

[55] A cartoon in the *Daily News*, 'Taking the Lady to Vote', pictured a huge 'modern woman' leading a much smaller man to the polling booth: the caption announced that 'Women voters have a majority of almost 2,000,000 over men': *Daily News*, 24 May 1929, 10.

everyday life of the housewife and the world of party politics was also continued. On the day of the general election in November 1935, for example, the *Daily Mirror* reminded female readers that 'You fought hard for the vote. Use it. Your vote may mean all the difference between comfort and misery in millions of homes'.[56] On the editorial page, meanwhile, the main article, by regular feature-writer Ursula Bloom, was headlined 'Women! Today It's Up To You!': 'This is a woman's election. Its trend will be decided by women and its canvassing has been very largely accomplished by women. Women's influence is enormous . . . the future lies in her hands'.[57] In the *Daily Herald*, meanwhile, Mary Sutherland, the chief woman's officer of the Labour Party, was invited to dispel any remaining doubts that the election was not of any relevance to women: 'Politics will not leave her alone. Decisions of Governments come right inside her home, to help or hinder her, and she is neglecting the interests of her home if she fails to take an interest in politics. No woman can be a good housewife or a good mother unless she is a good politician.'[58] On polling day an editorial implored women to vote, and vote early—although not before they had 'got the children off to school and the house tidied up'.[59] And in the *Mail* a political correspondent declared that women were more active citizens than men: 'women are taking more interest in this election than men . . . Women are asking more intelligent questions than men . . . There are more volunteer women workers at the committee rooms than men.'[60] The assumption that the decisions of female electors would be informed by their sex still retained much of its potency.

The main element missing from the 1918 election was a successful female candidate. This was not for want of press support: on polling day the *Mail* advised undecided voters in constituencies where women were standing that they should vote for her if there was 'any doubt' about the male candidates, 'if only because the new houses for the people have got to be provided and women naturally know more about houses than men'.[61] When women MPs did enter the House of Commons they were portrayed in a similar way to the female voters: it was expected that they would bring a valuable 'feminine' perspective to political debate. When Lady Astor took her seat in December 1919, the *Mail* anticipated 'a large increase in the number of women members, where there is so much legislative work for which they are peculiarly qualified waiting for them to do'.[62] These 'peculiar qualifications' seemed to be confirmed in May 1922 when Mrs Wintringham intervened in a debate on the

[56] *Daily Mirror*, 14 Nov. 1935, 1.   [57] Ibid. 10.   [58] *Daily Herald*, 9 Nov. 1935, 10.
[59] *Daily Herald*, 14 Nov. 1935, 10.   [60] *Daily Mail*, 14 Nov. 1935, 9.
[61] *Daily Mail*, 14 Dec. 1918, 4.   [62] *Daily Mail*, 2 Dec. 1919, 6.

revenue duties placed on hooks and eyes to point out that such fastening devices were increasingly being replaced by elastic. Such an insight, the *Mail* argued, would not have come from an all-male assembly. 'There are certain aspects of life with which women are obviously more competent to deal than men,' observed an editorial; 'we have been accustomed for so many years to hear only the man's point of view in public discussions that the shrewd common sense of a woman, on her own subjects, is as refreshing as it is novel.'[63] The first women MPs were usually treated fairly generously, but they found it impossible to avoid being marked out by their sex, which could prove frustrating.[64] Close attention was often paid to their clothing and appearance; indeed when the *Express* reported Lady Terrington's intention to wear her fur coat and pearls if elected to Parliament, she unsuccessfully sued the paper for misrepresenting her words.[65] At times, male journalists were so seduced by female candidates and activists that their political messages were obscured. An *Express* correspondent in 1924, for example, could not disguise his fascination with Ramsay MacDonald's daughter Ishbel, who was campaigning for her brother: 'It is easy to understand the enthusiasm for Miss Macdonald, even in so hopeless a fight. The blue eyes sparkle so infectiously, the dark curls so romantically. Ishbel, with her brilliant colouring, is so wholly, healthily English that it is exceedingly difficult to suspect her politics . . .'[66] And when women MPs were invited by the press to discuss their views, it was almost invariably directed at female readers or focused on 'women's issues'. During the 1922 campaign, Mrs Wintringham wrote a series of columns for the *Daily News* to encourage women to vote for the Liberals, and similar features was included by other papers at subsequent elections.[67] These female political figures appeared to be one of most effective means of reaching out to women readers, and their special 'expertise' was rarely to be 'wasted' on more general political articles.

Constructing the Female Voter: The 'Prudent Housewife'

Each paper reshaped its political discourse after 1918 in an attempt to include and engage the female electorate. In their appeals to women to study the issues and become actively involved in political campaigns, and also in their

---

[63] *Daily Mail,* 9 May 1922, 8.

[64] Cheryl Law notes Nancy Astor and Ellen Wilkinson's frustrations on this point: *Suffrage and Power: The Women's Movement 1918–28* (London: I. B. Tauris, 1997), 208.

[65] *Daily Express,* 3 Dec. 1923, 1, for the original report; 12 Nov. 1924, 1, for the court verdict. For other examples of the attention paid to appearance, see *Daily Express,* 25 Oct. 1918, 2; 16 Oct. 1924, 3.

[66] *Daily Express,* 21 Oct. 1924, 3.   [67] *Daily News,* 1–13 Nov. 1922.

emphasis on the potential power of the 'women's vote', the popular papers often sounded very similar. They varied significantly, however, in precisely how they 'feminized' their political rhetoric. The stereotypes that were mobilized, the 'female' priorities that were identified, and the policies that were recommended to improve the position of women, all differed according to the political persuasion of the paper. Editors and journalists picked from the selection of gendered images at their disposal—from the 'prudent housewife' to the 'caring mother' via the 'guardian of morality' and the 'peace lover'—and found various ways to shape their material around them. The widespread use of such stereotypes inevitably imposed certain restrictions. Despite protestations that women should interest themselves in the full range of political subjects—'everybody's question is a woman's question', proclaimed the *Mail* in 1923—in practice, the papers highlighted a set of topics that they regarded as being of especial concern to female electors.[68] Food prices, housing, health and welfare, education, and marriage reform were consistently presented as 'women's issues'. Each paper competed to persuade their female readers that the party or policy they supported offered the best prospect of prosperity.

The right-wing papers, the *Mail*, the *Express*, and (at least until the mid-1930s) the *Mirror*, placed the image of the cautious 'domestic chancellor' at the heart of their political discourse.[69] The housewife, responsible for family expenditure, was portrayed as seeking above all low prices, low taxes, and economic stability: these were the essential preconditions for maintaining a decent standard of living. The basic duty of governments was to maintain an iron control of the budget in the manner of the nation's women. In Northcliffe and Rothermere's Anti-Waste campaign against high prices and taxes after the war—largely the consequence of government 'squandermania', they claimed—the housewife naturally became a prominent figure. A *Daily Mail* editorial in February 1920 noted the 'widespread anxiety and alarm felt by women at the continued rise in prices'. The paper urged women to act: 'Many women ask us what they are to do. They have enormous power; of the 21,392,000 voters in this country no fewer than 8,479,000 are women. Let them use this power. The best and most practical way of using it is . . . for them to write to their members of Parliament. Government extravagance is the first cause of high prices.'[70] To ease the process of writing, the *Mail* suggested the

---

[68] *Daily Mail*, 26 Nov. 1923, 15.

[69] The official literature of the Conservative Party was very similar in this respect: see D. Jarvis, 'Mrs Maggs and Betty: The Conservative Appeal to Women Voters in the 1920s', *Twentieth Century British History*, 5/2 (1994), 129–52.   [70] *Daily Mail*, 23 Feb. 1920, 6.

exact words the postcard of complaint should use.[71] Over the next few days the 'squandermania' crusade was modulated into 'Women's War on Waste' and the 'Housewives' Agitation', and the sample postcard was reprinted. 'Everywhere women are uniting and agitating against the extravagance of the government, the cost of living, and the soaring prices of necessities,' claimed the *Mail*. 'Every woman should send a protest postcard to her MP.'[72] Similar appeals were made in the *Mirror*. The campaign was reprised two years later when the *Mail* demanded a reduction in income tax. The large number of women who signed the paper's 'giant petition' was, an article claimed, 'a striking illustration of the interest which women electors are taking in practical politics'.[73] When a general election was finally held in November 1922, the paper returned to the language of housewifery and made explicit parallels between the domestic budget and national finances:

Every woman who has a vote should use it today in the interests of efficient national housekeeping. Economy, good management and all those other essentials that help towards the smooth running of a home are equally important to the upkeep of the country. The housewife who records her vote for the candidate who stands for such ideals is helping to ensure the prosperity of the nation and indirectly the prosperity of her own home.[74]

'Good management', according to this conservative discourse, meant that money was not to be wasted on idealistic schemes. The 'domestic chancellor' was instinctively cautious and knew only too well the dangers of 'excessive' spending on 'extravagances'. 'Practical commonsense is the characteristic of the [female] sex,' noted Constance Ingram in the *Mirror*, 'and to hear Labour demand that a million new houses be built at once does not inspire confidence.'[75] Emilie Peacocke, writing in the *Express* in 1922, agreed: 'There are certain points in the Labour social programme which appeal sentimentally and theoretically to many women, but with their shrewd common sense and practical outlook women know that this is not the time for risking daring social experiments.'[76] The day after Peacocke's article, a *Daily Mirror* cartoon portrayed the 'British housewife' defending her home from interfering and impractical 'Bolshies' (Fig. 4.3).[77]

Yet while the 'good housewife' controlled her expenditure carefully, she also had certain expectations of her standard of living and her rights as a consumer. The right-wing popular papers placed great importance on defending these

---

[71] Ibid. 7.   [72] *Daily Mail*, 25 Feb. 1920, 7.
[73] *Daily Mail*, 1 May 1922, 9.   [74] *Daily Mail*, 15 Nov. 1923, 15.   [75] *Daily Mirror*, 9 Dec. 1918, 7.
[76] *Daily Express*, 8 Nov. 1922, 8.   [77] *Daily Mirror*, 9 Nov. 1922, 7.

FIG. 4.3. Conservative newspapers like the *Daily Mirror* warned housewives that they would no longer be in charge of their homes if the Labour party was elected, because it was full of 'disguised Bolshies' hoping to intervene and redistribute private wealth

interests. Immediately after the war, the *Express* called on the government to reduce restrictions on the domestic market: 'both wholesaler and retailer have lost incentives to labour, and the unfortunate consumer in the person of the wife or mother who does the shopping suffers from their inertia'.[78] A week before polling in the 1922 general election, the *Express* replaced its

[78] *Daily Express,* 4 Dec. 1918, 4.

regular women's page feature on 'modern housecraft' with an article arguing that political mismanagement was directly responsible for jeopardizing opportunities for women to rid themselves of domestic drudgery and enter the new age of 'modern housewifery': 'High prices are stifling the legitimate ambitions of the woman at home. She cannot afford the comforts and improvements to the home which modern enterprise has made available to those who have the money to pay for them.'[79] While the *Express* sought to channel the consumerist instincts that it attributed to its female readers, the *Mail* in 1924 went even further by warning that the practicalities of shopping would be transformed for the worse under socialism: 'Socialists talk about "nationalising" food supplies and shops . . . Government control means hundreds of officials, waste, extravagance, and inefficiency. Result: High prices—which you would pay! Any loss of money from running the shops extravagantly would have to be borne by the taxpayer—that is you!'[80]

The widespread middle-class discontent at the rising prices and economic dislocation of the immediate post-war years (which had produced alarmist press articles about the 'New Poor' and the 'Death of the Middle-Class'[81]) provided the ideal context in which to develop this rhetoric of 'political housekeeping'. The conventional attributes of the 'domestic chancellor'—prudence and economy—could be prescribed as the solutions to the nation's ills without stretching credibility too far. But this was a flexible discourse that could be adapted to a variety of circumstances, and it continued to form the basis of much press commentary throughout the period. The housewife became as important a figure in the *Mail* and the *Express*'s Empire Free Trade campaign at the end of the 1920s as she had been in the earlier anti-waste crusade. Unemployment, rather than high prices, was now regarded as the central problem; and the lack of protective tariffs for industry, rather than government 'extravagance', the suggested cause. Here the housewife could ease the situation by 'shopping imperially'. While the government dithered, women could act:

There is no actual tariff yet. But at all costs she must, wherever possible, buy British, thus setting up an imaginary tariff wall for herself . . . Every woman should spend as much as she can afford, always remembering, however, that every pound expended on foreign scents, cosmetics and clothes is contributing to a trade balance that is already weighted against her country.[82]

---

[79] *Daily Express*, 8 Nov. 1922, 3.   [80] *Daily Mail*, 15 Oct. 1924, 9.
[81] *Daily Mail*, 22 Oct. 1919, 5; *The Times*, 11 Nov. 1919, 11.   [82] *Daily Mail*, 18 Sept. 1931, 10.

Using the language of professionalism so frequently found on the women's pages, readers were told that 'what the housewife has to do now is a far more difficult job than buying as cheaply as she can; she must buy as well and as scientifically as she can in the light of all the knowledge to be amassed on the subject'. Indeed, 'like the war years, this financial crisis gives a golden chance to feminine intelligence'.[83] But 'buying British' entailed no real sacrifice: 'there are opportunities in every shop for each purchase to be a British article at a price no greater, when quality is compared, than the price of a similar article made abroad'.[84] The needs of the family and the nation were not contradictory.

If 'shopping imperially' was one solution to the crisis, equally vital was helping to maintain credit and the value of the pound. Articles explained 'What the Stable Pound Means to the Housewife' in 'commonsensical' terms, underlining that it was far more than 'a mysterious happening connected with high finance'.[85] During the election campaign of October 1931, the *Express* argued that the destruction of business confidence and financial liquidity would have the same impact as post-war 'squandermania':

Today the pound is worth twenty shillings all through Great Britain. The housewife can buy with it twenty shillings' worth of groceries and foodstuffs. If the Socialists were to win on Tuesday there would be such a destruction of credit, such a worldwide flight from the pound, that she might by the end of the week be able to buy ten shillings' worth of food for a pound, but much more likely she would be able to buy five shillings' worth.[86]

In a similar fashion, the *Mirror* appealed to the 'guardians of the domestic purse': 'if the purse is stuffed with worthless paper, what becomes of the home?'[87] This plea to the housewife to prevent the 'destruction of credit' became almost as common during the 1930s as the warnings against 'extravagance' in the previous decade.

Constructing the Female Voter: The 'Compassionate Mother'

The conservative press constructed in their columns a flattering picture of prudent, economical, practical, and patriotic housewives whose interests were identical to those of the nation as a whole. Everyday concerns about price levels and the availability of goods were taken seriously and placed at the forefront of political campaigns. On the left, the *News* and the *Herald* countered with

---

[83] Ibid.   [84] *Daily Mail,* 25 Sept. 1931, 5.   [85] *Daily Mail,* 9 Sept. 1931, 7.
[86] *Daily Express,* 24 Oct. 1931, 8.   [87] *Daily Mirror,* 27 Oct. 1931, 7.

their own gendered discourse. These papers made different sets of connections and employed other 'feminine' stereotypes. While they also used the language of housewifery and challenged conservative claims about high prices and credit, at the centre of their rhetoric was the image of the 'compassionate mother', whose overriding concern was for the health of her family and the prospects of her children. From this perspective, 'women' wanted constructive reforms such as better housing, welfare benefits, and improved education. The 'economy' of the 'domestic chancellor' could only be practised once a decent quality of life had been assured. The question that 'every women wants answered', according to parliamentary candidate, *News* columnist, and popular novelist Annie S. Swan (Mrs A. Burnett Smith) in 1922, was 'Where are those houses they promised? . . . How can we rear worthy citizens in slum areas? It is impossible.'[88] Two days later Hilda Trevelyan Thomson, the wife of a Liberal candidate, suggested that the maternal instinct that united women could prove an irresistible electoral force now that they had been enfranchised:

There is no human power on earth that can thrust aside a woman's will and intelligence when it has as the driving force behind it the divine love of children and home. They have at last a powerful weapon they have learnt how to wield, and they mean to use it for the defence of their children and the children of future generations.[89]

'The Children—Do Not Deprive Them of Their Chance', pleaded Mrs Wintringham, while a day before polling a banner headline announced that 'Women Can Turn Out the Hard-Faced Men'.[90] Whereas *Express* readers in 1922 had been warned against being won over by sentiment, the *News* denounced the Coalition as cold-heartedly putting war and retrenchment above family welfare: 'Women want decent homes and a chance for the children—Who spoiled the plans for providing houses? Who saved money on schools and spent it in wars in Mesopotamia, Russia and Ireland? The men who rushed themselves into Parliament four years ago—Vote Liberal this time.'[91] And when the prominent eugenicist Dr C. W. Saleeby was invited to address the female readers of the *Herald* the following year, the rhetoric was similar: 'Women are the natural mothers and nurses of life. They are nature's trustees of the future . . . Vote against candidates who approve of and who will maintain the "economy" of the late Government which starved health and

---

[88] *Daily News*, 6 Nov. 1922, 9.   [89] *Daily News*, 9 Nov. 1922, 4.
[90] *Daily News*, 13 Nov. 1922, 4; 14 Nov. 1922, 6.   [91] Ibid.

education . . . Vote against the men who make a waste of young life and call it thrift.'[92]

Especially in the early 1920s, the *Herald* did try to ensure that its articles for women did not just rely on these feminine stereotypes. Whereas the *Mail* and the *Express* reduced their economic discussions to the language of 'housewifely common sense', the *Herald* encouraged women to master policies in full. 'I find the women extraordinarily interested in the capital levy,' declared the Labour MP Margaret Bondfield in December 1923, determined as always not to rely on specifically 'feminine' appeals: 'It is a mistake to suppose that women cannot follow these financial arguments. At any rate, in those towns where the Women's Cooperative Guild and the women's sections of the Labour Party have been accustomed to meet the amount of political theory which they have managed to imbibe is really astonishing.'[93] The paper recognized, moreover, that many women were not actually housewives and mothers, and advised politicians to take seriously their role as workers: 'While the Tories and Liberals are straining every nerve to capture the woman's vote, they are forgetting the composition of this large figure. Of the 8,000,000 who are entitled to vote, a large percentage consists of actual workers in industry.'[94] Many of these women, argued the *Herald*, would be attracted by Labour's policies for better employment conditions, in particular their defence of the Trade Board regulations that protected a large number of female workers.

While such voices did not entirely disappear, however, they became less prominent as articles increasingly invoked the ideal of the 'caring mother'. During the economic crisis of 1931, the paper placed the welfare of children at the heart of its case against unemployment benefit cuts: 'What woman will give her vote for that cutting of the tiny income of the very poor which means, not figuratively but in hard fact, less food and less clothing for thousands upon thousands of children?'[95] Similarly, in the final days of the election campaign of 1935, each of the three major *Herald* political features directed at women effectively addressed the housewife and mother. Jennie Adamson's first appeal was to 'the well-being of your children';[96] Mary Sutherland's article, headlined 'Defend Your Shopping Basket', was illustrated by a large picture of a housewife with a small child, and claimed that only five pence of every shilling paid in tax was 'spent on things that add to the security of her home and the welfare of her children';[97] and Mary Ferguson's contribution used the conventional language of 'compassionate femininity' to declare that 'Women Will Say Never

---

[92] *Daily Herald*, 4 Dec. 1923, 7.   [93] *Daily Herald*, 1 Dec. 1923, 4.
[94] *Daily Herald*, 4 Dec. 1923, 6.   [95] *Daily Herald*, 22 Oct. 1931, 8.
[96] *Daily Herald*, 6 Nov. 1935, 10.   [97] *Daily Herald*, 9 Nov. 1935, 10.

Again' to the suffering of the last few years. Having spoken to many women, Ferguson revealed that 'they have told me that they want the new Government to be more human than the last. They want it to think in terms of human beings, human sufferings, hunger, despair in idleness, agony at the threat of another war.'[98]

The distinctions between the 'feminized' political discourses of the left- and right-wing newspapers should not be drawn too starkly. The *Daily News–News Chronicle* and the *Daily Herald* did also employ the language of housewifery and addressed women's concerns about high prices and taxation.[99] The *Herald* connected the housewife's spending power less to the cost of goods and the burden of taxation than to wage levels and unemployment. The housewife 'has the spending of the worker's wage; she is the biggest employer of labour in the country. The smashing wage reductions of the past three years have restricted her power to buy goods, thereby restricting the home market, creating unemployment, and at the same time bringing want into millions of homes.'[100] Equally, the conservative newspapers occasional used maternal imagery and appealed to womanly 'compassion', although, as Chapter 6 shows, more commonly in relation to the issues of war and peace than social reform. Nevertheless, the differences in style were important and unmistakable.

The Flapper Vote Campaign

There was one notable occasion when the rhetoric used by the *Daily Mail* and the *Daily Mirror* differed significantly from, and indeed jarred uncomfortably with, their usual 'feminized' conservative political discourse, namely during the Flapper Vote campaign in 1927–8. Since 1918 the press had generally sought to include and guide the female voter, emphasizing the importance of her political contribution. During this crusade, however, the *Mail* and the *Mirror* protested vehemently that women under the age of 30 were not worthy of full citizenship. From March 1927 Baldwin's plans to equalize the franchise were denounced at every possible opportunity: 'Nothing could be madder than at this present moment yet further to extend the franchise. But by adopting this ridiculous proposal of "votes for flappers" Ministers are preparing to add millions of irresponsible voters to the total of electors.'[101] Daily headlines implored the government to 'Stop the Flapper Vote Folly'; the measure was censured as 'worthy of Bedlam' and if passed, the *Mail* warned darkly that it

---

[98] *Daily Herald*, 12 Nov. 1935, 17.   [99] For example, *Daily News*, 4 Nov. 1922, 7.
[100] *Daily Herald*, 4 Dec. 1923, 1.   [101] *Daily Mail*, 30 Mar. 1927, 10.

'may bring down the British Empire in ruins'.[102] Attacks continued throughout the year, long after other papers had dropped the issue. Even when the bill passed through the Commons in March 1928 with a resounding 377 vote majority and with only ten dissensions, the *Mail* and the *Mirror* refused to concede: instead they tried to exploit the supposed divisions within the Conservative Party: 'Flapper Vote Bill Sensation—146 Missing Conservatives—Party Dissension Talk'.[103] Pursuing what was clearly a lost cause, the papers were in danger of appearing isolated from the public opinion that Northcliffe had been so careful to monitor.

Why were the *Mail* and the *Mirror* so adamant in their opposition to the equalization of the franchise in 1927–8? They had, after all, devoted many column inches over the previous decade to the task of courting undecided women voters and encouraging them to take an interest in public affairs. Nor did the conservative press harbour a visceral dislike of 'modern young women'; as Chapter 2 has demonstrated, they were frequently full of praise for their achievements, and even while editorials and political articles were criticizing the 'irresponsibility' of the 'flapper voter' in 1927–8, other features were encouraging young women to set their sights high when choosing their careers. Certainly, the fact that equalization would place the female electorate in an overall majority explained some of the anxieties. The *Mail* suggested that Baldwin's reform meant 'Rule-by-Women' and that it would 'transfer political power in Britain for all time from the male to the female sex'.[104] Nevertheless, as I have argued at length elsewhere, the dominant motivation for the Flapper Vote campaign was not anti-feminism, but anti-socialism.[105] The driving force behind the campaign was the proprietor of the *Mail* and the *Mirror*, Lord Rothermere, a man whose political activities throughout the inter-war years were dictated by his passionate hatred of the Labour Party. He was delighted when the *Mail* secured the coup of printing the Zinoviev letter days before polling for the 1924 general election, and his desire to find a long-term solution to the problem of socialism led to an interest in fascism and the regime of Mussolini (whom he celebrated as 'The Leader Who Saved Italy's Soul' in May 1927).[106] Examining the rhetoric of the Flapper Vote crusade, it is clear that the prospective voters were regarded with suspicion not so much because they were women, but because they were young and likely to be

---

[102] *Daily Mail*, 31 Mar. 1927, 10; 7 Nov. 1927, 10.   [103] *Daily Mail*, 31 Mar. 1928, 11.

[104] *Daily Mail*, 30 Mar. 1928; 18 Nov. 1927, 11.

[105] A. Bingham, ' "Stop the Flapper Vote Folly": Rothermere, the *Daily Mail* and the Equalisation of the Franchise 1927–28', *Twentieth Century British History*, 13/1 (2002), 17–37.

[106] *Daily Mail*, 2 May 1927, 10.

employed.[107] In an open letter to Baldwin on the *Mail*'s main news page, Rothermere distinguished between the more mature (and, implicitly, home-based) women and the 'flapper':

Unlike the other women voters on the register, something approaching five million of the women it is now proposed to enfranchise are industrial workers, nearly all of whom are subject to the discipline of politically active trade unions. At least three out of four of these women voters would be swayed by the class influences surrounding them and would vote for the Socialists.[108]

Such claims were wildly inaccurate: of the $5^1/_4$ million women to be enfranchised by the 1928 Act, both those who were over 30 and those who were under 30 and married, outnumbered single working women in their twenties.[109] The underlying logic of Rothermere's rhetoric ensured, however, that the class nature of the legislation had to be emphasized. Almost a month after the campaign had started, after all, the *Mail* had discarded any pretence that their opposition was based on anything other than party political calculation: 'The case against Votes for Flappers is really to be compressed into this: that Socialists are convinced such a measure will place them in power for many years and will mean for them the capture of a host of Conservative seats at the next general election.'[110]

The Equal Franchise Bill was regarded by the *Mail* and the *Mirror* primarily as a matter of party 'tactics' rather than as an issue of equality affecting relations between the sexes. Defending the 'public' against the socialist threat was always the overall goal, and the anti-feminist rhetoric of 1927 was largely a tool for this purpose. The crusade was also the product of the heightened class and party tensions that followed the General Strike in May 1926. Previous discussions of franchise reform in 1924 and 1925 had not provoked the same reaction;[111] after the strike, however, when the country 'was still bleeding in every limb from the wounds inflicted upon it by Socialism', Rothermere was determined that there be a period of consolidation and retrenchment.[112] Instead, this bill promised 'the exclusion of the Conservatives from office for a generation and the misgovernment of the country at a most critical point in English history'.[113]

---

[107] See also D. Jarvis, 'Behind Every Great Party: Women and Conservatism in Twentieth Century Britain', in Vickery (ed.), *Women, Privilege and Power*, 297.

[108] *Daily Mail*, 18 Nov. 1927, 11.

[109] According to the figures supplied by the Home Secretary, William Joynson-Hicks, in the Commons debate on the second reading of the Equal Franchise Bill, 29 Mar. 1928: 215 H.C. Debs. 5s, col. 1369.

[110] *Daily Mail*, 27 Apr. 1927, 10.   [111] *Daily Mail*, 4 June 1924, 8; 24 Oct. 1924, 6; 21 Feb. 1925, 7.

[112] *Daily Mail*, 1 Apr. 1927, 10.   [113] *Daily Mail*, 20 Apr. 1927, 10.

The other popular papers, meanwhile, supported the equalization of the franchise. The attitude of the *Daily Herald* and the *Daily News* was entirely predictable: they had long called for an end to the discrimination against women in the electorate.[114] The backing given by Beaverbrook's *Express* was more significant. After some initial uncertainty, the paper came down decisively in favour of conceding the vote at 21, and by the time of the 1929 election campaign gave lavish praise to the new generation of voters:

> Our conviction is firm that they value the privilege which has been extended to them, and that they will use it intelligently, with more independence and with a greater sense of responsibility than accompanies most men when they enter the polling booth. The leaders of the political parties need not fear the frivolity of the new voters.[115]

Once the voting had been completed, H. V. Morton informed *Express* readers that these predictions had been realized. Women had amply demonstrated their competence, and disproved the hostile stereotypes used against them:

> There is a type of man whose masculinity is flattered by the assumption that woman are tender, half-witted things fated to blunder on any stern occasion . . . But yesterday in the casual surroundings of the polling stations . . . women went to vote with that grim deliberation that is part of their mental make-up . . . If you expect me to tell you that they giggled or made eyes or behaved as 'flappers' are expected to behave you will be disappointed . . . they [voted] like people who had made up their minds long ago . . . the women went about the business of voting solemnly, responsibly and thoroughly.[116]

The Flapper Vote campaign should not be seen as a predictable manifestation of the anti-feminism of the conservative press. It was actually a product of the idiosyncratic political views of Lord Rothermere: his overwhelming fear of socialism forced the *Mail* and the *Mirror* into such a stubborn defence of the status quo that they had to sacrifice their usual attempts to cultivate female voters and risk alienating many of their own readers. As other papers gleefully pointed out, Rothermere was effectively criticizing an important section of his own audience.[117] Such hostility could not, however, be maintained. In 1929, as we have seen, the *Mirror* used the influx of new electors as the pretext for a series of political features for women.[118] Soon free of the proprietorship of Rothermere, moreover, it steered a more moderate course. And while the *Daily Mail* occasionally grumbled at the size and make-up of the electorate during the 1930s,[119] the desire to influence its decisions was sufficiently strong that

[114] *Daily Herald*, 14 Apr. 1927, 4; *Daily News*, 14 Apr. 1927, 6.
[115] *Daily Express*, 30 Mar. 1928, 1; 23 May 1929, 10. See also *Sunday Express*, 20 Nov. 1927, 12.
[116] *Daily Express*, 31 May 1929, 9.   [117] *Daily Herald*, 16 Apr. 1927, 5.
[118] *Daily Mirror*, 27 May 1929, 7.   [119] *Daily Mail*, 15 Jan. 1934, 10.

material aimed at women returned. The Flapper Vote crusade was not typical of the political discourse of the inter-war press, then, but a rather startling exception.

Stereotypes and Silences?

If the aggressive rhetoric of 1927–8 was unusual, the more subtle inequalities in the treatment of male and female voters should not be overlooked. While the popular papers made genuine efforts to include women within the political realm after 1918, there were still a variety of assumptions and silences that continued to stereotype and restrict the female citizen. Repeatedly associating women with a particular set of issues—whether price levels, taxation and consumption, or welfare reforms, housing, and education—inevitably suggested that other topics were not so relevant to women or so amenable to 'women's understanding'. 'She may not particularly care whether we sign a treaty with Albania or not because the whole thing is too distant,' argued Morton Wallace in the *Mirror*, 'but every housewife cares very considerably whether the price of sugar is to be 2 *d.* per pound cheaper or not.'[120] Important questions of fiscal strategy, industrial policy, and union legislation, for example, were frequently regarded as of little interest to women, and even when they were presented to female readers it was often in such a way as to reinforce this political 'separation of spheres'. Such topics were reduced to practicalities as quickly as possible, and while this helped to engage those who were not particularly interested in the background causes or the broader debate, it gave no encouragement to others seeking more theoretical detail. Examining the 1931 economic crisis for female readers, Helen Fraser in the *Mail* briefly declared her support for 'scientifically graded' tariffs. 'But these are views on the larger issue,' she noted, and moved swiftly on: 'We British housewives—I have no patience with the woman who is too "intellectual" to be a competent housewife—have to cope with the crisis here and now.'[121] Indeed, it was even suggested that women had little real need for involved political discussion, for they voted intuitively. Celebrating the Conservative victory in the 1924 election, a *Mail* editorial praised the contribution of the female electorate: 'Women are by nature a conservative force because they have an innate sense which detects folly and danger by instinct. It is an instinct which serves them better than any verbal logic, and in this case they knew by that instinct that their country's life was threatened.'[122]

---

[120] *Daily Mirror*, 29 Oct. 1924, 5.   [121] *Daily Mail*, 18 Sept. 1931, 10.
[122] *Daily Mail*, 31 Oct. 1924, 8.

Portrayed as housewives and mothers, women were repeatedly advised to consider the best interests of their family first; their own aspirations and demands aside from the family were rarely given similar attention. 'Vote for the sake of your men, your children, yourselves,' implored the *Mail* in 1918, reflecting the order of priorities it ascribed to its female readers.[123] 'Women are not thinking of their own comfort,' commented Mary Ferguson in the *Herald* in 1935, 'but because the "National" Government broke its pledge to fight the battle of the poorest and trampled upon women and children they are furiously angry.'[124] 'For the sake of our loved ones do realise that today is no time for light thinking,' agreed Ursula Bloom in the *Mirror*.[125] It was in the *Mirror*, indeed, that this type of appeal reached its fullest expression, when in 1945 female electors were encouraged to consider the wishes of absent servicemen and 'Vote for Him'.[126] Of course, men were also reminded to think of their families, but other interests such as wages, working conditions, and job prospects usually took precedence. The popular papers made grand claims about the potential power of the 'women's vote', but this power was usually to be expressed in bringing down prices or improving children's quality of life; in comparison, the prospect of women combining to reduce their own inequalities in relation to men received scant coverage.

Some feminists directly accused the press of neglecting the interests of women. In November 1923 an article in *Time and Tide* argued that 'Only one paper gives anything approaching fair and adequate space to reports of matters which concern the protection of children or equality of opportunity between men and women or of meetings held by non-party women's organisations. That paper is the *Manchester Guardian*.'[127] Similarly, Virginia Woolf in *Three Guineas* drew attention to Philippa Strachey's charge that there had been a press 'conspiracy of silence' around the endeavours of the women's movement in 1937 to remove a provision in the Contributory Pensions Bill which introduced a differential income limit for male and female entrants. Woolf looked forward to a time when a rich woman would 'run a daily newspaper committed to a conspiracy, not of silence, but of speech'.[128]

In some respects, these criticisms were unfair. The news values of the popular newspapers ensured that minority political organizations, unless particularly favoured by the proprietor or unusually eye-catching (such as the

---

[123] *Daily Mail*, 14 Dec. 1918, 7.   [124] *Daily Herald*, 12 Nov. 1935, 17.

[125] *Daily Mirror*, 14 Nov. 1935, 10.   [126] *Daily Mirror*, July 1945.

[127] *Time and Tide*, 23 Nov. 1923, cited in D. Spender (ed.), *Time and Tide Waits for No Man* (London: Pandora, 1984), 258.

[128] Virginia Woolf, *Three Guineas* (first pub. 1938; London: Penguin, 1993), 293–4, 192.

suffragettes), would struggle to receive regular or substantial coverage. The *Manchester Guardian* was produced for a very different audience from that of the *Mail* or the *Express*: these papers were far more concerned with the latest celebrity gossip or murder case than reform meetings. And with editors continuing to reduce the amount of 'heavy' political material throughout the 1930s, more and more issues were being condensed into 'snippet form'. This made it all the more difficult for a women's movement no longer united under the striking banner of 'Votes for Women' to obtain attention. Given that the *Mirror* only devoted 4 per cent of its total editorial space to political, social, and economic news and features in 1937, for example, it is unsurprising that there was no mention of the campaign to revise the Contributory Pensions Bill.[129] Within these constraints, moreover, there was neither a blanket 'conspiracy of silence' nor a consistent hostility towards feminism. As has been noted, a number of prominent feminists wrote articles for the popular papers, including Ray Strachey, Lady Rhondda, Vera Brittain, and Winifred Holtby. If the Pensions Bill controversy received little coverage, other reforms were specifically highlighted. In 1931, for example, even the *Daily Mail* found space to include editorials supporting two measures put forward by the women's movement, namely Eleanor Rathbone's bill to improve the situation of widows by preventing disinheritance, and international proposals to amend nationality legislation for the benefit of married women.[130] In November 1935 the *Daily Mirror* not only discussed the policies of the Women's Freedom League, but also sought to underline the paper's appeal to advanced opinion by printing on its news page a letter from a female reader thanking the paper for raising the issue of equal pay for equal work: 'as a woman worker myself I was keenly interested in the whole article. May I be allowed to congratulate you on the progressive nature of your paper?'[131] The *News* and the *Herald* frequently carried reports of the activities of organizations such as the National Union of Societies for Equal Citizenship and the Women's Cooperative Guild, while the Women's Institute received publicity and support from the conservative papers. By emphasizing the importance of women's political contribution, moreover, the press did encourage an engagement with public affairs.

On the other hand, the contemporary feminist case against the press was by no means entirely unfounded. There were instances when large-scale feminist activity went completely unreported. Discussing the equalization of the franchise in April 1927, for example, the *Mail* argued that 'no one

---

[129] Four per cent was the figure found by the Royal Commission: *Report*, 249.
[130] *Daily Mail*, 24 Mar. 1931, 10; 25 Mar. 1931, 11; 25 May 1931, 8–9.
[131] *Daily Mirror*, 5 Nov. 1935, 9; 9 Nov. 1935, 4.

demanded it, with the exception of a small handful of zealots'; yet had the paper covered the impressive rally in Hyde Park the previous July readers might have known different.[132] In the 1930s attempts to resuscitate the question of equal pay received only very occasional coverage. While conservative papers could be sympathetic to moderate 'new feminist' proposals focusing on marriage and motherhood, they were far less amenable to the more challenging egalitarian agenda. The language of 'rights' was an uncomfortable one: the *Mirror* wrote of its frustration at continuing feminist references to the battle for 'those silly old rights we've heard so much about'.[133] The *Express* praised the Federation of Women's Institutes because 'it speaks with a woman's voice and works in a woman's way'; it 'has no bone to pick, and has no "cause" to make its voice strident'.[134] Similarly, the *Mail* was relieved that the WIs were not 'forcing a pretentious urban feminism upon the countryside'.[135] A number of voices argued that not only were changes in position happening quickly enough as a result of the 'emancipation' brought by war, women now had the political power to remedy grievances themselves without the aid of 'crusading' organizations. And if the conservative papers did allow feminists to put their opinions, they also printed some fairly strong condemnations of feminism.[136]

On the left, the *Herald* was far more enthusiastic about egalitarian policies, but, as the content analysis suggests, the achievement of sexual equality was invariably relegated well below defending the interests of the 'working class'— and these interests were usually conflated with those of male trade unionists. The heavily contested question of the position of women teachers, to take one example, received less attention in the *Herald* than in some of the conservative papers because space was devoted instead to the more general issue of working-class access to education.[137] Similarly, the defence of male wage rates usually took precedence over the topic of equal pay for women. On party matters, too, voices were not always equal. Editorial material sometimes betrayed the assumption that wives would automatically fall in behind the leadership of the male unions. During the 1923 election campaign, for instance, an editorial announced that 'if the transport workers and miners of this country, with their wives, vote Labour on Thursday, a Labour Government will be returned to power'.[138] Indeed, frustrations on this matter were revealed when George Lansbury received complaints in 1924 that the conference of the Communist

---

[132] *Daily Mail*, 14 Apr. 1927, 10. The unreported rally in Hyde Park occurred on 3 July 1926.

[133] *Daily Mirror*, 19 June 1935, 11.   [134] *Daily Express*, 15 May 1929, 3.

[135] *Daily Mail*, 15 May 1929, 12.

[136] e.g. *Daily Express*, 28 May 1929, 10; *Daily Mirror*, 19 June 1935, 2.

[137] e.g. *Daily Herald*, 2–4 Apr. 1929; compare *Daily Mail*, 3 Apr. 1929, 9.

[138] *Daily Herald*, 3 Dec. 1923, 6.

Party was given greater attention than that of the Labour Women's sections.[139] The *Herald* was rarely negative about the cause of women's rights, it merely failed to give it the prominence it could have done, especially as the paper covered politics more extensively than the rest of the popular press.

More broadly, however, newspapers often failed to live up to their own election rhetoric. While proclaiming the importance of women becoming involved in politics—'no woman can be a good housewife or a good mother unless she is a good politician'[140]—the content analysis shows that once the 'news value' of a new female electorate faded, 'women's issues' and female candidates became less prominent. More significantly, if women had so many important political interests as a result of their domestic roles, it was difficult to understand why these did not receive more attention throughout the year on the women's pages. The 'ideal home' of the women's pages was usually presented as attainable by educated consumption, 'professional' housewifery techniques, and a 'companionate marriage'; only during 'crusades' or election campaigns did the political dimensions of such issues as price and wage levels, medical facilities, or marital rights emerge from the shadows. The popular press generated a self-fulfilling prophecy: assuming that women disliked or did not understand political material, they provided little to persuade them otherwise. Women were mobilized only when it was in the papers' own interests, and then they were usually discursively confined to a particular set of women's issues.

The overall impact of this 'feminized' political discourse was double-edged. On the one hand, conventional stereotypes were reinforced, for women voters and politicians were almost invariably presented through a gendered lens, as bringing a 'female perspective' to politics. Female voters were addressed as housewives and mothers, and they were encouraged to display 'womanly' virtues such as compassion, prudence, and practicality. Unclear or anxious about what the political interests of the single, 'modern young woman' might be, journalists after 1929 generally persevered with the types of rhetoric developed over the previous decade and made few attempts to address this large constituency directly. On the other hand, entry into the political sphere inevitably had a major impact on perceptions of femininity. For all the grand Victorian oratory about woman's 'supreme moral influence', or claims about women's capacity to shape decisions 'behind the scenes', observing women actually

---

[139] Daily Herald Papers, LP/DH/335, George Lansbury to J. S. Middleton, 23 June 1924. It should be noted, however, that these complaints were shown to be unfounded.

[140] *Daily Herald*, 9 Nov. 1935, 10.

casting votes and standing for Parliament was a profound turning point. Newspapers now had to include women not just in the feature pages but also in the political columns. For Vera Brittain, the publicity obtained by female parliamentary candidates was of almost incalculable value:

the sight of a woman effectively occupying a platform and winning widespread allegiance for her party provides the best evidence that life, as much for women as for men, may be a thing of dignity and beauty, of leadership and power. Anti-feminist prejudice, and that inferiority complex which is the most enervating influence that women have still to contend with, are alike disappearing in the constituencies where women candidates have fought.[141]

For Emmeline Pethick-Lawrence, looking over her life in 1937, the awareness that 'women as citizens are making the Government of the day anxious about the next election because of their protest about the rising cost of food' seemed to sum up the 'revolution of thought that has taken place with regard to women'.[142] If the numbers of women MPs had been fairly disappointing, equal enfranchisement was still sufficiently recent by the end of the period for commentators to assume that the nation had yet to witness the full expression of the 'women's vote'. This political power remained a crucial component of the widespread beliefs in modernity and female 'emancipation'. The restrictions and inequalities that still faced women in politics are far clearer to the historian than they were to most contemporaries.

[141] *Manchester Guardian*, 5 June 1929, cited in P. Berry and A. Bishop (eds.), *Testament of a Generation: The Journalism of Vera Brittain and Winifred Holtby* (London: Virago, 1985), 113.
[142] E. Pethick-Lawrence, *My Part in a Changing World* (London: Gollancz, 1938), 345, 347.

5

The Gendered Gaze: Fashion,
the Female Body, and Sexual Morality

From the turn of the twentieth century, the gradual acceptance of display advertising, and the evolution of techniques to reproduce photographs rapidly and cheaply, transformed the appearance of the daily newspaper. During the inter-war years, popular papers developed a recognizably modern layout as part of their drive to increase circulation. Columns of unbroken text in one typeface were replaced by a more fragmented and visually attractive format in which the reader was guided by prominent headlines and 'cross-headers', and articles were broken up by photographs, cartoons, and illustrated advertisements. The number of words per issue was reduced as editors filled space with appealing and striking photos and sketches. Northcliffe told his staff in June 1920 that he was 'more and more coming to the conclusion that the public judge the paper by the pictures, and the best paper can be marred by bad pictures';[1] by the 1930s the layout of the popular papers contrasted dramatically with that of the 'minority' press.[2] This illustrated press put the female body under scrutiny as never before. Women were not necessarily pictured more often or more prominently than men: news photography inevitably reproduced the numerical gender disparity in public life when displaying the 'people in the headlines', and men as well as women featured in advertisements and cartoons. Nevertheless, women were portrayed in a very different way from men. Women were repeatedly put on view not for what they had achieved but for what they were wearing or for how they looked; the reader was invited

---

[1] Bodleian Library, Oxford, MS Eng. hist. d. 303–5, Northcliffe Bulletins, 1 June 1920.

[2] These developments are described in detail in S. Morison, *The English Newspaper 1622–1932* (Cambridge: Cambridge University Press, 1932), ch. XVI; D. LeMahieu, *A Culture for Democracy: Mass Communication and the Cultivated Mind in Britain between the Wars* (Oxford: Clarendon Press, 1988), 253–73; and M. Conboy, *The Press and Popular Culture* (London: Sage, 2002), ch. 6.

to examine the clothed body and the smiling face in aesthetic terms. Newspapers were peppered with photographs of society women displaying the latest fashions, cinema actresses exuding 'sex appeal',[3] and young workers showing off their latest beachwear; adverts presented female models, both photographed and sketched, in everything from underwear to fur coats. Pictures of pretty women became central to the identity of the popular press. As the Political and Economic Planning (PEP) *Report on the British Press* observed in 1938, 'a popular newspaper, indeed, might almost be defined as one which features a photograph of the first bathing belles of the season on Easter Tuesday morning'.[4]

The increased prominence of the female body, not only in press illustrations but also in the flurry of articles that accompanied them, had a double-edged impact. On the one hand, it facilitated the rapid diffusion of that iconic image of the 1920s, the short-skirted, tubular-shaped 'flapper' with cropped hair. It is difficult to underestimate the power of this image in reinforcing the view that women had been transformed by the experience of war and were now asserting their independence and equality. Short hair and skirts became basic symbols of modernity, and they offered a visual reminder on a daily basis of the apparent transformation of femininity. Debates on these fashions became, in effect, contests about the 'proper' place of women, and the general support of the press for them—essential for advertising reasons, if nothing else—was another sign of its willingness to come to terms with modernity. Freedom from restrictive social conventions appeared to be a corollary of this new freedom from restrictive clothing, and there was also widespread press support for a relaxation of the suffocating rules of propriety, and for moves towards more 'companionate' forms of marriage.

On the other hand, the photographs of 'bathing belles' and 'glamorous lovelies' inevitably strengthened the belief that women had a special decorative role in society and should expect to be judged on their appearance. By the end of the period women were sexualized as never before in the press, with the *Daily Mirror* in particular placing titillating material at the centre of its strategy to win over working-class male readers. Women's page features often placed new burdens on women as they were invited to aspire to the appearance of cinema stars. Cosmetics, previously regarded as unnecessary and rather unrespectable, were redefined as essential beauty aids, and the self-discipline of

---

[3] 'Sex appeal' was a new phrase 'with a tremendous vogue' in the 1920s: R. Graves and A. Hodge, *The Long Week-End: A Social History of Great Britain 1918–39* (first pub. 1940; Harmondsworth: Penguin, 1971), 136; J. Ayto, *Twentieth Century Words* (Oxford: Oxford University Press, 1999), 173.

[4] Political and Economic Planning (PEP), *Report on the British Press* (London, 1938), 155.

slimming and health regimes was suggested as a replacement for tight-laced corsets. Advertisements emphasized that 'unattractive' women would fail to win, or to hold, the man of their dreams. And while 'Victorian' prohibitions on heterosexual mixing were derided, traditional double standards of morality remained evident. Although husbands were increasingly reminded of the need to provide companionship, advice columnists still often held women largely responsible both for maintaining the health of married relationships and for ensuring that there were no 'lapses' outside wedlock. The definition of the 'family newspaper' that editors developed in this period permitted the exhibition of women for the titillation of male readers but restricted discussion of birth control and venereal disease.

This chapter will show how the popular press tried to cater for its diverse market by simultaneously satisfying women's interest in fashion advice, delivering sexy images for male readers, and exploiting the post-war controversies about female appearance and morality.

Editorial Policies and Pressures

The Appeal to Women: Fashion Advice and Advertisements

Fashion advice had been a staple of women's magazines since the late eighteenth century and was a major feature in the women's pages of the popular press from the first issue of the *Daily Mail* in 1896.[5] As the content analysis makes clear, it received more coverage in the women's sections than any other topic throughout the period, and very rarely comprised less than a quarter of the total content (see the Appendix). Fashion was regarded as a subject which could attract much-sought-after young women, who would then, it was hoped, become long-term newspaper readers. Also of interest to some older women, it offered a perfect complement to the material on housewifery and motherhood. As Hamilton Fyfe, a pupil of Northcliffe and later editor of the *Herald*, noted, women's pages advised 'mother how to make a pudding and her daughter how to look fashionable'.[6] Fashion advice was repeatedly found to be popular with readers, both in the anecdotal surveys of the 1920s and in the more sophisticated research of the 1930s. PEP's survey revealed that 'beauty articles were read rather more than average' by women, while Mass

[5] M. Beetham, *A Magazine of her Own? Domesticity and Desire in the Woman's Magazine 1800–1914* (London: Routledge, 1996), 31–4; *Daily Mail*, 4 May 1896, 7.
[6] H. Fyfe, *Sixty Years of Fleet Street* (London: W. H. Allen, 1949), 169.

Observation discovered a female interest rate of 87 per cent in sewing patterns and 56 per cent in beauty aids.[7]

Even more significantly, retailers of women's clothing were vital advertisers in the press. Contracts from department stores and drapers could be extremely lucrative: the first two firms to spend over £100,000 in a year in the *Daily Mail* were Harrods and the Barker group, while in 1924 the latter agreed to take out a full page in the *Express* every day for a year.[8] 'Drapery and department store' advertising was the single largest category of expenditure in the press in 1935 (excluding an amalgamated group of 'other trade and technical advertising').[9] The importance of this class of advertising was impressed on editorial staff time and again, to the extent that even the most old-fashioned journalists came to recognize its value. Characterizing the conventional chief sub-editor, Hamilton Fyfe observed that 'His conviction is that newspapers are bought for the news they contain and for no other reason, except perhaps—he will admit grudgingly—the dress and drapery advertisements of the big stores, which make an undeniable appeal to women.'[10] When Beaverbrook was told in 1928 that the *Express* had received almost twice as much revenue from drapery advertisers as its rivals, he declared the information worthy of a news story in the paper.[11] Five years later an eight-page women's supplement in the Scottish *Express* was approved largely because it would 'contain all Glasgow and Edinburgh drapers' advertising'. The interest from these stores raised the prospect that the supplement 'could be made to pay for itself'.[12]

This significance as both a circulation and an advertising tool ensured that fashion features were treated very seriously. Less than two weeks after the signing of the Armistice, Northcliffe was urging his editor to rearrange the layout of the *Mail* (still restricted by newsprint shortages) and expand the women's section: 'I trust that we shall soon find room for Miss Ascough's drawings once or twice a week and for a good dress article.'[13] Northcliffe frequently sought opinions from women on the suitability of the fashion advice and he did not hesitate to pass on their criticisms: Idalia Villiers-Wardell was told that the hats

[7] PEP, *Report*, 252; Bodleian Library, Oxford, X. Films 200, Mass Observation Archives, File Report 3005, 'Reading the *Daily Herald*', June 1948, 22.

[8] British Library, Northcliffe Papers, Add. MS 62214, Faulkener to Northcliffe, 2 Sept. 1920; M. Aitken (Lord Beaverbrook), *Politicians and the Press* (London: Hutchinson, 1926), 82.

[9] N. Kaldor and R. Silverman, *A Statistical Analysis of Advertising Expenditure and of the Revenue of the Press* (Cambridge: Cambridge University Press, 1948), 123–7. [10] Fyfe, *Sixty Years*, 154.

[11] House of Lords Record Office, Beaverbrook Papers, H/54, E. J. Robertson to Beaverbrook, 16 Apr. 1928. [12] Beaverbrook Papers, H/99, Max Aitken to Beaverbrook, 3 Jan. 1933.

[13] Northcliffe Bulletins, 22 Nov. 1918.

she recommended were 'not quite-up-to-date', while Bessie Ascough discovered in 1922 that she only drew 'for tall people'.[14] Nor was fashion confined to the women's pages. The photographs of society debutantes, titled women, and film stars that appeared throughout the paper were regarded as being of interest to women as a guide to the latest trends. Northcliffe was furious in June 1921 when he learnt that production errors had led to the *Mail*'s photographs being printed faintly: 'This is a great mistake especially where costumes are concerned. Women insist upon seeing details of dresses.'[15] By the late 1920s reports on the latest fashions were regular features of the main news pages of all of the popular papers except the *Herald*. J. B. Priestley famously observed that working-class women increasingly looked 'like actresses' in this period; Graves and Hodge similarly remarked of the late 1920s that 'it was now at last possible to mistake working-class girls for titled ladies, if one judged by dress'.[16] As advertisers recognized, the fashion features and photography of the daily press, combined with similar material in women's magazines, played an essential role in enabling a far more rapid diffusion of fashion trends.[17]

The necessity for newspapers to 'keep up with the fashions' and to attract advertisers who prospered from rapid shifts in clothing styles ensured that the short skirts and backless dresses that provoked controversy in the 1920s were not generally opposed by the press. Newspapers could hardly afford, in Billie Melman's phrase, to 'deride' the appearance of young women.[18] As we shall see, criticisms were included to provide talking points, but on the women's pages at least, new fashions were usually accepted. Newspapers explicitly encouraged women to take advantage of the mass-produced clothing and cosmetics that were coming onto the market. The press presented these changes as a 'democratization' of fashion: features outlined how readers could look like glamorous film stars. Indeed, it was not a rejection of modern fashion but an all too enthusiastic embrace of it that was more characteristic, and arguably more problematic. There was little criticism of the constant shifts in what was fashionable and insufficient appreciation of the pressures placed upon women encouraged to live up to the expectations of cinema and the fashion industry. During the Royal Commission inquiry, accusations were made that pressure from hosiery manufacturers led to the *Express* criticizing women without stockings as being

---

[14] Northcliffe Papers, Add. MS 62220, Northcliffe to Idalia Villiers-Wardell, 7 Nov. 1913; Northcliffe Bulletins, 27 Apr. 1922.   [15] Northcliffe Bulletins, 15 June 1921.
[16] J. B. Priestley, *English Journey* (first pub. 1934; London: William Heinemann, 1937), 401; Graves and Hodge, *Long Week-End*, 174.
[17] A. J. Greenly, *Psychology as a Sales Factor*, 2nd edn. (London: Pitman, 1929), 51.
[18] B. Melman, *Women and the Popular Imagination in the Twenties: Flappers and Nymphs* (Basingstoke: Macmillan, 1988), 17.

unattractive. This claim was denied, and there is no way of checking its veracity; nevertheless, the suspicion itself is revealing and indicative of the close relationship between newspapers and fashion advertisers.[19]

The Appeal to Men: 'Sex Appeal'

It is clear that popular newspaper editors were conscious of an explicitly female gaze which would scrutinize photographs and fashion sketches; at the same time they were aware of another gaze, that of the heterosexual male, which would often be looking at the same pictures. There was a long tradition, especially in the Sunday market, of providing sexual content. Popular newspapers exploited the inexhaustible supply of stories of adulterous behaviour and crimes of passion from the law courts, while W. T. Stead's infamous investigation of 1885 into child prostitution—serialized as 'The Maiden Tribute of Modern Babylon'—demonstrated how moral crusading could be combined with titillating reporting.[20] Advertising and photography introduced a new dimension to this familiar press strategy. 'I have no use for a man who cannot appreciate a pretty ankle,' Northcliffe told his news editor Tom Clarke, '. . . certainly not on my newspapers. We must not let our outlook get too middle-aged.'[21] In his bulletins to the *Mail* he frequently reminded his staff of the need to display glamorous women and he was critical when his picture editor picked out what he regarded as 'common-looking ugly wenches'.[22] In August 1920 he encouraged the editor to compete with the 'picture papers': 'A few attractive ladies would make the paper look better. The public well know where to find these for they only appear in the *Daily Mirror* and the *Daily Sketch*.'[23] When a photograph of Polish women soldiers appeared the following day he was furious: 'Pictures of attractive English ladies would have been much more to the point. I am almost weary of repeating this.'[24] Over at the *Express* the editor Ralph Blumenfeld admitted to Beaverbrook in 1919 that the paper relied on 'mild forms of pornography' to maintain its circulation.[25] Nor were the less sensational left-wing papers above this type of appeal. As Hew Richards, the

---

[19] Royal Commission on the Press, *Minutes of Evidence* (London: HMSO, 1948), Day 5, Cmd. 7325, 5; denial Day 16, Cmd. 7364, 14.

[20] A. Humphries, 'Coming Apart: The British Newspaper Press and the Divorce Court', in L. Brake, B. Bell, and D. Finkelstein (eds.), *Nineteenth Century Media and the Construction of Identities* (Basingstoke: Palgrave, 2000), ch. 14; G. Savage, 'Erotic Stories and Public Decency: Newspaper Reporting of Divorce Proceedings in England', *Historical Journal*, 41/2 (1998), 511–28. On Stead, see J. Walkowitz, *City of Dreadful Delight: Narratives of Sexual Danger in Late Victorian London* (Chicago: University of Chicago Press, 1992), ch. 3.   [21] T. Clarke, *My Northcliffe Diary* (London: Victor Gollancz, 1931), 246.

[22] Northcliffe Bulletins, 1 Aug. 1920.   [23] Northcliffe Bulletins, 5 Aug. 1920.

[24] Northcliffe Bulletins, 6 Aug. 1920.

[25] Beaverbrook Papers, H/44, Blumenfeld to Beaverbrook, 22 Jan. 1919.

historian of the *Herald*, notes, when the paper launched its photo page in February 1926, 'the mix of something newsy, something sporty and at least one pretty girl became the norm'.[26] Once the *Herald* became more commercial in the 1930s, moreover, staff complained that any socialism had to be included 'on the back of a bathing beauty'.[27] Several firms also began to use images of glamorous women in their press advertising campaigns, even where such images appeared rather incongruous (see Fig. 5.1). A. P. Braddock, a publicity expert, observed in his 1933 handbook that 'Pictures of girls and women form a large percentage of the principal studies for [advertising] posters . . . A sex appeal is often thus made.'[28] Once the initial uproar over displaying women's underwear in popular newspapers had subsided (see Chapter 1), lingerie advertisements also gradually became more graphic, with photographs of models replacing cropped sketches. While these were obviously directed at women, editors were not unaware that male eyes strayed across the columns to them. In both the editorial and advertising columns, women were increasingly being displayed for male titillation.

It was only when the *Daily Mirror* reinvented itself in the mid-1930s, however, that a popular daily truly sought to capitalize on the strategy of sex and sensationalism that had proved so successful in the Sunday market, most notably for the *News of the World*.[29] Hugh Cudlipp, one of the architects of the *Mirror*'s 'tabloid revolution', remembered unapologetically that 'Glamorous young ladies smiled out of the picture pages, and there were even examples of beauty unadorned.'[30] Features such as 'So You Want to Be an Artist's Model?', for example, were transparently little other than an excuse to titillate with a nude picture and descriptions of women in various states of undress (see Fig. 5.2).[31] What Cudlipp described as 'the sexual misdemeanours of the populace' were reported more 'audaciously' than in other papers, and some cartoons began to rely on a more overtly sexual sense of humour.[32] By November 1937 Walter Layton, the editor of the *News Chronicle*, could dismiss the *Mirror* in an internal memo as a paper which was 'over sex-conscious'.[33] Nevertheless, as the

[26] H. Richards, 'Conscription, Conformity and Control: The Taming of the Daily Herald, 1921–30', D.Phil. thesis (Open University, 1992), 175.

[27] F. Williams, *Dangerous Estate: The Anatomy of Newspapers* (first pub. 1957 London: Longmans, Green, 1958), 198.

[28] A. P. Braddock, *Applied Psychology for Advertisers* (London: Butterworth, 1933), 101; see also 106.

[29] On the *News of the World*, see C. Bainbridge and R. Stockdill, *The News of the World Story: 150 Years of the World's Bestselling Newspaper* (London: HarperCollins, 1993).

[30] H. Cudlipp, *Publish and be Damned! The Astonishing Story of the Daily Mirror* (London: Andrew Dakers, 1953), 115. [31] *Daily Mirror*, 12 Sept. 1938, 12. [32] Cudlipp, *Publish and be Damned!*, 66.

[33] Trinity College, Cambridge, Walter Layton Papers, Box 89, Walter Layton memo to Directors, 9 Nov. 1937.

FIG. 5.1. By the 1930s, some advertisers used images of
attractive women to draw attention to their announcements,
even when they had no relationship to the product

TO BE AN

plenty of jobs coming in, hardly a day to myself—and happy indeed.

Now and again I run into girls I knew in the old City days.

I know they look at me strangely—as if I'd come from an entirely different world. A round of cocktail parties, suppers at the Dorchester, expensive dates and so on.

And I know the reason they look at me like that.

If they only knew why I am able to wear good clothes—a costly squirrel cape, or a hat which has hardly been out of a Mayfair salon five minutes. The clothes I wear I am often able to buy from the firm which has photographed me in them for a quarter of their actual price.

I have earned up to £25 a week, can still do it at certain times of the year when spring, summer and winter fashion advertisements have to be drawn up.

This is how we get paid.

A Mayfair dressmaker pays £2 2s. a day for a mannequin A commercial artist pays the same fee for a girl who poses for a camera

Best paid are the jobs for which we pose for nudes.

The fee here is three guineas—a guinea more than a pose with our clothes on.

Modelling in the nude is held to be pretty popular among models. It generally means a day in the fresh air, since these photos are generally taken in the country.

I often go down to a well-known nudist colony for a series of poses.

We do not hold that this is "shameful" work. It is all a part of our day, and we are never asked to pose for a picture which we'd be ashamed to show our own mothers.

Posing in the nude for an artist is a job which is now fairly rare for the model.

Four hours at 5s. an hour is the standard rate of pay for this kind of work.

And now you may ask what sort of a private life a model leads to-day.

The idea that every job means another "date" for the diary is wrong.

The proof of this is I married the man I love three years ago. He was nothing whatsoever to do with my work.

Most of the men I work for know I am married and that I have a tiny baby, just six months old.

I have been in demand as a model just as much since I married as when I was single.

I am a wife and mother of a tiny baby.

★

Sometimes I look like £5,000 a year, but my clothes don't cost me that.

★

As mannequins we get paid £2 2s. a day.

★

Best jobs are those where we pose in the nude. There's nothing shameful in it.

★

Fig. 5.2. From the mid-1930s, the *Daily Mirror* gave increasing prominence to titillating photographs and articles

Mirror's circulation grew, pressure was mounting on other papers to follow suit. Only six months before Layton's memo, Collin Brooks, the editor of the *Mail*'s Sunday sister paper, the *Sunday Dispatch*, found that his manager at Associated Newspapers was demanding measures to revive flagging sales. 'Having heard Rothermere talk of the success of the *Mirror* with sensationalism and pornography he now held that . . . that was what we needed.'[34] Brooks resigned rather than move the paper 'downmarket' in this way.

The *Mirror*'s strategy was supported by market research findings suggesting the circulation potential of sexy material. Before the 1930s evidence had only been anecdotal; Northcliffe told his staff in 1920, for example, that 'a well-known public man said to me yesterday "I have had to drop the *Daily Mail* in order to get the *Daily Mirror* bathing pictures."'[35] By the end of the period Mass Observation and others were backing up the instincts of journalists on this matter. Asked what he liked about the *Mirror* in 1938, for example, one respondent 'candidly' revealed that he enjoyed 'its so-called "sex" photos. I dislike the *Sketch*. It is not modern. I don't only want "All the news and pictures fit to print" [the slogan of the *Daily Sketch*]. I want the other side as well.'[36] (Others were not so dissatisfied by the *Sketch*'s more conservative tastes. One of its readers admitted that 'I like the pictures of nice-looking girls. I'm quite disappointed if there aren't any when I open the paper in the morning.'[37]) The *Mirror*'s 'Jane' was also found to be hugely popular. Despite being a cartoon—or perhaps because of it, for this meant that pictures of her could be more revealing—she was voted third favourite 'pin-up' in a survey of servicemen carried out for *Picture Post* in 1944. 'Many of us follow her adventures with more interest than, for instance, the war against Japan,' confided one private.[38] As its circulation soared the *Mirror* demonstrated, as the *Express* editor Arthur Christiansen observed ruefully, that 'sex is the surest recipe for circulation'.[39]

The Need for Respectability: The 'Family Newspaper'

If 'sex appeal' was undoubtedly a useful tool, it was one that had to be used cautiously and with moderation. Editors and proprietors were acutely aware of the dangers of alienating readers and advertisers, and, at least before the *Mirror* adopted its new, brash identity, were anxious to retain an air of respectability.

[34] N. J. Crowson (ed.), *Fleet Street, Press Barons and Politics: The Journals of Collin Brooks, 1932–40* (London: Royal Historical Society, 1998), 191.   [35] Northcliffe Bulletins, 23 July 1920.
[36] Mass Observation, File Report A11, 'Motives and Methods of Newspaper Reading', Dec. 1938, 21.
[37] Mass Observation, File Report 126, 'Report on the Press', May 1940, 6.
[38] *Picture Post*, 22 Sept. 1944: see Mass Observation, File Report 2156, 'What is a Pin-up Girl?', Sept. 1944.
[39] A. Christiansen, *Headlines All my Life* (London: Heinemann, 1961), 237.

Norman Angell, an experienced journalist who worked with Northcliffe before the First World War, found that 'the Chief' recognized 'that every man (and woman) was prurient and liked pornography; but he knew also that most of them (in England at least) had their puritan side, and had a certain idealism about the proper relation of the sexes'.[40] While Northcliffe was determined that his papers did not become too 'middle-aged', he tried to ensure that they remained within well-defined boundaries. When they overstepped this mark, he was fiercely critical. In 1921, for example, Bernard Falk, the editor of the *Weekly Dispatch*, later renamed the *Sunday Dispatch*, received a message that one of his photographs was too revealing: Northcliffe 'did not like the picture of Miss Noreena Feist, it is vulgar and inelegant. (Enough is as good as a feast)'.[41] 'Vulgarity'—the sign of a paper going so far 'downmarket' that it would lose its wider influence—was to be avoided at all costs: 'The *Daily Mail* is popular but not vulgar,' he announced.[42]

This sensitivity was partly a response to attacks from politicians, religious leaders, and organizations such as the Mothers' Union that the popular press was a corrupting force in society. Hamilton Fyfe was conscious of the damage done by the comment of the archbishop of Canterbury, Cosmo Lang, that 'cheap newspapers' were a 'menace to the home'.[43] The sensational coverage of divorce proceedings had provoked criticism since the establishment of the Divorce Court in 1857, and a campaign directed by Sir Evelyn Cecil finally led to these reports being curtailed by the 1926 Judicial Proceedings (Regulation of Reports) Act.[44] This Act was passed despite the fact that definite examples of press obscenity could not be identified. Sir Arthur Steel-Maitland accepted that 'there is hardly a single obscene detail in reports of divorce cases which could be made subject to the present law', but he still believed that 'the cumulative effect of these divorce cases cause the harm'.[45] These words were echoed two decades later in the course of the Royal Commission inquiry, when Robert Ensor questioned R. Clough, the editor of the *Newcastle Journal*, about sex-related features:

Ensor: You can fill the pages day after day and week after week with material of that sort, and though you cannot put your finger on anything salacious, the whole effect is nevertheless demoralising?

Clough: Yes.

Ensor: Is it stimulating the sex side very much?

Clough: Yes.[46]

---

[40] N. Angell, *After All: The Autobiography of Norman Angell* (London: Hamish Hamilton, 1951), 119.

[41] Northcliffe Papers, Add. MS 62229, to Falk (undated), mid-1921.

[42] Northcliffe Bulletins, 22 May 1921.   [43] Fyfe, *Sixty Years*, 78.

[44] National Archives, Kew, LCO/2/775; Savage, 'Erotic Stories'.   [45] Savage, 'Erotic Stories', 522.

[46] Royal Commission, *Minutes*, Day 13, Cmd. 7351, 9.

The fact that there were few concrete examples of 'salacity' was a sign that newspapers were trying to deny ammunition to their critics and remain within the bounds of decency. More broadly, the popular press defended itself by rejecting these charges and portraying itself as suitable for the whole family. On many sexual matters, and especially on subjects for which titillating copy was difficult to produce, newspapers tended to err on the side of caution. Marie Stopes, for example, did receive a significant amount of press coverage—the birth of her son in 1924 reached the front page of the *Express*[47]—but her books and her birth control campaign were rarely discussed in any detail. When she opened her first clinic in Holloway, North London, in March 1921, for example, it was not reported in the *Mail*, the *Express*, or the *Mirror*. The *Daily Mirror* replied to her letter giving advance warning of the event by explaining that the subject was 'inappropriate for discussion or publicity' in a 'family newspaper'.[48] Hamilton Fyfe revealed that birth control was one of three topics the press sought to avoid if at all possible (the others were religion and the folly of gambling).[49] Catholic readers were certainly liable to take offence: indeed, the *News of the World* was officially banned in Ireland between 1930 and 1937 for its editorial line on this issue.[50] During the 1920s, the *Daily Herald* was the only national daily consistently to accept birth control advertisements, but this was not without resistance from both the circulation and the advertisement managers. 'Their publication does undoubtedly tend to injure the prestige of the paper,' argued the former in May 1928, and Poyser, his advertising colleague agreed: 'These advertisements do not look nice, and give the appearance of something furtive about that particular corner of the paper in which they appear.'[51] The paper's policy committee overruled these objections: but after the paper was taken over by the commercial publisher Odhams in 1929, the policy was changed. When Stopes's Constructive Birth Control Society tried to place an advert in March 1932, they were refused with the explanation that the board had decided such material would lose the paper readers.[52]

The press was similarly cautious about discussing venereal disease. Although Northcliffe encouraged the *Mail* not to turn a blind eye to the issue—'Ours is not, as some people in the office seem to think, the Children's Newspaper, and

[47] *Daily Express*, 28 Mar. 1924, 1.

[48] J. Rose, *Marie Stopes and the Sexual Revolution* (London: Faber & Faber, 1993), 144; Stopes's frustrations with the press are clearly revealed in her correspondence: e.g. British Library, Marie Stopes Papers, Add. MS 58699, fos. 33, 53, 54, 75.   [49] Fyfe, *Sixty Years*, 217.   [50] PEP, *Report*, 208.

[51] Bodleian Library, Oxford, X. Films 77/6, Daily Herald Papers, LP/DH/544, Circulation Manager's Report, 21 May 1928; Advertisement Manager's Report, 21 May 1928.

[52] Marie Stopes Papers, Add. MS 58598, fo. 75, M. Poyser to G. B. Higgs, 8 Mar. 1932; fo. 76, memo by G. B. Higgs, 11 Mar. 1932.

the more you suppress the facts about this disease, the more it will spread,' he told his staff in 1920—nor did he want to give it undue prominence.[53] When the paper mentioned a case of gonorrhoea two weeks later, he commented that 'I am glad to see that we have at length plucked up the courage to help to do good but I by no means desire these cases should be emphasised.'[54] Robert Graves and Alan Hodge believed that venereal disease was still effectively a 'tabooed subject' for the press.[55] Even when the Ministry of Health sought to publish an advert highlighting the rising incidence of venereal disease during the Second World War, the Newspaper Proprietors' Association objected to use of popular terminology such as 'pox', 'clap', and 'sex organs'. The ministry agreed to make amendments, but the *Express* still refused to print it: it was determined to remain faithful to its status as a 'family newspaper'.[56]

When the *Mirror* broke ranks in the mid-1930s to pursue its deliberately 'sensational' line, other papers actively sought to distance themselves from it. The *Express* reminded readers of its respectability, and stoutly defended its record before the Royal Commission in 1948. E. J. Robertson, the chairman of Express Newspapers, outlined Beaverbrook's basic policies: 'always make the paper clean in the sense that no pornography should be in; keep all salacious things out. Our test is that our papers should be such that we should never be ashamed of our daughters reading them, and I defy anybody to find any-thing that we have done contrary to that rule.'[57] The *Express* editor Arthur Christiansen privately accused the *Mirror* of hypocrisy. In a letter to Tom Driberg, his former colleague, in 1943, he observed sarcastically: 'It is wonderful how solicitous the *Daily Mirror* is for the boys [i.e. servicemen]. They work up their sex desires by publishing sexy pictures in the overseas edition, and campaign against V.D. in preparation for their return.'[58] Looking back over his career, Christiansen was proud to maintain that his *Express* 'had more of everything, except for bosom pictures and smutty reports'.[59]

The *Daily Sketch* was even more eager than the *Express* to demonstrate its virtue. Launching a 'Clean and Clever' campaign, it resolved not to print any 'sensational, ribald and pornographic pictures' and published letters from clergymen supporting its principled stand.[60] This purity crusade reached

---

[53] Northcliffe Bulletins, 12 May 1920.   [54] Northcliffe Bulletins, 29 May 1920.
[55] Graves and Hodge, *Long Week-End*, 104.
[56] *Daily Mirror*, 19 Feb. 1943, 2–3; *Newspaper World*, 27 Feb. 1943, 17, 19; Cudlipp, *Publish and be Damned!*, 207–8.   [57] Royal Commission, *Minutes*, Day 16, Cmd. 7364, 29.
[58] Christ Church, Oxford, Tom Driberg Papers, E1, fo. 13, Christiansen to Driberg, 8 Mar. 1943.
[59] Christiansen, *Headlines*, 177.
[60] The *Sketch* produced an advertising campaign highlighting these letters, e.g. *Daily Telegraph*, 23 June 1938, 21.

the level of farce over a photograph of the Canadian skater Barbara Ann Scott. When the *Mirror*'s Sunday sister publication, the *Pictorial*, was accused of doctoring the photograph to chop inches off Scott's underwear for 'salacious' purposes, the paper gleefully revealed that in fact the *Sketch*'s stablemate, the *Sunday Graphic*, had added on material to protect its readers' sensibilities.[61] Women's bodies were becoming the measure of a paper's respectability.

If papers differed over how far they would exploit sexy material and photographs, however, all of them displayed women differently from men. Most journalists unself-consciously regarded heterosexual desire as 'normal' and women as the sex to be admired. Pictures of 'bathing belles' were regarded as perfectly natural and little more than a 'bit of fun'. 'Pornography'—the charge levelled at the *Mirror*—was held to entail the unnecessary inclusion of salacious detail or gratuitously revealing photographs. But this contest between 'respectability' and 'pornography' could not disguise the fact that women were increasingly displayed for the male gaze throughout the press, even in the so-called 'family newspapers'. Sporting photographs of men might have operated as celebrations of the male body—and Christiansen pointed out to his staff after the Second World War that some women admitted that they were disappointed if there was not a picture of the cricketer Dennis Compton somewhere in their paper—but in almost every case they were portrayed focused on their pursuit.[62] Attractive women, on the other hand, did not need to demonstrate any other ability to be included. Smiling at the camera, they invited the reader's gaze and their own objectification. Northcliffe underlined this distinction when discussing photographs in cinema features: 'If you are using film pictures, they should either be charming ladies or action pictures.'[63] The respectability that was deemed essential to most papers was defined selectively to preclude discussion of 'controversial' issues such as birth control and venereal disease, but not to prohibit a cultural heterosexuality in which women were regarded as 'sex objects' and men were encouraged to view them in these terms.

Inter-War Debates

Modern Fashions

These various impulses of the popular press to provide fashion advice to women, to present pictures of attractive women, and to create 'talking points'

---

[61] Cudlipp, *Publish and be Damned!*, 115–17.   [62] Christiansen, *Headlines*, 163.
[63] Northcliffe Bulletins, 20 Oct. 1919.

out of issues of respectability, combined to generate huge interest in the conspicuous shifts in women's appearance that occurred over these years. Even
when space was severely limited during the war, the short skirts and uniforms
that many women donned on the home front provoked comment in both news
pages and correspondence columns. This simpler and less cumbersome
wartime attire seemed to offer yet more evidence of the opportunities the conflict was providing for women to break free from traditional restrictions and to
challenge notions of propriety. The ending of newsprint restrictions after 1918
enabled the return of the women's pages, and, encouraged by the increasing use
of photography, the new fashions of the 1920s were put under unprecedented
scrutiny. Short skirts and, later, short hair came to be regarded as expressions of
the changed character of 'modern women' and were frequently elevated into
symbols of modernity in the press. The subject was debated far beyond the
fashion columns: women's appearance had become a major news story.

Less than a week after the signing of the Armistice, Florence Kilpatrick in the
Daily Mail encouraged women to resist any return to restrictive pre-war styles.
The prospect that tight skirts would become the next fashion filled her with
worry:

we, daughters of freedom, are expected to walk the broad earth in that! . . . the time has
arrived to shake off the despot . . . Let us refuse to countenance this outrageous fashion. Land Girls, who have known the comfort of breeches; will you consent to be
pinioned in this way? Munitionettes, fellow war workers, all who have learned to
out-distance men in the fierce race for the omnibus, will you fall back into unequal
contest?[64]

Helen Newton in the *Daily News* agreed entirely, and predicted that henceforth
women would demonstrate a more discerning attitude to their clothing:

Before the war, fashion was a word that threw its magic spell over nearly every class of
women. No matter how ugly or ridiculous a hat or frock might be, if it were 'the
fashion' it was gladly worn by sensible women as well as by silly ones. But these four
years of war have taught most of us women the foolishness of wearing uncomfortable
and unsightly clothes just because fashion ordered it and I think it will be a very long
time before we see any such extravagances again.[65]

The assumption that styles of dress had a powerful influence upon behaviour went almost unchallenged. It seemed to be entirely natural to connect the
changes in fashions with the perceived shift in the character of young women.
Joan Kennedy in the *Mirror* was representative of this line of thought:

[64] *Daily Mail*, 15 Nov. 1918, 2.   [65] *Daily News*, 2 Dec. 1918, 8.

The waistline is almost a thing of the past, so corsets do not count. Short sleeves are coming in and dresses are diminishing at both ends . . . Modern dress certainly encourages freedom of movement, and along with freedom of movement goes freedom of mind—for mind and body work in partnership.[66]

For critics of the 'loose' behaviour of young women, the solution was evident. 'There is nothing like a tight corset for the purpose of putting a stop to the noisy "hoydenism" of the modern girl,' wrote 'Vespes' in response to Kennedy's article.[67] The battle-lines drawn up in months after the Armistice remained fiercely contested for the next two decades. Supporters of modern freedoms defended 'rational' dress from the assaults of those who believed that women had lost their femininity and charm by loosening corsets and cropping skirts and hair. At stake was nothing less than the moral balance of the nation—'a long skirt is followed by a long train of evil', announced the *Mail* in 1921—and the role of women in society.[68] In 1931 the National Union of Societies for Equal Citizenship carried by a large majority a resolution deploring the return of the long skirt. Mary Stocks declared after the meeting—in a statement that was reported by the press—that 'the coincidence between the freeing of women from hampering dress and the freeing of women in politics was really no co-incidence at all'.[69]

The popular press generally covered these issues in two distinct ways. In the fashion columns of the women's pages, where women were writing almost exclusively for women, the latest styles were usually reported enthusiastically and unfussily. Readers were given information about 'The New Bareback Fashion', advice on how to 'Choose Your Shingle', and a preview of 'Fashion Novelties from Monte Carlo'.[70] Here the emphasis was upon keeping up to date with shifting trends, and crucially in terms of attracting advertising revenue, discussing new clothes that were entering the department stores. (See Figure 5.3 for a good example of the acceptance of modern fashions.) Comparisons with older modes of dress were usually favourable:

Close-fitting clothes, neat hosiery, small hats, they compel admiration. At middle-age women retain the suggestion of youth . . . our grandmothers were drab with their monotonous black or dull, uninteresting colours, their pride in minute, wasp-like waists, fussy dolmans, and long-hair difficult to keep tidy . . . Compare them with the woman of today, with her altered outlook, her sparing use of frills, her support of fresh air and all it stands for.[71]

---

[66] *Daily Mirror*, 3 May 1919, 5.   [67] *Daily Mirror*, 6 May 1919, 5.
[68] *Daily Mail*, 9 Nov. 1921, 8.   [69] *Daily Mail*, 14 Mar. 1931, 9.
[70] *Daily Mirror*, 12 May 1919, 3; *Daily Express*, 14 Nov. 1924, 4; *Daily Mail*, 3 Mar. 1926, 15.
[71] *Daily Mail*, 30 June 1926, 15.

It's Your
AFTERNOON DRESS that COUNTS
By ODETTE

Slightly longer frocks that can be worn at afternoon parties, dinner-restaurants, and the cinema.

MUCH interest just now is centred on the type of dress that can be worn, under a fur coat or with one of the short jackets that are so becoming and fashionable, for formal afternoon and informal evening occasions.

Such dresses should have no frills or draperies about the corsage that would get crushed under a heavy or close-fitting coat, and consequently many of the features of the new mode will have to be avoided. There is no reason, however, why a frock with a close, unbroken outline and flat shoulder and neckline should not be as smart as anything that is required for day wear.

The dress at the extreme left of the sketch has the skirt of dull velvet attached to the upper part (which is of finely crocheted filet mesh net in silk to match) in a diagonal line which starts well above the waistline at the left side and dips to the hip at the other side. Both skirt and lower sleeves appear to be buttoned to the corsage.

tion to the winter wardrobe. It makes a distinctive finish to a collarless cloth coat, and can be left on the shoulders when the coat is removed to decorate an otherwise plain dress.

The next figure shows a dress which strikes quite a new note this season, when nearly every gown shows a combination of two or more colours.

With Triple Collar

It is of Burgundy red woollen crêpe de Chine, and the theme of the double basque is carried up into the corsage in a most effective way. It has a very original triple collar, in georgette of the same shade as the dress, which fastens at the back and can be removed when a coat is put on. The cuffs, which match the collar in material and design, are also detachable.

In cold weather, when a heavy fur coat is worn, chills are frequently caught by removing it in an indifferently heated room. The remaining sketch shows the ideal toilette for general afternoon wear with a fur coat in really cold weather.

FIG. 5.3. The women's pages of newspapers kept readers fully up to date with the latest fashions

FIG. 5.4. Cartoonists frequently contrasted pre- and post-war fashions,
reinforcing the perception that modern women were markedly different from
their predecessors (by W. K. Haselden; *Daily Mirror*, 7 September 1938, 6)

Elsewhere in the paper, however, editors sought to exploit the wider controversies surrounding these fashions, providing as they did excellent opportunities for colourful, illustrated copy. Leader-writers offered their opinions on skirt and hair length while journalists canvassed the views of notable figures. Photographers were sent to search out examples of daring post-war innovations such as the backless dress, and cartoonists produced numerous sketches which played on the contrasts between old and new fashions (see Figs. 2.3 and 5.4). Doctors were invited to give their 'medical' verdicts: some proclaimed the virtues of more practical clothing while others identified 'Shivering Women' damaging their health with 'winter outfits' that 'weigh 7 lbs'.[72] Clerical attacks on 'immodest dress' were also given prominence.[73] When Parisian designers indicated their desire to lengthen skirts in April 1922, the *Daily Mail* launched a full-blown campaign, headlined the 'Battle of the Skirts', which lasted well over a month. It was clear that the paper was on the side of brevity—'the short skirt is common sense', Northcliffe told his staff, and headlines declared enthusiastically that 'Active Women Want Them Short'—but Northcliffe was experienced enough to know that it was controversy that enticed newspaper

---

[72] *Daily Mail,* 23 May 1919, 6; 27 Nov. 1923, 7.
[73] e.g. *Daily Mail,* 17 Feb. 1920, 5; *Daily Express,* 11 July 1925, 9.

readers.[74] 'Give all opinions,' he told his news editor, Tom Clarke. 'It will be a terrific discussion.'[75]

By deliberately stoking up controversy and repeatedly underlining the significance of the contrast between 'old' and 'new' fashions, the press was drawing attention to the challenge posed by the post-war generation. Time and again, newspapers returned to this theme of modernity when considering fashions. Articles frequently portrayed clothing as being the measure of women's freedom. When the 'hobble skirt' was spotted on the fashion horizon in September 1923, for example, the *Mail* challenged its female readers to reveal the strength of their attachment to their new liberties:

The threat of the hobble skirt's return will inspire alarm among the modern generation of women who play games . . . We have now to see whether the emancipation of women has altered the position; if she submits to the hobble skirt it will be proof that the emancipation is only skin deep. The mere male would never allow his trousers to be frilled, or distended with whalebone, or slit up the side.[76]

This test was passed—indeed, over the next few years women raised the stakes yet further by cropping their 'crowning glory'. Shorter hair, in combination with the fashionable slim silhouette, appeared to give visual confirmation of the convergence of the sexes. Supporters of the new styles again used a rhetoric of modernity and convenience to defend themselves against accusations that they were losing their femininity: 'their hair adds greatly to that appearance of trimness which is characteristic of all ranks of society' in the post-war world, noted the *Mail*'s women's page. A writer in the *Mirror* argued that not only was short hair hygienic and easy for active women to manage, 'it helped on the equality of the sexes since, with the permanent wave, "doing the hair" took less time than it takes a man to shave'.[77]

These debates were reprised in the early 1930s, when beach trousers became the new subject of contention. Hannen Swaffer in the *Herald* was yet another to regard modern fashions as the manifestation of a more assertive generation:

At Margate, where the bathing machines once waited in a row . . . there is now a wonderful bathing pool to which young women walk down in trousers—scores of them. It is the latest sign of the challenge of New England . . . Not one girl looked embarrassed, nervous or modest. They wore them as though it was their right . . . They had seen girls doing it on the films, and now they were doing it for themselves. I am all for it. If I can wear trousers, why can't a girl?[78]

[74] Clarke, *Northcliffe Diary*, 263; *Daily Mail*, 20 Apr. 1922, 10.   [75] Clarke, *Northcliffe Diary*, 263.
[76] *Daily Mail*, 6 Sept. 1923, 8.   [77] *Daily Mail*, 30 June 1926, 15; *Daily Mirror*, 2 June 1934, 21.
[78] *Daily Herald*, 4 Aug. 1931, 6.

The attitude of the *Mail* on this issue shows how notions of respectability were shifting. Although wholeheartedly in favour of the short skirt, Northcliffe in 1921 made clear to his staff that he did not like 'the constant reference in the Paper to women in breeches. Many learned people think that masculinity in women is interfering with the British birth rate . . . If we keep suggesting masculinity in women, that type of woman will increase.'[79] By 1931, however, an editorial was prepared to accept that changes in the relationship between the sexes were such that this prohibition could no longer be maintained: 'an age that has discovered that woman is sufficiently like man to share in most of his occupations will be slow to deny her the use of the garments he has found convenient'.[80] (The beach trousers were also accepted by the women's pages, as Figure 5.5 shows.) But such admissions did not prevent papers from continuing to stir up controversy. The day after its editorial on the matter, the *Mail* revealed 'Women's Divided Views', and when a vicar declared in 1939 that women's trousers were 'the last step in the degradation of a nation before it is overtaken by calamity', the *Express* gleefully sent a correspondent to his church.[81] Reporting that no trousered women were in evidence for the Sunday service, the reporter wryly noted that a 'Man in Sports Shirt Took Front Pew'.[82]

Opponents of inter-war fashions, like this vicar, continued their struggle because they were convinced that these trends represented deeper truths about modern society. In their attacks on the 'mere functionality' of short skirts and cropped hair, for example, a number of critics revealed wider anxieties about a soulless mass society. Who would provide colour and inspiration if the 'Angel in the House' was not cultivating her charms? One writer in the *Mail* looked back in 'a spirit of tender regret' to the 'days when every woman, in expression and in clothes, preserved her individuality'; now, he was convinced that 'the time is approaching . . . when women will look as much alike as men have done since they cast off the velvet and wig . . . The standardisation of clothes has given women a standardised expression of face.'[83] A contributor to the *Express* in 1929 outlined at length the case that women were sacrificing the most precious aspects of femininity to compete with men:

The rush of modern life is mainly responsible for the lack of good grooming that one notices among women . . . modern women's debt and credit account for the past few years would read something like this did she ever bother about her accounts: Gains— The Vote, Equal Pay, Independence; Losses—Beauty, Charm, Good Dressing . . .

---

[79] Northcliffe Bulletins, 30 May 1921.   [80] *Daily Mail*, 22 May 1931, 8.
[81] *Daily Mail*, 23 May 1931, 7; *Daily Express*, 19 Aug. 1939, 9.   [82] *Daily Express*, 21 Aug. 1939, 5.
[83] *Daily Mail*, 27 Oct. 1924, 8.

FOR THE SUN-SEEKERS

A RIOT OF PYJAMA SUITS —BEACH HATS
by Jennifer

THE shops have high hopes of a glorious, sun-drenched summer.

You have only to look at the vast array of beach wear to see that they are buoyed up with optimism about the weather.

A big manufacturer of bathing suits told me recently that the two and three-piece suits are selling well, especially those which include long, full trousers.

The Younger Set are favouring the short knicker suits with pert little coats lined with Terry towelling in some lovely colour.

"And why shouldn't beach suits become as popular here as abroad?" said a member of this firm to me one day while the rain was pouring down and an east wind penetrated to one's very bones.

I murmured something about our unspeakable climate and how wretched it is to walk on wind-swept beaches in bathing kit.

He told me then how the British manufacturers are now making suits specially for the English summer, wet or fine.

Three-piece and four-piece suits of soft, warm wool in place of the thin cotton fabrics.

THE SAILOR VOGUE

"The trouser vogue is here," he said. "It will be seen everywhere during the holiday months. Not only on the bathing beaches, but in country bungalows and gardens."

"Everything to match" is another slogan, and each suit is provided with its accompanying coat, cap, sun-hat, shoes and bag.

The most useful thing is to buy one entire outfit in a two-colour scheme. With this as a basis you can ring the changes by having two different-coloured swimming caps, with scarf, shoes and etceteras.

The trousers vary in shape. The most popular are certainly the wide-legged sailor ones. Others are decorated with bands, or spots, embroideries or inserted pleats.

There is the suit of Persian outline with the trouser legs caught in tightly round the ankles.

Colours are marvellous. You will see a white suit "trimmed" with coral-coloured spots, a little jacket bound with the coral colour and

Navy blue stockinet beach suit with wide trousers, tunic blouse and white scarf-tie with blue polka dots.

beneath the suit itself the "swimmer." Venetian green, surf, and the French "matelot" colours—red, blue and white—are greatly favoured.

If you are a bathing fiend then it is advisable to get two or even three "swimmers." While one is drying the others are there for use, either for the water or sun-bathing.

Never have I seen such a collection of beach hats as there are this year.

Some are of quite modest proportions—others of fantastic size. I measured one, and without exaggeration it was a yard across.

There are linens, natural and coloured, stitched cretonnes and cambries, but most novel and amusing of all are the cartwheel shapes of light-as-thistledown basket straw.

FAIRY TALE HATS

Some are plain, others in clear gay shades. Raffia decorates many, or the straw will be woven into queer little designs. You will see some with one side of the brim in bright green and the other in equally bright blue.

Outstanding among all these by no means ordinary hats was an enormous Spanish model, with chimney-pot crown cut off square like a Welsh hat, allied to a huge brim from

---

TO-MORROW—

—Jennifer's article will deal with Space-Saving Furniture

---

each side of which dangled the most curious little straw blobby tassel.

And most of these fairy-tale hats are priced under ten shillings.

Sandals are the shoe fancy of the moment. The beach ones are made of plaited leather or thick canvassy linen. They are all given names like the "Cleopatra" or the "Eastern."

But sandals are not confined to beach wear. There are the indoor sandals of various shapes like the plain grecians just slit down the sides, generally in velvet with contrasting coloured heels—fairly low. Shebas are made in crêpe de Chine, with big tufts of curled ostrich feathers on the low-cut vamps, while the pompeiians are much more elaborate with intertwined straps.

This beach suit of golden brown has sand-coloured contrasts. Notice the inset pleats in the trousers and the jaunty sleeveless coat. (Wolsey.)

FIG. 5.5. Although too unfeminine for some observers, beach trousers were praised by newspapers' fashion columnists like Jennifer in the *Daily Mirror* (*Daily Mirror*, 4 May 1931, 23)

women do not realise how much they have lost during the past few years in their quest for personal independence.[84]

Similarly, Mary Burdett in the *Mirror* argued that only a return to Victorian fashions could restore both the elegance and the modesty that were lacking in modern women. The crinoline dress, she claimed, was the 'essence of femininity' enhancing grace and charm:

Could not some enterprising dress designer make an effort to bring back a modified form of the crinoline dress . . . By returning to the crinoline we would . . . pave the way for a revival in manners. Women would cease to be caricatures of the opposite sex, but instead would assiduously cultivate that womanly charm now, alas, almost extinct.[85]

Such pleas were coming to seem ever more old-fashioned, however, and merely served to sharpen the definition of the 'modern generation' against 'Victorianism'. Placed amidst photographs of 'bathing belles' and cinema stars keen to show off their 'sex appeal', as well as adverts and women's page features displaying the latest trends, these were voices from another era in newspapers committed to modernity.

A New Morality?

The freeing of women from restrictive forms of dress seemed to be an essential part of a wider loosening of 'Victorian' proprieties. Ray Strachey believed in 1928 that 'the chaperon has vanished with the crinoline, and freedom and companionship between the sexes have taken the place of the old uneasy restraint'.[86] The approach of the press to this apparent relaxation of moral codes mirrored its treatment of the changing fashions: newspapers were generally on the side of modernity, but were determined to generate talking points and headlines in the process. Mrs Gordon Stables, writing in the *Express* in May 1919, provided a typical example of a women's page article celebrating the new social opportunities: 'the girl of today has to thank the war for her emancipation from the restrictions which bad, sad old Mrs Grundy sought for so long to place upon her masculine friendships. And this emancipation is to spell for her a widened outlook on life as well as a far profounder understanding of her fellow man.'[87] Women were occasionally allowed to express an active sexuality with an openness that would have been considered improper before

---

[84] *Daily Express*, 24 May 1929, 5.   [85] *Daily Mirror*, 1 June 1934, 12.
[86] R. Strachey, *The Cause: A Short History of the Women's Movement in Great Britain* (London: G. Bell, 1928), 387.   [87] *Daily Express*, 7 May 1919, 3.

the war. A 'Flapper', contributing to the main feature page of the *Express*, proclaimed that

My one terror in life is the thought that the time will come when my skirts will have to be at least two inches longer than they are now . . . I know that my shapely legs are the admiration of pale young City men . . . I make my own pleasure, supply my own excitement, manufacture my own thrills . . . No ordinary natural man can resist me. I have made it my study not only to attract, but also to hold in bonds that no one can break. I am a flapper, a coquette, and every man is my slave.[88]

Such boldness was unusual, but the fact that this article could be published without any editorial word of condemnation or qualification was a sign of the significant shifts in public discussions of sex that had been encouraged by the work of Marie Stopes and other sexologists and marriage reformers.[89] Features on the cinema, which were becoming increasingly prominent in the popular press, also had the effect of bringing sexuality further to the forefront of public discourse. Stars such as Rudolph Valentino were explicitly developed as 'heartthrobs' for female audiences, while articles called on film directors to 'Give English "Vamps" a Chance' to prove their 'sex appeal' and allure in major films.[90]

As with post-war fashions, however, nothing was more effective than controversy in emphasizing that old mores were being challenged. Once again, the *Daily Mail* was at the forefront, choosing to whip up a debate on the practice of 'mixed bathing'.[91] When Donald Clark, a councillor from Tonbridge, Kent, declared in 1920 that mixed bathing on beaches was 'the worst public scandal of our so-called civilisation', that women swam purely 'for the purposes of display', and that 'much of the unrest in the country is due to the barbarous licence in women's dress', he came to the attention of the staff of the *Mail*.[92] Tom Clarke, the news editor, recalled suggesting 'half-jestingly' to Northcliffe that the paper

ought to commission the councillor to go round the seaside resorts and write his views of what the bathing costumes were, and what he thought they should be. 'Capital', cried the Chief. 'Arrange it at once. Plan a tour and pay all his expenses. Send a first-class reporter with him to help him . . . Send a photographer too . . . It will be one of the best holiday-season features we have had for years.'[93]

---

[88] *Daily Express*, 2 May 1923, 6.

[89] M. Collins, *Modern Love: An Intimate History of Men and Women in Twentieth Century Britain* (London: Atlantic Books, 2003), ch. 2.   [90] *Daily Express*, 6 Mar. 1928, 10.

[91] The issue of 'mixed bathing' is discussed in C. Horwood, ' "Girls Who Arouse Dangerous Passions": Women and Bathing, 1900–39', *Women's History Review*, 9/4 (2000), 653–73. On the *Mail*'s interest in the subject, see 659–62.   [92] His articles in the *Mail* repeated these charges, e.g. *Daily Mail*, 14 Aug. 1920, 3.

[93] Clarke, *Northcliffe Diary*, 162–3.

For Northcliffe, this was, as Tom Clarke recognized, a 'deliberate move in his campaign for brightness in the paper'. But the controversy that was initiated was not only long-lasting—reports on this issue were still being filed at the end of the decade—it was also significant in focusing attention on shifting notions of morality. Robert Graves and Alan Hodge recalled the campaign twenty years later as a reflection of the increasing acceptance of modernity as 'lively progress'.[94] By presenting Councillor Clark as a representative of Victorian propriety and then turning him into little more than a figure of ridicule, the *Mail* was helping both to undermine 'traditional' standards and to clarify definitions of 'modern behaviour'. When some of what Tom Clarke described as the 'older school' *Mail* journalists complained that the feature was 'not only frivolous, but also getting near the pornographic', Northcliffe was unrepentant: 'Everybody is reading these articles . . . We must not become too respectable.'[95] Nevertheless, Northcliffe's instinctive populism was also supplemented by more sophisticated arguments defending mixed bathing and drawing on recent sexological literature. January Mortimer, a regular *Mail* columnist, was given the task of outlining the basic editorial line. The campaign against mixed bathing, she argued, was fed by 'two of the deadliest moral poisons in our society—namely prudery and prurience'. Referring to the work of Havelock Ellis—still regarded in some quarters as 'indecent'—Mortimer continued that

An aesthetic perception of the human body, which has always been regarded by morally educated people as beautiful and marvellous, is one of the chief safeguards of purity . . . The simple and charming pictures of girls bathing and dancing on the seashore which appear almost daily in the newspapers indicate that we, as a people, are awakening to the fact that the 'human form divine' is actually beautiful . . . The mixed bathing cult is a means of refining public morals and not, as the unthinking imagine, an incentive to vice.[96]

As with the skirt controversy, observers in the mid-1930s looked back on these disputes as if they were from another era. The *Mirror* could barely contain its mirth when it discovered in 1935 that the Ministry of Health had been forced to instruct a local council that its regulations on female bathing costumes were unrealistic given modern fashions. An editorial pointed out that 'it is now impossible to buy the serge tunic-and-knickerbockers outfit held to be decent in that remote age' and asked its readers: 'Are there any buried by-laws anywhere requiring bustles or even crinolines for the promenade?'[97]

[94] Graves and Hodge, *Long Week-End*, 110.   [95] Clarke, *Northcliffe Diary*, 163.
[96] *Daily Mail*, 27 July 1920, 6.   [97] *Daily Mirror*, 26 June 1935, 11.

If 'Victorian' restrictions on heterosocial mixing came under attack, so too did the supposedly 'Victorian' inegalitarian model of marriage. By the early 1920s papers across the political spectrum supported legislation to end the 'double standard of morality' that was enshrined in the divorce system. The *Mail* consistently backed the reforming efforts of the former Lord Chancellor, Lord Buckmaster, declaring in 1920 that the 'existing divorce law is causing an immense amount of domestic suffering and unhappiness which can be relieved by wise and humane legislation'.[98] In 1923 the *Herald* welcomed the Matrimonial Causes Act, equalizing the grounds of divorce, as a recognition of 'Common Justice to Women', while the *News* presented the Act as further evidence that 'justice and more humane ideas in regard to women . . . are steadily making headway in the House of Commons'.[99] The *Express* and the *Mirror* both accused opponents of the reform as being guilty of hypocrisy.[100] The notion of 'companionate marriage', introduced in 1928 by the American authors Ben Lindsey and Wainwright Evans in their work *The Revolt of Modern Youth*, also received publicity in the press; the *Express* could begin an article on Lindsey in 1931 with the claim that 'everybody has heard of "Judge" Ben Lindsey'.[101] But many others had already argued that husbands would have to treat 'modern wives' differently. Indeed, some of the long-standing demands of the women's movement were once again being advocated in the name of modernity rather than 'feminism'. 'A Cambridge Man', writing a major feature article for the *Mail* in 1928, was representative of this tendency:

It never seems to have occurred to our ancestors that marriage could be an affair between equals. It was the man that mattered then, and the Happy Couple were not, as we see it, a couple at all . . . Men have ceased to be the only piece in the game, and with women an equal social unit, marriage has become a very different enterprise . . . The demand is companionship, and that is the main reason why a man and a girl marry nowadays.[102]

Problem and advice columns, which became increasingly common on women's pages during the 1930s, tended to reinforce the idea that emotional compatibility and companionship were at the heart of lasting relationships. And, as Chapter 7 demonstrates, husbands were warned that they had to continue to work on their marriage rather than taking their wives for granted.

Calls for a reformulation of marital relationships inevitably provoked a reaction. 'Let us hear less talk of "equality" in marriage,' pleaded a frustrated

---

[98] *Daily Mail*, 16 Nov. 1920, 6; see also *Daily Mail*, 8 Nov. 1922, 8.

[99] *Daily Herald*, 3 Mar. 1923, 1; *Daily News*, 3 Mar. 1923, 1.

[100] *Daily Express*, 3 Mar. 1923, 6; *Daily Mirror*, 5 Mar. 1923, 7.

[101] *Daily Express*, 1 Mar. 1928, 3; 2 Oct. 1931, 7.   [102] *Daily Mail*, 17 Mar. 1928, 10.

Mrs James Rodney in 1931: 'Every woman who loves naturally wants to be protected, guided and even ordered sometimes. She longs to have her husband's "I won't allows" and it is all nonsense thinking there can be any joy in the marriage where each goes an individual way.'[103] It was clear, however, that those championing modernity were dictating the terms of this debate about marriage. Returning to this theme two months later, Rodney accepted both that marital practices had already changed, and that her solution was 'Victorian'. 'Should husbands reassert their lost authority', she asked, 'and become masterful once more?' Her answer was in the affirmative: 'Wives have had it far too much their own way,' she announced, imploring them instead to 'Be More Victorian'.[104] But an appeal to rediscover 'Victorian' ways was easy to discredit and outmanoeuvre when the language of modernity associated the customs of older generations with repression and restriction. As with the fashion controversy, criticisms of post-war gender roles remained, but they were covertly undermined by their context in papers that had clearly come to terms with the central features of 'modern life'.

Women as Decoration

In a number of ways, then, popular newspapers both accepted and supported a 'modern' conception of femininity in which women were freed from restrictive attire and what Ray Strachey described as the 'hampering conventions' of an earlier age.[105] Every photograph and sketch of a 'flapper' with cropped hair and a short skirt subtly reinforced the perception that women had made a break from the past, and these perceptions were sharpened by press controversies that underlined the significance of these shifts. While space was by no means denied to critics of modernity, they were inevitably on the defensive in papers heavily committed both to retaining young readers and to including fashion advertising and cinema publicity. Yet the profundity of these changes was in many respects exaggerated by contemporaries. For if women had cast aside some of the more elaborate and physically restrictive fashions, it was far more difficult to escape from the underlying ideas defining them as the decorative sex, and they continued to be judged on their appearance far more than men. Indeed, slightly more liberal attitudes to the depiction and discussion of 'sex appeal' ensured that women were sexualized in press photography as never before.

This tendency can be seen clearly in the *Mail* controversies examined earlier. When Northcliffe contrived the Battle of the Skirts campaign, he was

103 *Daily Mail*, 4 June 1931, 17.   104 *Daily Mail*, 3 Aug. 1931, 15.
105 Strachey, *The Cause*, 389.

helping to bring into focus a modern femininity which he supported, within limits; yet he was also well aware that he was displaying these same 'modern women' for male titillation. Tom Clarke recalled the instructions of his proprietor:

Get plenty of sketches by well-known artists—photographs and drawings illustrating the comparisons between the long and the short skirts. Get hold of back numbers of *Punch*, with illustrations of the ugly long skirts of a decade ago. Print as many as you can. Get people like Arthur Ferrier and Gladys Peto to draw pictures of the modern girl in her alluring short skirt. Plenty of legs . . . don't forget, plenty of pictures and sketches of pretty ankles.[106]

The mixed bathing features were also deliberately designed to provide sexy material. The photographer sent to accompany Councillor Clark was told to return with 'plenty of pictures of pretty bathing girls'—and indeed the older staff were not the only ones to complain that some of the material was verging on the 'pornographic', with several readers sending in letters of protest.[107] For all January Mortimer's fine words about a chaste celebration of the 'human form divine', Northcliffe was clearly exploiting the tastes of a prurient market.

The Armistice predictions that fashion would no longer cast 'its magic spell over nearly every class of woman' seemed to have little impact on the presentation of new trends. If post-war styles were more practical, women's page 'experts' continued to portray them as dictated from 'above', with readers ignoring them at their peril. The *Mirror* in May 1919, for example, outlined 'Dame Fashion's Peace Terms' and the 'Decrees for the Coming Summer'.[108] Fashion was still a coercive and unsympathetic force to which women were advised to submit even if they were not always entirely convinced themselves. Joan Beringer in 1934 discussed the forthcoming changes in necklines:

For many months now we have accustomed ourselves to the throttle neck mode. And how convenient this fashion has been to the woman who has something to conceal, only that woman knows! . . . It will be with mixed feelings, then, that many women will look forward to wearing the low-cut formal gown once more. But wear it they will.[109]

The need for a constant stream of material to fill fashion columns ensured that some suggestions verged on the bizarre. The *Daily Express* outlined in 1926, for example, the 'Arms-Akimbo Fashion' that was being used to show off capes:

---

[106] Clarke, *Northcliffe Diary*, 262–3. [107] Ibid. 163. [108] *Daily Mirror*, 12 May 1919, 4.
[109] *Daily Mail*, 17 Jan. 1934, 19.

The 'Washerwoman Pose', in which the aspirant to the height of fashion assumes an arms-akimbo attitude which at one time would have been considered inelegant, if not vulgar, is daily gaining in popularity. It keeps pace with the advance of the cape vogue, which makes a great appeal to women in search of smart summer wraps . . .[110]

Of course, there was a large element of fantasy in these features. Journalists were well aware that the vast majority of their readers could not possibly afford most of the fashions that were displayed. Nevertheless, there were vicarious pleasures to be enjoyed in discovering what would be worn by society ladies at Ascot, Cowes, and court, or by film stars at premières. In this sense, as Sally Alexander points out, the media and advertising were only fulfilling genuine audience demands and enabling women to dream of more glamorous lifestyles. Women often customized cheaper or home-made clothing using ideas from fashion columns, allowing both a sense of participation and an expression of individuality. Readers did not necessarily conform in the way the texts invited, and clothing remained a means of making personal statements.[111] At the same time, the expectations of female beauty that were generated by this material could place burdens on all women. An editorial in the *Mail* suggested that an attractive appearance was such an essential female virtue that it was worth teaching in schools: 'It is as important for women to be charming as to be good housewives, and therefore there is a great deal to be said for teaching girls, as many schools have begun to do, how to cultivate good taste in dress—how, that is, to make the best of the materials they can command.'[112] As Haselden observed light-heartedly in a cartoon for the *Mirror*, the media's concern to find 'beauty' meant that it risked losing sight of 'reality': the 'plain man' found it difficult to reconcile 'the thousands of beautiful girls proved to exist' by the *Mirror's* photographs 'with his daily experiences in tubes and such-like public places'.[113]

The women's pages emphasized the double role of decoration and domestic worker both implicitly and explicitly. As the content analysis demonstrates, the subjects of fashion and housewifery dominated the columns. The duties of the ideal wife were also spelt out in detail. Jane Gordon in the *News Chronicle*, for example, used the increasingly pervasive language of psychology to explain the consequences if the correct balance between the work of housewifery and the cultivation of beauty was not achieved:

[110] *Daily Express*, 10 July 1926, 9.

[111] S. Alexander, 'Becoming a Woman in London in the 1920s and 1930s', in ead., *Becoming a Woman and Other Essays* (New York: New York University Press, 1995).

[112] *Daily Mail*, 2 May 1921, 6.   [113] *Daily Mirror*, 5 Apr. 1919, 7.

It is not really fair to your husband to keep his home nice at the expense of your personal appearance. You may entertain beautifully, but if your hands are rough and red, your husband will succumb, either consciously or unconsciously, to an inferiority complex. If when you first marry you make up your mind to give yourself an hour's beauty treatment every Friday evening you will be at your best for the weekends when your husband will be free to admire you.[114]

Indeed, the expectations of what women should do to manage their appearance were in some ways increasing. In particular, these years saw a marked shift in press attitudes towards the use of cosmetics.[115] Vera Brittain recalled that up until the First World War, make-up was regarded, in middle-class circles at least, as the sign of an 'amateur prostitute'.[116] In the early post-war years, women's page contributors maintained a stern dislike of cosmetics. 'Don't Camouflage', advised Leslie Scott in the *Express* in 1919:

I'm not an aged relic of Early Victorian days, for nobody hates a shiny nose or a greasy countenance more than I do . . . [But] no cosmetics under the sun, however alluring the advertisements, are going to do Dame Nature out of her job. And for the preservation of that complexion, clean water, a judicious use of pure soap, fresh air and regular exercise beat all the sham inventions absolutely hollow.[117]

'Do not "paint" or "rouge",' agreed 'FS' in the *Mail* the following year. 'These methods of growing roses in the garden of the face are very bad. They injure the skin and produce a coarse, artificial effect.'[118] 'When a woman makes up . . . the face has a smooth, waxen look like some hairdresser's dummy,' argued Mrs Adrian Ross in the *Mirror*. 'It is just a painted face, pretty in a way, shallow and soulless.'[119] In November 1922, meanwhile, Hilda Nield in the *Daily News* censured modern 'doll girls': 'The present day use of over much and often very badly selected powder, rouge and such "face colourings", lip sticks and eye pencils by girls of schoolgirl age has nothing to excuse it. It is foolish and pitiable and more than a little sickening.'[120]

By the end of the 1920s, however, the balance of opinion was very different. 'Exercise and Cleanliness Are Great Factors, But You Mustn't Neglect Make-Up' was the headline of a *Mirror* article in May 1929 in which the actress Clare

---

[114] *News Chronicle*, 12 Nov. 1935, 5.
[115] On the take-up of cosmetics, see I. Zweiniger-Bargielowska, 'The Body and Consumer Culture', in ead. (ed.), *Women in Twentieth Century Britain* (Harlow: Longman, 2001), 187–8. On similar changes in America, see M. Pumphrey, 'The Flapper, the Housewife and the Making of Modernity', *Cultural Studies*, 1/2 (May 1987), 179–94, esp. 189–90; K. Peiss, 'Making Up, Making Over: Cosmetics, Consumer Culture, and Women's Identity', in V. de Grazia and E. Furlough (eds.), *The Sex of Things* (Berkeley: University of California Press, 1996). [116] V. Brittain, *Testament of Youth* (first pub. 1933; London: Virago, 1986), 429.
[117] *Daily Express*, 7 May 1919, 3. [118] *Daily Mail*, 13 July 1920, 11.
[119] *Daily Mirror*, 24 May 1921, 7. [120] *Daily News*, 7 Nov. 1922, 2.

Hardwicke offered her expert advice: 'In my opinion make-up is a modern necessity. No woman can do without it, for even if her skin is perfect, she needs a certain amount of cream and powder to preserve its beauty.'[121] Only the previous week another feature had declared 'Oh These Beauty Aids! Believe in Them and They'll Do What They Claim—But You Must Have Faith'.[122] 'Don't Economise with Beauty Aids', agreed Diana Wynyard in the *Express*.[123] 'Gone is the old convention that young girls should not make-up,' remarked the paper's women's page in 1932; 'that would be impossible under the glaring modern lights and wearing modern colours and dresses.'[124] Although men might protest that cosmetics are unnecessary, another *Express* contributor noted, 'just look at the women he admires and you will see that they do not practise his preachings any more than you do'. Whereas previously it had been claimed that nature could not be surpassed, now the 'imperfections' of the natural appearance needed to be supplemented: 'So long as your facial beauty looks natural, and not painted on, he will be perfectly prepared to admire it and ask no questions. Cosmetics, after all, are intended primarily to make us look healthy; to supplement natural colour deficiencies.'[125]

The influence of Hollywood seems to have been the most important cause of this shift in attitudes towards cosmetics. As Joan Beringer argued in the *Mail* in 1935, after the war 'cinema took over the role of instructor' in matters of beauty, and women sought to emulate the heavily made-up stars: 'every woman sees a wish picture of herself in the glamorous heroine of the film she is watching'.[126] By the Second World War surveys found that 90 per cent of women under 30 applied cosmetics.[127] Keeping up with this interest in grooming, women's page features recommended increasingly detailed and rigorous beauty routines. 'Personal beauty treatment is like good housekeeping,' observed Jane Gordon in the *News Chronicle*: 'it has to be tackled every day, but many women are inclined to be a little unreasonable about this . . . No beauty treatment is permanent any more than dusting is permanent.'[128] The number of 'essential' techniques and aids were multiplying. Electrolysis was recommended as the 'best method' for removing hairs on the lip and chin.[129] Women over 30 were warned to 'Look Out for Beauty's Danger Points', but were consoled with information about useful remedies: 'Incipient lines on the face can be defeated by patting in special anti-wrinkle creams at night . . .

---

[121] *Daily Mirror*, 25 May 1929, 16.   [122] *Daily Mirror*, 18 May 1929, 16.

[123] *Daily Express*, 22 Oct. 1931, 5.   [124] *Daily Express*, 9 Feb. 1932, 5.

[125] *Daily Express*, 8 May 1935, 5.

[126] *Daily Mail*, 7 May 1935, 23; see also J. Stacey, *Stargazing: Hollywood Cinema and Female Spectatorship* (London: Routledge, 1994).   [127] Zweiniger-Bargielowska, 'The Body and Consumer Culture', 187.

[128] *News Chronicle*, 4 June 1934, 5.   [129] *News Chronicle*, 26 Oct. 1933, 5.

There are special reducing lotions that can be used for the double chin and the pad at the back of the neck.'[130] Advertisements reiterated these messages, offering products that would enable an alluring appearance to be maintained. Without them, it was suggested, women might miss out on the partner of their dreams. Wenlo White's tone was typical: '1-2-3 And Ugly Hair Is Gone! Men hate superfluous hair. Ugly hair growths on the arms or even faintly showing through silk stockings, disgust a man so much that he can never find a woman attractive who suffers in this way.'[131] Winifred Holtby assumed that she would be immune from the blandishments of these beauty advertisements, but, as she confessed in May 1935, found herself struck by the occasional doubt:

I admit that after reading the more luscious advertisements in the daily and weekly press, I feel my convictions a little shaken . . . So powerful, so skilful and so universal is the propaganda, stabbing our most tender vanities, stirring our most sensitive secrets, hitting all the most delicate susceptibilities of our nature, that I think she must be a robust woman who is not occasionally stricken by these qualms.[132]

There were also increasing pressures on women to maintain a slim figure. In 1923 a contributor to the *Daily News* revealed her frustrations on this matter in an article headlined 'Thin Women—How They Irritate Their Stout Sisters'. 'This is the willowy woman's day,' she observed. 'She gazes upon us from books and hoarding advertisements . . . The public print teems with methods for reducing flesh.'[133] Slimming advice certainly appeared to be becoming more prominent on newspaper women's pages, with self-discipline rather than 'tight-lacing' now required to produce the desired silhouette. A variety of experts from doctors to athletes were called in to offer their hints.[134] The tone was not always sympathetic, such as when Lady Kitty Vincent told the *Express* how to 'Skip and Be Slim': 'With few exceptions, we are all born with good figures; they are our natural birthright and Nature meant us to keep them. We lose them through our own laziness, and let me be candid, our own greed. There is absolutely no reason why we should not all be as sylph-like at eighty as at eighteen.'[135]

This is not to claim that there were no dissenting voices. Some criticized 'This Fetish of the Filleted Figure',[136] while Jane Gordon was rather more charitable on the subject of weight than she was on wrinkles. Searching for fashions suitable for larger women in 1935, she declared that 'It is nothing short

---

[130] *News Chronicle*, 11 June 1934, 5.   [131] *Daily Herald*, 7 Aug. 1931, 11.

[132] W. Holtby, 'The Best of Life', *Good Housekeeping* (May 1935), cited in P. Berry and A. Bishop, (eds.), *Testament of a Generation: The Journalism of Vera Brittain and Winifred Holtby* (London: Virago, 1985), 87–8.

[133] *Daily News*, 21 Feb. 1923, 2.

[134] e.g. *Daily Express*, 20 Oct. 1933, 5; 15 Feb. 1937, 14; *Daily Mail*, 1 May 1931, 19; *Daily Mirror*, 24 May 1937, 22.   [135] *Daily Express*, 8 July 1926, 5.   [136] *Daily Mail*, 24 Apr. 1928, 19.

of cruel to brand a woman's figure as "difficult" just because she gets generous marks from a weighing-machine and tape measure.'[137] Nevertheless, she recognized the reality of the situation: 'This weight and measurement persecution has been going on for so many years that no one dares stand up against it.' Film columns began to discuss openly the figures of female stars. The *Express* noted in 1935, for example, that Mae West had lost weight for the film *Goin' to Town*, and, when featuring Ann Sheridan in 1939, disclosed her weight, height, bust, and waist size.[138] By the end of the 1930s it became common to supply the so-called 'vital statistics' of female film stars. Such women were held up as aspirational models for newspaper readers, and advertisements and fashion columns revealed how to emulate the stars— but the difficulty of doing so without their resources and expert support was usually underplayed.

The left-wing press did little to challenge the assumption that women had a special duty to maintain an attractive appearance. In the 1920s, certainly, the *Herald* devoted less space on its women's page to fashion and beauty than other papers. Of thirty-five samples used for content analysis, only in six cases were fashion and beauty not the largest category, and four of these were in the *Herald* (1919, 1923, 1927, and 1931). Nevertheless, in each of these *Herald* samples, fashion and beauty still accounted for about a quarter of the total space. The distinctive feature of the paper's columns throughout the 1920s was a determination to present the latest styles in ways that would be affordable to a less wealthy class of reader: 'Why shouldn't the working-woman take a pride in dainty headwear as well as the leisured lady who has little to do but wonder what suits her best? Any of these pretty caps can be easily made from scraps of lace, net or ninon, and such work is a fascinating pastime for winter evenings'.[139] There was a corresponding reluctance to celebrate the fashions of society women at the traditional events of the 'season'. Scathing captions below pictures from Ascot in June 1925 criticized the ostentation of the spectators: 'while official figures were revealing the increasing suffering of the working class, "Society" was flaunting its wealth, mostly unearned, at Ascot'.[140] Yet the underlying attitudes of the *Herald*'s material were similar to those of the rest of the press. In April 1927, for example, the paper suggested 'A New Hat for Easter': 'It is true that a new hat has a tonic effect on a woman. You must have something new for Easter, and, if it won't run to a whole new outfit, spend what you can spare on a hat. Here are three sketches from a shop

[137] *News Chronicle*, 1 Nov. 1935, 5.   [138] *Daily Express*, 3 May 1935, 8; 29 Aug. 1939, 15.

[139] *Daily Herald*, 6 Jan. 1921, 7.

[140] *Daily Herald*, 17 June 1925, cited in Richards, 'Conscription, Conformity and Control', 170.

window.'[141] After the Odhams relaunch in 1930, the differences narrowed even further. The tone of Mary Grace's report from Ascot in May 1930 offered a dramatic contrast to that of 1925:

Ascot is the great fashion parade of the year. As many people go to look at the dresses as at the horses. To a dressmaker an Ascot success means a very great deal. For it will be copied and recopied for months to come. Ascot fashions are thus of interest to every woman, as they soon become in more economical forms the fashions for all.[142]

On the subjects of cosmetics and slimming, the paper was entirely conventional. And throughout the 1930s both the *Herald* and the *News Chronicle* displayed the same enthusiasm for printing photographs of 'bathing belles' and alluring film stars as their competitors. There was to be no mainstream press opposition to the sexualization and scrutiny of women.

The Persistence of the Double Standard?

If the left-wing papers did not disrupt assumptions about female appearance, they were rather more willing than the rest of the daily press to explore the more liberal attitudes to the discussion of such issues as birth control and sexuality. For despite their celebrations of an end to 'Victorian prudery' evident in such features as the Mixed Bathing campaign, and the welcoming of more egalitarian patterns of marriage and divorce, the conservative papers remained very suspicious of more far-reaching challenges to traditional morality. Women continued to be valued according to their sexual purity, and they were held responsible for maintaining sexual proprieties. Mary Boazman in the *Mail* argued that

A girl cannot sow her wild oats as a man has been accustomed to do. Her experience must be too dearly bought . . . Its young girls are the nation's very precious jewels. Upon their purity and sense of right depends the future well-being of the nation, and the pity is great if either is injured by careless guardianship.[143]

In the *Mirror*, similarly, young women were warned to 'guard against any indiscretion in yourself or in your young man'. After all, 'there is a certain moral standard to be observed even though at times it may be hard . . . Do not put yourself under conditions whereby your natural desires tend to be unduly aroused . . . Men despise in their hearts the girls who make themselves cheap.'[144] From this perspective, pre-marital sex was the fault of girls who *made*

141 *Daily Herald*, 2 Apr. 1927, 7.   142 *Daily Herald*, 26 May 1930, 5.
143 *Daily Mail*, 13 July 1920, 6.   144 *Daily Mirror*, 13 Nov. 1935, 12.

themselves cheap: boys, with their greater levels of sexual desire, could hardly be blamed for succumbing to temptation. The expert advice on the increasingly prominent problem columns sometimes reinforced such attitudes. Dorothy Dix in the *Mirror* criticized an unmarried nurse when she asked what to do about a male doctor who was trying to court her: 'It is very unwise of you to allow this doctor to come and see you and I strongly advise you to consider your good name. Conduct of this sort is one of the unforgivable sins in hospitals.'[145] Cyril James, writing in the same paper, even went so far as to claim that women were ultimately responsible for many sexual crimes:

I set out to find how many 'decent' girls would, without invitation, speak to me and strike up an acquaintanceship . . . I met ten women—'nice girls' as we call them, and in each instance they made my acquaintanceship first . . . What fools girls can be! . . . What can [welfare workers] hope to do in face of this reckless search for a good time at any cost?[146]

At the same time as printing pictures of sexy women for male consumption, newspapers emphasized the importance of women controlling their sexuality. The press was also very reluctant to discuss the physical and biological aspects of sex, and thereby reinforced the widespread female ignorance about the body. Women's magazines began to give advice about sex after the success of Marie Stopes's *Married Love*, but newspapers seemed to have retained a more cautious attitude, conscious of their mixed audience of all ages.[147] When Isabel Hutton, a doctor, tried to secure press publicity for her sex education pamphlet *The Hygiene of Marriage*, for example, the editor of a popular daily told her that 'we never touch sex stuff'.[148]

In the context of these silences surrounding sex and sexuality, James Douglas's famous denunciation of Radclyffe Hall's lesbian novel *The Well of Loneliness* in the *Sunday Express* in 1928 was highly unusual. Editors generally regarded lesbianism as an unsuitable subject for publicity, but Douglas, who had sustained a long-running campaign against 'sex novels', was determined to obstruct what he regarded as a perverted attempt by 'inverts' to undermine Christianity itself:[149] 'We must protect our children against their specious fallacies and sophistries. Therefore, we must banish their propaganda from our book-shops and libraries. I would rather give a healthy boy or a healthy girl a

---

[145] *Daily Mirror*, 4 Mar. 1936, 25.   [146] *Daily Mirror*, 2 Dec. 1936, 12.

[147] L. Hall, *Sex, Gender and Social Change since 1880* (Basingstoke: Macmillan, 2000), 108; C. L. White, *Women's Magazines 1693–1968* (London: Joseph, 1970), 107–8.

[148] Hall, *Sex, Gender and Social Change*, 111.

[149] On these events, see D. Souhami, *The Trials of Radclyffe Hall* (London: Virago, 1999), 167–230; A. Travers, *Bound and Gagged: A Secret History of Obscenity in Britain* (London: Profile, 2000), ch. 3.

phial of prussic acid than this novel. Poison kills the body, but moral poison kills the soul.'[150] This episode should not be taken as the start of a crusade against lesbianism, however. The suspicion of single women as potential 'inverts' has been considerably overstated, for most newspapers disliked even to make the suggestion.[151] Only four months after Hall's obscenity trial, for example, there was a high-profile court case involving a woman masquerading as a man, the infamous 'Colonel Barker'. Despite the recent controversy, however, the press made no explicit mention of sexual perversion, instead portraying Barker merely as an 'eccentric' and indeed almost coming to admire her skills as an impostor.[152] Nevertheless, on those occasions when it was discussed, homosexuality was clearly presented as 'unnatural' and 'wrong'. Press psychologists advised parents to ensure that their children were socialized to have 'a healthy interest in the opposite sex' and were provided with 'healthy opportunities' to make such acquaintances.[153] With 'good' parenting, 'perversion' could be avoided.

The *Daily Herald* and the *Daily News–News Chronicle* undoubtedly shared many of these conservative attitudes, but they were more willing to explore controversial issues. Both papers offered support to birth control pioneers, even if, in the early-1920s, it was sometimes less explicit than they might have wished. When Marie Stopes lost her libel action in March 1923, a *News* editorial backed her decision to seek an appeal: while maintaining that 'we have nothing to say as to the rightness or wrongness of birth control', they defended Stopes's right to advocate it.[154] The same day, however, a feature article by Alban Widgery indicated the paper's real attitude when it concluded that 'constructive birth control gives a new ray of hope for humanity'.[155] The *Herald* was similarly cautious about coming out directly in favour of contraceptive advice, but by printing readers' letters on the subject and giving information about clinics it gave the issue more coverage than the conservative press.[156] In

---

[150] *Sunday Express*, 19 Aug. 1928, 10. Douglas had earlier condemned D. H. Lawrence's *Women in Love* in similar terms: it was, he claimed in 1915, more dangerous than an epidemic disease: 'they destroy the body, but it destroys the soul'; *The Star*, 2 Oct. 1915, 4, cited in S. Hynes, *A War Imagined: The First World War and English Culture* (London: Bodley Head, 1990), 61–2.

[151] Deirdre Beddoe, for example, observes that in this period 'A distinct phobia of lesbians emerged, and single women lived in fear of being labelled sexually deviant': D. Beddoe, *Back to Home and Duty: Women between the Wars 1918–1939* (London: Pandora, 1989), 4. See also S. Jeffreys, *The Spinster and her Enemies: Feminism and Sexuality 1880–1930* (London: Pandora, 1985), chs. 8 and 9; and C. Law, *Suffrage and Power: The Women's Movement 1918–28* (London: I. B. Tauris, 1997), 206–7.

[152] J. Vernon, ' "For Some Queer Reason": The Trials and Tribulations of Colonel Barker's Masquerade in Interwar Britain', *Signs*, 26/1 (Autumn 2000), 37–62; A. Oram and A. Turnbull (eds.), *The Lesbian History Sourcebook* (London: Routledge, 2001), 15, 38–9.   [153] *Daily Mirror*, 9 Nov. 1935, 10.

[154] *Daily News*, 2 Mar. 1923, 4.   [155] Ibid.

[156] e.g. *Daily Herald*, 3 Mar. 1923, 2; 5 Mar. 1923, 2; 6 Mar. 1923, 5.

1930, moreover, the paper played an important role in forcing the Ministry of Health to publicize its decision to allow local authority maternal welfare clinics to provide birth control instruction in certain circumstances. Richard Soloway, the leading historian of this subject, concludes that 'the *Daily Herald* was more sympathetic to birth control than any other newspaper in the country'.[157] The *News* and the *Herald* also covered the activities of the national and international groups combating venereal disease and prostitution more fully than the other popular dailies.

Both papers attacked censorship and silence on sexual issues. Responding to complaints about 'sex plays', the *News* theatre critic declared that 'drama should be based on life, and whether we like it or not, the questions of marriage and divorce are big questions that cannot be ignored'.[158] The *Herald* censured Hollywood—and much of the press could have been included as well—for its hypocrisy on matters of sexual morality: 'Every "movie fan" . . . knows that ten transatlantic pictures out of ten show Virtue (in a short frock) triumphant over Vice (in a slightly shorter one) in the final 'close-up'. But Vice has invariably had a good look in all the same, for the heights of Hollywood are built on the tried commercial foundations of sex appeal.' Yet at the same time as exploiting this 'sex appeal', the editorial continued, serious attempts to consider pressing sexual issues were denounced as 'immoral': 'Is sexual "dolling-up" to pass muster as Morality, whilst discussion of sex-problems comes under the ban?'[159] The following year the *Herald* stood against the suppression of *The Well of Loneliness*. Its literary editor, Arthur Dawson, reviewed the novel as a 'profound and moving study of a profound and moving problem' and gave Radclyffe Hall the opportunity to defend herself from the accusations of the *Express*.[160] Attempting to cultivate mass readerships, both the *Herald* and the *News* continued to tread cautiously and indeed to exploit 'sex appeal' themselves; nevertheless, they did on some issues use their influence to challenge notions of 'morality' that discriminated against women.

Despite encouraging a conception of modernity that portrayed post-war women as more independent and equal than ever before, the popular press maintained and even strengthened underlying assumptions about appearance and sexuality that buttressed gender difference. Modernity was constructed as a culture of greater sexual openness that contrasted with 'Victorian' prudery,

---

[157] R. Soloway, *Birth Control and the Population Question in England, 1877–1930* (Chapel Hill: University of North Carolina Press, 1982), 311–12, 196.   [158] *Daily News*, 12 Mar. 1921, 8.

[159] *Daily Herald*, 13 Apr. 1927, 4.

[160] *Daily Herald*, 20 Aug. 1928, 4; 21 Aug. 1928, 1; 24 Aug. 1928, 1, 4.

but there were widespread silences about the disparities of power between the sexes that ensured that these greater freedoms would be exploited in profoundly unequal ways. Women were increasingly sexualized and subjected to the male gaze in the press, but the opportunities for the expression of an active and assertive female sexuality remained limited. Pictures of women designed for a heterosexual male audience became entrenched in the popular press, and it was inevitable that when competition intensified in the 1960s and 1970s, this device would be exploited more fully. The 'page three girl' that would eventually become the defining symbol of the *Sun* was a natural progression from the 'bathing belle' regarded by PEP in 1938 as the characteristic feature of the popular press. And when sexual difference is made so visually conspicuous, it perhaps becomes more difficult to sustain the wider case for sexual equality.[161]

[161] On this point, see P. Holland, 'The Politics of the Smile: "Soft News" and the Sexualisation of the Popular Press', in C. Carter, G. Branston, and S. Allan (eds.), *News, Gender and Power* (London: Routledge, 1998).

6

Patriotism and Citizenship: The Gendered Languages of War and Peace

Late Victorian and Edwardian notions of gender were, as many historians have recognized, significantly influenced by the increasing prominence of the Empire in British culture. Imperial adventurers and conquerors such as Gordon, Rhodes, and Kitchener were held up as paragons of manliness. Baden-Powell, the hero of Mafeking, explicitly encouraged the nation's youth to learn the virtues of the Empire-builders through his dramatically successful scouting organizations. A chivalrous, nationalistic, muscular, stoic masculinity was celebrated in the best-selling fiction of such writers as G. A. Henty, Rider Haggard, and Rudyard Kipling.[1] Women, meanwhile, were exhorted to raise the standards of motherhood: 'national efficiency' and imperial strength required a healthy and patriotic generation of citizens and soldiers.[2] The pre-war popular press both reflected and contributed to this climate of opinion. Kennedy Jones revealed that the imperialism of the *Daily Mail*—soon imitated by the *Mirror* and the *Express*—was a conscious strategy agreed by Northcliffe and himself at the outset: 'We discovered at once an abounding desire for knowledge on all matters affecting the Empire. We realized that one of the greatest forces, almost untapped, at the disposal of the Press was the depth and volume of public interest in Imperial questions.'[3] Patriotic coverage of the Boer

---

[1] J. Tosh, *A Man's Place: Masculinity and the Middle-Class Home in Victorian England* (New Haven: Yale University Press, 1999), pt. 3; G. Dawson, 'The Blond Bedouin: Lawrence of Arabia, Imperial Adventure and the Imagining of English-British Masculinity', in M. Roper and J. Tosh (eds.), *Manful Assertions: Masculinities in Britain since 1800* (London: Routledge, 1991); J. A. Mangan and J. Walvin, Introduction, in id. (eds.), *Manliness and Morality: Middle-Class Masculinity in Britain and America, 1800–1940* (Manchester: Manchester University Press, 1987); A. Warren, 'Popular Manliness: Baden-Powell, Scouting and the Development of Manly Character', ibid.; K. Surridge, 'More than a Great Poster: Lord Kitchener and the Image of the Military Hero', *Historical Research*, 74/185 (Aug. 2001), 298–313.

[2] A. Davin, 'Imperialism and Motherhood', *History Workshop Journal*, 5 (Spring 1978), 9–65.

[3] K. Jones, *Fleet Street and Downing Street* (London: Hutchinson, 1920), 146.

War took the *Mail*'s circulation above 1 million copies for the first time, and Jones encouraged the paper to devote 'at least double the amount' of space previously thought necessary to record colonial events and the courageous exploits of British pioneers.[4] Indeed, the overseas edition of the *Mail* founded and organized an Overseas Club pledged to defend the 'greatest Empire in the world' by maintaining 'the heritage handed down to us by our fathers'. Able-bodied men were encouraged to learn how to bear arms; the final lines of the club's motto implored members to 'Pray God our greatness may not fail through craven fears of being great.'[5] Norman Angell, editor of the Paris-based *Continental Daily Mail* until 1912 despite his pronounced anti-war views, later recalled how the contemplation of any form of pacifism was regarded as a sign of weakness and effeminacy: 'it was not merely the implication of crankery which made it difficult for any man to state the case for the avoidance of war. There was the implication of a want of manliness, virility, in such an attitude. You were necessarily a coward.'[6] The *Mail* repeatedly called for an expansion of the Navy and infamously stoked fears of European war in 1909 when it commissioned Robert Blatchford to warn readers about the growing threat that Germany posed to Britain.[7] The anti-German sentiment was so striking and belligerent that the liberal *Star*—the *Daily News*'s evening sister paper—would claim in 1914 that 'Next to the Kaiser, Lord Northcliffe has done more than any living man to bring about the war.'[8]

The Great War itself encouraged all the main popular papers, except the *Daily Herald*, to rally around the banner of nation and Empire. Press coverage of the military campaign emphasized the heroism and courage of the British soldiers, and critical or pessimistic reporting, if not censored, was usually felt to be inappropriate.[9] (Only in 1920, for example, could the renowned war correspondent Philip Gibbs publish his thoughts on the *Realities of War*—a work released in the United States under the even more revealing title of *Now it Can*

---

[4] Ibid. 147. See also G. R. Wilkinson, 'Purple Prose and the Yellow Press: Imagined Spaces and the Military Expedition to Tirah, 1897', in D. Finkelstein and D. M. Peers (eds.), *Negotiating India in the Nineteenth Century Media* (Basingstoke: Macmillan, 2000).

[5] British Library, Northcliffe Papers, Add. MS 62222, fos. 91–92, circulars from Evelyn Wrench, 27 Aug. 1910, Nov. 1910.

[6] N. Angell, *After All: The Autobiography of Norman Angell* (London: Hamish Hamilton, 1951), 159.

[7] A. J. A. Morris, *The Scaremongers: The Advocacy of War and Rearmament 1896–1914* (London: Routledge & Kegan Paul, 1984). The Blatchford articles were printed on 13–24 Dec. 1909; reprinted as a penny pamphlet, they sold 1.6 million copies by 22 Jan. 1910: S. Koss, *The Rise and Fall of the Political Press*, ii (London: Hamish Hamilton, 1984), 134.

[8] S. J. Taylor, *The Great Outsiders: Northcliffe, Rothermere and the Daily Mail* (London: Weidenfeld & Nicolson, 1996), 143.

[9] M. Farrar, *News from the Front: War Correspondents on the Western Front* (Stroud: Sutton, 1998).

Be Told.[10]) Newspaper editors as a result became prime targets of attack in the eyes of bitter soldier–poets for 'glorifying' the conflict.[11] Yet if militarism and nationalism were reinforced while the war was being fought, the scale and brutality of events on the Western Front, only gradually understood in their entirety, inevitably generated a reaction after 1918. The assumptions of 'imperial masculinity' were soon subjected to fierce criticism in the *Daily Herald* and the *Daily News*, and by the late 1920s even the conservative papers were re-evaluating traditional attitudes. During the 1930s there was a widespread disillusionment with the grand rhetoric and 'high diction' of war and Empire as it became clear that the huge sacrifices had not secured a lasting peace. An 'anti-heroic' atmosphere was perhaps not as pervasive as some historians have claimed, but the press portrayal of the international crises of the 1930s differed significantly in tone from the coverage of pre-1914 tensions. Only the *Daily Mail*, increasingly drifting away from the political mainstream, stood apart from these developments and was seduced by the temptations of more 'virile' fascist forms of leadership.

Many press commentators rested their hopes for lasting peace after 1918 on the inclusion of the female voice in public affairs. Ever since Aristophanes women had been associated with the prevention of war: the life-giving and nurturing qualities of femininity had traditionally been contrasted with the masculine predisposition for violence and dominance. But now not only were an unprecedented number of women apparently united in a community of grief, they were also armed for the first time with the vote to influence policy. Papers from across the political spectrum frequently reported the ceremonies of remembrance from the perspective of sorrowful mothers and gave space to women's condemnations of warfare. Yet this gendered 'pacificist'[12] critique was rarely allowed to develop beyond a fairly superficial level and could not transform entrenched attitudes. As circumstances changed in 1938–9, the critique was increasingly marginalized, and women were encouraged to mobilize in preparation for another war.

This chapter will demonstrate how the shadows of wars past and future shaped press gender discourse, and in particular how notions of 'patriotism', 'glory', and imperial manliness were rethought in this period. By the time of the Sudetenland crisis and the eventual countdown to war in 1938–9, the idealistic

---

10 S. Hynes, *A War Imagined: The First World War and English Culture* (London: Bodley Head, 1990), 284.

11 Ibid. 118, 173–4, 384.

12 I use this term in the sense outlined by Martin Ceadel, e.g. in his recent work *Semi-Detached Idealists: The British Peace Movement and International Relations 1854–1945* (Oxford: Oxford University Press, 2000), 6–8: seeking the abolition of war, but recognizing that states will have to be reformed in various ways first.

nationalism of 1914 had been rewritten as a cheerfully cynical spirit of defiance against Hitler's attempted domination of Europe.

Editorial Policies and Pressures

Defending Imperialism and Internationalism

Most of the main newspaper proprietors and editors in this period held passionate views on Britain's imperial and international position, and their attitudes inevitably had a major impact upon the content of their papers. For Northcliffe, Rothermere, and Beaverbrook, maintaining and strengthening the bonds of Empire was of the utmost significance for British prosperity. In his first editorial as a newspaper proprietor, having taken over the *Evening News* in 1894, Northcliffe pledged to 'preach the gospel of loyalty to the Empire' and he retained that aspiration until his death.[13] For Beaverbrook, a Canadian, 'the cause of Empire is the greatest issue in public life', and, as he told the Royal Commission in 1948, it was the mainspring of his newspaper 'propaganda' efforts.[14] Rothermere's disgust at Conservative concessions in India, meanwhile, was one of the main reasons for his interest in fascism. The world-views of all three of these men had been shaped by pre-war imperialism, and the continuing influence in particular of Beaverbrook and Rothermere over the *Express*, the *Mail*, and the *Mirror* ensured the persistence of a rather idealized vision of the Empire and the heroic qualities of its inhabitants. These press barons remained convinced that a strong Empire required a manly and virile population and encouraged their papers to foster patriotic ideals. They were absolutely certain both of the rightness of the British cause in the First World War and of the suitability of what Samuel Hynes describes as the 'official rhetoric' of the war, the 'set of abstractions'—such as Honour, Glory, Heroism, and Sacrifice—that expressed traditional martial and patriotic values, and which were so important in delineating contemporary ideals of masculinity.[15] The *Mail* signified its commitment to this rhetoric by altering its front-page slogan to the words 'For King and Country'. By 1918 all three proprietors were—to the concern of many MPs—officially involved in the running of the war (Northcliffe and Beaverbrook in propaganda positions, Rothermere at the RAF) and had staked their reputations on a successful outcome. In the clashes

---

[13] Jones, *Fleet Street*, 132.

[14] House of Lords Record Office, Beaverbrook Papers, H/104, Beaverbrook to Strube, 2 May 1934; Royal Commission on the Press, *Minutes of Evidence* (London, 1948), Day 26, Cmd. 7416, 4–5.

[15] Hynes, *A War Imagined*, 109–10.

of the 1920s and 1930s over how the Great War was to be understood, these conservative papers defended—although not completely or unthinkingly—the traditional values of nation and Empire.

Nevertheless, the press barons also shared the widespread revulsion at the unprecedented bloodshed of the war. Rothermere himself was particularly affected by the loss of his two elder sons.[16] While certain that the defence of British interests in 1914 had necessitated the defeat of Germany, Rothermere and Beaverbrook became convinced that involvement in another European war would undermine the British Empire. This belief created an underlying tension in their position that was difficult to resolve: while determined to encourage a strong, well-armed, manly nation and Empire—and, in the case of Rothermere, admiring the virile nationalism of the fascist states—they were forced into what appeared a rather craven appeasement of German and Italian expansionism in the 1930s.

On the other side of the post-war cultural divide stood the *Daily Herald*. George Lansbury's socialist and pacifist beliefs ensured a critical view of the conflict against Germany, both while it was being waged and subsequently. The *Herald*—only 2 years old at the outbreak of the war—had been forced to struggle through the war years as a weekly pamphlet with a tiny circulation of some 40,000, and had been threatened with government suppression when it called for workers to follow the example of the Bolsheviks.[17] After the war it became a magnet for pacifist, left-wing, feminist, and internationalist thinkers such as Bernard Shaw, Siegfried Sassoon, Robert Graves, Evelyn Sharp, and Rose Macaulay. The Lansbury tradition was maintained until the Odhams relaunch in 1930 by the editorship of William Mellor, a conscientious objector during the war (and one of the founders of the British Communist Party).[18] With such contributors, the *Herald* led the way in criticizing the rhetoric and attitudes of nationalism and imperialism, and the gendered ideas that were inextricably bound up with them. The liberal *Daily News–News Chronicle*, while never sharing the pacifist inclinations of the *Herald*, and generally supportive of the government during the war, developed a strong internationalist flavour in the 1920s and was also open to writers critical of conventional patriotism. Like the *Herald*, it gave a significant amount of coverage to the activities of women's peace organizations.

---

[16] Taylor, *The Great Outsiders*, 194–5.

[17] D. Griffiths (ed.), *The Encyclopedia of the British Press* (London: Macmillan, 1992), 360.

[18] H. Richards, 'Conscription, Conformity and Control: The Taming of the *Daily Herald*, 1921–30', D.Phil. thesis (Open University, 1992) 191.

The Desire for Colour and Contrast: The Use of Gendered Imagery

If editors recognized that mass audiences had a limited interest in domestic politics, they were even more aware that readers often had a short attention span when faced with 'heavy' foreign affairs material. As early as 4 June 1919 Northcliffe was reminding his staff that the public were sated with comment about the peacemaking process: 'What the public wanted this morning was more of the horses. They are not talking about St Germain, but about Epsom.'[19] Readership surveys found foreign politics to be one of the least-liked categories of news, especially among women.[20] The editorial team responsible for the transformation of the *Mirror* in the mid-1930s was certainly conscious of this lukewarm attitude. Hugh Cudlipp cheerfully admitted that 'as a general rule . . . day-to-day developments in international affairs received scant attention'.[21] Even the *News Chronicle*, which aspired to provide relatively comprehensive news coverage, was making severe cuts in the number of its foreign correspondents at the end of the 1930s to save money.[22] In this context of limited knowledge and uncertain reader interest the popular press frequently succumbed to the temptation to present the international situation in bold, bright colours. Where Britain was involved, the conservative press in particular tended to fall back on a rather uncritical chauvinism and appeal to the sense of British superiority. The rhetoric of 'honour', 'glory', and 'patriotism' was used not only because it was sincerely felt, but also because it offered a simple, convenient shorthand which rendered further explanation unnecessary. Elsewhere, the emphasis tended to be on the dramatic and elements of 'human interest'. Lord Copper's instructions to Boot about the coverage he expected of the Ishmalian civil war in Evelyn Waugh's *Scoop* were often uncomfortably close to the truth: 'a few sharp victories, some conspicuous acts of personal bravery on the Patriot side and a colourful entry into the capital . . . We shall expect the first victory about the middle of July.'[23]

This type of reporting, built around stark dichotomies and contrasts, encouraged many contributors to employ gendered language and analogies. Contrasting the timid imperial policy of post-war governments with the

---

[19] Bodleian Library, Oxford, MS Eng. hist. d. 303–5, Northcliffe Bulletins, 4 June 1919.

[20] Political and Economic Planning, *Report on the British Press* (London, 1938), 250; J. Curran, A. Douglas, and G. Whannel, 'The Political Economy of the Human Interest Story', in A. Smith (ed.), *Newspapers and Democracy: International Essays on a Changing Medium* (Cambridge, Mass.: MIT Press, 1980), 318–19.

[21] H. Cudlipp, *Publish and be Damned! The Astonishing Story of the Daily Mirror* (London: Andrew Dakers, 1953), 64.

[22] British Library of Political and Economic Science, LSE, Gerald Barry Papers, File 4, 'Economics in Editorial Expenditure', memo 1938–9.

[23] E. Waugh, *Scoop* (first pub. 1938; Harmondsworth: Penguin, 1967), 42.

supposed assertiveness of their Victorian predecessors, for example, Rosita Forbes, writing in the *Daily Mail* in 1931, accused ministers and their supporters of displaying an effeminate weakness:

the modern is obsessed by other people's feelings . . . Old John [Bull] was a bully and respected for it . . . all this must be the fault of a new brand of English man . . . Funny, old, obstinate, arrogant, intolerant, inflexible, John Bull ruled a vast portion of the world for the undoubted benefit of its inhabitants and for an unsophisticated ideal represented by the flag . . . He believed in fair play, but he made the rules and enforced their observance . . . it was a greater Britain than we know today.[24]

Such arguments relied upon, and consolidated, pre-war notions of manly British imperialists courageously defending the national interest. At the same time, the *Daily Express* could deride the League of Nations during the crisis over Japanese aggression in Manchuria as 'the Geneva Governess', a 'feminine' institution unable to assert its authority: 'The League of Nations, caught between China and Japan, is like nothing so much as a timid governess trying to assert herself over two turbulent charges. She has told them both not to be naughty, and is now only wishing that she had nerve enough to attempt a good hard slap.'[25] The *Mail* was similarly critical of 'Dame Geneva', easily seduced in cartoons by rogues such as the overly idealistic 'Rainbow Chaser'.[26] As discussed below, the *Mail* explained its sympathy for fascism in terms of its admiration for the 'manliness' and 'virility' of Mussolini, Mosley, and Hitler; other papers structured foreign affairs coverage around 'masculine' interventionist and 'feminine' pacificist viewpoints. There were increasing difficulties in sustaining these contrasts by the late 1930s, with the usually belligerent and conventionally patriotic conservative press becoming the staunchest defenders of appeasement, and the left-wing papers beginning to advocate internationalist intervention. Nevertheless, the basic patterns were clear. Whereas gendered language was rarely employed by the 'minority' press in its foreign affairs coverage, it suited the demands of popular journalism, and this helped to bring to the surface the gender assumptions of the writers.

Maintaining Optimism: Circulation, Advertising, and Government Pressure

Editors knew that foreign affairs coverage had to be simplified and brightened if it was to appeal to a mass audience; they also believed that readers tended to

---

[24] *Daily Mail*, 2 Mar. 1931, 12.   [25] *Daily Express*, 16 Oct. 1931, 10.
[26] *Daily Mail*, 15 Dec. 1936, 10.

react badly to excessively gloomy material. The stagnation of the *Mail*'s circulation in the 1930s was attributed by colleagues to Rothermere's extreme pessimism about Britain's international position.[27] Maintaining advertising revenue was, as always, an important consideration. Advertisers hoped above all for a settled international situation in which consumers could feel confident; European tensions inevitably produced a decline in demand for many types of goods. The responsibility of advertising pressure for the continued optimism of certain popular papers in the late 1930s—most notably the *Daily Express,* which persisted with its infamous There Will Be No War campaign well into 1939—was much debated at the time.[28] This is not the place to review the evidence in full, but, despite the 'not guilty' verdict delivered by the Royal Commission in 1949, it seems likely that commercial considerations did encourage newspapers occasionally to play down the threat from Hitler.[29] Collin Brooks's diary recorded a conversation with Beaverbrook in 1935 which was very revealing:

We talked of Rothermere's belief in an imminent war, and Beaverbrook was insistent that we kept it out of the papers. 'I agree,' I said, 'But I feel that Rothermere is right.' 'Does it matter, Brooks?' 'From the angle of selling ink and paper at a profit, no. But from the angle of a man with a mission, yes . . .' He grinned, impishly. 'A paper can't afford to prophesy disaster, can it?'[30]

These editorial calculations were reinforced by the information management policies of the Chamberlain government.[31] As Stephen Koss points out, inflammatory journalism was commonly held to be a contributory factor in the outbreak of the Great War, and officials were determined that the press should not be encouraged to raise tensions.[32] There were also fears about the reaction of the British people. In August 1938 C. Tower, a member of the *Yorkshire Post* staff, informed his editor, Arthur Mann, of the substance of his conversations with Sir Robert Vansittart and Lord Halifax at the Foreign Office:

[27] Collin Brooks's diary (3 Apr. 1935), for example, records the view of Rothermere's colleagues that 'too much insistence upon the imminence of war and the need for defence is harming the papers'; N. J. Crowson (ed.), *Fleet Street, Press Barons and Politics: The Journals of Collin Brooks 1932–40* (London: Royal Historical Society, 1998), 95.

[28] See e.g. the criticisms of Henry Wickham Steed in *The Press* (Harmondsworth: Penguin, 1938), 249–50; T. Harrison, 'The Popular Press?', *Horizon* (Aug. 1940); and the allegations of Francis Williams, Michael Foot, Kingsley Martin, and others to the Royal Commission on the Press, *Minutes of Evidence*, Day 3, 7, 10, etc.

[29] Royal Commission on the Press, *Report* (London: HMSO, 1949), Cmd. 7700, 135–8.

[30] *Journals of Collin Brooks*, 4 Apr. 1935, 96.

[31] These are outlined in detail by R. Cockett, *Twilight of Truth: Chamberlain, Appeasement and the Manipulation of the Press* (London: Weidenfeld & Nicolson, 1989).

[32] Koss, *Rise and Fall*, 543–6.

the 'popular' papers are not discouraged from talking rather more optimistically, the explanation given to me being that if they were warned off that line they would immediately become sensationally pessimistic and might create in advance the very conditions of popular panic upon which Nazis are known to reckon as one of their weapons.[33]

Such external pressures help to explain the relatively muted nature of newspaper rhetoric at the end of the 1930s. As much effort was expended on encouraging women to fulfil their role as consumer—trying to 'make them feel it would be a good thing to buy a new dress or washing machine', Francis Williams, editor of the *Herald* in the late 1930s, remarked bitterly to the Royal Commission in 1948—as to preparing men to undertake their 'male' duty to defend the nation.[34] Even Walter Layton, the committed internationalist and anti-fascist editorial director of the *News Chronicle*, was prepared to smooth the harsh edges of Hitler's rhetoric during the crisis of September 1938.[35] As for the *Mail*, the contrast with its pre-1914 patriotic belligerence was stark. This 'epidemic of self-restraint'[36] across Fleet Street was an important discouragement to grand pronouncements about the 'heroic masculinity' of British citizens.

Inter-War Debates

Understanding the Great War: The Persistence of Traditional Values

In his survey of the depiction of military force in the Edwardian press, Glenn Wilkinson concludes that before 1914 war was portrayed by newspapers as 'both beneficial and desirable to the societies engaged in it'.[37] Popular theories of 'social Darwinism' encouraged the view that warfare was a necessary test of a nation's male population, and a protection against 'degeneration'. A *Daily Mirror* editorial in April 1904, for example, breezily accepted involvement in colonial skirmishes in Tibet, Nigeria, and Somaliland, against the backdrop of increasing tensions with Germany, as proof of English virility: 'That England is always at war shows an amount of energy and superabundant spirits that go a long way to demonstrate that we are not a decaying race. Three little wars

[33] Bodleian Library, Oxford, Arthur Mann Papers, MS Eng. c. 3274, Foreign Affairs File, fos. 31–2, C. Tower to Arthur Mann, 12 Aug. 1938.

[34] Royal Commission, *Minutes of Evidence*, Day 3, Cmd. 7318, 4.

[35] D. Hubback, *No Ordinary Press Baron: A Life of Walter Layton* (London: Weidenfeld & Nicolson, 1985), 162–4. [36] Koss, *Rise and Fall*, 546.

[37] G. Wilkinson, '"The Blessings of War": The Depiction of Military Force in Edwardian Newspapers', *Journal of Contemporary History*, 33/1 (1998), 98.

going on, and the prospect of a large one looming before us, we take quite as a matter of course.'[38]

The popular press entered the conflict with Germany in 1914 with a combination of patriotic superiority and faith in the manliness of its people. 'England Expects That Every Man Will Do His Duty' ran a streamer headline on the front page of the *Express* on 5 August.[39] If 'England had grown fat and slothful with prosperity', the paper declared, '. . . Germany's threat has called to life again the England of Henry V, the England of Drake . . . the England of Nelson.'[40] The following month H. G. Wells, discussing in the *Daily Chronicle* the likely impact of aeroplanes on the war, predicted that the new machines would generate 'The Most Splendid Fighting in the World' and provide Englishmen with the opportunity to live up to the glorious heroes of the past: 'One talks and reads of the heroic age and how the world has degenerated. But indeed this is the heroic age, suddenly come again. No legendary feats of the past, no battles with dragons or monstrous beasts, no quest or feat that man hitherto attempted can compare with this adventure, in terror, danger and splendour.'[41] With (alleged) German atrocities in Belgium depicted in full brutal detail, newspapers portrayed the war in traditional terms as a chivalrous crusade in which all men should enlist to protect defenceless women and children from rape and pillage.[42] Dispatches from the front throughout the war continued to emphasize the heroic achievements of the British and imperial troops whatever the painful reality. Philip Gibbs's report from the first day of the campaign at the Somme, for example, described in detail the 'splendid valour' of the soldiers and the success of their exploits. 'The spirit of our men is so high that it is certain we shall gain further ground.'[43]

Yet as the losses mounted and the failures of the Gallipoli and Somme offensives demonstrated the difficulty of finding a way out of the bloody stalemate, this self-confident patriotism was severely tested. Gibbs was soon writing in a markedly more bitter vein: 'If any man were to draw the picture of those things or to tell them more nakedly than I have told them . . . no man or woman would dare to speak again of war's "glory", or of "the splendour of war", or any of those old lying phrases which hide the dreadful truth.'[44] By the end of 1917 the *Daily News* feared that the traditional certainties were collapsing: 'The

---

[38] *Daily Mirror*, 5 Apr. 1904, 5, cited in Wilkinson, 'The Blessings of War', 101. This editorial is also cited by Hugh Cudlipp as evidence of the *Mirror*'s early 'jingoism': *Publish and be Damned!*, 14.

[39] *Daily Express*, 5 Aug. 1914, 1.   [40] *Daily Express*, 6 Aug. 1914, 4.

[41] *Daily Chronicle*, 9 Sept. 1914, 4.

[42] Such atrocities were publicized as early as 6 Aug. 1914: *Daily Mail*, 6 Aug. 1914, 4; *Daily Express*, 6 Aug. 1914, 1.   [43] *Daily Chronicle*, 3 July 1916, 1; 4 July 1916, 1.

[44] *Daily Chronicle*, 16 July 1916, cited in Hynes, *A War Imagined*, 111.

spirit of the nation is darkening. Its solidarity is crumbling. We began this war with a splendid faith in our aims and with a unity of moral purpose that was priceless . . . but our faith has grown dim.'[45]

If the triumph of November 1918 eventually offered a vindication of national strength, it was clear that war and military service could never be regarded in the same way again. It is in this context that Alison Light and Judy Giles have described the inter-war period as an 'anti-heroic' age of the 'little man', 'psychologically exhausted by the demands of imperial masculinity' and 'content with his garden, home and domestic ideals'.[46] In a number of respects their arguments are persuasive, and calls for the redefinition of masculinity were made in the columns of the press. Nevertheless, the persistence of traditional values and language, especially in the 1920s, should not be overlooked. Wartime bravery and 'sacrifice' continued to be glorified in the well-worn phrases of the 'high diction': the nation was exhorted to prove itself worthy of the 'heroic slain' and the public were encouraged to 'pay tribute to the gallant Dominion troops who so readily responded to the Empire's call and won renown on many a hard-fought field'.[47] 'Kitchener's men', the original volunteers, remained secure in their status as 'the pick of the nation's manhood'.[48] After the signing of the Versailles peace treaty on 7 May 1919, the *Express* declared that the

greatest grandeur of England is now and here . . . No man . . . should ever forget that he is in some sense set apart in the eyes of history both from those who came before 1914 and those who come after, because he was privileged to serve his country in her greatest need and speed her to her greatest glory.[49]

The belief that military service was the finest expression of manliness and the ultimate test of 'national character' clearly lived on. The day after the remembrance ceremonies in 1924, for example, Richard Viner in the *Express* voiced the feelings of inadequacy felt by many too young to serve in the trenches:

We waited and waited [to reach the age of military service], but all that came was a resentment against our dreadful uselessness . . . So yesterday, besides our reverence, besides our homage, there was, perhaps, a little resentment in our hearts, a little envy of those who had the years to prove their manhood. For somehow, it seems, we are not such men as they are.[50]

[45] *Daily News*, undated editorial, end of 1917, cited in Hynes, *A War Imagined*, 222–3.
[46] A. Light, *Forever England: Femininity, Literature and Conservatism between the Wars* (London: Routledge, 1991), 8–10; J. Giles, *Women, Identity and Private Life in Britain 1900–50* (Basingstoke: Macmillan, 1995), 21.   [47] *Daily Express*, 11 Nov. 1918, 4; 3 May 1919, 1.
[48] *Daily Express*, 12 Nov. 1918, 2.   [49] *Daily Express*, 8 May 1919, 4.
[50] *Daily Express*, 12 Nov. 1924, 8. George Orwell would later admit to feeling 'a little less than a man' for

The following year the *Express* drew attention on its front page to 'The Modern Tired Young Man', whose 'distinctive characteristic is a lack of masculinity': 'his voice is weary and affected, his pose is feminine, his outlook anaemic, and his general attitude to life bloodless'.[51] Crucially, these men came from the generation 'who never saw the flash of guns or the gleam of bayonets at dawn' and had thus not proved their manliness; 'men in their thirties who fought in the trenches find this type of youth intolerable', the paper commented grimly, 'they have nothing in common'. The *Express* feared that this was the 'penalty the world is paying for the wave of masculinity that spent itself in death during five years of war'. Yet there was little sympathy for the young men themselves: 'if he goes abroad he will become the worst advertisement this country could put forward'.[52] Traditional masculinity was, it seemed, infinitely preferable to this foppishness and effeminacy. The articles drew a flurry of correspondence. One writer protested that he was no shirker: it was the 'greatest regret of himself and thousands of other young "youths about town"' that they had never witnessed the 'flash of guns or the gleam of bayonets'.[53] An ex-serviceman was unconvinced, declaring that 'if we had another war I feel sure that modern girls would be more competent to take their place in the trenches than modern young men'.[54] Despite their differing views, both accepted that true manliness was forged in the fires of conflict.

The valiant exploits of the 'war generation' were celebrated by regular serializations of their autobiographies and journals. The *Sunday Dispatch* proudly announced in 1930, for example, that it would provide a platform for Captain Kettle, 'hero of brilliant exploits on every front', who 'in the form of a racy narrative . . . has just written his personal war memoirs'.[55] But the press also highlighted fresh examples of brave endeavour, grateful for evidence that modern men were not all 'foppish' and 'anaemic'. When Flight Lieutenant Kinhead, the commanding officer of the High Speed Section of the RAF, was killed carrying out a rash manoeuvre in 1928, the *Express* welcomed the 'eagerness' of his comrades to fill the vacancy and erase the memory of his accident. Their enthusiasm was a vindication of British manliness:

Hundreds put in their application the moment the official invitation was issued. That is as it should be, and, among the youth of Britain, one may fairly hope, will always be. Success for them, as for all who are salted with the right spirit, is much less of a

having been too young to fight: 'My Country Right or Left', first pub. in *Folios of New Writing* (Autumn 1940), repr. in S. Orwell and I. Angus (eds.), *The Collected Essays, Journalism and Letters of George Orwell*, i: *1920–40* (Harmondsworth: Penguin, 1970), 589.

[51] *Daily Express*, 8 July 1925, 1.   [52] *Daily Express*, 6 July 1925, 8; 8 July 1925, 1, 9.
[53] *Daily Express*, 8 July 1925, 8.   [54] Ibid.   [55] Advertised in the *Daily Mail*, 24 May 1930, 12.

stimulus and inspiration than is a splendid failure they are determined to retrieve. It is this 'courage never to submit or yield' that carries the world on from one triumph to another.[56]

Only months earlier the *Mail* had argued in similar terms that the military could demonstrate to the world that Englishmen had not 'gone soft'. The triumphant showing of the Army in a series of tests in the United States, an editorial asserted, revealed that 'treated severely, the English of the present day are not degenerate, but have the right to hold their heads up high'.[57] A daring reconnaissance mission of the northern ice floes in 1931 provided further evidence: 'If proof were needed that our young men are as brave and as hardy today as they were in the most glorious epochs of our past, it is supplied by the record of the British Arctic Air Route Expedition on which so much attention is centred at the moment.'[58]

Serialized fiction and cartoons in newspapers continued to satisfy the demand for fantasies of virility and daring. As Graham Dawson has argued, the rejection of war and its 'high diction' by the literary elite, as described by Paul Fussell, should not blind us to the 'continuing centrality of war adventure stories and their versions of heroic masculinity' in more popular media.[59] These stories were often transposed to imaginary situations that had less potentially distressing associations than French battlefields. The *Daily Mirror*, for example, advertised C. T. Stoneham's 'thrilling jungle adventure' as 'a real he-man's serial', an uplifting contrast to 'feminine' 'sex-problem' fiction.[60] The paper's 'Garth' and 'Buck Ryan' cartoons unashamedly depicted ideals of lion-hearted masculinity. One reader told Mass Observation that he 'wanted a body like Garth's'. Hugh Cudlipp believed that this feature allowed the 'short and skinny' vicariously to enjoy superhuman strength and the attentions of female admirers.[61] Orwell's observations about 'Boys' Weeklies' could easily have been extended to include some of this newspaper fiction: old values lingered and society appeared to have been frozen in 1910.[62]

Indeed, the *Mail*, the *Express*, and the *Mirror* sought to encourage their younger readers to aspire to a form of 'imperial masculinity' by continuing to support the scouting movement. Children's supplements included articles penned by Baden-Powell himself, ranging from 'a yarn especially for those who long for Adventure Overseas' to explanations of 'How to Know the Ropes'.[63]

---

[56] *Daily Express*, 26 Mar. 1928, 10.   [57] *Daily Mail*, 2 Jan. 1928, 8.

[58] *Daily Mail*, 30 Apr. 1931, 10.   [59] Dawson, 'Blond Bedouin . . .', 120.

[60] *Daily Mirror*, 16 Nov. 1935, 4.   [61] Cudlipp, *Publish and be Damned!*, 73–4.

[62] G. Orwell, 'Boys' Weeklies', *Horizon* (May 1940), cited in Orwell and Angus (eds.), *The Collected Essays*, 505–31, quotation at 528.   [63] *Daily Mail*, 5, 12 Dec. 1936, in children's suppl.

In 1927 the *Mail* called for Baden-Powell to be recognized in the king's birthday honours. His organization, an editorial asserted, 'has now for nearly twenty years served the cause of good citizenship and manly ideals. It has taught enormous multitudes of boys to be self-reliant, loyal, honourable and patriotic. It has given them a zest for the outdoor life which is peculiarly desirable in the case of a city-bred population such as ours.'[64] The chief scout's success, opined another contributor, was guaranteed because he 'based his conception upon the romance and adventure for which every healthy boy craves'. The maintenance of a healthy model of masculinity was sufficiently important for the paper to claim that 'few living Englishman have done more for their generation than Sir Robert Baden-Powell'.[65]

Understanding the Great War: Re-evaluating Masculinity

Yet if the language and values of a heroic 'imperial masculinity' had by no means disappeared from the columns of the popular press, it was impossible to disguise that the realities of the war and its aftermath had exposed them to dangerous criticism. At first, the attacks came from expected quarters. The *Herald*, as soon as it relaunched as a daily in March 1919, sought to puncture the rhetoric of the conservative press. The paper highlighted the political and social realities obscured by the appeal to patriotism and military valour, pointing out that, in contrast to the stirring tales of propaganda and fiction, wartime sacrifice and service did not guarantee lasting security or even recognition for working men. It argued that the war had been a fundamental betrayal of working-class interests, a time when the 'peace and happiness of the world' had been allowed to fall into the 'murderous hands of a few cynical old men'.[66] The Versailles treaty was denounced as 'a dangerous peace' that would 'make new wars inevitable';[67] its aim was simply 'to make the world safe for Plutocracy'.[68] 'They'll Cheat You Yet Those Junkers', warned the *Herald*'s first headline of 1921 in a play on the *Mail*'s slogan of 1919—but the 'Junkers' in question were not Germans but the bosses of British industry, as 'Want, Misery and Unemployment' continued into the new year.[69] The real enemies were the profiteers at home, not foreign workers. Britons must recognize their 'kinship with the defeated Germans'.[70] The ideal of manliness put forward in these

---

64 *Daily Mail*, 7 May 1927, 10.
65 *Daily Mail*, 20 Apr. 1927, 9. See also *Daily Mirror*, 1 Aug. 1924, 5, 8–9.
66 *Daily Herald*, 11 Nov. 1919, 1.   67 *Daily Herald*, 9 May 1919, 4.
68 *Daily Herald*, 8 May 1919, 1.   69 *Daily Herald*, 1 Jan. 1921, 1.
70 *Daily Herald*, 2 May 1919, 4.

columns was one of a peaceful, educated, international, 'human brother-hood': 'The working-class the world over is one; and when it is divided against itself, every section must pay the penalty. Woe always to the workers, unless they learn the lesson and do unite, without distinction of creed or race or colour.'[71]

But as the economic difficulties continued, and the dreams of a country 'fit for heroes' evaporated, this sense of disillusionment spread beyond the pages of the *Herald* into the liberal press. An editorial in the *Daily News* in November 1922 drew a bitter contrast between the acclaim received by soldiers during the war and the exclusion and poverty facing them on their return:

The ex-soldiers—the men who won the war—sell matches from door to door; their children huddle in the rat-infested slums; the miners—heroes of many a thrilling dis-patch from the front—struggle desperately to keep themselves and their families alive on 26s. a week; the agricultural labourers—some of our best regiments—sink back into the sodden misery of a poverty to which the bare decencies of life are luxuries. And men . . . patter platitudes about patriotism and about the 'prestige' of a country in which such things are done.[72]

Ten days later, reporting on the 11 November services of commemoration, the paper concluded that 'if Armistice Day is to establish a tradition . . . it will be the tradition that there are no war-winners, least of all among those who are sent forth to win it'.[73] Here was the antithesis of the heroic tradition that H. G. Wells had predicted would be renewed in 1914. Meanwhile, Annie Swan suggested that warfare, far from energizing the 'higher' manly virtues of patriotism, dutiful service, and self-sacrifice, actually encouraged the 'lower' animal instincts:

The cost of war is death to the body, and alas! oft-times death to the soul of those who escape physical death. Many families are suffering today from the lowering of the moral standard—from the masquerade of licence calling itself liberty—homes have been broken up, vows forgotten, happiness ended. War, while it may make an appeal to the heroic side of nature, also gives rein to the baser passions.[74]

Swan warned darkly that an experienced soldier had told her that 'if women only knew what war is really like, how base it is, they would be so appalled that they would make an end of it for all time'. Unlike the dashing men of fiction, soldiers were in danger of becoming desensitized 'brutes'.

The codes of 'imperial masculinity' were also subject to scrutiny in the con-servative press, although usually in the course of articles of social observation

---

[71] *Daily Herald*, 10 Jan. 1921, 4.   [72] *Daily News*, 1 Nov. 1922, 4.
[73] *Daily News*, 11 Nov. 1922, 4.   [74] *Daily News*, 2 Nov. 1922, 7.

rather than overtly political critiques. Diana Bourbon, a regular feature-writer in the *Express*, in 1924 lamented that such pressure was put on men to control their emotions and maintain a 'stiff upper lip'. The war had demonstrated that 'a manly man, capable of winning the V.C. or D.S.O., could still know abject physical fear as completely as any woman—and have no reason to be ashamed of the knowledge'. She hoped that boys would no longer be 'taught to worship brute strength' and learn instead that 'a little feminine sensitiveness' could be compatible with manliness.[75] In the correspondence generated by the *Express*'s criticism of the 'Modern Tired Young Man' in 1925, several writers rejected the paper's assumptions about 'proper' masculinity, and argued that the war and its aftermath highlighted the need to rethink traditional values. 'R.P.', for example, claimed that modern youth were determined to treasure cerebral qualities above strength and valour: they were more intelligent and artistic, and were 'non-militarist' in outlook.[76] 'Two Modern Young Men' joined in this defence. 'The carnage of the Great War', they argued, had had a profound effect on contemporary man: it 'sickened him of brutalities, and he has to seek expression in a manner as far remote as possible from brutality'.[77] Perhaps the images of the British citizen in the post-war cartoons of the conservative press can be seen as one manifestation of this revulsion from 'brutality'. As Sian Nicholas has observed, Poy's 'John Citizen' in the *Daily Mail* of the 1920s, and Strube's 'Little Man' in the *Express*, offered a stark contrast to the traditional manly figure of John Bull: private and domesticated, these unassuming figures wanted a 'quiet life' undisturbed by the demands of the state (see Figs. 6.1 and 6.4).[78] This shift certainly did not go unnoticed: one right-wing Tory even accused Strube of helping to undermine Conservative values by drawing the 'Little Man' rather than 'the good robust character' of John Bull.[79]

The re-evaluation of masculinity was further encouraged by the popularization of psychology. The harmful psychological effects of war became a commonplace among press doctors. 'Before the war women were allowed a certain licence in the display of nerves,' noted the *News Chronicle* medical expert; 'their weakness was attributed to femininity and the trials and boredom of running a

[75] *Daily Express*, 20 Oct. 1924, 8.   [76] *Daily Express*, 13 July 1925, 8.   [77] Ibid.

[78] S. Nicholas, 'From John Bull to John Citizen: Images of National Identity and Citizenship on the Wartime BBC', in R. Weight and A. Beach (eds.), *The Right to Belong: Citizenship and National Identity in Britain 1930–1960* (London: I. B. Tauris, 1998), 37–8.

[79] An accusation made by the unsuccessful Conservative candidate Summers after the 1945 general election: Beaverbrook Papers, H/117, E. J. Robertson to Beaverbrook, 6 Oct. 1945. Ten years later Geoffrey Gorer, discussing the decline of aggressive behaviour in Britain, wrote of the 'remarkable change . . . from John Bull to John Citizen': G. Gorer, *Exploring English Character* (London: Cresset Press, 1955), 17.

FIG. 6.1. Poy's John Citizen, a retiring suburban taxpayer, offers a marked contrast
to the vigorous and hearty figure of John Bull as a representation of the nation.
This cartoon offers a critique of the Lloyd George government's 'squandermania',
with Sir Eric Geddes's electricity generation scheme on the River Severn likened
to an unnecessarily extravagant hat demanded by a spendthrift wife

home.' Now, however, 'neurotic men appear to be as numerous as women. Post-war neurasthenia—the result of wounds, shell shock, or searing war experience—is a well-recognised condition which deserves all the sympathy it commands.'[80] An inability to cope with the demands of war and live up to the example of military heroes was no longer stigmatized simply as 'effeminacy' and 'cowardice'; men could display weakness without completely compromising their masculinity.[81]

[80] *News Chronicle*, 4 Nov. 1935, 5.
[81] M. Smith, 'The War and British Culture', in S. Constantine, M. W. Kirby, and M. Rose (eds.), *The First World War in British History* (London: Edward Arnold, 1995), 177.

The public understanding of the horrors of the front line was, as a number of historians have demonstrated, significantly improved by the wave of war books that were published at the end of the 1920s (including works by Robert Graves, Siegfried Sassoon, and Erich Remarque).[82] The *Herald*, unsurprisingly, gave considerable publicity to these accounts. Extracts from Remarque's *All Quiet on the Western Front* were printed during the election campaign of 1929, and the paper championed Graves's *Goodbye to All That*: 'Never Has the War Myth Been More Fearlessly Exploded', concluded Egon Wertheimer.[83] P. L. Mannock told readers how such books treated 'war with a grim and often horrible intimacy . . . destroying much of its hollow and spurious glory', and awaited similar films to portray 'war in its ghastly futility of mud, blood and demoralisation'.[84] Much more revealing of how these critiques were entering the mainstream, however, was the fact that the *Sunday Express* was the first paper to serialize *All Quiet on the Western Front* at length. The serialization was sensationally successful and appeared to tap the increasingly widespread 'pacificist' sentiment described by Martin Ceadel.[85] The circulation manager informed Beaverbrook in September 1929 that Remarque's book was 'a winner and the best single thing for circulation that the *Sunday Express* has ever done'; the following week he observed that 'all Fleet Street seems to envy us just now'.[86] The impact was certainly noted in journalistic circles and similar publications followed: Stefan Zweig's *The Case of Sergeant Grischa* was another 'debunking' novel to be serialized. The male protagonists of these works were sensitive, vulnerable, and sickened by the immense bloodshed around them: they were the highest literary expressions of the anti-heroic reaction to the war and a complete contrast to the manly conquerors of Henty and Haggard stories. By bringing these books to a wider audience, the press played a notable part in reinforcing and deepening the anti-war mood.

Indeed, as a growing sense of crisis enveloped Europe in the early 1930s and war broke out between China and Japan, the robust idealism and 'high diction' of 1914 were conspicuous by their absence. The rhetoric of the conservative press had come to resemble in a number of ways the left-wing and liberal critiques of the previous decade. The *Express* in February 1932, for example, contemplated the 'war weariness of the human race':

---

[82] Hynes, *A War Imagined*, ch. 21; A. Gregory, *The Silence of Memory: Armistice Day 1919–46* (Oxford: Berg, 1994), 118–21.

[83] *Daily Herald*, 28 May 1929, 3; 29 May 1929, 3; Richards, 'Conscription, Conformity and Control', 290.

[84] *Daily Herald*, 23 May 1930, 6.   [85] Ceadel, *Semi-Detached Idealists*.

[86] Beaverbrook Papers, H/64, Russell to Whelan, 8 Sept. 1929; Russell to Beaverbrook, 14 Sept. 1929.

Even the soldiers have lost faith in slaughter. And the civilians have learned that in modern warfare no one wins. War is out of date. It is old-fashioned, despite the embellishments of scientific invention. It has become a tragic absurdity. The will to war still exists in many breasts, but the game is not what it was. When the tank becomes ridiculous in men's eyes and the bombing airplane no more romantic than a criminal's 'life preserver' the days of world warfare will be numbered.[87]

Similarly, when the *Express* produced a photographic history of the First World War the following year, warfare was portrayed as the 'crucifixion of youth' rather than as the testing ground of manliness. An editorial described the volume as 'perhaps the most dreadful book of bloodshed ever printed. There is no glamour left in war after turning these pages.'[88] '300 Stark Photographs Tear the Veil of Romance from the War', declared one headline; George Lansbury, by then leader of the Labour Party, announced that 'The *Daily Express* has undoubtedly produced the best anti-war document I have ever seen.'[89] The sort of unthinking militarism and conservatism that was now widely regarded as having triumphed during the First World War was satirized in Beaverbrook's other daily paper, the *Evening Standard*, in David Low's 'Colonel Blimp' cartoons, which appeared regularly from 1934. ('If I wanted to attack the officer class very successfully,' complained Captain Frederick Bellenger, the Labour MP, in the Commons in 1942, 'I would employ the methods adopted by David Low in his cartoons of "Colonel Blimp".'[90]) When Hitler remilitarized the Rhineland in March 1936, the *Mirror* could do little more than share the disgust of the *Express* at old ideals, and pray that war could be avoided:

Who will be caught again by lying twaddle about war to end war, and about our sacred honour and our solemn oath? The futile pacts and obsolete treaties may lie in pieces wherever Hitler or anybody else has thrown them. Better flimsy fragments of imbecile documents on the ground than millions of rotting bodies of young men.[91]

By the late 1930s the Great War was widely understood as a tragic waste: the conflict had not destroyed militarism and brought peace, but merely transferred problems to another generation. Although the anti-heroic atmosphere was not all-encompassing, the bitterness and disillusionment evident in the

---

[87] *Daily Express*, 11 Feb. 1932, 8.   [88] *Daily Express*, 21 Oct. 1933, 2, 10.

[89] *Daily Express*, 20 Oct. 1933, 3; 24 Oct. 1933, 9.

[90] *Parliamentary Debates*, 378 H. C. Deb., 5th ser., 26 Mar. 1942, col. 2300. For examples of Low's Colonel Blimp cartoons, see P. Seymour-Ure and J. Schoff, *David Low* (London: Secker & Warburg, 1985).

[91] *Daily Mirror*, 9 Mar. 1936, 13.

language of press commentators had significantly tarnished the shiny ideals of pre-1914 'imperial masculinity'.

Reinvigorating 'Imperial Masculinity'? The Daily Mail *and Fascism*

One paper, the *Daily Mail*, stood somewhat apart from these currents of opinion. Its political policy directed by the increasingly erratic Lord Rothermere, the paper displayed considerable sympathy for fascism even when its violent character had become clear. Throughout the 1920s the *Mail* had admired Mussolini for attempting to build a barrier against socialist advance in Europe, and the Italian leader was celebrated as a positive example to British politicians; he was nothing less than the 'greatest figure of our age'.[92] During the 1930s Rothermere's frustration with the 'ineffectiveness' of parliamentary democracy deepened, and resulted in the *Mail* coming out in support of Mosley's British Union of Fascists (BUF) in January 1934. In his article 'Hurrah for the Blackshirts', Rothermere described Italy and Germany as 'beyond all doubt the best-governed nations in Europe today' and recommended fascist reforms in Britain.[93] While open propagandizing for the BUF lasted only six months before differences of opinion forced a split,[94] Rothermere and the *Mail* did little to conceal their continued approval of Hitler and Mussolini's domestic policies.

Rothermere was interested in fascism as a means of remedying what he perceived to be a loss of the virility and active patriotism that had previously marked the British Empire and its leaders. As his confidant Collin Brooks recalled, 'He was convinced that Britain had entered a phase of decline, had lost her old militant virtues, and, in her softness, was lusting after the strange idols of pacifism, nationalisation and everything which would sap self-reliance.'[95] The series of concessions made to colonial opinion in India were 'craven' and 'sentimental', a symbol of the nation's 'decadence'.[96] In their shared diary, Rothermere and Brooks lamented the passage of the India Bill in 1935 with a revealing metaphor: affronting 'all the old Imperial Spirit of the race' the measure seemed 'like the last, mis-shapen, abortive child of the Mother of Parliaments already entering the madness of her

[92] *Daily Mail*, 28 Mar. 1928, 10. For other examples of the *Mail*'s support for Mussolini, see 17 Sept. 1923, 5; 2 May 1927, 10; 28 Apr. 1928, 12. [93] *Daily Mail*, 15 Jan. 1934, 10.
[94] Rothermere and Mosley's public exchange of letters (printed in the *Daily Mail*, 14 July 1934) signalled the end of the relationship. On this, see M. Pugh, 'The British Union of Fascists and the Olympia Debate', *Historical Journal*, 41/2 (1998), 529–42.
[95] C. Brooks, *Devil's Decade: Portraits of the Nineteen Thirties* (London: Macdonald, 1948), 145.
[96] *Daily Mail*, 19 Mar. 1931, 12; 16 Apr. 1931, 10; *Brooks Journals*, 24 July 1935, 121–2.

menopause'.[97] The failure to maintain the nation's armed strength was a further sign of the 'incapacity of the old men who rule our country'. 'Britons of a generation ago', the *Mail* observed darkly, 'were more alert in such vital matters.'[98] They understood that 'weakness is never honoured or respected'.[99] Another editorial, critical of the League of Nations, warned that '"Collective Security" is the phrase which has disarmed us and which is hampering our efforts to regain strength.' This was because patriotic feeling could only be mobilized for the purposes of Empire: 'no sane youth burns to guarantee a system which would throw British manhood into the trenches to safeguard San Salvador or some other League member whose frontiers only school teachers know'.[100] The *Mail* decided to act itself: in 1935 it established and publicized a National League of Airmen, to encourage 'a rapid advancement in our air force strength'.[101]

The contrast between the decisive masculinity of the fascist leaders and the effeminacy of British politicians was constantly reiterated. Invited by the *Mail* to discuss the appeal of Mussolini, Oswald Mosley resorted to gender imagery: 'Englishmen who have long suffered statesmanship in skirts can pay him no less, and need pay him no more, tribute than to say "Here at least is a man".'[102] Rothermere was similarly positive about Hitler. He made clear his disdain for the 'old women of both sexes' who circulated hysterical reports of Nazi excesses and ignored the 'immense benefits' guaranteed by the regime.[103] Hitler and Mussolini had overseen a 'gigantic revival of national strength and spirit'. Hundreds of thousands of people in Britain, Rothermere declared when announcing the *Mail*'s support for the BUF, 'would like to see their own country develop that spirit of patriotic pride and service which has transformed Germany and Italy.'[104] The admiration for Germany's vigorous imperialism was evident in Rothermere's suggestion that Tanganyika, the Cameroons, and Togoland be returned to it: 'We cannot expect a nation of "he-men" like the Germans to sit forever with folded arms under the provocations and stupidities of the Treaty of Versailles . . . To deny this mighty nation . . . a share in the work of developing backward regions of the world is preposterous.'[105]

The arguments of Rothermere and the *Mail* were riddled with inconsistencies. Nazi Germany was praised for its virility, but also feared for the danger it posed to Britain. There was a passionate wish to avoid war, but also a glorifi-

---

[97] *Brooks Journals*, 31 May 1935, 113.   [98] *Daily Mail*, 2 Jan. 1934, 10.

[99] *Daily Mail*, 17 Jan. 1934, 10.   [100] *Daily Mail*, 15 Dec. 1936, 10.

[101] P. Addison, 'Lord Rothermere and British Foreign Policy', in C. Cook and G. Peele (eds.), *The Politics of Reappraisal* (London: Macmillan, 1975), 200–1; Taylor, *The Great Outsiders*, 309.

[102] *Daily Mail*, 1 Feb. 1932, 10.   [103] *Daily Mail*, 10 July 1933, 10.

[104] *Daily Mail*, 15 Jan. 1934, 10.   [105] *Daily Mail*, 21 Mar. 1934, 12.

cation of military strength and the tools of conflict (new destroyers were announced in large headlines with undisguised awe and appreciation: 'New £7,000,000 Battleship—Wonders of HMS Nelson—Nine 16in Guns and Bomb-Proof Deck—Huge Armoured Tower'[106]). Rothermere was essentially an old-fashioned imperialist who found it difficult to come to terms with the altered post-war climate of opinion. His rhetoric relied on dated conceptions of 'imperial masculinity' and national virility, and he believed that fascism might be the only way to preserve such ideals in an increasingly hostile environment. The stagnation of the *Mail's* circulation throughout a decade in which other papers rapidly gained readers exposed the limited appeal of this type of language. Other newspapers responded by attempting to reveal fascist 'manliness' as uncivilized brutality. The *Daily Herald* had long sought to equate right-wing Conservatism with fascism and the spectre of violence. A cartoon published at the time of the East Fulham by-election in 1933, for example, denounced the Conservatives as the 'Treat 'Em Rough Party', with a woman representing 'the housewives of England' sporting two black eyes obtained at the hands of the 'He Men' Tories.[107] The rough treatment of hecklers at the BUF's ill-fated Olympia rally in June 1934 was reported in great detail by the press and ensured that the brutality of the movement became a major issue: 'One woman was picked up after being ejected from the building. Her clothes had been torn nearly off her back and there was scarcely a visible portion of her body which was not covered with blood.'[108] Fascists were labelled as 'aboriginal', 'cave-men', 'war-mongers', and 'sabre-rattlers': insensitive, militaristic men whose values belonged to an age that had passed.[109] Another tactic was simply to ridicule the fascist claims of virility and strength. Describing the 'Blackshirts' Dismal March', held shortly after the banning of political uniforms, the *News Chronicle* questioned the manliness of the participants: 'the loss of their black shirts seemed to have taken all the stuffing out of the men. They appeared to be what most of them probably were: a miscellaneous assortment of weedy clerks, not 30 per cent of whom would be passed for the Army, or even as Scoutmasters.'[110] It seems clear that the *Mail* lost the propaganda battle on this issue. The failure of the paper to capture the public imagination with its advocacy of a 'remasculinization' of society provides further evidence that notions of patriotism and national service had moved on.

---

[106] *Daily Mail*, 25 Apr. 1927, 11. [107] *Daily Herald*, 25 Oct. 1933, 8.
[108] *News Chronicle*, 12 June 1934, 9. [109] e.g. *News Chronicle*, 14 July 1937, 8; 14 June 1934, 2.
[110] *News Chronicle*, 5 July 1937, 1.

'Feminine Instincts': A Barrier to Future War?

If the impact of the Great War on notions of masculinity was uncertain and fiercely contested, there was a far greater unanimity in the press about the reaction of women to the conflict. In what was one of the most pervasive and stable sets of gendered stereotypes in the period, commentators across the political spectrum agreed that the slaughter in the trenches had outraged 'feminine' nurturing and mothering instincts and united women in grief for lost husbands, sons, friends, and relatives. While there were differences of opinion over how it might be achieved, all assumed that peace would become a pre-eminent concern for the newly enfranchised female citizens. Asked by the *Daily Mirror* only weeks after the Armistice to assess women's likely contribution to politics, for example, Eva Gore-Booth predicted that

It seems likely that those who, through the ages, have been taught that their business was to be the guardians of their homes, and the cherishers of human life in its weakest phases, will bring some of the old constructive spirit into their new sphere of action and welcome the idea of a league of disarmed nations to protect the peace of the world.[111]

Writing in the *Herald* during the election campaign of December 1923, Dr C. W. Saleeby used almost identical imagery to rally female voters:

Women are the natural mothers and nurses of Life. They are Nature's trustees of the future. Men tend to fight and roam and spend and bluster and destroy; women to protect and nourish, to love and to save. Men make wars and women make homes.[112]

The public apparatus of commemoration constructed in the aftermath of the war was directed above all at the nation's grieving women. As Adrian Gregory has demonstrated, the bereaved mother—rather than the ex-serviceman—'was the pre-eminent subject of Armistice Day in the United Kingdom'.[113] This emphasis was certainly reproduced in the press, and it became standard practice to narrate remembrance ceremonies from the perspective of women. 'As one Armistice Day after another slips past,' noted a *Daily Mail* editorial in November 1921, 'women's remembrance of the dead deepens in devotion':

The pilgrimage to the Cenotaph in the cold hours of yesterday was supremely a pilgrimage of mothers . . . In the Abbey it is the women who weep quietly, each alone. Everywhere it is the women who remember, with an intense concentration or

---

[111] *Daily Mirror*, 5 Dec. 1918, 5.   [112] *Daily Herald*, 4 Dec. 1923, 7.
[113] Gregory, *Silence of Memory*, 40.

sorrow for lost husband or child. Men talk of wars which may come. Women think only of a war that is past. There is one safeguard for world peace—the strongest. It is women's undying remembrance of sorrow which is war's pitiless legacy to all wives and mothers of men.[114]

Time and again, this painful maternal memory of loss was offered as the justification for a female stand against war. In the following year's Armistice Day edition, the *Express* printed the thoughts of 'A Soldier's Mother':

If these young mothers only knew what I have known, that blank dead end to all the secret ambitions and joys of motherhood, surely they would band themselves together in a fixed determination that they at least would never be robbed as I was robbed. The hands of women linked together the world over could stop war.[115]

The potency of this appeal is suggested by the fact that in a paper of a very different political complexion, almost a decade later, the language remained very similar. Another unnamed mother 'whose son was killed in the last war'—this was the only qualification required to command attention—pleaded to the female readers of the *Herald* to preserve peace:

Mothers, I tell you if ever you permit war again you are potential enemies of your sons. You protect your son from harm in his babyhood. Safeguard his manhood with passionate and ceaseless effort to prevent war! . . . We have now a voice both in the home and in the world outside which we have gradually won for ourselves during the last fifty years. We ought to form a Mother's National, or International League for the Prevention of War.[116]

Even Ray Strachey, a feminist not inclined to indulge in nebulous rhetoric about sexual difference and usually suspicious about generalizations about women, accepted the assumptions behind these articles. 'If there can be said to be a special women's point of view upon anything', she told the *Daily News* in 1923, 'perhaps the business of fighting is that thing':

women are not themselves fighters . . . they get no compensation whatever for their suffering. It is all pure loss; while to men, even with their greater suffering, there is the satisfaction of duty done . . . all over the world women are likely to provide an enthusiastic body of support for the ideals of peace, and for any concrete steps towards a reduction of the chances of war.[117]

Press commentators frequently claimed to have found evidence that women were beginning to translate this shared hostility to war into effective political action. A *Daily News* editorial argued that the success of pacifists in the 1922 general election was attributable in part to 'the women electors' anti-war

---

[114] *Daily Mail,* 12 Nov. 1921, 6.   [115] *Daily Express,* 11 Nov. 1922, 6.
[116] *Daily Herald,* 4 Aug. 1931, 1, 8.   [117] *Daily News,* 26 Feb. 1923, 4.

fervour'.[118] Seven years later an *Express* editorial suggested that the success of women's organizations in the United States in holding up the government's Navy Bill might herald a new era:

As a portent of the growing power of women in national and international affairs the incident . . . is deeply significant. There is no country where women have the vote in which similar vetoes or obstacles may not be experienced on issues which they conceive to be essentially moral issues; women may then easily work and vote as a sex. Nobody pays much attention to the present League of Nations. But an International League of Women, actively vehement in the politics of all countries, would be a power indeed. It might come very near to abolishing war for ever.[119]

Others discerned what they took to be a crucial turning point in the unexpected defeat of the National Government candidate in the East Fulham by-election of 1933.[120] Yet although women's pleas for peace received a considerable amount of attention in the press, the gendered critique of war was rarely developed beyond a fairly superficial level. Always seeking to connect with the 'average' mother, and assuming that she lacked interest in the precise developments of the diplomatic situation, articles tended to rely on simple generalizations and the domestic language of maternal and wifely love. Those women's organizations that were actively involved in the League of Nations and other international forums—such as the Women's International League for Peace and Freedom—were often overlooked in favour of reports on this more pervasive, though unorganized, female opposition to war. The lack of engagement with the actual, shifting world of international affairs gave the arguments a rather timeless quality, which, although superficially seductive, ensured that there were rarely any specific recommendations for positive action. Indeed, an almost identical rhetoric could be mobilized on either side of the political debate. In the run-up to the 1935 general election, for example, Jennie Adamson in the *Daily Herald* used familiar language to criticize Baldwin's £200 million rearmament package: 'Don't forget that heavy arms are an incitement to war . . . You don't want to lose your sweetheart. You don't want your husband to march away to some battle front. You don't want your brothers and your sons to be maimed and slaughtered because a "National" Government ruined our chances of collective security.'[121] The *Mirror*, on the other

[118] *Daily News*, 17 Nov. 1922, 4.

[119] Undated *Daily Express* editorial, May(?) 1929, quoted in the June 1929 issue of *Pax International*, the magazine of the Women's International League for Peace and Freedom (WILPF); cited in G. Bussey and M. Tims, *Pioneers for Peace: Women's International League for Peace and Freedom 1915–65* (London: WILPF, 1980), 80–1.

[120] See e.g. the *Herald* editorial entitled 'The Revolt of the Women', 23 Oct. 1933, 8; and the *News Chronicle*, 23 Oct. 1933, 2, and 27 Oct. 1933, 10.   [121] *Daily Herald*, 6 Nov. 1935, 10.

hand, supported the rearmament programme as the best way of securing inter-national stability. Yet it too made an appeal to the female instincts for peace in what was described as the 'women's election': the housewife and mother suffered most from war, it declared, and 'for the sake of our loved ones', she would 'put peace before party' and support Baldwin.[122] Employed so frequently, the radical dimensions of the rhetoric—in the sense of reorienting the world around a different, 'feminine' set of values—were often obscured and the words became mere platitudes.

Occasionally, particular policies and institutions were criticized, and the contrast was telling. Ursula Bloom's open letter to the foreign secretary, Anthony Eden, in the *Mirror* in 1936 took the usual point of departure: 'I am the mother of a son who is of fighting age, I believe my fears are the fears of every other mother in the Empire, and I speak for the other mothers.' Yet, unusually, she continued by censuring Eden's conduct in the Rhineland crisis and developed a wider attack on the bastions of male power:

you are being aggressive. You are undoubtedly a young man who is possessed of the fetish of the old school tie. You are bombastic and behave in a manner that is extremely foolish . . . You would tell me that Waterloo was won on the playing fields of Eton. I would tell you that the Empire will be lost if we cannot forget an era which we have outlived. The world is changing. The old school tie is becoming the old fool tie . . . The spirit of the old tradition will not stand the strain of a second claim upon it.[123]

Bloom's arguments, drawing attention to the competitive masculinity instilled by public schools, foreshadowed those of Virginia Woolf in *Three Guineas*. Revealingly, however, the article was prefaced by a disclaimer from the paper: 'It is essential that all opinions, however provocative, should be discussed . . . Do you agree with her?' This showed the limitations of this 'feminine' anti-war rhetoric. Presented in a generalized form on Armistice Day or during general elections, it could command widespread support and sympathy. Yet when a more radical cutting edge was developed, and a call was made for the reform of specific attitudes and policies, it was no longer accorded the status of being the 'woman's perspective', but became instead a controversial and 'provocative' position to be debated (and, implicitly, to be regarded with scepticism). Campaigners such as Vera Brittain, who maintained a radical feminist–pacifist position up to, and throughout, the war against Hitler, found themselves increasingly marginalized in the press. As early as 1933 Brittain suspected that she was having some articles rejected for being 'too pacifist', and she found it

---

[122] *Daily Mirror*, 14 Nov. 1935, 10.   [123] *Daily Mirror*, 11 Mar. 1936, 12.

very difficult to obtain space by the end of the decade.[124] Arguably, she was only defending many of the sentiments prominently expressed over the previous two decades; as circumstances changed, however, she was perceived to be challenging the 'national interest'.

The Daily Mirror *and the Sudetenland Crisis*

These developments in the gendered language of war and peace emerge clearly in the *Daily Mirror*'s coverage of the Sudetenland crisis of September 1938. The *Mirror* was in many respects the most dynamic popular paper of the late 1930s, refashioning its approach and rapidly gaining readers; it also had the most individual perspective on foreign affairs, uncommitted either to 'appeasement', like the *Mail* and the *Express*, or to collective security through the League of Nations, like the *News Chronicle* and the *Herald*. The *Mirror*'s commentary on the crisis, supplementing the main news columns and editorials, was dominated by two of its star columnists: the plain-speaking Cassandra (William Neil Connor) and the women's feature-writer Eileen Ascroft (whose recent 'Charm School' series had been so successful that the paper turned it into a book).[125] Cassandra and Ascroft were writing for different sections of the readership and developed two clearly gendered styles and positions. Both naturally wanted to avoid war, and by the end of the crisis both would declare their willingness to support military intervention against Hitler; but along the way their emphases diverged significantly.

On 5 September 1938 Ascroft's article was a lament for the horrors of the world. The headline summed up her thoughts: 'I was feeling sad on Friday— Sad at the sight of men suffering from the effects of a war that ended 20 years ago—Sad at the thought that war was perhaps once again so near . . . In a tiny hamlet I found Sanctuary'.[126] Her column had for some time been entitled 'Sanctuary', for it offered a haven of (female) kind-heartedness and hope in a world of (male) dictatorship and violence. The following week the anti-war feeling became more prominent: 'This is a page of Peace . . . Take the hate out of your hearts and let them beat in sympathy with all men.'[127] Employing a language informed by Christian feminism, she called for the reformation of masculinity: 'Let us kill within us the morbid fascination of war which sadly lies in the heart of nearly every man.' 'Why', she asked, 'can't

---

[124] A. Bishop (ed.), *Vera Brittain: Diary of the Thirties 1932–39. Chronicle of Friendship* (London: Victor Gollancz, 1986), 22 Aug. 1933, 146. On Brittain's pacifism, see P. Berry and A. Bishop (eds.), *Testament of a Generation: The Journalism of Vera Brittain and Winifred Holtby* (London: Virago, 1985), 38–42.

[125] On 'Cassandra', see R. Connor, *Cassandra: Reflections in a Mirror* (London: Cassell, 1969).

[126] *Daily Mirror*, 5 Sept. 1938, 9.   [127] *Daily Mirror*, 13 Sept. 1938, 9.

we devote as large a part of our national budget for the organisation of peace . . . as we do for war?'[128] With no solution in sight the following week, the gendered rhetoric reached its fullest expression. 'Yesterday', ran the headline, 'Eileen Ascroft went to Westminster Abbey and joined the women who knelt before the Unknown Warrior's tomb, and she says . . . this was my prayer'. The prayer was one that found 'its echo in the heart of every woman in England today':

O Lord . . . we, the women of England, are on our knees to You today . . . The storm clouds gather all around us and men talk and argue about peace and war. And we are afraid for our husbands and our sons and our dear ones. We are prepared to see them fight for justice—but we long for peace . . . Hear the united prayer of the women of Europe. We are mothers, Lord, who have cherished and loved our children . . . We are wives . . . we are sweethearts . . . we are friends.[129]

These columns expressed powerful and sincere sentiments of a kind that had not received similar space or respect on the eve of the First World War. Editors in 1938 were clearly far more convinced than their counterparts of 1914 of the need to give due recognition and attention to what they assumed to be the 'women's perspective'. Yet the limitations of this approach are once again obvious. The distinction was maintained between the men who 'talk and argue' and the women who prayed. These prayers were based on the traditional female concern for family and friends: there was relatively little discussion of the actual issues under dispute, and merely a general advocacy of spending more on the 'organisation of peace'. Ascroft created a discursive 'Sanctuary', and the female voice remained confined to it, rather isolated from the detail of the unfolding crisis.

Cassandra, on the other hand, was all too keen to share his inside knowledge of the diplomatic war of nerves. As a leading (male) columnist he had been sent by the paper on fact-finding journeys to the cities at the centre of the dispute, Berlin and Prague, before returning to reveal his thoughts.[130] Cassandra's language was as far from the 'high diction' of pre-1914 imperial manliness as it was from the contemplative, 'feminine' style of Ascroft. His was the voice of 'common sense', cynical, blunt, and practical, the 'ordinary man' in the pub; in the *Mirror*'s words, he provided 'realistic writing unadulterated with sentiment or jingoism':[131]

the ordinary German has not the slightest desire to get behind a gun and put the sights on an Englishman. And I, for my part, know of nobody in this country

---

[128] Ibid.   [129] *Daily Mirror*, 20 Sept. 1938, 9.
[130] In his final pre-war visit, in Aug. 1939, 'Cassandra'–Connor was arrested by the Gestapo and held for several hours': Connor, *Cassandra*, 42.   [131] *Daily Mirror*, 15 Sept. 1938, 14.

who wants to blast hell out of Fritz. Yet here we are whooping along for a war that'll make the last scrap seem like a nursemaid's tiff . . . I think we are on top of a volcano.[132]

In contrast to Ascroft, Cassandra was ferociously critical of particular people and policies. He condemned as 'callous' *The Times*'s suggestion that the total secession of the Sudeten territories be considered, for example, and explained the proposal as a manifestation of the 'irresponsible' influence of the 'pro-German Cliveden mob', that 'rich clique, born and bred in the selfish cradle of the ruling classes' who were trying to masquerade as the voice of Britain.[133] Cassandra's patriotism involved a loyalty to the 'common man' rather than the British establishment. (When, in 1941–2, Cassandra and the *Mirror*'s support for the troops turned into criticism of the way the war was being conducted, there were furious criticisms from the government.[134]) Nevertheless, the desire to achieve justice in Czechoslovakia was not just a form of masculine bravado. He refused to indulge in the language of heroism and patriotic sacrifice, and specifically referred to the way in which Remarque's *All Quiet on the Western Front* had exposed the old platitudes. He was quite prepared to reveal his own terror: 'I myself, born in the year 1909, am ripe for the plucking. I am strong. I am able. And I can kill, if given a good gun and enough fear. Maybe I'm a fool, but, dear God, how I want to live!'[135]

He also rejected portrayals of the Czechs as a virtuous, pure (feminine) people, who, like the Belgians in 1914, required assistance from chivalrous (masculine) Britain:

The Czechs hate the Germans. Let no one be deceived about that. When a comparatively weak country appears about to be the victim of aggression from an immensely more powerful state, all the sob sisters of the world get together and scream poor little Belgium, or Abyssinia, or China, or Czechoslovakia, or anything else that's in the sentimental slush bag . . . Let me tell you here and now, that the Czechs hate the Germans with a hatred that would burn holes in the corrugated-iron roof of a mission-hall.[136]

Such statements can be contrasted with the language of Eileen Ascroft, who, when war appeared to be imminent, justified it in terms of an everyday dispute involving any mother's child:

I hate the misery of little people, ground under the heel of a bully. Especially when every new humiliation seems only to feed the appetite of that bully for more arrogant

---

[132] *Daily Mirror*, 8 Sept. 1938, 12.   [133] *Daily Mirror*, 9 Sept. 1938, 15.
[134] Cudlipp, *Publish and be Damned!*, chs. 21–3.   [135] *Daily Mirror*, 15 Sept. 1938, 14.
[136] *Daily Mirror*, 14 Sept. 1938, 12.

triumphs. And I know that there is only one way to deal with a bully—and that's to pay him back in his own coin, to knock him down before he can hit you.[137]

Cassandra and Ascroft in their columns exemplified many of the trends of inter-war discourse. Cassandra articulated a cynical, pragmatic masculinity, sceptical of grand rhetoric, traditional heroism, and the blandishments of the establishment, but also proudly patriotic and determined not to see grave international injustices go unpunished. Ascroft used the language of domesticity and maternal love to pray for peace. When war loomed once again, in August 1939, her prayer was reprinted, and the women of Britain were urged to plead for a non-violent solution to the crisis.[138] Ultimately, though, she did not fundamentally question the wisdom of male leadership. 'Women play no part in the decisions of wars and great armies. We know that, and we are content to leave these things to our men, trusting them to decide what must be done for justice and freedom.' If the men did conclude that conflict was unavoidable, she promised that 'we women will not be found wanting'.[139]

Preparing for War

Eileen Ascroft's acceptance that military force would be justified against Hitler was representative of a wider shift at this time in which women were portrayed less as the 'guardians of peace' than as dutiful citizens mobilizing for war. When the Auxiliary Territorial Service called for 25,000 female recruits in September 1938, the *Mirror* proudly reported that 'Britain's women throughout the length and breadth of the country flocked in their thousands to enrol,' determined to defend the nation: 'if danger comes, the modern girl will play an even bigger part than her mother did last time'.[140] During the last war, another article recalled, 'No Sacrifice Was Too Great' for the women on the home front. The author agreed that there was no question that their daughters would live up to the challenges ahead: 'What will women do? They will take over men's jobs. They will watch and wait . . . We know their bravery.'[141] Over the course of the next year all of the popular papers gave considerable publicity to women's role in the war preparations, and the 'female' language of peace remained muted. 'This is Miss England 1939', declared the front page of the *Express* above a picture of a woman stitching plane wings at an aircraft factory at Hanworth.[142] 'Their Hearts Are in the Air', proclaimed the *Mail* about the women of the National Women's Air Reserve, 'very business-like in their white

---

[137] *Daily Mirror*, 27 Sept. 1938, 9.   [138] *Daily Mirror*, 25 Aug. 1939, 11.
[139] *Daily Mirror*, 28 Aug. 1939, 9.   [140] *Daily Mirror*, 28 Sept. 1938, 3.
[141] *Daily Mirror*, 29 Sept. 1938, 19.   [142] *Daily Express*, 13 May 1939, 1.

overalls'.[143] It was accepted that women would play a subordinate and supportive role in any future conflict, and the idea that women could be used in
front-line service does not seem to have been seriously entertained. Nevertheless, papers highlighted how women were being given greater responsibilities
than in the Great War. Mona Friedlander, who was featured across the press in
May 1939, typified the strides made since 1918: this 'twenty-five year old
England international ice hockey player', noted the *Express*, 'has become
Britain's first woman air-taxi pilot . . . Soon she will be flying at night over
London as a target for the searchlights of the anti-aircraft brigades.'[144]

But it was clear that women would not only play a greater role in the
prosecution of the war, they would also be exposed to its dangers as never
before. The potential threat of aerial bombardment had received huge publicity in the press throughout the 1930s and it was widely recognized that the previous stark dichotomy between the front line and the home front would be
blurred in modern warfare.[145] When a Mrs Gameson described a dream for the
Mirror in which she and her daughter followed her husband into the Army, the
paper's expert Pamela Rose replied that the 'meaning is too obvious' to require
detailed explanation: 'it is the women's point of view about war. If another
comes, it won't be fought in the trenches. We shall all be in it.'[146] Women were
expected to concern themselves not just with their own safety, but also with
that of their children. Women's pages explained the details of evacuation and
air-raid procedures, and encouraged women to ensure that children did not
develop 'crisis nerves'.[147] Although there was some sympathy for 'crisis-
puzzled' mothers anxious about parting from their children, articles tended
to assume that women would be able to call on deep reserves of strength and
'rally to the cause'.[148]

Appeals to men to mobilize were often couched in traditional terms: 'Work
to protect the women and children of your own land,' implored the *Mirror*,
'defend your home, your street and your town against the bomb and the aerial
torpedo.'[149] But the idealism of 1914 was conspicuously absent, and aggressive
posturing seemed unsuitable. When the Labour MP George Buchanan wrote
to Gerald Barry, the editor of the *News Chronicle*, asking to contribute an
article on the preparations for war, he noted that there had been little of the

---

[143] *Daily Mail*, 8 May 1939, 5.
[144] *Daily Express*, 12 May 1939, 13; see also *Daily Mail*, 12 May 1939, 13.
[145] As early as August 1928 the *Mail* discussed the 'bombers no one can stop', and in July 1931 it cautioned
that 'London is at the mercy of air raiders'. There were frequent warnings thereafter: *Daily Mail*, 18 Aug. 1928,
8; 24 July 1931, 12; 2 Jan. 1934, 10; 15 Dec. 1936, 10; *Daily Mirror*, 29 June 1935, 10, etc.
[146] *Daily Mirror*, 12 Sept. 1938, 13.   [147] *News Chronicle*, 11 May 1939, 4.
[148] *Daily Express*, 31 Aug. 1939, 11, 7.   [149] *Daily Mirror*, 17 Sept. 1938, 28.

'flamboyancy' that marked the previous conflict: the mobilization 'is not yet covered with a horrid glamour or Rule-Britannia-ism'.[150] Instead, commentators celebrated the good-natured, if rather cynical, sense of humour supposedly shared by British men (in contrast to the stereotypical dour efficiency of the Germans). Judy Giles has suggested that masculine heroism was, in the inter-war years, rewritten as optimism and endurance.[151] This certainly captures the tone of much newspaper commentary in 1938 and 1939. The commercial and diplomatic incentives to maintain a positive outlook have already been highlighted, and they merely reinforced an already existing distaste for the rhetoric of the old 'imperial masculinity'. As late as 7 August 1939 the *Express* confidently predicted on its front page that there would be 'No War This Year'.[152] Even after the Molotov–Ribbentrop pact, the paper declared that 'the position is not critical yet'.[153] During the crisis the *Express* portrayed a steadfast nation at ease with itself and remaining cheerful despite the gloomy international outlook. Sent out to test the atmosphere of the crowds in London towards the end of August 1939, the *Express* reporter Hilde Marchant declared 'You Can't Stop Those Cockney Wisecracks': 'The Londoner is crisis hardened . . . no war will stop a Cockney from wisecracking . . . It's grand to be in London.'[154] The following day she expanded on the atmosphere in the 'real London':

Every day Berlin announces that London is terrified. It may be that their informants can speak only pidgin English, for listening into the street conversation you get the impression that the city is accepting the crisis with incredible calm and humour. It is not that we are ill-informed on the danger—just that we are ready for friends or enemies.[155]

Strube's cartoons reinforced this image of a calm nation: one depicted his famous 'Little Man' very deliberately lighting a cigarette while being shot at from all sides by 'Propaganda', 'Rumours', 'Scares', and 'Tension' (see Fig. 6.2).[156] Such were the qualities of a nation 'united by the love of liberty and not marshalled by force and oppression'.[157] The contrast with the cruel, humourless Germans was underlined by another cartoon which showed two soldiers studying a book taken from a shelf labelled 'Atrocity Stories', one commenting 'Here's one we've not used since 1870.'[158] The *Mirror* provided similar reports of an undaunted population, describing how 'cheerfulness was

[150] Gerald Barry Papers, File 9, George Buchanan to Gerald Barry, 27 Aug. 1939.
[151] Giles, *Women, Identity and Private Life*, 21.   [152] *Daily Express*, 7 Aug. 1939, 1.
[153] *Daily Express*, 22 Aug. 1939, 8.   [154] *Daily Express*, 25 Aug. 1939, 11.
[155] *Daily Express*, 26 Aug. 1939, 4.   [156] *Daily Express*, 29 Aug. 1939, 8.
[157] *Daily Express*, 30 Aug. 1939, 8.   [158] *Daily Express*, 29 Aug. 1939, 6.

Fig. 6.2. Strube's 'little man' (similar to Poy's John Citizen) is here shown embodying the
phlegmatic attitude of the British in the face of rumours of imminent war

the keynote of Britain's people in the hours of crisis yesterday'. The paper called
on its readers to draw heart from this resolute mood: after all, it declared, in the
past 'we've always come smilin' through'.[159] The *News Chronicle*, meanwhile,
offered five shillings for each comic anecdote from mobilizing servicemen, and
boasted that even floods 'have not dampened the humour of the men in
camp'.[160]

On the left, there was a particular determination that support for a campaign against Hitler should not be corrupted by militarism or jingoism.
Colonel T. A. Lowe, writing in the *Herald*, emphasized that the modern soldier
was not just a blindly patriotic 'tough guy' but a 'hard-working artisan, a skilled
craftsman and a self-respecting citizen' simply carrying out his duty to protect
Europe from dictatorship.[161] Similarly, Walter Layton insisted at a *News
Chronicle* policy conference in July 1939 that 'we should give as much space as
possible to interesting stories of the new militia, etcetera, but should avoid any
implied glorification of war . . . We should stress the idea of service to the
nation and the necessity of ultimately forming some plan for achieving

159 *Daily Mirror*, 25 Aug. 1939, 16–17.   160 *News Chronicle*, 9 Aug. 1939, 3.
161 *Daily Herald*, 8 May 1939, 10.

peace.'[162] But it was Cassandra in the *Mirror* who provided the clearest exposition of the realistic and pragmatic approach to war, free of the elevated rhetoric of 1914. War was 'obscene, murderous, bestial [and] profoundly evil', he wrote, and should not be presented as a Christian crusade. Invoking the name of God was 'blasphemy unbounded'. 'When the triggers start going off,' he continued, 'I'll do some shooting myself to save my skin': 'I'll not be in it for love, for money, for glory or for honour, but because the most detestable regime since the days of Attila the Hun wants to carve up our way of life to fit its own evil purpose.'[163] If the First World War and its aftermath destroyed the high ideals of its participants—'the Great War was meant . . . to make the world safe for democracy, and it established dictatorships throughout Europe', noted the *Express* bitterly in 1939—the cynical humour and restrained patriotism of 1939 offered a defence against similar disillusionment.[164]

Newspapers were just as determined in September 1939 as they had been in August 1914 to encourage men to serve the nation and protect British interests, but the ideals and expectations of masculinity that accompanied the patriotic rhetoric had been significantly re-evaluated in the intervening years. The appeal of 'imperial masculinity' undoubtedly remained in popular culture, and soldiers had by no means lost all of their glamour. Nevertheless, both the social costs of the militaristic ideal, and the individual difficulty of achieving that type of heroism, were more widely recognized. As the following chapter suggests, sportsmen and film stars offered new aspirational models of masculinity which could compete with the mighty imperial conquerors of the past. The way in which the *Mail*'s fascist rhetoric of imperial manliness jarred in the 1930s underlined how sensibilities had changed. As with the political material surveyed in Chapter 4, while the 'female perspective' was far more prominent than ever before, it remained rather crudely stereotyped and restricted to certain topics. War was viewed as a disturber of domestic peace, a wrecker of family ties, and its deeper roots usually went unexamined. Female journalists were given new opportunities to write on foreign affairs, but they were encouraged to use personal experience rather than knowledge of the diplomatic situation. As war loomed, the limitations of this approach became increasingly obvious.

[162] Trinity College, Cambridge, Walter Layton Papers, Box 89, fo. 37, Notes on Policy Conference No. 31, 21 July 1939.
[163] *Daily Mirror*, 30 Aug. 1939, 16.   [164] *Daily Express*, 4 Aug. 1939, 8.

7

Masculinity: Ideals and Anxieties

By the 1930s the popular daily press had embraced the female reading audience so conspicuously that it was difficult to regard newspapers any longer as directed above all at men. For some observers this was a matter of great regret. For others, however, it signalled a commercial opportunity. In December 1935 C. Arthur Pearson Ltd, the publishing company established by the founder of the *Daily Express*, launched *Men Only*, the first lifestyle magazine in Britain specifically for men, to try to capitalize on a perceived gap in the market. The new magazine was necessary, argued its editor, because the rest of the media was effeminate, offering only 'castrated nonsense'. Every daily paper was now afraid to 'fully and fairly support' the 'man's point of view' in case it lost the 'draper's advertisements'.[1] These claims were, of course, grossly exaggerated. While features and advertising directed at women had certainly dramatically increased in importance, men continued to dominate editorial positions and the 'man's point of view' remained well-entrenched in many parts of the paper—as the prevalence of 'bathing beauties' indicated.

Nevertheless, *Men Only's* accusations do perhaps bring into relief the changed circumstances in which masculinity was articulated in the daily press. Whereas *Men Only* could respond to contemporary fears about the 'feminization' of society by championing an uncomplicated 'rugged masculinity', and denouncing both the activities of the 'modern woman' and the 'effeminate' charms of suburban domesticity, such an editorial approach was inappropriate for daily newspapers committed to a much broader audience of both sexes and reliant on advertising aimed at domestic consumers. Popular newspapers carried a variety of different images of men and masculinity, and not all of them were particularly positive or reassuring. If masculinity was not as heavily con-

---

[1] J. Greenfield, S. O'Connell, and C. Reid, 'Fashioning Masculinity: *Men Only*, Consumption and the Development of Marketing in the 1930s', *Twentieth Century British History*, 10/4 (1999), 457–76, quotations at 462–3.

tested as femininity in this period, there were nevertheless a number of different ideas about what the character of the 'modern man' was, or should be, and these were debated far more freely in the popular daily press than in a magazine such as *Men Only*.

Confirmation that newspapers had not been symbolically 'castrated' was provided by the press coverage of sportsmen and film stars, which, at a time when many perceived traditional manliness to be under threat, offered regular celebrations of male virility, power, and finesse. The protagonists of the sporting field and the silver screen would have shaped the male imagination without the intervention of the press, but the significance of popular newspapers in raising the profile and esteem of these fantasy figures should not be underestimated. Sportsmen and film stars became far more than skilled professionals, admired by eager fans: instead they were portrayed as national heroes or epitomes of style and glamour, and were often elevated above cabinet ministers and dignitaries on the front pages. In a period when imperial adventurers and military leaders were losing some of their appeal as models of masculinity, sportsmen embodied similar manly qualities in a less threatening and controversial environment. Similarly, when the emotional and sexual aspects of (marital) relationships were being increasingly scrutinized, film stars offered men a master-class in the arts of 'sex appeal' and charisma. Invested by the press with iconic status, actors and sportsmen offered a modern focus for aspirations of manliness.

But if newspapers could celebrate a self-confident masculinity in the arenas of leisure and fantasy, a rather different picture inevitably emerged when the realities of everyday life were under the spotlight. The economic dislocation and mass unemployment that beset the nation from 1920 generated concerns about contemporary masculinity. The conservative press expressed fears that the provision of unemployment benefit would erode the initiative, independence, and desire to provide for a family that supposedly typified British men, and create instead a pool of 'soft', 'effeminate' layabouts. The fact that 'modern women' seemed to be advancing in many spheres of employment reinforced the perception that the traditional 'breadwinner' model was under threat. On the left, meanwhile, the *News* and the *Herald* responded with the accusation that modern, machine-led capitalism was frustrating and stultifying a generation of male workers; faced with a loss of job security and denied any meaningful input into working processes, many men seemed unable to forge a satisfying identity through employment.

Modern masculinity was also being defined in the increasingly prominent newspaper features offering advice about personal relationships and domestic arrangements. Subjects traditionally confined to women's magazines were now debated before a mixed audience and many articles outlined ideals of 'companionate' marriage and educated parenthood that expected a more 'domesticated' masculinity. Problem pages criticized those men who shirked their responsibilities at home, and columnists warned husbands and fathers that they should be actively and regularly involved in family life if they were to keep their wives happy and bring up their children properly.

This chapter will show how the popular press discussed masculinity in a variety of different contexts, creating a spectrum of male heroes and villains and debating how men should come to terms with economic and social change.

Editorial Policies and Pressures

'Manly' Heroes: Sportsmen

Sport was a central ingredient in the development and success of the popular newspaper. From the 1880s, when the spread of the telegraph enabled evening papers to boost circulations by publishing the latest racing and football results, editors came to recognize that coverage of a major sporting event was second only to a big crime story in terms of attracting irregular readers.[2] Innovations and improvements in sports reporting were constantly sought. Special football editions became a regular feature of Monday papers, and pools and betting guides soon followed in midweek. Popular sports columnists were vital members of the editorial staff and could command handsome salaries: Tom Webster, the *Mail*'s sports cartoonist, in 1924 became the most well-paid cartoonist in the world, while Trevor Wignall of the *Express* earned a 'huge salary'.[3] By the 1930s football, cricket, and boxing, in particular, were receiving press attention on a scale never before seen. Women's sports were covered in reasonable depth—especially tennis and golf—but this was clearly a male domain. Readership surveys repeatedly found that while sports pages were the favourite pages for male readers, 'practically no women like the sports items'.[4] Robert Ensor was typical in considering the sports section to be, in effect, the 'man's

---

[2] L. Brown, *Victorian News and Newspapers* (Oxford: Clarendon Press, 1985), 98, 124–5.

[3] D. Griffiths (ed.), *The Encyclopedia of the British Press* (London: Macmillan, 1992), 587; A. Chisholm and M. Davie, *Beaverbrook: A Life* (London: Hutchinson, 1992), 212.

[4] Bodleian Library, Oxford, X. Films 200, Mass Observation, File Report A11, 'Motives and Methods of Newspaper Reading', Dec. 1938, 3, 15; File Report 3005, 'Report on Reading the *Daily Herald*', June 1948, 24, 33; quotation from File Report 1339, 'Report on *Daily Express* Readership', June 1942, 18.

page'.[5] Unlike the women's page, however, its importance came to be symbolically underlined by its location at the back of the paper, balancing the 'serious' news at the front. Some husbands, it was observed, pulled out the central sections of the newspaper to give to their wives: they were then left with the 'meat' of the paper.[6] Indeed, a number of men informed Mass Observation that they chose their paper solely for its sports reporting.[7] Sport was such a major feature of male conversation that even those with little interest sometimes felt obliged to keep themselves informed. One respondent told Mass Observation that he had 'never been able to stir up any lasting feelings for sport', but he scanned the sports pages nevertheless: 'one must be keen on the Test'.[8]

The importance of the sports section to the popular paper was underlined daily at the editor's conference. Having listened to the requirements of the news editor, Hamilton Fyfe recalled, attention turned to the sporting editor: 'Whatever space he demands is pretty sure to be granted. Probably he is too much occupied to appear at the conference: he sends a deputy, who states his requirements. They are seldom challenged. He has regularly, as of right, greater space than is given to any other subject; he often supplies matter for the principal news page as well.'[9] Analysing the 'news space' of the *Daily Mail* and the *Daily Mirror* in 1927 and 1937, the Royal Commission on the Press discovered, to its dismay,[10] that the coverage of sport far exceeded that of 'political, social and economic news', even when international and imperial news were included. In 1937, indeed, there was twice as much space devoted to sports reports in the *Mail*, and four times as much in the *Mirror*, than there was to 'serious' news about politics, society, and the economy.[11]

As several historians have noted, sport was very significant in the formation of masculine identity.[12] It offered an arena in which individual male skill and strength could be unashamedly celebrated, at the same time as glorifying comradeship and team spirit in the absence of women and the 'feminine'. For Virginia Woolf, this veneration of athleticism represented the inequality of the

---

[5] R. C. K. Ensor, 'The Press', in Sir Ernest Barker (ed.), *The Character of England* (Oxford: Clarendon Press, 1947), 419.

[6] H. H. Aldridge to Royal Commission, Royal Commission on the Press, *Minutes of Evidence* (London, 1948), Day 22, Cmd. 7398, 28.   [7] Mass Observation, File Report A11, 13.   [8] Ibid. 5.

[9] H. Fyfe, *Sixty Years of Fleet Street* (London: W. H. Allen, 1949), 148.

[10] Royal Commission on the Press, *Report* (London: HMSO, 1949), Cmd. 7700, 131.

[11] Ibid., app. VII, table 4, 250.

[12] e.g. R. McKibbin, *Classes and Cultures: England 1918–51* (Oxford: Oxford University Press, 1998), ch. IX; R. Holt, *Sport and the British* (Oxford: Clarendon Press, 1989), Conclusion; D. Sabo and S. Curry Jansen, 'Images of Men in Sport Media', in S. Craig (ed.), *Men, Masculinity and the Media* (Newbury Park, Calif.: Sage, 1992); S. Humphries and P. Gordon, *A Man's World: From Boyhood to Manhood 1900–1960* (London: BBC Books, 1996), 16, 54–5, 178–9.

sexes in society: 'it is the masculine values that prevail. Speaking crudely, foot-ball and sport are "important"; the worship of fashion, the buying of clothes "trivial".'[13] Analysing the 'male culture' of the London medical schools in the inter-war years, Carol Dyhouse has remarked that 'it is difficult to exaggerate the importance of athletics [and] team sports'. Opposing the entry of female graduates into these male preserves, university spokesmen articulated fears that women would 'undermine the athletic life' of the schools, and produce 'ath-letic paralysis'. Such claims were more than empty excuses; as Dyhouse observes, the substance to these anxieties can be gauged by reading the college histories, which were full of tributes to past sporting heroes and essentially operated as 'hymns' to the male body.[14] Newspaper sports pages performed a similar function in the wider culture. For the *Daily Express* in 1928, for example, a weekend of top sport was enough to prove that fears about national effemina-cy were misplaced. Previewing the Varsity Boat Race and the Grand National, the paper assured readers that 'Both are hard, pounding, merciless struggles, not to be engaged in by any one, man or beast, who is not in perfect training and has not the stoutest heart. When people talk of the age as going soft let them think of the Grand National and the Boat-Race and be comforted.'[15]

Sporting prowess was regarded as a basic indicator of 'national character', vital to the health and well-being of the country. In such conceptions of the 'nation' and its 'character', women and 'feminine' qualities were implicitly excluded. There was no mention of the role of women when, little more than a week after the Armistice, the *Express* drew an explicit connection between military victory and the Englishman's love of sport:

It was sport which helped to win the war. It was racing which gave us the horses. It was football which gave us thews and sinews and quickness and dash. It was cricket which taught us the teamwork and the spirit of the game. It was boxing which gave us the stamina and the punch behind the final knock-out blow. Always a nation of sportsmen, we shall now be more a nation of sportsmen than ever; and to secure an A1 people for an A1 Empire it is the duty of the authorities to give every possible facility for the recon-struction of sport.[16]

There were similar silences and exclusions when the *Mail* called for public support of the amateur boxing championships. The noble art of pugilism, it argued, demonstrated the best attributes of the nation, and taught each gen-eration how to embody the national character:

[13] V. Woolf, *A Room of One's Own* (first pub. 1929; London: Penguin, 1993), 67.
    [14] C. Dyhouse, 'Women Students and the London Medical Schools, 1914–39: The Anatomy of a Mascu-line Culture', *Gender and History*, 10/1 (Apr. 1998), 117, 125–6.   [15] *Daily Express*, 31 Mar. 1928, 10.
    [16] *Daily Express*, 21 Nov. 1918, 4.

It would be a bad day for this country if this manly and typically English sport became too commercialised and if the amateur championships ceased to arouse real interest . . . boxing not only requires skill and strength, and is therefore an admirable training, but it calls for those qualities of good temper and sportsmanship which are peculiarly British.[17]

The *Mirror*, too, agreed, with this assessment of sport's place in national life:

Games have become a necessity, and we do not perhaps realise what a national pleasure and boon they are both to players and spectators alike . . . Who said we were a nation of shopkeepers? It may be so, but we are wicketkeepers and goalkeepers as well—and that perhaps is one secret of our good fortune and well-being.[18]

The *Herald*, typically, punctured the sense of complacency about the national well-being by pointing out that the sporting activities of working-class children were inhibited by their 'imprisonment' in the 'sordid surroundings' of ugly and evil towns, the litter of 'industrial capitalism'. Yet, campaigning for the provision of playing fields, the paper shared the vision of English character being improved by male sporting activity. It was a 'national duty' to secure the provision of adequate spaces for such sport.[19]

In order to provide a comprehensive coverage, the popular papers reported on almost every form of sporting endeavour. Some sports, though, clearly attracted greater respect than others, because they involved a more obvious display of 'manliness'. Discussing which games fathers should encourage their sons to take up, a 'sporting doctor' in the *Express* enunciated this usually unspoken hierarchy. Golf and tennis, he argued, were 'not recreations at which a vigorous and healthy youth should be encouraged to make himself proficient'. They did not require the strength and exertion of rugby, cricket, and other field sports, and were 'too individualistic', not fostering the 'team spirit'.[20] It is no coincidence that these were the two sports most commonly played by women: if women could participate at a high level, it suggested that the sport verged on the effeminate.[21] The 'sports doctor' also dismissed indoor sports requiring only skill rather than strength. Masculinity had to be proven in the outdoors with displays of athleticism: 'I hope he will not trouble about billiards. Darkened rooms, stuffy atmospheres, and generally unhealthy surroundings are no good to a boy.'[22] The children's sections of the *Express* and other papers usually provided advice for young boys on how to play the

---

[17] *Daily Mail,* 7 Apr. 1927, 10.   [18] *Daily Mirror,* 24 June 1935, 13.
[19] *Daily Herald,* 6 May 1927, 4.   [20] *Daily Express,* 21 Oct. 1931, 6.
[21] Alec Gunn, a pupil at Sherborne School in the early 1930s, remembered that 'not being a team game, it [tennis] was considered effeminate'; cited in Humphries and Gordon, *A Man's World,* 54.
[22] *Daily Express,* 21 Oct. 1931, 6.

more 'manly' games: sporting activity was accepted to be an essential part of becoming a man.[23]

The rhetoric of the 'sports doctor' has echoes of Baden-Powell's scouting movement, and indeed sport was often regarded as imperial adventure modulated into the domestic urban arena.[24] Sports reports often celebrated warrior-like attributes and drifted into military metaphors. The *Mail* described the FA Cup as a 'long-drawn-out struggle in which some club or another must meet with a knock-out blow in every round'.[25] 'We had a grand 20 minutes or so of he-man stuff,' purred a *Daily News* rugby correspondent in 1935, 'in which neither side gave or asked for quarter.'[26] Proving such virility on the sports field was more attractive than ever after the mechanized slaughter of the trenches had made military heroism so difficult to contemplate.

New types of sport were especially welcomed if they required the sort of uncommon bravery and 'manly' skill that typified heroes of the past. When the *Daily News* sent Iris Downing to report on the growing attraction of speedway racing, she produced the sort of report which exemplified the affirmation of masculinity that men could receive in sport. Men turned into 'gladiators' and 'knights' jousting in front of an enraptured crowd of female admirers:

> When I got used to the noise I found I was really being thrilled . . . It was difficult to imagine that after the race [the riders] probably went back to quiet suburban homes . . . Their diet should be fire and brimstone . . . Last night I felt that the women who cheered the riders so enthusiastically were a little like those who cheered on the gladiators . . . I came away full of admiration for the skill and the nerve displayed by these modern knights of the Speedway Track.[27]

The editorial demand for 'human interest' ensured that the sports reporting of this period gradually moved away from broad descriptions of the pattern of play towards a focus on individual personalities and performances, and this inevitably encouraged the creation of heroes.[28] The England cricketer Jack Hobbs was perhaps the main beneficiary of this in the 1920s, receiving widespread adulation for his numerous century-making innings. David Low compared him with the great figures of history in a light-hearted, but revealing, cartoon in the *Star*. In a 'Gallery of the Most Important Historical Celebrities', Hobbs was pictured towering over Caesar, Columbus, Mahomet and Lloyd

---

[23] e.g., *Daily Express*, 1 May 1931, 4.

[24] A. Warren, 'Popular Manliness: Baden-Powell, Scouting and the Development of Manly Character', in J. Mangan and J. Walvin (eds.), *Manliness and Morality: Middle-Class Masculinity in Britain and America, 1800–1940* (Manchester: Manchester University Press, 1987).   [25] *Daily Mail*, 18 Apr. 1927, 6.

[26] *Daily News*, 11 Nov. 1935, 18.   [27] *News Chronicle*, 8 June 1934, 11.

[28] J. Hill, *Sport, Leisure and Culture in Twentieth Century Britain* (Basingstoke: Palgrave, 2002), 11.

FIG. 7.1. The sportsman as national hero: Low shows how England
batsman Jack Hobbs was capturing the public imagination in the mid-
1920s. In 1925, Hobbs broke W. G. Grace's record of first-class centuries.
He later became the first professional sportsman to be knighted

George, as well as Adam and Charlie Chaplin (see Fig. 7.1).[29] Here was sport
as the new form of warfare and conquest, the new religion. Subtitled 'It', the
piece also hinted that leading sportsmen possessed the indefinable qualities of
charisma and sexual allure—typified at the time by 'It' girl Clara Bow—as
well as, or as a result of, their athleticism and skill. Sportsmen combined, then,
traditional heroism with a more modern type of appeal. A Tom Webster
cartoon in the *Mail* in 1931 similarly celebrated the pantheon of sporting heroes
that Britain had produced, with Hobbs, the boxer Jim Driscoll, and the
motor-racers Sir Henry Segrave and Sir Malcolm Campbell portrayed as
embodying the best of a proud 'Land of Hope and Glory'.[30]

[29] *Star*, 18 Aug. 1925, 3, pictured in C. Seymour-Ure and J. Schoff, *David Low* (London: Secker &
Warburg, 1985), 63.
[30] *Daily Mail*, 21 Oct. 1931, 14.

Male supremacy on the sports pages was, however, by no means entirely secure. As Chapter 2 noted, press commentators frequently remarked on the increasing proficiency of 'modern women' at a range of sports. Athleticism and team spirit, it seemed, were no longer exclusively male qualities. The anxious responses to such challenges offer clear evidence of the sense of shared masculinity that was involved. As early as 1921 'The Pilgrim', a regular contributor to the *Daily News*, argued that 'football is now the only festival left to men', other sports having been 'invaded' by women. In what was surely a rhetorical flight of fancy, the writer claims to have sat next to the only woman in the crowd during a recent international match. She was an 'accidental spectator', having come with her newly-wed husband—he 'had not yet reached that stage of emancipation at which a man may safely say: "I am going to a football match" '—but she could not understand the charms of the 'beautiful game': 'Long before half-time she was sitting silent, completely ignored among 40,000 men, a forlorn and disconsolate figure, face to face with the disquieting revelation that there are mysteries a woman cannot penetrate, and that she could not hope to recognise her husband till the match was over.' 'The Pilgrim' continued with a salute to the 40,000 members of the crowd: they 'were the defenders of the last remaining stronghold of men'.[31] In retrospect, it is obvious that his embattled tone was hardly necessary: for all the eye-catching achievements of some young women, sport continued—continues—to be a very male-dominated arena.[32] Instead, the article reaffirms the reality of contemporary fears of effeminacy, and suggests how useful sport was in combating them.

'Manly' Heroes: Film Stars

Just as the generous coverage of sport helped the footballer and the cricketer to become significant male role models and admired exemplars of masculinity, so too the column inches devoted to film stars assisted the rise of another set of male fantasy figures. Both Northcliffe and Beaverbrook recognized the popularity of the cinema to newspaper readers and demanded that it be reported fully. Writing to the editor of the *Daily Mail* in July 1919, Northcliffe made his position clear: 'I wish we had more film matter with pictures. I had no notion the topic of public conversation among all classes films have become.'[33] He

---

[31] *Daily News*, 14 Mar. 1921, 5.

[32] McKibbin notes that working-class women in particular remained 'deeply alienated' from most sports: *Classes and Cultures*, 384.

[33] British Library, Northcliffe Papers, Add. MS 62200, Northcliffe to Marlowe, 6 July 1919.

soon asked for 'film notes' to appear daily.[34] Almost a decade later Beaverbrook was insisting that the *Express* had not done enough to reorder its cultural priorities. The cinema, in his opinion, was superseding the theatre, as it was far more glamorous and exciting. John Gordon, the editor of the *Sunday Express*, received a memo that 'Lord Beaverbrook advises you to give more space to the cinema than to the theatre. At present there is far too much given to the theatre. The public is not interested. The theatre is too dull.'[35] Where the *Mail* and the *Express* led, other papers followed, and by the 1930s large amounts of space were being given over to report not only films, but the stars themselves. Robert Ensor, describing the tendencies of the inter-war press in 1947, claimed that 'film-stars came to be for the popular Press nearly the most important persons living; and a "romance" between two of these idolized beings was an event which few could outclass in attraction'.[36] The Royal Commission two years later similarly expressed its distaste that such papers presented 'the matrimonial adventures of a film star as though they possessed the same intrinsic importance as events affecting the peace of a continent'.[37] But the popular press had little desire to undermine the mystique and glamour that was carefully cultivated by film companies, and elevated a handful of cinema stars to such an exalted status that they inevitably shaped gender identities and aspirations. The power of female celebrities to set fashions has been widely remarked, and the male equivalent should not be overlooked. When Hannen Swaffer told readers of the *Herald* how the men at Margate were donning American 'doughboy' caps in order to imitate their favourite film heroes, he was reporting on a tendency which his paper and its competitors had done much to encourage.[38]

Film stars tended to portray a different type of masculinity than the sportsman. Handsome and sophisticated, they did not perform in an all-male arena, but rather won male admiration and envy by exhibiting the sort of charm that won the hearts of beautiful women. It was on this perceived 'sex appeal' that newspapers usually focused, to the extent that the above (hostile) commentators believed that stories of their romances and 'matrimonial adventures' were taking over the pages of the press. Rudolph Valentino pioneered the role of male film superstar when he shot to fame in *The Sheik*: popular newspapers helped to build up his allure and featured him on their front pages.[39] Pictures

---

[34] Ibid., Northcliffe to Marlowe, 17 Sept. 1919.
[35] House of Lords Record Office, Beaverbrook Papers, H/49, memo to John Gordon, 28 Oct. 1928.
[36] Ensor, 'The Press', 419.   [37] Royal Commission, *Report*, 131.
[38] *Daily Herald*, 4 Aug. 1931, 6.
[39] e.g., *Daily Express*, 16 Mar. 1923, 1; *Daily Mirror*, 16 Mar. 1923, 1.

and reports suggested an almost unrivalled virility and magnetism. The *Daily News*, for example, told how 'A tall, lean figure, wearing with proud distinction the flowing white garments of the East, has entranced the hearts of hundreds of thousands of young ladies throughout the world'.[40] Valentino's career was cut short by his untimely death in 1926—Graves and Hodge observed wryly that 'half the female population seemed to be his widow'—but his image retained a significant power: five years later the *Express* included him in their suggestions for the 'Ideal Husband.'[41] Nevertheless, the press soon had plenty of other leading men with which to dazzle readers. Antonio Moreno, the star of the hit film *It* alongside Clara Bow, became a press favourite, with his publicity including a piece in the *Weekly Dispatch* in 1927 telling the inside stories about his numerous 'film loves';[42] nine years later it was Errol Flynn who was featured by the *Mail* as 'Romantic Actor Number 1'.[43] Numerous other leading men, from James Cagney to Humphrey Bogart, received considerable attention.

Newspapers played along with the attempts of studios to generate hype. When a major Hollywood star came to London, the papers often treated him as sexually charged royalty. The arrival in 1931 of John Gilbert, 'Filmland's £2000-A-Week Lover', rated a front-page story in the *Daily Express*. This 'idol of twenty million women', the 'screen's greatest lover' was received by a guard of honour consisting of 'twenty-seven ravishing blondes, brunettes and red-heads'; despite almost fighting women off, though, and admitting that he 'adored' them, Gilbert proved his cool manliness by simply requesting a game of golf and a beer.[44] Described in such terms, it is hardly surprising that these stars became fantasy figures imitated by thousands of men. When Tyrone Power came to London in 1939, the *Express* revealed how he had to notify Scotland Yard of his route 'all because he has a beautiful face that everyone recognises'; he kept on being made 'prisoner' by his 'girl fans'.[45] Here was a new breed of heroes causing hysteria, it seemed, merely by their dashing good looks and suave manner. In general, the press neither exposed the careful marketing machinery employed by the studios, nor did they question the public images created for the stars—there was no hint of Tyrone Power's homosexuality, for example. After all, both newspapers and their advertisers benefited financially from the interest in cinema.

In some ways, these handsome male stars were the equivalent of the glam-

---

[40] *Daily News*, 21 Feb. 1923, 6.

[41] R. Graves and A. Hodge, *The Long Week-End: A Social History of Great Britain 1918–1939* (first pub. 1940; Harmondsworth: Penguin, 1971), 136; *Daily Express*, 1 May 1931, 5.

[42] Article advertised in the *Daily Mail*, 22 Apr. 1927, 12.   [43] *Daily Mail*, 28 Dec.1936, 4.

[44] *Daily Express*, 21 Oct. 1931, 1.   [45] *Daily Express*, 17 Aug. 1939, 3.

orous leading ladies, and were undoubtedly objects of a female heterosexual gaze. Yet whereas female stars tended to be *defined* by their appearance, the good looks of the male heroes were presented as only one part of a desirable 'manly' package; men were able to admire them without discomfort because they were usually portrayed as tough, dominant, and virile. As McKibbin suggests, 'Hollywood's celebration of competitive individual achievement . . . attracted young men.'[46] This aspect of the film star could appeal even to conservative commentators. The *Mail* reported eagerly the Labour MP Colonel Wedgwood's praise of vigorous cinema heroes: 'The he-man . . . is the essence of the American film. He is the self-made man who struggles to the top. He is a type we want more of and a jolly good example to set before our young people.'[47]

It was upon this manliness and virility that many journalists focused. Some even suggested that the film star offered a useful model for the nation's leaders. On the eve of the 1929 general election, G. W. L. Day in the *Express* argued that candidates resembling cinema heroes would have considerable success, especially among the new young female voters: 'All in a space of a few years we have had the Apache, the Strong Silent Man, the Cave Man, the Sheik, and the Bull-Dog Man . . . The fact is that today women are fixing their choice on a virile type of man . . .'[48] Alongside the military heroes Colonel Lawrence (of Arabia) and Rear-Admiral Evans, Day suggested that Rudolph Valentino might provide a popular template for the national leader sought by women. Two days later the *Daily Mirror* picked up on this theme. The reaction of women to a number of films, an editorial concluded, had indeed demonstrated the popularity of the 'forceful and direct methods of their heroes. A brutal hand and a loud voice went straight to the feminine heart'. Nevertheless, it warned, political candidates were advised to 'beware of the dominating touch . . . The technique of politics, apparently, is subtler than the technique of love.'[49] Whether or not film stars offered any clues to politics, however, they were undoubtedly significant in setting standards of masculinity, as demonstrated by the 1931 *Daily Mirror* cartoon 'Up, Clerks, and At 'Em!', which gently satirized the gap between fantasy and reality (see Fig. 7.2).

Despite the conspicuous manliness of most male film stars, anxieties about 'effeminacy' remained, with some fearing that the virility of most actors would be undermined by the industry's concern with appearance and romance. British newspapers picked up accusations in the American press that Valentino

---

[46] McKibbin, *Classes and Cultures*, 433.   [47] *Daily Mail*, 13 Apr. 1927, 8.
[48] *Daily Express*, 15 May 1929, 10.   [49] *Daily Mirror*, 17 May 1929, 9.

FIG. 7.2. Haselden shows the influence of the cinema stars as models of masculinity, while at the same time underlining how distant the fantasy world of these film heroes can be from everyday life

encouraged 'foppishness' among men.[50] The *Daily Express* in 1932 voiced its concern that screenwriters were allowing romantic story lines to predominate, and were not giving male protagonists sufficient opportunity to demonstrate their bravery:

Last year a fine record was taken of the Himalayan expedition that conquered Mount Kamet, the second highest peak in the Empire. No producer will look at it. It has no

[50] *Daily Mail,* 24 Aug. 1926, 10.

'plot'. It has no 'love interest'. It merely deals with adventure, hairbreadth escapes that are real instead of fabricated, indomitable pluck, triumphant achievement.[51]

Such complaints were rare, but, as with 'The Pilgrim's' diatribe about the 'feminization' of sport, they revealed how important these arenas were for the demonstration of masculinity.

Inter-War Debates

Mass Unemployment and Fears of Effeminacy

If manliness was being amply demonstrated on the sports field and the cinema screen, some press observers believed that many men were not fulfilling their basic responsibilities closer to home—namely working hard and functioning as the family breadwinner. The unemployment that became entrenched in Britain after the collapse of the post-war boom in 1920 provoked a notable amount of agonizing and anxiety in the press. Unemployment was not, of course, a new phenomenon, nor was concern about and criticism of 'scroungers' who supposedly shirked work and tried to obtain poor relief.[52] Nevertheless, there were two novel elements which ensured that the problem obtained greater prominence than ever in this period. Firstly, the scale and persistence of unemployment in the staple export industries was unprecedented, and the issue became one which could not be ignored or dismissed, as it had sometimes been in the past. Secondly, post-war governments undertook significant new responsibilities in the provision of unemployment insurance and benefits. With the nation's finances under considerable strain after a hugely expensive war, these costly benefit commitments inevitably became controversial.[53] Unemployment thus remained high on the political agenda throughout the period.

For the conservative papers, committed to the capitalist system, the causes of prolonged depression lay not in the overall economic structure but rather in the failures of individuals within it. Governments of all hues received a significant portion of the blame, for 'squandering' money, imposing high taxes, or failing to introduce tariffs. But such serious dislocation seemed to indicate failures within the workforce as well—and some contributors believed that there was a widespread tendency to shirk hard work. 'Have We Lost the Work

---

[51] *Daily Express*, 5 Feb. 1932, 8.

[52] As discussed, for example, in J. Burnett, *Idle Hands: The Experience of Unemployment 1790–1990* (London: Routledge, 1994).   [53] Ibid., ch. 6.

Habit?' asked E. F. Forster in the *Daily Mirror* in 1924. Young men, he argued, expected everything to become 'easier and easier' in the modern world, and failed to apply themselves: they 'are willing to take the honour, the glory and the cash, but they shrink from the idea of taking trouble'.[54] The following year the *Daily Express* agreed that 'there appears to be a general indisposition to face the necessity of working more and playing less':

Work is too often regarded as an evil, not as a good . . . The mood of this post-war period is hostile and antipathetic to the old gospel of work. Carlyle is unfashionable. Samuel Smiles is a laughing stock . . . There are other cures for our national distresses and anxieties, but there is no cure which is so simple and so universally applicable as the gospel of hard work.[55]

This was not exclusively a male problem—as Chapter 2 demonstrated, working-class women were also accused of 'scrounging'—but because the male breadwinner remained, in the eyes of most journalists, at the heart of the nation's economic system, it was upon men and masculinity that the spotlight was turned. It was no coincidence that the *Express*'s editorial was printed in the same week as the paper's attack on the 'Modern Tired Young Man'. It was one of the characteristics of this unsavoury figure that he disdained honest labour: 'He is not a worker. All he asks is to be allowed to drift fatuously through life admiring the neckties, the high-necked jumpers and the Oxford trousers of his tribe.' His main requirement of employment was that it entailed only 'easy hours'.[56] This critique of modern youth was constructed around a particular type of urbane, upper-middle-class graduate—but the claim that hard work was being avoided throughout the country inevitably suggested that this effeminacy was spreading. The 'foppish' young man was therefore an economic, as well as a cultural, enemy. His polar opposite, and the heroes of the conservative press, were self-made millionaires such as Lord Nuffield, Lord Leverhulme, Lord Reading—and, of course, Beaverbrook, Northcliffe, and Rothermere. The *Express* celebrated the former trio in 1926 as 'The Men Who Dared': there was, insisted an editorial, 'increasing scope for the boy who is born a nobody but who has grit, enterprise and the capacity for work'.[57] Lord Nuffield was described by the *Mirror* as possessing 'the zeal of a boy adventurer, all the savvy of [his] rivals combined, and all the courage of a team of forest-bred lions'.[58] Class-based inequalities were frequently obscured while the suggestion was made that success was a reflection of inner qualities, of 'manliness'. 'As human beings we all have certain rights,' observed John Blunt in the

---

[54] *Daily Mirror*, 5 Aug. 1924, 5.   [55] *Daily Express*, 10 July 1925, 8.
[56] *Daily Express*, 8 July 1925, 9; 6 July 1925, 8.   [57] *Daily Express*, 14 July 1926, 8.
[58] *Daily Mirror*, 1 Dec. 1936, 12.

Mail, 'but as individuals we rise and fall according to what is in us. The weak go to the wall.'[59]

The *Mail* focused above all upon what it perceived to be the damaging effects of the 'dole'. Besides being an intolerable burden on industry and the taxpayer, it was 'demoralizing', the 'ruin of youth' and a 'breeder of discontent', and was 'undermining energy and destroying that independence of spirit which used to be the hallmark of the Englishman'.[60] The initiative and vigour responsible for Victorian prosperity and wartime victory was being sapped by short-sighted governments. In a fictional series by C. J. Cutcliffe Hynes in the *Mail* discussing the topics of the day, a businessman explained how 'the post-war man simply won't do our office work at any price the business can stand. He finds the dole a softer job.'[61] 'Soft' men were essentially unsexed—and the suggestion that society was being feminized was underlined by the business-man's assertion that he had to employ women to do his firm's work instead. John Blunt soon returned to this theme of the 'softness' of the unemployed. They were 'so comfortable', taking the 'line of least resistance':

It is a pity for a man to be too tame and unadventurous . . . when I think of all the unemployed and poorly employed young men in this country I am astonished that more of them do not strike out for themselves and try to make their own way. They will, naturally, be able to think of endless excuses against any drastic decision, but there always arrives the time when they have got to face the real problem: are we prepared to chance it or are we not?[62]

Attacks redoubled as the depression deepened in 1931. The *Mail*'s special cor-respondent Montague Smith filed a series of reports about the 'Dole Menace' which threatened to destabilize the country's economy.[63] 'Victims of hard times', lamented an editorial, 'are apt to think that the best way of restoring prosperity is not any irksome labour on their part but a quick and simple oper-ation performed by someone else in a Government department'.[64]

Although the conservative press usually maintained in their reports the traditional distinction between the 'deserving' and 'undeserving' poor—'the respectable workman who wants work and cannot get it has nothing in com-mon with these hardened and shameless dole-mongers', argued the *Express* in 1925[65]—they often gave the impression that the labour movement was, directly or indirectly, encouraging 'scrounging'. In the *Mail*, Collinson Owen, discussing 'Why Men Are Bored', claimed that 'his own leaders have so

[59] *Daily Mail*, 26 Apr. 1927, 8.   [60] *Daily Mail*, 8 Oct. 1924, 7; 1 May 1925, 9; 12 Feb. 1925, 8.
[61] *Daily Mail*, 12 Apr. 1927, 10.   [62] *Daily Mail*, 10 May 1927, 6.
[63] *Daily Mail*, 4 Mar. 1931, 10.   [64] *Daily Mail*, 17 Apr. 1931, 12.
[65] *Daily Express*, 8 July 1925, 8.

bemused him with the iniquities of capital that he has lost all belief in the dignity, and even the joy of labour'.[66] Less than a week after the *Mail* had 'revealed' the Independent Labour Party's 'Dole-For-All-Plan', the *Express* noted that if the leaders of the trade unions had their way 'the relief of unemployment would no longer be on a contributory basis' and youths coming out of schools 'would be able to say, "I can get something for nothing. Why should I work?"'[67] Such trade unionists, the editorial continued, overlooked the vital fact that 'in work, and work alone, are true happiness and prosperity to be found'. Unless these doctrines were resisted, the *Express* suggested, the nation would lose its strength and virility.

Critiques of Capitalism

The *Daily Herald* repeatedly dismissed these reports of effeminate 'dole' scroungers and irresponsible unions. Unemployment was not the result of individual failings, but the inevitable consequence of an iniquitous and inefficient economic system:

There has been a tendency in some circles to regard every benefit receiver as a malefactor. The view has been spread that the unemployed do not want employment. In some minds the facts that men have fought for work in the docks, that hundreds apply where one vacancy is advertised, have not been able to shake that view. For the fair-minded, a different view is inescapable—the view that the unemployed man or woman is out of work through no personal fault, but because a disorganised industry has no use for them.[68]

For the *Herald* it was not the 'dole', but capitalism itself, that was emasculating the workers. 'Deskilling', 'Taylorism', and recurrent unemployment were gradually eroding the position of the male breadwinner. Visiting the 'underworld' of London in 1923, Vivian Brodzky painted a bleak picture of men stripped of their dignity and independence, no longer able to provide for their families: 'thousands of England's best workers and citizens are slowly being dragged into the abyss of degradation, losing the skill and cunning of their crafts, their health and their manhood, and becoming street sellers, beggars, and, in some cases, more or less criminals.'[69]

The paper pointed out that the benefit system itself ensured that it was difficult for workers to retain any sense of pride and respectability. The household means test, imposed by the National Government in 1931, submitted claimants

---

[66] *Daily Mail*, 14 July 1931, 9.   [67] *Daily Mail*, 1 May 1931, 5; *Daily Express*, 7 May 1931, 8.
[68] *Daily Herald*, 24 Aug. 1931, 8; see also 1 Aug. 1935, 8.   [69] *Daily Herald*, 12 Dec. 1923, 6.

to a 'degrading inquisition', a 'Star Chamber' which treated the unemployed 'not only as paupers, but almost like criminals'.[70] But even those with work risked losing their self-esteem and individuality, because of the carefully controlled regimes of modern factories. Profiling Henry Ford for the *Herald*, Harold Laski observed that 'Men in the Ford Factory cease to be men. They are the recipients of objects to be assembled. For so many hours a day they cease to have personality . . . One doubts whether he [Henry Ford] realises the psychological price the worker has to pay for the autocratic discipline of the factory.'[71] Women toiled in such dehumanizing factories, too, but because it was assumed that most would leave the workforce at marriage or motherhood, these conditions were not regarded as being quite so damaging. Only through socialism and industrial reform, the *Herald* suggested, would workers obtain both the financial security and the opportunity to develop skills that were essential elements of masculine identity. The nationalization of industry would allow 'the workmen's self-respect and sense of responsibility [to] increase'; he would also have 'an increasing voice in matters concerned with the organisation of work'.[72]

While commentators in other papers were sceptical of these socialist solutions, they ensured that readers were left with little doubt as to the devastating effects that long-term unemployment was having on the male workforce. Men 'rotting in idleness', argued Trevor Allen in the *Mirror*, 'is the curse of our generation'. The depression 'has robbed good men of initiative and self-respect, made them depressed and embittered'.[73] Cassandra, visiting Durham and Chester-le-Street in 1936, labelled the area the 'Land of Pity Me': 'All the men look old—you soon forget the joy of youth near Pity Me . . . There's no spirit left. There's no incentive.'[74] In the *News Chronicle* a 'family doctor' warned that not only were the unemployed themselves psychologically damaged by their loss of work, younger men 'may be affected both in nerves and physique by the mental trauma of the parent'.[75] In the same paper J. B. Priestley voiced his concern that society was in 'imminent' danger because of the 'sense of frustration and despair deep down inside men, who because they cannot find a way to live properly either turn into mere machines . . . or explode into violence and cruelty and wild unreason'.[76] Without meaningful employment, it seemed, men were incomplete and unable to find their identity.

Problem pages addressed the tensions generated by the inability of men to fulfil the breadwinner role. One expert advised a female correspondent whose

---

[70] *Daily Herald*, 27 Oct. 1931, 1.　　[71] *Daily Herald*, 9 May 1931, 8.
[72] *Daily Herald*, 9 Nov. 1935, 16.　　[73] *Daily Mirror*, 13 Nov. 1935, 7.
[74] *Daily Mirror*, 2 Dec. 1936, 14–15.　　[75] *News Chronicle*, 4 Nov. 1935, 5.
[76] *News Chronicle*, 14 Aug. 1939, 8.

husband was upset by her going out to work, despite the fact that her wages were essential for family survival. The burdens placed upon men by their provider status were not fundamentally questioned and the couple was simply expected to come to terms with them:

You must learn to take this resentment as a perfectly natural reaction of a husband who would, of course, like to give you everything himself, but can't. Make it clear to him that you are working (as he is) for your mutual happiness and for the greater comfort of you both. But don't delay in explaining this. You may need a lot of patience but, if you appeal to his sense of fair play, I'm sure you can win.[77]

The *News Chronicle* reminded women not to hand money to men in public: 'If it is a woman's treat pass the money surreptitiously. It is very embarrassing for a man to be with a woman and have to endure the agony of her paying the bill before the gaze of onlookers.'[78]

   One logical solution to these financial hardships, as some feminists recognized,[79] was embracing a more flexible sexual division of labour, and this was occasionally discussed in the press. The *Express* in 1931 reported on 'Britain's Heroic Mothers' engaged in employment while the 'out-of work "Dad" takes her place at home'. But the problems were presented as being grave:

There cannot be, I think, a more difficult life than that of the woman who goes to work each day while her husband, unemployed, gives an eye to the home. She has need of unfailing tenderness and consummate tact to soften the hard truth that it is she who plays the part of the man, while he, poor soul, makes shift to take her place between looking for jobs.[80]

The *Mirror* also published a prominent feature article on a couple that 'had an "experiment in marriage" thrust upon them by necessity'. While the wife left home to work, her unemployed spouse was left to 'wash the dishes, cook the meals, and scrub the house clean'. The couple involved actually pronounced the 'experiment' a success—but only because the man was 'unprejudiced [and] morally brave'.[81] The suggestion that masculinity could survive the strain of unemployment was also tempered by the fact that the husband soon found another job. In general, swapping gender roles was rarely considered to be a serious option. Although men were increasingly expected to offer some assistance around the home, few contributors regarded full-time domesticity as suitable for men.

---

   [77] *Daily Sketch*, 8 July 1937, 22.   [78] *News Chronicle*, 14 July 1937, 5.
   [79] See e.g. R. Strachey, 'Changes in Employment', in ead. (ed.), *Our Freedom and its Results* (London: Hogarth, 1936), 169–70.   [80] *Daily Express*, 7 May 1931, 3.   [81] *Daily Mirror*, 14 Nov. 1935, 12.

Indeed, the fact that some women were able to find employment when men could not offered a further challenge to the male identity.[82] Although popular papers did not, in general, oppose advances in female employment, the perception that 'modern women' were 'invading' male realms inevitably produced some expressions of anxiety and resentment. A few commentators were unable to accept that men were being outperformed by women, and rationalized female success in terms of the unfair deployment of 'feminine wiles'. A contributor to the *Express* in 1924 claimed that the successful female businesswoman

uses all the battery of her sex—her charm, and the atmosphere of womanhood . . . When she tries to fight [men] with their weapons, she may be hopelessly outclassed; but when she sticks to her own (given her for such a different purpose) they are children in her hands.[83]

'Women have a weapon which men cannot wield in the fight for recognition,' agreed James Douglas in the same paper four years later:

They have beauty and charm. Men are not always invulnerable against female coquetry. A male clerk, for instance, cannot captivate his employer by a bewildering glance or a dazzling smile . . . Men are creatures of sentiment, and women are able to exploit their sentimentality. There are only a few remaining barriers which protect men against their natural instinct to surrender to feminine entreaty. These barriers are crumbling, and men will soon be deprived of all their defences.[84]

The male teaching union, the National Association of Schoolmasters (NAS), meanwhile, was able to tap into fears of national effeminacy to obtain some sympathy in the conservative press for its proposals that the number of female teachers should be restricted, since 'no woman can train a boy in the habits of manliness'.[85] A *Mirror* editorial admitted in 1927 that 'for the time being we are on the side of the President [of the NAS]', while the *Mail* accepted that 'the advantages of masculine control for boys even of tender years are immeasurable'.[86] In particular it was deemed that sport, that vital crucible of masculinity, was 'best directed' by male teachers.[87] Such open hostility to the 'feminization' of a profession was, however, relatively infrequent; whereas articles in *Men Only* freely criticized 'The Gate-Crashing Sex' and pleaded for 'No More Women in My Office', popular newspapers continued to offer careers advice to women (although, as the content analysis suggests, this was

---

[82] S. Alexander, 'Men's Fears and Women's Work: Response to Unemployment in London between the Wars', *Gender and History*, 12/2 (July 2000), 401–25.   [83] *Daily Express*, 14 Oct. 1924, 8.

[84] *Daily Express*, 17 Mar. 1928, 8.

[85] *Daily Mirror*, 18 Apr. 1927, 7. On the NAS, see A. Oram, *Women Teachers and Feminist Politics 1900–1939* (Manchester: Manchester University Press, 1996), 57–67.

[86] *Daily Mirror*, 18 Apr. 1927, 7; *Daily Mail*, 8 Apr. 1931, 8.   [87] *Daily Mail*, 3 Apr. 1929, 10.

becoming less extensive in the 1930s).[88] If the perceived success of 'modern women' served to place the difficulties of parts of the male workforce into relief, the press generally focused the resulting hostility against government policy, the unions, dole 'scroungers', or the evils of capitalism rather than against women.

A 'Domesticated' Masculinity?

The gradual shift in the popular press away from a diet of public affairs news to 'human interest' features on domestic life and personal relationships inevitably brought male behaviour in the roles of lover, husband, and father under scrutiny as never before. Problem columns and women's page pieces provided a regular commentary on what was required of men in the private sphere, and this material was frequently supplemented by editorials and feature-page articles. As Maurice Edelman observed of the 1930s *Daily Mirror*, popular papers had become 'a school of manners, a *carte du tendre*, a guide to every sentimental problem'.[89] Previous chapters have noted that this was a period of changing expectations about the nature of personal relationships, with the advocacy of a more equal, 'companionate' form of marriage and more educated and active parenting. Improving housing conditions were making the domestic space more attractive, while suburbanization and the erosion of traditional kinship and homosocial networks also had the effect of encouraging the 'privatization' of family life.[90] Popular newspapers, broadly supportive of these developments and keen to promote domestic consumption, sought in this context to articulate a more domesticated modern masculinity. Such material offered a significant contrast to the late Victorian and Edwardian tendency, described by John Tosh, to disparage domesticity for men.[91] In constructing this ideal, however, many negative aspects of masculinity were exposed to criticism, stimulating further fears that men were being undermined.

A. J. Hammerton has shown how abusive husbands entered the pages of the late Victorian press in reports of court proceedings as public interest in the regulation of marriage grew.[92] This practice continued and was extended in the

---

[88] *Men Only* (Dec. 1935, Feb. 1936), cited in Greenfield et al., *Fashioning Masculinity*, 467.

[89] M. Edelman, *The Daily Mirror: A Political History* (London: Hamish Hamilton, 1966), 42.

[90] D. Gittins, *Fair Sex: Family Size and Structure 1900–39* (London: Hutchinson, 1982), 52–3; M. Collins, *Modern Love: An Intimate History of Men and Women in Twentieth Century Britain* (London: Atlantic Books, 2003), ch. 2.

[91] J. Tosh, *A Man's Place: Masculinity and the Middle-Class Home in Victorian England* (New Haven: Yale University Press, 1999), ch. 8 (which is entitled 'The Flight from Domesticity').

[92] A. J. Hammerton, 'The Targets of "Rough Music": Respectability and Domestic Violence in Victorian England', *Gender and History*, 3/1 (Spring 1991), 40–1.

inter-war period, with newspapers increasingly decisive in their condemnation of violence against women. Several features highlighted the difficulties faced by wives seeking to separate from dangerous men, and the *Mail* invited a barrister to confirm that 'Wives May Not Be Beaten'.[93] In the *Express*, James Douglas advised women to leave alcoholic husbands: 'She can administer to her husband the only shock which may arouse his manhood, galvanise his conscience, and stimulate his shame. Let him come back to a wifeless home . . . If she cannot save her drunken husband, she can save herself.'[94]

The most significant feature of these years, however, was the increasing insistence not merely that certain negative aspects of marriage, such as violence and abuse, were unacceptable, but more positively that a genuine companionship between husband and wife was desirable. If, as Elizabeth Marc suggested in the *Mail*, a career was so precious to many 'modern women' that it was 'only to be sacrificed if the lure of love is overwhelming', it appeared inevitable that women would become more discerning in their choice of partners.[95] Husbands would have to prove their emotional compatibility and commitment. Women were 'no longer content . . . to sit at home in the evening while their lords and masters go to the club', noted another contributor to the *Mail*. 'They demand far greater attention than they have ever received before.'[96] When the *Express* carried out a survey in 1931 to discover the characteristics of the 'Ideal Husband', the paper claimed to have demonstrated that attitudes were definitely changing:

The modern girl, with her greater freedom and fuller knowledge of people and the world in which she lives, has evolved for herself a new standard by which to judge the man into whose hands she gives her life . . . She has a grip of the realities . . . Although a number of women still wish a man to be 'master in his own house' they are in a minority, and a very large proportion of them like the household to be run on a partnership basis, with a husband ready to sympathise and help with domestic responsibilities.[97]

Only a few months later, when the *Mail* discussed the opinion of Dr Theodore van de Velde, the author of the best-selling *Ideal Marriage*, that men should assert their authority over their wives, the paper's reporter found that his view was 'rejected by married couples of all ages as an anachronism'.[98]

Some men clearly felt threatened by these changing expectations. 'I want a helpless wife,' a male correspondent told the *Mirror*'s problem columnist Dorothy Dix in 1938. 'I don't want one of these independent young women

[93] *Daily Mail*, 7 Nov. 1922, 8; 5 Nov. 1927, 10.   [94] *Daily Express*, 1 Nov. 1930, 8.

[95] *Daily Mail*, 10 Sept. 1923, 8.   [96] *Daily Mail*, 1 Mar. 1928, 10.

[97] *Daily Express*, 6 May 1931, 5.   [98] *Daily Mail*, 21 Oct. 1931, 7.

who can stand on their own two feet, and hold down as good a job as I can, and maybe tell me where I can get off.' But Dix was unsympathetic, declaring that the man was old-fashioned and that 'clinging-vine wives are getting to be a rare specimen of flora in these days'. Warning about the dangers of unequal partnerships and the male tendency to self-aggrandizement, her article became little less than a popular exposition of Virginia Woolf's conception of woman as a 'mirror' to magnify man, as outlined in *A Room of One's Own*:

Above everything else, a man desires to feel superior to his wife. He wants to be bigger physically, stronger mentally, and to have her regard him as an oracle . . . [That] is why practically every married woman who achieves success in business or a profession loses her husband . . . Women rejoice in their husbands' triumphs . . . But men writhe under being known as their wives' husbands. The minute a man feels himself inferior to his wife he flees for compensation to some woman before whom he can strut and pose as a godling.[99]

Problem columnists repeatedly warned women against taking men at face value, explaining that superficial charm would not provide a reliable indication of the long-term compatibility that was now deemed essential for a successful marriage. Helen Hope in the *Daily News* cautioned women against falling for the dashing but insubstantial rogue: 'the fascination such men exert is purely physical. They inspire passion and little else.'[100] Suitable partners, she suggested, should exhibit sensitivity and good humour as well as glamour. Another columnist, Jane Doe, implored women not to trust suitors until they had properly proved their affection, and used some dramatic case studies to point out the 'extreme folly of taking men—however pleasant and genial—on their own valuation'. 'Any girl contemplating marriage', she suggested, should 'have every inquiry possible made about her lover.'[101]

Some contributors expressed doubts as to whether men would ever live up to the heightened expectations implicit in the ideal of the 'companionate' marriage.[102] Whatever the reality, these expectations certainly received considerable publicity and there were a significant number of press articles that did encourage husbands to display greater affection and properly fulfil the responsibilities of marriage. 'Why not make a pal of the wife?' suggested a contributor to the *Mirror* in 1919, arguing that a wife could provide better companionship than any male 'chum'.[103] 'Are you a good weekend husband?' asked an *Express* editorial in 1930:

---

99 *Daily Mirror*, 14 Sept. 1938, 22.   100 *Daily News*, 2 May 1925, 4.
101 *Daily Mirror*, 2 May 1919, 7.   102 e.g. Dorothy Dix in the *Daily Mirror*, 14 Sept. 1938, 22.
103 *Daily Mirror*, 9 May 1919, 7.

Do you see to it that your wife is included in some of the fun you enjoy, or do you treat your home merely as a week-end hotel in which you tip no one? Your wife does not want to spoil your holiday. But she does resent being left to herself until you come home from golf or tennis and then proceed to fall asleep over the evening newspaper. Try to remember how you acted when you were courting her.[104]

When the *Daily Herald* invited Sir Ellis Hume-Williams, the famous divorce lawyer, to reveal the secrets of a happy marriage the following year, he too recommended that husbands pay attention to the emotional needs of their wives:

A woman does not like to be taken too much for granted. She likes to be courted after her wedding as well as before it . . . He forgets that she needs more than material comfort. A woman must live—that is, she must have change, adventure, admiration, affection—all the things which break up the monotony of her existence. And if her husband takes no trouble to see that she has these, then as often as not she looks elsewhere to find them.[105]

The warning in the final sentence was significant. Once again, it was implied that modern women would seek to break out of an unhappy marriage. Feature articles advised how such an eventuality could be avoided, outlining 'How to Hold a Wife',[106] reminding husbands to 'Praise Your Wife'[107] and to 'Kiss Your Wife',[108] and even explaining 'How to Write the Perfect Love Letter': 'Contrary to the popular idea, cave-man stuff does not impress the average woman. Consequently, a touch of humility in a lover does not go amiss' (see also Fig. 7.3).[109] More concretely, men were warned that their wives were unlikely to be content if they were not allowed some measure of financial autonomy. 'A wife ought to have money of her own to spend as she pleases,' insisted James Douglas. 'The husband who spends all the money is a fool as well as a knave.'[110] When a woman wrote to the *Mirror* to complain that her husband would not give her any money even though she had been forced to give up her old job, Dorothy Dix was highly critical of his 'niggardliness': she advised her to tell him that 'he has at least to pay you a servant's wages for doing his cooking and washing and ironing, or else you are going back to your old job, or into someone else's kitchen, where you will get pay envelopes on Saturday night'.[111]

Men were sometimes encouraged to demonstrate their commitment to the

---

[104] *Daily Express*, 24 May 1930, 8.   [105] *Daily Herald*, 19 Aug. 1931, 8.
[106] *Daily Mail*, 5 January 1928, 6.
[107] *Sunday Express*, 8 May 1927, as advertised in the *Daily Express*, 7 May 1927, 5.
[108] *Daily Sketch*, 1 Sept. 1938, 24.   [109] *Daily Express*, 3 Feb. 1933, 10.
[110] *Sunday Express*, 27 Nov. 1927, 12.   [111] *Daily Mirror*, 28 May 1937, 26.

Let the men in your life see this page

4 ways to madden a woman

You may like a boisterous romp, holding your girl friend as though you were dancing with a sawdust doll, whistling over her shoulder, but your partner won't care for it.

You feel swell showing off how many people you know, excusing yourself to have a word with old so-and-so half the time. But you'll not have another opportunity of leaving this girl alone at the dinner table. She's not come out to watch you while you stand about talking to other people.

Maybe you like to show off your strength. But you won't impress a girl by spending the entire evening balancing the furniture on your nose-end. If you were to stop fooling you'd see the glazed look in her eye. You're docketed as a first-rate bore.

And this, you will find, is final. If you want never to be asked round again, try out your clever stunts. This man showed a girl how he could tread out a burning cigarette without damaging the carpet. Found the carpet rated higher than his society.

FIG. 7.3. By the 1930s, popular newspapers provided a substantial amount of advice on domestic life and personal relationships. Material of this kind emphasised that men had to be thoughtful and considerable suitors if they were to attract women. 'Modern wives' sought compatibility and friendship, and could not be taken for granted

marriage by contributing to the domestic work. The notion that 'manliness' precluded such efforts was rejected:

There are lots of happy homes scattered throughout the length and breadth of the land. They are usually those in which the husband does not mind a bit taking his share in keeping the house nice and doing a little to help with the housework . . . It's just such friendly deeds that make a happy home, and keep alive the flame of love on which marriage was based.[112]

By the mid-1930s the *Express* included a weekly column entitled 'Man About the House', which gave advice on the domestic improvements and repairs for which men were expected to feel responsible. Those husbands who failed to shoulder any of the burdens were criticized. A woman who complained to the *Express* women's page that her 'husband won't grow up' and that he did not realize that 'running a house and a family is a two-man job [*sic*]', for example, was heard with considerable sympathy.[113]

Men were expected to involve themselves actively in the domestic sphere not only with their wives but also with their children. 'Likes children' was a significant criterion for the 'ideal husband' in the *Express* survey of 1931, and 'scientific' advice reinforced the desirability of this characteristic. Childcare experts and psychologists claimed that men had an indispensable role to play in parenting, and that failing to discharge their responsibilities could have very damaging consequences:

Fathers must take their share in the life of the home—and take it seriously. Home is the little world that prepares for the big world. If the little world is a world of women without men—a 'fatherless' world—then the child is ill-equipped to go out into life and mix with both sexes. The father must sacrifice a little time from his business, or golf, or whatever it is, in order to be a real father and set an example of manhood to his children.[114]

Fathers should not be restricted to imposing discipline, warned the *Daily Herald*'s 'nursery expert': 'Daddy's homecoming should be the exciting end of the day, not an event to be dreaded.'[115] Instead, fathers were advised to engage in such tasks as ensuring that young boys were able to harness their energy and restlessness: 'High spirits can't be bottled up, they must have an outlet some time. And this is the time when the wise father takes over the job of guiding these active spirits into proper channels. It is a mistake for the mother to try to do too much in this respect . . .'[116]

---

112 *Daily Herald*, 22 Feb. 1923, 7.
113 *Daily Express*, 12 May 1939, 15.
114 *Daily Mirror*, 16 Nov. 1935, 14.
115 *Daily Herald*, 8 Feb. 1932, 5.
116 *Daily Herald*, 4 May 1939, 15.

Clearly, the burden of bringing up children remained largely with the mother. Nevertheless, many press commentators were convinced that fathers were embracing their duties with enthusiasm. 'There has never been a time in the history of mankind when children were better off or more cared for,' observed an *Express* editorial in 1926: 'The cult is not confined to the mothers, it extends to the fathers and the fathers' friends, so that the average man is beginning to feel that the day has been wasted of which he does not spend some time in child worship.'[117] Six years later the *Herald* agreed: 'As soon as daddy's key is heard in the door, there are orders to "come up at once".'[118] Of course, the historian is likely to regard such grand claims with considerable scepticism, and oral evidence suggests that such active and involved fathers were not common outside the suburban middle classes in this period.[119] Nevertheless, the articulation of these ideals was significant, and perhaps helped to prepare the way for the more domesticated working-class masculinity observed by sociologists such as Wilmott and Young in the 1950s.[120] Moreover, these articles suggest that the widespread inter-war belief that the sexes were converging was not merely a reflection of the apparent success of women in 'male' spheres: it was also a response to the perception that men were increasingly comfortable in the 'feminine' world of the family.

It is clear that some journalists in this period were genuinely concerned about the prospect of national 'effeminacy'. The Great War, mass unemployment, and the political and legal gains made by women combined to offer a significant challenge to the assumptions and expectations embodied in many pre-war notions of manliness, and brought a number of commentators close to despair. On the other hand, it is hardly surprising that aspects of what later historians have described as a 'crisis in masculinity' received attention in the press.[121] The persistence of male power was not, of course, a news story in the same way that challenges to it were, and 'foppish youth' provided eye-catching copy in just the same way as did the 'modern woman'. In reality, the continued dominance of men in every sphere of public life was silently reaffirmed day after day in the pictures and reports of male politicians and businessmen. And if the elabora-

---

[117] *Daily Express*, 12 July 1926, 8.   [118] *Daily Herald*, 8 Feb. 1932, 5.

[119] Humphries and Gordon were struck by 'how little' fathers of this generation had to do with bringing up their children: *A Man's World*, 179. See also C. Langhamer, *Women's Leisure in Britain, 1920–1960* (Manchester: Manchester University Press, 2000), 146–53.

[120] P. Wilmott and M. Young, *Family and Kinship in East London* (first pub. 1957; Harmondsworth: Penguin, 1986), 27–30. For a discussion of the 'domesticated masculinity' of the 1950s, see S. Brooke, 'Gender and Working-Class Identity in Britain during the 1950s', *Journal of Social History*, 35 (2001), 781, 784.

[121] Greenfield, et al., 'Fashioning Masculinity', 459.

tion of increasing male responsibilities in the domestic sphere created a potential tension with more active and heroic fantasies of masculinity, these con-
tradictions remained far less complex than the multiple expectations of
femininity—'modern woman', worker, housewife, 'sex symbol', and loving
mother. Although anxieties were persistent in the press, the discussion of the
'modern young man' never reached anything approaching the pervasiveness of
that relating to the 'flapper' or 'modern young woman'. When war loomed in
1939, moreover, the press was confident that the nation's men were ready, if
necessary, to face the German threat. The concerns about manliness should
perhaps be seen not as the manifestations of a 'crisis', then, but as inevitable
by-products of the gradual evolution of masculinity in this period.

Conclusions

It is time that someone wrote a book, or at least a Hogarth essay, in defence of the popular press. For I suspect that the *Express*, the *Mail* and the *Herald* do not really get half the credit they deserve. It is all very well to say, as everyone says almost every day, that they constitute the gravest of our national perils, that they exploit mass fear and mass selfishness, that compared to them the devil himself is a clean-minded purveyor of the strict, honest and sober truth. But is it not also just as true to say that they are on the whole considerably in advance of some half of their readers?

(M. Haig (Lady Rhondda), 'In Defence of the
Popular Press', in *Notes on the Way*, 1937)

The popular press has always been an easy target for educated critics. As daily newspapers extended their circulations and moved to the forefront of popular culture in the inter-war years, commentators of all persuasions denounced their vulgarity, commercialism, and superficiality. The Leavises lamented the 'cheap gratification' offered by the press and held it responsible for ensuring that reading was 'now often a form of the drug habit'.[1] John Middleton Murry, the editor of *The Adelphi*, argued that the mass newspaper was based on the 'total rejection of all notion of moral value. No matter what the demand is, supply must be created to fulfil it.'[2] When Harold Nicolson took a job at the *Evening Standard*, he found that his literary reputation started to suffer and feared that he would 'never be taken seriously again'. 'I never foresaw that writing for the Press would be actually so degrading,' he wrote in his diary; 'the moment I cease to be unhappy about it will be the moment when my soul has finally been killed.'[3] Evelyn Waugh, similarly disgusted by his short experience

---

[1] Q. D. Leavis, *Fiction and the Reading Public* (first pub. 1932; London: Chatto & Windus, 1965), 117, 7; see also F. R. Leavis, *Mass Civilisation and Minority Culture* (Cambridge: Gordon Fraser, 1930).

[2] J. Middleton Murry, 'Northcliffe as Symbol', *The Adelphi*, 1/1 (Oct. 1930), 15.

[3] *Harold Nicolson: Diaries and Letters 1930–39*, ed. N. Nicolson (London: Collins, 1966), 44, 58.

of Fleet Street, fictionalized his observations in *Scoop*. Even some of those who enjoyed a long career in popular journalism came to despise their work. 'What shallowplates and vulgarians produce our great daily papers,' observed Collin Brooks; he felt that 'journalism in the Rothermere group' was simply 'purpose-less buffooning' and valued his articles for the *Sunday Dispatch* as 'less than the dust'.[4] Attacked by those on the left for political bias and crass consumerism, and by those on the right for immorality and undermining cultural hierarchies, an unusually broad consensus of the literary elite ranged itself against the 'mass' press.[5]

Such entrenched attitudes have left a powerful legacy. There remains a reflex assumption in much of the historiography that the content of the popular press is inevitably crude and reactionary, and not worth taking particularly seri-ously. In the field of gender studies, this is compounded both by the specific comments about press hostility to women made by influential inter-war figures such as Ray Strachey and Virginia Woolf, and by the expectations generated by more recent feminist research which has shown how the media has consist-ently stereotyped and restricted women. Although some recent gender histori-ans have taken a more nuanced view of popular fiction, women's magazines, and films, the press has remained a common focus of disapproval. In some respects, these criticisms are justified. There were, undoubtedly, persistent gendered inequalities in the press. As Mary Agnes Hamilton noted, inter-war newspapers were often guilty of portraying 'women as separate and odd items in the catalogue of humanity', and of making general pronouncements 'cover-ing and expressing them all, such as would at once be dismissed as absurd if enunciated about men'.[6] Whereas men were usually regarded as independent public citizens, women continued to be defined by their family relationships, and the 'interests' and 'needs' of women were repeatedly conflated with those of 'housewives' and 'mothers'. In press photography and advertising, moreover, women were also increasingly sexualized and offered up for male consumption. Those who hoped along with the *Manchester Guardian* that 'the time is approaching when [men and women] will both be regarded as human beings sharing the same human interests' would have been disappointed by the con-tinued tendency of popular papers to highlight sexual difference in almost any arena, from politics to personal relationships.[7]

---

[4] N. J. Crowson (ed.), *Fleet Street, Press Barons and Politics: The Journals of Collin Brooks 1932–40* (London: Royal Historical Society, 1998), 62, 67, 201.

[5] See also K. Williams, *British Writers and the Media 1930–45* (Basingstoke: Macmillan, 1996), 48–61.

[6] M. A. Hamilton, 'Changes in Social Life', in R. Strachey (ed.), *Our Freedom and its Results* (London: Hogarth, 1936), 256.   [7] *Manchester Guardian*, 2 Jan. 1928, 2.

On the other hand, this did not amount to a coherent policy of anti-feminism, nor to a 'backlash' aiming to re-establish 'traditional' gender roles after the blurring experienced during the Great War. There has been a tendency of critics of the press to overestimate its coercive powers. Although newspapers had a significant influence on contemporary attitudes, the press was in no position to impose 'patriarchy' and 'domesticity' on an unwilling female population. When Deirdre Beddoe, for example, argues that women were 'manipulated' by the media 'to embrace the role of housewife and mother and to scorn other role models', she is surely underplaying the ability of the public both to resist unwelcome images and also to influence the output of the media through their purchasing power.[8] Editors were keenly aware of the need to satisfy a wide variety of different readers. They provided a range of material and a number of different perspectives in their newspapers; the sort of monolithic, propagandist publication suggested by Beddoe would have been unappealing and unpopular. Gender roles were the subject of intense debate between the wars, and this was reflected in the press. Undoubtedly, there was a considerable amount of material about housewifery and motherhood—but there were also numerous features about careers for women and female achievements in the public sphere. If anti-feminist articles were printed, so too were explicitly feminist ones. Writers such as Ray Strachey, Lady Rhondda, Vera Brittain, and Winifred Holtby were regular contributors to the popular press—Sylvia Pankhurst, indeed, was even given a platform to defend single motherhood.[9] When Virginia Woolf opened her newspaper in *A Room of One's Own* to discover Lord Birkenhead arguing that women lacked literary talent, she might also have noted that even the *Mail*, at that time campaigning against the 'flapper vote', reported female authors rebutting these claims.[10] Of course, each paper had its own particular sympathies, but even in 'conservative' papers readers were exposed to authors as challenging as Havelock Ellis, Freud, and Remarque.

In any case, there was a widespread perception that a return to pre-war patterns was impossible. Most editors and journalists assumed that society—and gender relations—had been irrevocably changed by the shattering experience of the war, and that the main task ahead was to understand and come to terms with, rather than condemn, 'modernity'. The powerful conviction that the sexes were set on a gradually converging path ensured that desperate denuncia-

[8] D. Beddoe, *Back to Home and Duty: Women between the Wars, 1918–1939* (London: Pandora, 1989), 9.

[9] *Daily Mirror*, 4 Nov. 1935, 10.

[10] V. Woolf, *A Room of One's Own* (first pub. 1929; London: Penguin, 1993), 48; *Daily Mail*, 13 Mar. 1928, 9; 20 Mar. 1928, 21.

tions of female enfranchisement or greater social freedoms for women generally appeared to be both foolish and futile. Circulation and advertising pressures both reinforced this acceptance of modernity. Far from being marginalized, the achievements of female pioneers—from Lady Astor and Ivy Williams to Amy Johnson and Suzanne Lenglen—were often given generous coverage and regarded as pointers to a more equal future. Women were prompted to use their new political influence, encouraged to take advantage of modern fashions and social opportunities, advised how to enter previously closed professions. Domestic columns tried to demonstrate how housework could be made more rational and less time-consuming, enabling women to benefit from these broader horizons. Nor did newspapers simply buttress conventional forms of masculinity. Criticisms of 'imperial manliness' percolated throughout the press by the 1930s, and men were urged to respond to changing expectations by making more time to fulfil their responsibilities as husbands and fathers.

Many journalists overestimated the changes in the balance of gender relations. With the benefit of hindsight it is clear that anxieties about male power being undermined were overblown, that the re-evaluation of gender was limited, and that traditional hierarchies were by no means overturned. The Great War was not, in reality, as great a turning point as some contemporaries assumed, and, as previous chapters have demonstrated, many conventional attitudes were very resistant to revision. Indeed, the popular press, by focusing upon change and individual achievements, allowed some of the deeper social and cultural obstacles to equality to remain obscured and hence inadvertently encouraged some of the rather extravagant claims about the position of women. Nevertheless, if contemporaries exaggerated the radical nature of modernity, some historians have been equally guilty of selectivity in discussing this period. By concentrating, with some notable exceptions, on domesticity and the apparent weakness of feminism, the historiography has overstated the strength of social conservatism and the resilience of the 'separate spheres' model of gender relations. The female war-workers, voters, politicians, professionals, aviators, and sportswomen who were featured, and often celebrated, in the pages of the press did significantly challenge notions of what was 'appropriate' for women. Much of what had appeared so threatening when advocated by suffragists and 'new women' before 1914 seemed entirely uncontroversial by the 1920s. 'The new habits, the greater liberty, the more strenuous work, have not had the bad effect which the mournful predicted,' noted an *Express* editorial in 1923. 'Exercise, golf, dancing—even mild smoking—have made a real new woman of what was once considered and lampooned as a dreadful dream of the future—the New Woman.'[11]

Perhaps the most serious threat to greater equality came not from an attempt to resist these developments by championing domesticity, but from the increasing sexualization of women in the press that was a corollary of 'modern' freedoms. Glamorous images of women on photo pages and in adverts, coupled with a greater coverage of 'beauty aids' and slimming techniques, put new pressures on women to maintain an attractive appearance and reinforced the assumption that women were to be judged in aesthetic terms. The sexual objectification of women that would reach its full expression in the *Sun*'s 'page three girl' was already emerging in the 1930s and this was a tendency that inevitably made it harder for women to be treated equally in public life.

Lady Rhondda's plea that the popular press should be considered on its merits and not convicted on the basis of accusations from hostile witnesses is surely a salutary one. Historians studying the inter-war years have ignored or stereotyped the content of newspapers for too long. Reading these papers helps us to understand that contemporaries saw these decades not as an 'era of domesticity'[12] but as an important period of change and 'modernity' in gender relations.

[11] *Daily Express*, 3 May 1923, 6.

[12] This is how the period 1918–40 is labelled in M. Pugh, *State and Society: British Political and Social History 1870–1992* (London: Edward Arnold, 1994), ch. 13.

The Women's Pages

In order to obtain some detailed information about the material provided specifically for female readers, I conducted a content analysis of the 'women's pages' in each of my five newspapers. I surveyed papers from the first two weeks of May—a month that was neither close to Christmas nor in the so-called 'silly season'—at four-yearly intervals, providing a sample of 72 issues for each title (360 issues in total). I classified the material into eight categories, listed below, and calculated the number of column inches taken up by each:

- 'Fashion': Fashion, beauty, and cosmetics advice
- 'Housewife': Features on cookery, cleaning, household management, and domestic consumption
- 'Mother': Motherhood and childcare advice
- 'Work': Careers advice and articles about working life
- 'Position': Articles about women's changing social and political position
- 'Relations': Advice about personal relationships
- 'Horoscope': Astrological features
- 'Others': Features that could not be classified in the above categories.

As with any content analysis, certain features proved difficult to classify and sometimes I split certain articles between two or more categories. The data should be treated as providing general indications rather than being 'scientifically' accurate. A certain amount of discretion was also required with the *Daily Mirror*, for it sometimes lacked the clearly defined 'women's section' possessed by other papers. In this case, material obviously directed towards women was collated from a number of pages. Otherwise, though, it should be emphasized that these totals refer only to the women's sections and do not include material on these topics found elsewhere in the newspaper. In practice, this restriction tended particularly to keep down the total for the 'fashion' category, the topic most likely to be covered in news columns and on photo pages. Relationship advice in separate problem columns or feature pages was also excluded, except, at times, for the *Mirror*.

The following charts display the results. Their implications are discussed in the main body of the text, but certain brief conclusions are worth highlighting. In almost every instance, the 'women's pages' were dominated by fashion–beauty and housewifery features. Fashion advice was the largest single category, comprising less than a quarter of the total space in only two of the fortnightly samples (and both of these were in the *Herald*); the prominence of material directed at the housewife and mother fluctuated rather more. Other notable trends include the declining frequency of articles on employment in the 1930s, and the rise of horoscopes and features on personal relationships towards the end of the period.

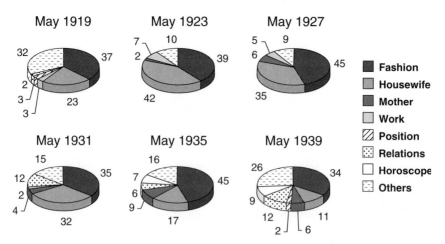

FIG. A1. Contents of the women's page, *Daily Express*, 1919–1939

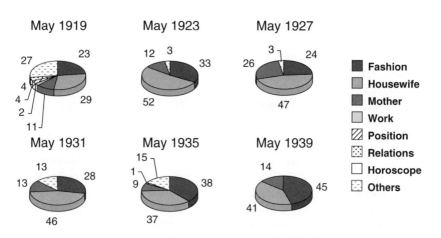

FIG. A2. Contents of the women's page, *Daily Herald*, 1919–1939

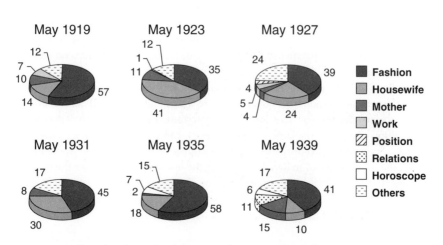

FIG. A3. Contents of the women's page, *Daily Mail*, 1919–1939

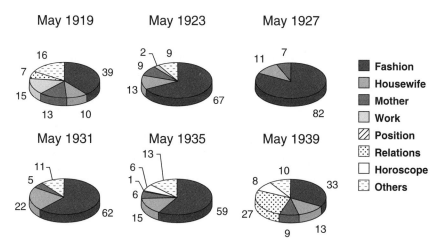

Fig. A4. Contents of the women's page, *Daily Mirror*, 1919–1939

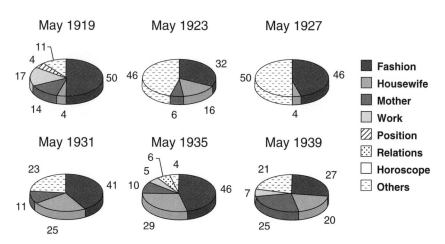

Fig. A5. Contents of the women's page, *Daily News–News Chronicle*, 1919–1939

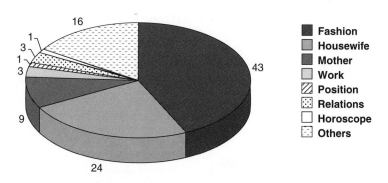

Fig. A6. Contents of the women's page in all samples, 1919–1939

BIBLIOGRAPHY

MANUSCRIPT SOURCES

Bodleian Library, Oxford

Arthur Mann Papers (MS Eng. c. 3274).
C. P. Scott Papers (X. Films 1643).
Daily Herald Papers, from Archives of the Labour Party (X. Films 77/6).
Evelyn Sharp Letters (MSS Eng. lett. c. 277, d. 278).
Geoffrey Dawson Papers.
Howell Gwynne Papers.
John Simon Papers (Correspondence with Lord Rothermere, Boxes 55 and 57).
Lord Northcliffe's Bulletins to the *Daily Mail* 1915–22 (MS Eng. hist. d. 303–5).
Mass Observation File Reports (X. Films 200).
Robert Ensor Papers.
Society of Women Journalists and Writers, Correspondence and Papers 1927–62 (MS Eng. hist. c. 1126).

British Library, London

Evelyn Wrench Papers (Add. MSS 59544).
Lord Northcliffe Papers (Add. MSS 62198–271).
Marie Stopes Papers (Add. MSS 58699, 58598).

British Library of Political and Economic Science, LSE, London

Gerald Barry Papers.

Christ Church, Oxford

Tom Driberg Papers.

House of Lords Record Office, London

Beaverbrook Papers (BBK C Series, 282–7; H Series, 43–113).

National Archives, Kew

LCO/2/775 Judicial Proceedings (Regulation of Reports).

Nuffield College, Oxford

Lord Cherwell Papers (Correspondence with Lord Rothermere).

Trinity College, Cambridge

Walter Layton Papers (Boxes 85–9).

PRINTED PRIMARY SOURCES

Diaries and Letters

BISHOP, A. (ed.), *Vera Brittain: Diary of the Thirties 1932–39. Chronicle of Friendship* (London: Victor Gollancz, 1986).

CROWSON, N. (ed.), *Fleet Street, Press Barons and Politics: The Journals of Collin Brooks, 1932–40* (London: Royal Historical Society, 1998).

GILBERT, M. (ed.), *Winston Churchill, v/1: Documents: The Exchequer Years 1922–29* (London: Heinemann, 1979).

NICOLSON, N. (ed.), *Harold Nicolson, Diaries and Letters 1930–39* (London: Collins, 1966).

SELF, R. (ed.), *Austen Chamberlain Diary Letters* (Cambridge: Cambridge University Press, 1995).

YOUNG, K. (ed.), *The Diaries of Sir Robert Bruce Lockhart 1915–38* (London: Macmillan, 1973).

Newspapers

Daily Chronicle
Daily Express
Daily Herald
Daily Mail
Daily Mirror
Daily News
Daily Sketch
Daily Telegraph
Evening Standard
Manchester Guardian
Morning Post
News Chronicle
News of the World
Observer
The Star
Sunday Dispatch
Sunday Express
The Times

Fawcett Library (now the Women's Library): Press Cuttings Collection, Reel 58

Press Industry Magazines and Annuals

Newspaper Press Directory
Newspaper World
The Writer
World's Press News

Other Magazines

The Adelphi
Home and Politics
John Bull
Punch, or, The London Charivari
Woman and Home

Reports etc.

Political and Economic Planning (PEP), *Report on the British Press* (London, 1938).
Royal Commission on the Press 1947–9, *Minutes of Evidence* (London: HMSO, 1948).
Royal Commission on the Press 1947–9, *Report* (London: HMSO, 1949), Cmd. 7700.

WORKS PRE-1945 AND ANTHOLOGIES OF PRE-1945 MATERIAL

AITKEN, M. (Lord Beaverbrook), *Politicians and the Press* (London: Hutchinson, 1926).
—— *Politicians and the War, 1914–16* (London: Thornton Butterworth, 1928).
BERRY, P., and BISHOP, A. (eds.), *Testament of a Generation: The Journalism of Vera Brittain and Winifred Holtby* (London: Virago, 1985).
BLUMENFELD, R. D., *The Press in my Time* (London: Rich & Cowan, 1933).
BRADDOCK, A. P., *Applied Psychology for Advertisers* (London: Butterworth, 1933).
BRAITHWAITE, B., and WALSH, N., *Home Sweet Home: The Best of Good Housekeeping 1922–39* (London: Leopard, 1995).
BRITTAIN, V., *Testament of Youth* (first pub. 1933; London: Virago, 1986).
CLARKE, T., *My Northcliffe Diary* (London: Victor Gollancz, 1931).
CRAWSHAY, M., *Journalism for Women* (London: Fleet Publications, 1932).
CUMMINGS, A. J., *The Press and a Changing Civilisation* (London: John Lane, 1936).
DARK, S., *The Life of Sir Arthur Pearson* (London: Hodder & Stoughton, 1922).
DEANE, P. (ed.), *History in our Hands: A Critical Anthology of Writings on Literature, Culture and Politics from the 1930s* (London: Leicester University Press, 1998).
ERVINE, St John, *The Future of the Press* (London: World's Press News, 1933).
FYFE, H., *Northcliffe: An Intimate Biography* (London: G. Allen & Unwin, 1930).
GIBBS, P., *Adventures in Journalism* (London: William Heinemann, 1923).
GRAVES, R., and HODGE, A., *The Long Week-End: A Social History of Britain 1918–1939* (first pub. 1940; Harmondsworth: Penguin, 1971).
GREENLY, A. J., *Psychology as a Sales Factor*, 2nd edn. (London: Pitman, 1929).
HAIG, M. (Lady Rhondda), *This was my World* (London: Macmillan, 1933).
—— *Notes on the Way* (London: Macmillan, 1937).
HARRISON, MAJOR G., with MITCHELL, F. C., and ABRAMS, M. A., *The Home Market* (London: G. Allen & Unwin, 1936; rev. and updated 1939).
HERD, H., *Bigger Results from Advertising* (London: P. Allan, 1926).
—— *The Making of Modern Journalism* (London: G. Allen & Unwin, 1927).

HOLTBY, W., *Women, and a Changing Civilisation* (London: John Lane, 1934).

JONES, K., *Fleet Street and Downing Street* (London: Hutchinson, 1920).

LANSBURY, G., *The Miracle of Fleet Street: The Story of the Daily Herald* (London: Labour Publishing, 1925).

LEAVIS, Q. D., *Fiction and the Reading Public* (first pub. 1932; London: Chatto & Windus, 1965).

MARLOW, J. (ed.), *The Virago Book of Women and the Great War* (London: Virago, 1998).

MORISON, S., *The English Newspaper 1622–1932* (Cambridge: Cambridge University Press, 1932).

MOSELEY, S., *Short Story Writing and Freelance Journalism* (London: Pitman, 1926).

ORWELL, S., and ANGUS, I. (eds.), *The Collected Essays, Journalism and Letters of George Orwell*, i: *1920–40* (Harmondsworth: Penguin, 1970).

PEACOCKE, E. H., *Writing for Women* (London: A. & C. Black, 1936).

PEEL, C. S., *Life's Enchanted Cup: An Autobiography* (London: John Lane, 1933).

PETHICK-LAWRENCE, E., *My Part in a Changing World* (London: Victor Gollancz, 1938).

RUSSELL, G., *Advertisement Writing* (London: Ernest Benn, 1927).

SMITH, W., *Spilt Ink* (London: Ernest Benn, 1932).

SPENDER, D. (ed.), *Time and Tide Wait for No Man* (London: Pandora, 1984).

STANNARD, R., *With the Dictators of Fleet Street* (London: Hutchinson, 1934).

STEED, H. W., *The Press* (Harmondsworth: Penguin, 1938).

STOTT, M. (ed.), *Women Talking: An Anthology from the Guardian Women's Page 1922–35, 1957–71* (London: Pandora, 1987).

STRACHEY, R., *The Cause: A Short History of the Women's Movement in Great Britain* (London: G. Bell, 1928).

——(ed.), *Our Freedom and its Results* (London: Hogarth, 1936).

WAUGH, E., *Scoop* (first pub. 1938; Harmondsworth: Penguin, 1967).

WOOLF, V., *A Room of One's Own* (first pub. 1929; London: Penguin, 1993).

—— *Three Guineas* (first pub. 1938; London: Penguin, 1993).

—— *A Woman's Essays: Selected Essays*, i, ed. R. Bowlby (London: Penguin, 1992).

SECONDARY WORKS POST-1945

ADDISON, P., 'Lord Rothermere and British Foreign Policy', in C. Cook and G. Peele (eds.), *The Politics of Reappraisal 1918–39* (London: Macmillan, 1975).

ALBERTI, J., *Beyond Suffrage: Feminists in War and Peace, 1914–28* (Basingstoke: Macmillan, 1989).

——'"A Symbol and a Key": The Suffrage Movement in Britain 1918–28', in J. Purvis and S. S. Holton (eds.), *Votes for Women* (London: Routledge, 2000).

ALEXANDER, S., 'Becoming a Woman in London in the 1920s and '30s', in ead., *Becoming a Woman and Other Essays* (New York: New York University Press, 1995).

——'Men's Fears and Women's Work: Responses to Unemployment in London between the Wars', *Gender and History*, 12/2 (July 2000), 401–25.

ALLEN, R., and FROST, J., *Daily Mirror* (Cambridge: Stephens, 1981).

—— *Voice of Britain: The Inside Story of the Daily Express* (Cambridge: Stephens, 1983).

ANGELL, N., *After All: The Autobiography of Norman Angell* (London: Hamish Hamilton, 1951).

AYERST, D., *The Guardian: Biography of a Newspaper* (London: Collins, 1971).

AYTO, J., *Twentieth Century Words* (Oxford: Oxford University Press, 1999).

BAINBRIDGE, C., and STOCKDILL, R., *The News of the World Story: 150 Years of the World's Bestselling Newspaper* (London: HarperCollins, 1993).

BANKS, O., *Faces of Feminism: A Study of Feminism as a Social Movement* (Oxford: Martin Robertson, 1981).

BARKLEY, W., *Reporter's Notebook* (London: Oldbourne, 1959).

BEAUMAN, N., *A Very Great Profession: The Woman's Novel 1914–39* (London: Virago, 1983).

BEAUMONT, C., 'Citizens not Feminists: The Boundary Negotiated between Citizenship and Feminism by Mainstream Women's Organisations in England, 1928–39', *Women's History Review*, 9/2 (2000), 411–29.

BEDDOE, D., *Back to Home and Duty: Women between the Wars 1918–39* (London: Pandora, 1989).

BEETHAM, M., *A Magazine of her Own? Domesticity and Desire in the Woman's Magazine 1800–1914* (London: Routledge, 1996).

BEHLING, L. L., *The Masculine Woman in America 1890–1935* (Urbana, ILL.: University of Illinois Press, 2001).

BENSON, J., *The Rise of Consumer Society in Britain 1880–1990* (London: Longman, 1994).

BLAND, L., *Banishing the Beast: English Feminism and Sexual Morality 1885–1914* (London: Penguin, 1995).

BOURKE, J., *Dismembering the Male: Men's Bodies and the Great War* (London: Reaktion, 1996).

BOURNE, R., *Lords of Fleet Street* (London: Unwin Hyman, 1990).

BOWDEN, S., and OFFER, A., 'The Technological Revolution that Never Was: Gender, Class, and the Diffusion of Household Appliances in Inter-War England', in V. de Grazia and E. Furlough (eds.), *The Sex of Things: Gender and Consumption in Historical Perspective* (Berkeley: University of California Press, 1996).

BOYCE, G., CURRAN, J., and WINGATE, P. (eds.), *Newspaper History from the Seventeenth Century to the Present Day* (London: Constable, 1978).

BRAKE, L., BELL, B., and FINKELSTEIN, D. (eds.), *Nineteenth Century Media and the Construction of Identities* (Basingstoke: Palgrave, 2000).

BRAYBON, G., *Women Workers in the First World War* (London: Croom Helm, 1981).

BRAYBON, G., and SUMMERFIELD, P., *Out of the Cage: Women's Experiences in Two World Wars* (London: Pandora, 1987).

BRENDON, P., *The Life and Death of the Press Barons* (London: Secker & Warburg, 1982).

BROOKE, S., 'Gender and Working-Class Identity in Britain during the 1950s', *Journal of Social History*, 35 (2001), 773–95.

BROOKS, C., *Devil's Decade: Portraits of the Nineteen Thirties* (London: Macdonald, 1948).

Brown, L., *Victorian News and Newspapers* (Oxford: Clarendon Press, 1985).

Bruley, S., *Women in Britain since 1900* (Basingstoke: Macmillan, 1999).

Burnett, J., *Idle Hands: The Experience of Unemployment 1790–1990* (London: Routledge, 1994).

Bushaway, B., 'Name upon Name: The Great War and Remembrance', in R. Porter (ed.), *Myths of the English* (Cambridge: Polity Press, 1992).

Bussey, G., and Tims, M., *Pioneers for Peace: Women's International League for Peace and Freedom 1915–1965* (London: WILPF, 1980).

Caine, B., *English Feminism 1780–1980* (Oxford: Oxford University Press, 1997).

Campbell, B., *The Iron Ladies: Why do Women Vote Tory?* (London: Virago, 1987).

Carey, J., *The Intellectuals and the Masses: Pride and Prejudice among the Literary Intelligensia 1880–1939* (London: Faber & Faber, 1992).

Carter, C., Branston, G., and Allan, S. (eds.), *News, Gender and Power* (London: Routledge, 1998).

Catterall, P., Seymour-Ure, C., and Smith, A. (eds.), *Northcliffe's Legacy: Aspects of the British Popular Press 1896–1996* (Basingstoke: Macmillan, 2000).

Ceadel, M., *Semi-Detached Idealists: The British Peace Movement and International Relations 1854–1945* (Oxford: Oxford University Press, 2000).

Chalaby, J. K., *The Invention of Journalism* (Basingstoke: Macmillan, 1998).

Chinn, C., *They Worked All their Lives: Women of the Urban Poor in England 1850–1939* (Manchester: Manchester University Press, 1988).

Chisholm, A., and Davie, M., *Beaverbrook: A Life* (London: Hutchinson, 1992).

Christiansen, A., *Headlines All my Life* (London: Heinemann, 1961).

Clarke, T., *Northcliffe in History: An Intimate Study of Press Power* (London: Hutchinson, 1950).

Cockett, R., *Twilight of Truth: Chamberlain, Appeasement and the Manipulation of the Press* (London: Weidenfeld & Nicolson, 1989).

Collins, M., *Modern Love: An Intimate History of Men and Women in Twentieth Century Britain* (London: Atlantic Books, 2003).

Conboy, M., *The Press and Popular Culture* (London: Sage, 2002).

Constantine, S., Kirby, M. W., and Rose, M. B. (eds.), *The First World War in British History* (London: Edward Arnold, 1995).

Craig, S., *Men, Masculinity and the Media* (Newbury Park, Calif.: Sage, 1992).

Crawley, A., *Leap before You Look: A Memoir* (London: Collins, 1988).

Cudlipp, H., *Publish and Be Damned! The Astonishing Story of the Daily Mirror* (London: Andrew Dakers, 1953).

—— *Walking on Water* (London: Bodley Head, 1976).

Curran, J., 'The Impact of Advertising on the British Media', *Media, Culture and Society*, 3/1 (1981), 43–69.

—— and Seaton, J., *Power without Responsibility*, 5th edn. (London: Routledge, 1997).

——Douglas, A., and Whannel, G., 'The Political Economy of the Human Interest Story', in A. Smith (ed.), *Newspapers and Democracy: International Essays on a Changing Medium* (Cambridge, Mass.: MIT Press, 1980).

——Smith, A., and Wingate, P. (eds.), *Impacts and Influences: Essays on Media Power in the Twentieth Century* (London: Methuen, 1987).

DAUNTON, M., and REIGER, B. (eds.), *Meanings of Modernity: Britain from the Late-Victorian Era to World War II* (Oxford: Berg, 2001).

DAVIDOFF, L., and WESTOVER, B., *Our Work, our Lives, our Words: Women's History and Women's Work* (Basingstoke: Macmillan, 1986).

DAVIES, A., *Leisure, Gender and Poverty: Working-Class Culture in Salford and Manchester* (Buckingham: Open University Press, 1992).

DAVIES, K., DICKEY, J., and STRATFORD, T. (eds.), *Out of Focus: Writings on Women and the Media* (London: Women's Press, 1987).

DAWSON, G., 'The Blond Bedouin: Lawrence of Arabia, Imperial Adventure and the Imagining of English-British Masculinity', in M. Roper and J. Tosh (eds.), *Manful Assertions: Masculinities in Britain since 1800* (London: Routledge, 1991).

DE BEAUVOIR, S., *The Second Sex* (first pub. 1949; London: Picador, 1988).

DE GROOT, G., ' "I Love the Scent of Cordite in your Hair": Gender Dynamics in Mixed Anti-Aircraft Batteries during the Second World War', *History*, 82/265 (1997), 73–92.

DYER, G., *Advertising as Communication* (London: Methuen, 1982).

DYHOUSE, C., *Feminism and the Family in England 1880–1939* (Oxford: Basil Blackwell, 1989).

—— 'Women Students and the London Medical Schools 1914–39: The Anatomy of a Masculine Culture', *Gender and History*, 10/1 (Apr. 1998), 110–132.

EDELMAN, M., *The Mirror: A Political History* (London: Hamish Hamilton, 1966).

ENGEL, M., *Tickle the Public: One Hundred Years of the Popular Press* (London: Gollancz, 1996).

ENSOR, R. C. K., 'The Press', in Sir Ernest Barker (ed.), *The Character of England* (Oxford: Clarendon Press, 1947).

FARRAR, M., *News from the Front: War Correspondents on the Western Front* (Stroud: Sutton, 1998).

FERGUSON, M., *Forever Feminine: Women's Magazines and the Cult of Femininity* (London: Heinemann, 1983).

FERRIS, P., *The House of Northcliffe* (London: Weidenfeld & Nicolson, 1971).

FIENBURGH, W., *25 Momentous Years: A 25th Anniversary in the History of the Daily Herald* (London: Odhams, 1955).

FINK, J., and HOLDEN, K., 'Pictures from the Margins of Marriage: Representations of Spinsters and Single Mothers in the Mid-Victorian Novel, Inter-War Hollywood Melodrama and British Film of the 1950s and 1960s', *Gender and History*, 11/2 (July 1999), 233–55.

FOWLER, B., *The Alienated Reader: Women and Romantic Literature in the Twentieth Century* (Hemel Hempstead: Harvester Wheatsheaf, 1991).

FOWLER, D., *The First Teenagers: The Life-Style of Young Wage-Earners in Inter-War Britain* (London: Woburn, 1995).

FOWLER, R., *Language in the News: Discourse and Ideology in the Press* (London: Routledge, 1991).

FRANCIS, M., 'The Domestication of the Male? Recent Research on Nineteenth and Twentieth-Century British Masculinity', *Historical Journal*, 45/3 (2002), 637–52.

FRIEDAN, B., *The Feminine Mystique* (London: Gollancz, 1963).

FUSSELL, P., *The Great War and Modern Memory* (New York: Oxford University Press, 1975).

FYFE, H., *Sixty Years of Fleet Street* (London: W. H. Allen, 1949).

GANNON, F. R., *The British Press and Germany 1936–39* (Oxford: Clarendon Press, 1971).

GILES, J., *Women, Identity and Private Life in Britain 1900–50* (Basingstoke: Macmillan, 1995).

GITTINS, D., *Fair Sex: Family Size and Structure, 1900–39* (London: Hutchinson, 1982).

GLUCKSMANN, M., *Women Assemble: Women Workers and the New Industries in Inter-War Britain* (London: Routledge, 1990).

GOTTLIEB, J., 'Suffragette Experience through the Filter of Fascism', in C. Eustance, J. Ryan, and L. Ugolini (eds.), *A Suffrage Reader: Charting Directions in British Suffrage History* (London: Leicester University Press, 2000).

GRAVES, P. M., *Labour Women: Women in British Working-Class Politics 1918–39* (Cambridge: Cambridge University Press, 1994).

GREENFIELD, J., and REID, C., 'Women's Magazines and the Commercial Orchestration of Femininity in the 1930s: Evidence from *Woman's Own*', *Media History*, 4/2 (Dec. 1998), 161–74.

——O'CONNELL, S., and REID, C., 'Fashioning Masculinity: *Men Only*, Consumption and the Development of Marketing in the 1930s', *Twentieth Century British History*, 10/4 (1999), 457–76.

GREER, G., *The Female Eunuch* (London: Paladin, 1971).

GREGORY, A., *The Silence of Memory: Armistice Day 1919–46* (Oxford: Berg, 1994).

GRIFFITHS, D. (ed.), *The Encyclopedia of the British Press 1422–1992* (London: Macmillan, 1992).

HADLEY, W. W. (ed.), *The Kemsley Book of Journalism* (London: Cassell, 1950).

HALL, L., *Sex, Gender and Social Change in Britain since 1880* (Basingstoke: Macmillan, 2000).

HAMMERTON, A. J., 'The Targets of "Rough Music": Respectability and Domestic Violence in Victorian England', *Gender and History*, 3/1 (1991), 23–44.

HARGREAVES, J., *Sporting Females: Critical Issues in the History and Sociology of Women's Sports* (London: Routledge, 1994).

HARRIS, J., *Private Lives, Public Spirit: Britain, 1870–1914* (Oxford: Oxford University Press, 1993).

HARRISON, B., *Separate Spheres* (London: Croom Helm, 1978).

——'Women in a Men's House: The Women MPs 1919–45', *Historical Journal*, 29/3 (1986), 623–54.

——*Prudent Revolutionaries* (Oxford: Clarendon Press, 1987).

HIGONNET, M. R., JENSON, J., MICHEL, S., WEITZ, M. C. (eds.), *Behind the Lines: Gender and the Two World Wars* (New Haven: Yale University Press, 1987).

HILL, J., *Sport, Leisure and Culture in Twentieth Century Britain* (Basingstoke: Palgrave, 2002).

HILL, M., *Women in the 20th Century* (London: Chapmans, 1991).

HOGGART, R., *The Uses of Literacy* (London: Chatto & Windus, 1957).

HOLT, R., *Sport and the British* (Oxford: Clarendon Press, 1989).

HORN, P., *Women in the 1920s* (Stroud: Alan Sutton, 1995).

HORWOOD, C., '"Girls Who Arouse Dangerous Passions': Women and Bathing 1900–39', *Women's History Review*, 9/4 (2000), 653–73.

HUBBACK, D., *No Ordinary Press Baron: A Life of Walter Layton* (London: Weidenfeld & Nicolson, 1985).

HUMPHRIES, S., and GORDON, P., *A Man's World: From Boyhood to Manhood 1900–60* (London: BBC Books, 1996).

HYNES, S., *A War Imagined: The First World War and English Culture* (London: Bodley Head, 1990).

JARVIS, D., 'Mrs Maggs and Betty: The Conservative Appeal to Women Voters in the 1920s', *Twentieth Century British History*, 5/2 (1994), 129–52.

JEFFERY, T., and MCCLELLAND, K., 'A World Fit to Live In: The *Daily Mail* and the Middle Classes 1918–39', in J. Curran, A. Smith, and P. Wingate (eds.), *Impacts and Influences: Essays on Media Power in the Twentieth Century* (London: Methuen, 1987).

JEFFREYS, S., *The Spinster and her Enemies: Feminism and Sexuality 1880–1930* (London: Pandora, 1985).

JONES, A., *Powers of the Press: Newspapers, Power and the Public in Nineteenth Century England* (Aldershot: Scolar, 1996).

JONES, H., *Women in British Public Life, 1914–1950: Gender, Power and Social Policy* (Harlow: Longman, 2000).

KALDOR, N., and SILVERMAN, R., *A Statistical Analysis of Advertising Expenditure and of the Revenue of the Press* (Cambridge: Cambridge University Press, 1948).

KEMP, S., and SQUIRES, J. (eds.), *Feminisms* (Oxford: Oxford University Press, 1997).

KENT, S. K., *Making Peace: The Reconstruction of Gender in Inter-War Britain* (Princeton: Princeton University Press, 1993).

—— *Gender and Power in Britain 1640–1990* (London: Routledge, 1999).

KOSS, S., *Fleet Street Radical: A. G. Gardiner and the Daily News* (London: Allen Lane, 1973).

—— *The Rise and Fall of the Political Press*, ii (London: Hamish Hamilton, 1984).

LANGHAMER, C., *Women's Leisure in England, 1920–1960* (Manchester: Manchester University Press, 2000).

LAW, C., *Suffrage and Power: The Women's Movement 1918–28* (London: I. B. Tauris, 1997).

—— 'The Old Faith Living and the Old Power There: The Movement to Extend Women's Suffrage', in M. Joannou and J. Purvis (eds.), *The Women's Suffrage Movement: New Feminist Perspectives* (Manchester: Manchester University Press, 1998).

LEE, A. J., *The Origins of the Popular Press in England 1855–1914* (London: Croom Helm, 1976).

LEE, H., *Virginia Woolf* (London: Chatto & Windus, 1996).

LEMAHIEU, D., *A Culture for Democracy: Mass Communication and the Cultivated Mind in Britain between the Wars* (Oxford: Clarendon Press, 1988).

LEWIS, J., *Women in England 1870–1950* (Brighton: Wheatsheaf, 1984).

——'Public Institution and Private Relationship: Marriage and Marriage Guidance, 1920–68', *Twentieth Century British History*, 1/3 (1990), 233–63.

——(ed.), *Labour and Love: Women's Experience of Home and Family 1850–1940* (Oxford: Basil Blackwell, 1986).

LIGHT, A., *Forever England: Femininity, Literature and Conservatism between the Wars* (London: Routledge, 1991).

LINTON, D., *The Twentieth Century Newspaper Press in Britain: An Annotated Bibliography* (London: Mansell, 1994).

McALEER, J., *Popular Reading and Publishing in Britain, 1914–50* (Oxford: Clarendon Press, 1992).

McDONNELL, J., *Public Service Broadcasting: A Reader* (London: Routledge, 1991).

McKIBBIN, R., *Classes and Cultures: England 1918–1951* (Oxford: Oxford University Press, 1998).

MANGAN, J., and WALVIN, J. (eds.), *Manliness and Morality: Middle-Class Masculinity in Britain and America, 1800–1940* (Manchester: Manchester University Press, 1987).

MARRIS, P., and THORNHAM, S. (eds.), *Media Studies: A Reader*, 2nd edn. (Edinburgh: Edinburgh University Press, 1999).

MARWICK, A., *Women at War 1914–1918* (London: Fontana, 1977).

——*The Deluge: British Society and the First World War*, 2nd edn. (Basingstoke: Macmillan, 1991).

MATTHEWS, J. J., '"They Had Such a Lot of Fun": The Women's League of Health and Beauty between the Wars', *History Workshop Journal*, 30 (1990), 22–54.

MELMAN, B., *Women and the Popular Imagination in the Twenties: Flappers and Nymphs* (Basingstoke: Macmillan, 1988).

MELMAN, B., (ed.), *Borderlines: Genders and Identities in War and Peace 1870–1930* (New York: Routledge, 1998).

MESSINGER, G. S., *British Propaganda and the State in the First World War* (Manchester: Manchester University Press, 1992).

MIDDLEMISS, K., and BARNES, J., *Baldwin: A Biography* (London: Weidenfeld & Nicolson, 1969).

MILLETT, K., *Sexual Politics* (New York: Doubleday, 1970).

MINNEY, R. J., *Viscount Southwood* (London: Odhams Press, 1954).

MITCHELL, D., *Women on the Warpath* (London: Jonathan Cape, 1966).

MORRIS, A. J. A., *The Scaremongers: The Advocacy of War and Rearmament 1896–1914* (London: Routledge & Kegan Paul, 1984).

NICHOLAS, S., 'From John Bull to John Citizen: Images of National Identity and Citizenship on the Wartime BBC', in R. Weight and A. Beach (eds.), *The Right to Belong: Citizenship and National Identity in Britain 1930–1960* (London: I. B. Tauris, 1998).

NORRIS, P. (ed.), *Women, Media and Politics* (New York: Oxford University Press, 1997).

O'MALLEY, T., and SOLEY, C., *Regulating the Press* (London: Pluto Press, 2000).

ORAM, A., 'Repressed and Thwarted, or Bearer of the New World? The Spinster in Inter-War Feminist Discourses', *Women's History Review*, 1/3 (1992), 413–34.

—— *Women Teachers and Feminist Politics 1900–1939* (Manchester: Manchester University Press, 1996).

——and TURNBULL, A. (eds.), *The Lesbian History Sourcebook* (London: Routledge, 2001).

PEISS, K., 'Making Up, Making Over: Cosmetics, Consumer Culture and Women's Identity', in V. de Grazia and E. Furlough (eds.), *The Sex of Things* (Berkeley: University of California Press, 1996).

POOVEY, M., *Uneven Developments: The Ideological Work of Gender in Mid-Victorian England* (London: Virago, 1989).

POUND, R., and HARMSWORTH, G., *Northcliffe* (London: Cassell, 1959).

PUGH, M., 'Politicians and the Woman's Vote 1914–18', *History*, 59 (Oct. 1974), 358–74.

—— *Women and the Women's Movement in Britain 1914–1959* (Basingstoke: Macmillan, 1992).

—— *State and Society: British Political and Social History 1870–1992* (London: Edward Arnold, 1994).

—— 'The British Union of Fascists and the Olympia Debate', *Historical Journal*, 41/2 (1998), 529–42.

—— 'The *Daily Mirror* and the Revival of Labour 1935–45', *Twentieth Century British History*, 9/3 (1998), 420–38.

—— *The March of the Women: A Revisionist Analysis of the Campaign for Women's Suffrage 1866–1914* (Oxford: Oxford University Press, 2000).

PUMPHREY, M., 'The Flapper, the Housewife and the Making of Modernity', *Cultural Studies*, 1/2 (1987), 179–94.

PURVIS, J. (ed.), *Women's History in Britain, 1870–1945* (London: UCL Press, 1995).

RAPP, R., and ROSS, E., 'The 1920s: Feminism, Consumerism, and Political Backlash in the United States', in J. Friedlander, B. W. Cook, A. Kessler-Harris, and C. Smith-Rosenburg (eds.), *Women in Culture and Politics* (Bloomington: Indiana University Press, 1986).

RASMUSSEN, J., 'Women in Labour: The "Flapper Vote" and Party System Transformation in Britain', *Electoral Studies*, 3/1 (1984), 47–63.

RICHARDS, H., *The Bloody Circus: The Daily Herald and the Left* (London: Pluto Press, 1997).

ROBERTS, E., *A Woman's Place: An Oral History of Working-Class Women 1890–1940* (Oxford: Basil Blackwell, 1984).

ROPER, M., and TOSH, J., *Manful Assertions: Masculinities in Britain since 1800* (London: Routledge, 1991).

ROSE, J., *Marie Stopes and the Sexual Revolution* (London: Faber & Faber, 1993).

ROSE, J., *The Intellectual Life of the British Working Classes* (New Haven: Yale University Press, 2001).

ROSEN, M., *Popcorn Venus: Women, Movies and the American Dream* (New York: Coward, McCann & Geoghegan, 1973).

Rowbotham, S., *A Century of Women: The History of Women in Britain and the United States* (London: Viking, 1997).

Rupp, L. J., *Worlds of Women: The Making of an International Women's Movemen* (Princeton: Princeton University Press, 1997).

Ryan, D. S., *The Ideal Home through the Twentieth Century* (London: Hazar, 1997).

Savage, G., 'Erotic Stories and Public Decency: Newspaper Reporting of Divorce Proceedings in England', *Historical Journal*, 41/2 (1998), 511–28.

Scott, J. (ed.), *Feminism and History* (Oxford: Oxford University Press, 1996).

Seymour-Ure, C., 'The Press and the Party System between the Wars', in G. Peele and C. Cook (eds.), *The Politics of Reappraisal* (London: Macmillan, 1975).

——and Schoff, J., *David Low* (London: Secker & Warburg, 1985).

Skidelsky, R., *Oswald Moseley* (London: Macmillan, 1975).

Smith, A., *New Statesman: Portrait of a Political Weekly 1913–31* (London: Frank Cass, 1996).

Smith, A. C. H., with Immirizi, E., and Blackwell, T., *Paper Voices: The Popular Press and Social Change 1935–65* (London: Chatto & Windus, 1975).

Smith H. L., *The British Women's Suffrage Campaign 1866–1928* (Harlow: Longman, 1998).

——(ed.), *British Feminism in the Twentieth Century* (Aldershot: Elgar, 1990).

Soland, B., *Becoming Modern: Young Women and the Reconstruction of Womanhood in the 1920s* (Princeton: Princeton University Press, 2000).

Soloway, R., *Birth Control and the Population Question in England, 1877–1930* (Chapel Hill: University of North Carolina Press, 1982).

Stacey, J., *Stargazing: Hollywood Cinema and Female Spectatorship* (London: Routledge, 1994).

Stevenson, J., *British Society 1914–45* (London: Allen Lane, 1984).

Stott, M., *Forgetting's No Excuse: The Autobiography of Mary Stott* (London: Faber, 1973).

Souhami, D., *The Trials of Radclyffe Hall* (London: Virago, 1999).

Summerfield, P., *Reconstructing Women's Wartime Lives: Discourse and Subjectivity in Oral Histories of the Second World War* (Manchester: Manchester University Press, 1998).

Surridge, K., 'More than a Great Poster: Lord Kitchener and the Image of the Military Hero', *Historical Research*, 74/185 (Aug. 2001), 298–313.

Taylor, A. J. P., *Beaverbrook* (London: Hamish Hamilton, 1972).

Taylor, S. J., *The Great Outsiders: Northcliffe, Rothermere and the Daily Mail* (London: Weidenfeld & Nicolson, 1996).

——*The Reluctant Press Lord: Esmond Rothermere and the Daily Mail* (London: Weidenfeld & Nicolson, 1998).

Thane, P., 'What Difference did the Vote Make?', in A. Vickery (ed.), *Women, Privilege and Power: British Politics, 1750 to the Present* (Stanford, Calif.: Stanford University Press, 2001).

Thesander, M., *The Feminine Ideal* (London: Reaktion Books, 1997).

THOM, D., *Nice Girls and Rude Girls: Women Workers in the First World War* (London: I. B. Tauris, 1998).

THOMPSON, J. LEE, *Northcliffe: Press Baron in Politics 1865–1922* (London: John Murray, 2000).

THURLOW, R., *Fascism in Britain: A History 1918–1985* (Oxford: Basil Blackwell, 1987). *The Times, The History of the Times*, iv/2: *1921–48* (London: *The Times*, 1952).

TINKLER, P., *Constructing Girlhood: Popular Magazines for Girls Growing Up in England 1920–1950* (London: Taylor & Francis, 1995).

TOSH, J., 'The Making of Masculinities: The Middle-Class in Late Nineteenth Century Britain', in A. John and C. Eustance (eds.), *The Men's Share* (London: Routledge, 1997).

—— *A Man's Place: Masculinity and the Middle-Class Home in Victorian England* (New Haven: Yale University Press, 1999).

TRAVIS, A., *Bound and Gagged: A Secret History of Obscenity in Britain* (London: Profile, 2000).

TUNSTALL, J., *The Media in Britain* (London: Constable, 1983).

—— *Newspaper Power: The New National Press in Britain* (Oxford: Clarendon Press, 1996).

TYLEE, C. M., *The Great War and Women's Consciousness: Images of Militarism and Womanhood in Women's Writings, 1914–64* (Basingstoke: Macmillan, 1990).

van ZOONEN, L., *Feminist Media Studies* (London: Sage, 1994).

VELLACOTT, J., 'Feminist Consciousness and the First World War', *History Workshop Journal*, 23(1987) 80–102.

VICKERY, A. (ed.), *Women, Privilege and Power: British Politics, 1750 to the Present* (Stanford, Calif.: Stanford University Press, 2001).

WADSWORTH, A. P., 'Newspaper Circulations 1800–1954', *Transactions of the Manchester Statistical Society*, Session 1954–5 (1955).

WALKOWITZ, J. R., *City of Dreadful Delight: Narratives of Sexual Danger in Late Victorian London* (Chicago: University of Chicago Press, 1992).

WALTER, N., *The New Feminism* (London: Little, Brown, 1998).

WEEKS, J., *Sex, Politics and Society: The Regulation of Sexuality since 1800* (London: Longman, 1981).

—— *Coming Out: Homosexual Politics in Britain from the Nineteenth Century to the Present*, rev edn. (London: Quartet Books, 1990).

WHITE, C., *Women's Magazines 1693–1968* (London: Michael Joseph, 1970).

WIENER, J. H. (ed.), *Papers for the Millions: The New Journalism in Britain, 1850s to 1914* (New York: Greenwood, 1988).

WILKINSON, G., 'Purple Prose and the Yellow Press: Imagined Spaces and the Military Expedition to Tirah, 1897', in D. Finkelstein and D. M. Peers (eds.), *Negotiating India in the Nineteenth Century Media* (Basingstoke: Macmillan, 2000).

WILLIAMS, F., *Dangerous Estate: The Anatomy of Newspapers* (first pub. 1957; London: Longmans, Green, 1958).

WILLIAMS, G., *Firebrand: The Frank Owen Story* (Worcester: Square One, 1993).

WILLIAMS, K., *British Writers and the Media 1930–45* (Basingstoke: Macmillan, 1996).

WILLIAMS, R., *The Long Revolution* (Harmondsworth: Penguin, 1965).

WILSON, E., *Adorned in Dreams: Fashion and Modernity* (London: Virago, 1985).

WILMOTT, P., and YOUNG, M., *Family and Kinship in East London* (first pub. 1957; Harmondsworth: Penguin, 1986).

WINSHIP, J., *Inside Women's Magazines* (London: Pandora, 1987).

WOLF, N., *The Beauty Myth: How Images of Beauty are Used against Women* (London: Chatto & Windus, 1990).

WOOLLACOTT, A., *On Her their Lives Depend* (Berkeley: University of California Press, 1994).

ZWEINIGER-BARGIELOWSKA, I. (ed.), *Women in Twentieth Century Britain* (Harlow: Longman, 2001).

UNPUBLISHED THESES

BENSON, T. S., 'Low and Lord Beaverbrook: The Case of a Cartoonist's Autonomy', Ph.D. thesis (University of Kent at Canterbury, 1998).

RICHARDS, H., 'Constriction, Conformity and Control: The Taming of the *Daily Herald*, 1921–30', D.Phil. thesis (Open University, 1992).

INDEX